Designing XML Internet Applications

W9-CSE-063

ISBN 0-13-616822-1

90000

9 780136 168225

SC 99

⟨!CFG OIM⟩ The Charles F. Goldfarb Series on Open Information Management

"Open Information Management" (OIM) means managing information so that it is open to processing by any program, not just the program that created it. That extends even to application programs not conceived of at the time the information was created.

OIM is based on the principle of data independence: data should be stored in computers in non-proprietary, genuinely standardized representations. And that applies even when the data is the content of a document. Its representation should distinguish the innate information from the proprietary codes of document processing programs and the artifacts of particular presentation styles.

Business data bases—which rigorously separate the real data from the input forms and output reports—achieved data independence decades ago. But documents, unlike business data, have historically been created in the context of a particular output presentation style. So for document data, independence was largely unachievable until recently.

That is doubly unfortunate. It is unfortunate because documents are a far more significant repository of humanity's information. And documents can contain significantly richer information structures than data bases.

It is also unfortunate because the need for OIM of documents is greater now than ever. The demands of "repurposing" require that information be deliverable in multiple formats: paper-based, online, multimedia, hypermedia. And information must now be delivered through multiple channels: traditional bookstores and libraries, the World Wide Web, corporate intranets and extranets. In the latter modes, what starts as data base data may become a document for browsing, but then may need to be reused by the reader as data.

Fortunately, in the past ten years a technology has emerged that extends to documents the data base's capacity for data independence.

And it does so without the data base's restrictions on structural freedom. That technology is the "Standard Generalized Markup Language" (SGML), an official International Standard (ISO 8879) that has been adopted by the world's largest producers of documents and by the World Wide Web.

With SGML, organizations in government, aerospace, airlines, automotive, electronics, computers, and publishing (to name a few) have freed their documents from hostage relationships to processing software. SGML coexists with graphics, multimedia and other data standards needed for OIM and acts as the framework that relates objects in the other formats to one another and to SGML documents.

The World Wide Web's HTML and XML are both based on SGML. HTML is a particular, though very general, application of SGML, like those for the above industries. There is a limited set of markup tags that can be used with HTML. XML, in contrast, is a simplified subset of SGML facilities that, like full SGML, can be used with any set of tags. You can literally create your own markup language with XML.

As the enabling standard for OIM of documents, the SGML family of standards necessarily plays a leading role in this series. We provide tutorials on SGML, XML, and other key standards and the techniques for applying them. Our books vary in technical intensity from programming techniques for software developers to the business justification of OIM for enterprise executives. We share the practical experience of organizations and individuals who have applied the techniques of OIM in environments ranging from immense industrial publishing projects to websites of all sizes.

Our authors are expert practitioners in their subject matter, not writers hired to cover a "hot" topic. They bring insight and understanding that can only come from real-world experience. Moreover, they practice what they preach about standardization. Their books share a common standards-based vocabulary. In this way, knowledge gained from one book in the series is directly applicable when reading another, or the standards themselves. This is just one of the ways in which we strive for the utmost technical accuracy and consistency with the OIM standards.

And we also strive for a sense of excitement and fun. After all, the challenge of OIM—preserving information from the ravages of technology while exploiting its benefits—is one of the great intellectual adventures of our age. I'm sure you'll find this series to be a knowledgable and reliable guide on that adventure.

About the Series Editor

Dr. Charles F. Goldfarb invented the SGML language in 1974 and later led the team that developed it into the International Standard on which both HTML and XML are based. He serves as editor of the Standard (ISO 8879) and as a consultant to developers of SGML and XML applications and products. He is based in Saratoga, CA.

About the Series Logo

The rebus is an ancient literary tradition, dating from 16th century Picardy, and is especially appropriate to a series involving fine distinctions between things and the words that describe them. For the logo, Andrew Goldfarb incorporated a rebus of the series name within a stylized SGML/XML comment declaration.

 # The Charles F. Goldfarb Series on Open Information Management

As XML is a subset of SGML, the Series List is categorized to show the degree to which a title applies to XML. "XML Titles" are those that discuss XML explicitly and may also cover full SGML. "SGML Titles" do not mention XML per se, but the principles covered may apply to XML.

XML Titles Available

Goldfarb, Pepper, and Ensign
▮ SGML Buyer's Guide™: Choosing the Right XML and SGML Products and Services

Megginson
▮ Structuring XML Documents

Leventhal, Lewis, and Fuchs
▮ Designing XML Internet Applications

McGrath
▮ XML by Example: Building E-commerce Applications

Goldfarb and Prescod *(Coming Soon)*
▮ The XML Handbook™

Jelliffe *(Coming Soon)*
▮ The SGML Cookbook

SGML Titles Available

Turner, Douglass, and Turner
▮ ReadMe.1st: SGML for Writers and Editors

Donovan
▮ Industrial-Strength SGML: An Introduction to Enterprise Publishing

Ensign
▮ $GML: The Billion Dollar Secret

Rubinsky and Maloney
▮ SGML on the Web: Small Steps Beyond HTML

McGrath
▮ ParseMe.1st: SGML for Software Developers

DuCharme
▮ SGML CD

Designing XML Internet Applications

- Michael Leventhal
- David Lewis
- Matthew Fuchs

Prentice Hall PTR, Upper Saddle River, NJ   07458
http://www.phptr.com

Library of Congress Cataloging-in-Publication Data

```
Leventhal, Michael.
    Designing XML Internet applications / Michael Leventhal, David
  Lewis, and Matthew Fuchs
       p.    cm. -- (The Charles F. Goldfarb series on open information
  management)
    Includes index.
    ISBN 0-13-616822-1
    1. XML (Document markup language)   2. Internet programming.
  I. Lewis, David.   II. Fuchs, Matthew.   III. Title.
  QA76.76.H94L46
  005.7'2--dc21                                            98-2850
                                                               CIP
```

Editorial/Production Supervision: *Eileen Clark*
Acquisitions Editor: *Mark Taub*
Marketing Manager: *Dan Rush*
Manufacturing Manager: *Alexis R. Heydt*
Cover Design: *Anthony Gemmellaro*
Cover Design Direction: *Jerry Votta*
Series Design: *Gail Cocker-Bogusz*

 © 1998 Prentice Hall PTR
Prentice-Hall, Inc.
A Simon & Schuster Company
Upper Saddle River, NJ 07458

Prentice Hall books are widely used by corporations and government agencies for training, marketing, and resale.

The publisher offers discounts on this book when ordered in bulk quantities. For more information, contact Corporate Sales Department, Phone: 800-382-3419; fax: 201-236-7141; email: corpsales@prenhall.com or write Corporate Sales Department, Prentice Hall PTR, One Lake Street, Upper Saddle River, NJ 07458.

All rights reserved. No part of this book may be reproduced, in any form or by any means, without permission in writing from the publisher.

Printed in the United States of America

10 9 8 7 6 5 4 3 2 1

ISBN 0-13-616822-1

Prentice-Hall International (UK) Limited, *London*
Prentice-Hall of Australia Pty. Limited, *Sydney*
Prentice-Hall Canada Inc., *Toronto*
Prentice-Hall Hispanoamericana, S.A., *Mexico*
Prentice-Hall of India Private Limited, *New Delhi*
Prentice-Hall of Japan, Inc., *Tokyo*
Simon & Schuster Asia Pte. Ltd., *Singapore*
Editora Prentice-Hall do Brasil, Ltda., *Rio de Janeiro*

All product names mentioned herein are the property of their respective owners.

Series logo by Andrew Goldfarb for EyeTech Graphics, copyright (C)1996 Andrew Goldfarb.

Series foreword and book foreword copyright (C)1998 Charles F. Goldfarb.

Opinions expressed in this book are those of the Author and are not necessarily those of the Publisher or Series Editor.

The Author of this book has included a diskette or CD-ROM of related materials as a convenience to the reader. The Series Editor did not participate in the preparation, testing, or review of the materials and is not responsible for their content.

A Sarah, mon coeur de jade

— Michael

To my parents: Robert and Louise

— David

To AYE as always – Annie, Yael and Elie

— Matthew

Contents

Chapter 3
XML and SGML Tools   80

Part Three

XML/SGML E-mail   355

Chapter 9
XML E-mail   356

I Part Four

XML and Java–
Parsers and APIs   389

Chapter 10
XML Parsers and Application
Programmer Interfaces   390

I Part Five

Future –
Agents and all that

Chapter 11
Input Gathering and Negotiation using XML

Foreword

The computer network is the essential information management tool of the modern enterprise. And like most things to do with information technology, networks have been changing rapidly.

A few years ago, networks were chiefly proprietary. The internet and the World Wide Web changed all that. They showed that systems based on open standards could be as robust and powerful as any other.

And since open standards cause competition to flourish, these new networks were less expensive as well. They were called *intra*nets because they applied *inter*net standards *within* a network, rather than among networks.

But it isn't just the Information Technology staff that appreciates intranets. End-users love them because intranets let them use their familiar Web browsers for internal corporate information—mail, news, bulletin boards, procedure manuals, and the like—and even for exchanging abstract data such as spreadsheets and data bases.

In fact, these more demanding data-centric applications have become a driving force behind the World Wide Web Consortium's adoption of a major new standard—XML—which promises to transform intranets radically. Unlike HTML, which basically describes how pages should look, XML can capture the actual meaning and structure of the underlying data.

Now skillful website designers who can "think the XML way" can add amazing amounts of intelligence, flexibility, and ease-of-use to their sites, while simplifying development and maintenance at the same time.

This book will teach you how to do those things for your own website.

Michael Leventhal, David Lewis, and Matthew Fuchs have had years of practical experience with XML and its parent technology, SGML. They will show you how to think about structured information the XML/SGML way, how to apply that thinking to intranet application design, and how to implement the applications. And they support their writing with actual running code on the CD-ROM.

Since earliest times, a net has simultaneously been a tool for the skillful and a snare for the unwary. *Designing XML Internet Applications* will give you the skills to cast your net without getting tangled in it.

Charles F. Goldfarb
Saratoga, CA
March, 1998

User's Guide

There is an extremely wide-range of information about XML in this book. But because we have chosen to organize the largest portion of it into programming projects, the reader may have to do some thumbing through the table of contents and index and some browsing to find all the bits of interest. We choose this approach because in our own experience our insights into design have come primarily to us when faced with concrete problems or even with the consequences of a poor design. So we feel that our presentation of XML design issues, topics, and standards is stronger for being presented within the project context.

While it is true that this a programming book much of the material will be of interest to non-programmers. Our goal even in the midst of technical discussions of programming is to highlight design issues which will provide insight into using XML to anyone concerned with software applications and the internet. There is also a great deal of material of direct interest to specialists in the production and dissemination of documents and designers of information systems.

This is not an introductory book although it should be of interest to readers with varying levels of experience. We do assume the reader already knows a fair amount about how the internet without XML works. Knowledge of XML is not assumed but some readers may find our introduction to it rather "steep sledding" and for those readers there is no shame in consulting an introductory text before or in parallel with ours. Other readers will find though that it all sinks in fairly rapidly once one works through some of the projects that actually do something with XML.

There is a general progression in the project material from easier to more complex applications of XML and from less to more rigorous utilization of XML concepts, tools, and standards. Our motivation for this was partly pedagogical and partly because we are addressing application designers and developers with different needs. But we would like to alert the reader again to the fact that a lot of our knowledge of XML is diffused throughout the project descriptions and we do think that many will find it profitable to follow the progression of the material.

Frankly, it is nigh impossible to write a book that will be absolutely up-to-date on every topic associated with XML. That said we worked until three deadlines past the deadline where our publisher threatened to have us shot to incorporate the latest developments in XML into this text. Our more general solution to this dilemma is to emphasize the problem space and design principles which will always be useful in working with XML and will give one a solid basis for understanding the evolutions in XML to come.

The CD-ROM contains most of the material presenting in the project chapters including source code, document type definitions, XML, stylesheets and so forth as well as the JDK, Perl, and the distributions of the public domain tools used in the text including AElfred, Jade, SP, sgrep, NXP, and SAX.

Acknowledgments

Our colleagues and friends Tim Bray and Jon Bosak are the two people most responsible for the genesis of XML and its incredibly rapid evolution into a W3C recommendation. We would like to express our admiration of these two excellent gentlemen and our thanks. Messrs. Bray and Bosak were joined in this undertaking by the other members of the W3C's XML editorial board and by other collaborators from around the world to whom we also render our deepest appreciation of their efforts.

We are indebted to the creators of various tools used in this book including Norbert Mikula (NXP), James Clark (SP and Jade), David Megginson (SAX), Pekka Kilpeläinen (sgrep), Jani Jaakkola (sgrep), Eleftherios Koutsofios (dotty), Stephen North (dotty), and Microstar Corporation (AElfred). Messrs. Kilpeläinen and Jaakkola also contributed an extensive and exacting review of the portion of our book on sgrep.

Aidan Killian contributed his keen insight and experience in reviewing portions of the manuscript. Henry Thompson and Ingo

Macherius graciously granted us permission to use illustrations created by them.

Stuart Culshaw, a European worth the weight of a Harrad's pork pie in gold, contributed important material to this book as did Gene Kan, our friend and colleague and a young man of exceptional talents.

Our apologies and thanks to our executive editor, Mark Taub, who, fortunately, knew when to brandish the brass knuckles, our production manager, Eileen Clark, who deserves a four week vacation on a sparkling Caribbean island, Mark, after coping with us, and all the staff at Prentice Hall who aided in the publishing of our book.

It has been a great honor for us to work with the series editor, Dr. Charles F. Goldfarb, inventor of SGML and grandfather of XML. Dr. Goldfarb may not be hesitant to apply the whip but he does so with such humor and intelligence that we didn't much mind our generally well-deserved flailings.

Matthew would like to thank Michael Leventhal for inviting him to co-author this book, David would like to thank Joan Bannan for her encouragement, support, and friendship, and Michael would like to thank Hoa Quach for sustaining him with countless bowls of pho ga and cups of tra gung prepared with lots of yeu.

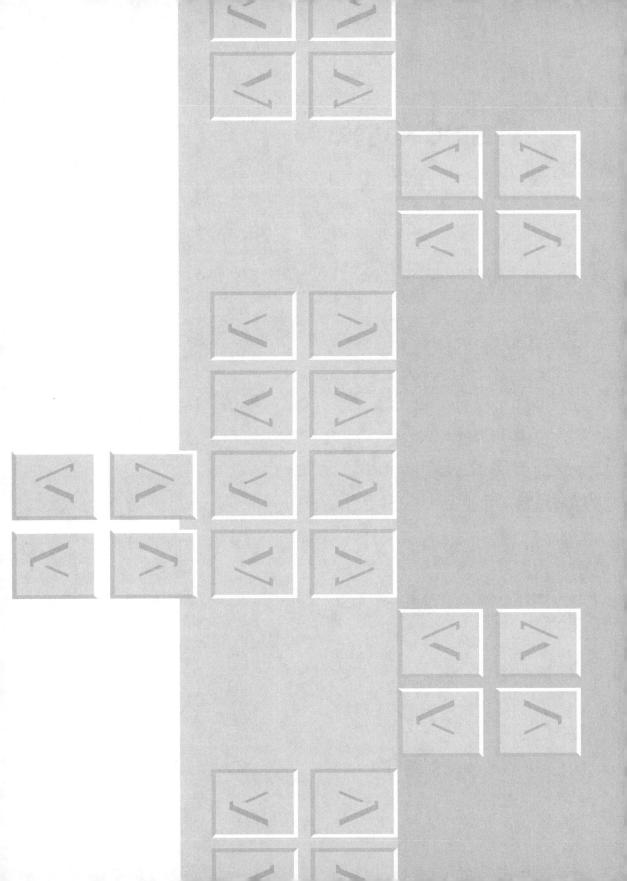

Part One

Internets, XML, and Tools

Internets

XML is a pivotal technology in the development of the Internet. In this first chapter we cover the philosophy behind XML and how it will affect your organization. This includes a new approach to documents and what we do with them. We will also include a roadmap of the rest of the book.

1.1 | Introduction

Despite the ever-changing panoply of tools, the reason businesses use computer technology remains the same: coordinate mission-critical resources and information to further the corporation's goals. From the "big iron" of the 1960s to the Internet of today, and on into the buzzwords of the future, this remains constant. Each new technology is measured ultimately by how it supports the corporation and is either kept or dropped (possibly after a fair amount of blood, hopefully not yours, is spilled) as this holds true.

The information systems world is awash in talk of corporate internets, intranets, and extranets, and companies across the globe are rushing to take advantage of this "new" technology. But in this rush, the technologies have been hyped to death with very little serious thought given to just what the Internet is used for. The user's goal, as in any corporate network, is to improve the information and resource sharing to further corporate objectives.

1.2 | Why XML

In this book we will introduce you to XML—the tool of choice for structured information in the networked age. We will show you how to use this important strategic technology to exploit the Internet to serve you. XML can not only help you in dealing with the new flashy buzzword technologies of the moment—such as groupware and the Internet—but also help insulate you from the booms and busts of the hot new products ready to drop in your lap in the future. Because we consider improving your life the primary goal of this book, we will not just blithely describe how to run a few products and then drop you but show just how XML can help you organize your information and resources better. We will introduce you to a *philosophy* of XML to help you get the most out of your Internet investment.

The ideas behind XML have been developing since the 1960s, culminating in the approval of XML's parent, SGML, as an international standard in 1986. SGML found its niches in publishing, defense contractors, and large multinationals (such as aircraft manufacturers). It was perceived (wrongly, its practitioners would claim) as a difficult technology for high-end systems by corporations with deep pockets. However, by the mid-1990s, large-scale transmission of SGML-based electronic documents around the World Wide Web had become commonplace through HTML (an SGML application built from the grass roots up). While HTML has played a key role in enabling the rapid development of the Web, the full power of SGML for the Internet remained largely untapped. In 1996 a working group under the aegis of the World Wide Web Consortium started developing XML, a streamlined version of SGML designed to simplify transmission of structured documents over the Web. In many ways XML is a "purification" of SGML, removing portions of it with limited application that complicate its very powerful and basically simple central ideas. Because of this, almost everything we have to say will apply equally to both and examples, except where explicitly stated, will conform to both. Unless the content clearly indicates otherwise the term "XML" will mean "XML and SGML."

But before getting into the nitty-gritty of XML and the Internet (in later chapters) we need to convince you to spend time and money implementing XML technology. We will approach this in two ways:

1. Describe the qualities of the ideal Internet—the Internet you hoped you'd get with just HTML, a Web server, and some browsers, or with your "Internet-in-a-box" solution, but didn't. Then we'll show you just how much closer you can get with XML, both the state of the art and future possibilities. There will be a small philosophical detour as we build the list of requirements. You can skip this, if you'd like, and get right to the list, but it will also explain how the pieces of this book fit together and show you how to lead your technology, rather than letting it lead you.

2. Tell you of all the whiz-bang possibilities XML has to offer. This gee-whiz approach shows you all the incremental capabilities you can have without having to "buy into" the whole concept (although you should buy the book).

In the end these are the same—it is the whiz-bang features which allow you to implement an Internet, and it is the Internet which makes those whiz-bang features useful.

1.3 | Structure of the Book

This book is divided into five parts.

In the first part we will introduce you to the XML universe. Here you will find a discussion of the role of XML in the internet and a quick-start on the XML recommendation and XML tools. We don't assume prior knowledge of either XML or SGML but our task here is not to provide an extended tutorial or reference on the language syntax. What we do do is develop the perspective of the XML internet application designer and provide any background that is needed to comprehend the subsequent chapters.

The next three parts consist of a series of projects using XML in actual internet applications. Working through the projects the reader will gain concrete experience in the design of XML applications, DTDs, and programming. We also delve into standards related to XML and the internet wherever relevant.

This first project spans five chapters as the construction of several types of components is involved including a bulletin board, forms processing tools, a search engine, and transformation filters.

Most of the work is done in Perl and the approach is less rigorous than that used in subsequent projects. Our intention here is to introduce XML programming in the most simple and "exposed" form possible.

We have chosen to use Perl in this first part for various reasons.

It is the closest thing we know of to a lingua franca for internet programmers, it is extremely compact allowing us to construct complete examples in relatively few lines of code, and, most significantly, Perl is the most versatile XML scripting language.

The second project implements SGML/XML email and digs into the topics of entity management, catalogs, MIME, and full-scale SGML/XML parsing. Code is presented in Perl and C++.

Lest the reader think we are Perl bigots the third project plunges us into Java and XML, building an application based on the Document Object Model and making use of an Java XML parser API. Java is the language in which most of the new XML internet infrastructure is being built.

The fifth and final section of the book takes a rigorous, formal look at the role of XML in software architectures and agents based on the paradigm of negotiation.

Full source code for all the projects has been included on the CD-ROM as have all the public domain tools used in the book.

1.4 | Let's Talk: Internets Are for Communicating

Shorn of its aura, the Internet is just a lot of sand-running programs and sending electrons on wires. However people do not knowingly spend enormous sums of money on such devices without some purpose in mind.

The essential business purpose of the Internet, never to be lost sight of, is communication. Before the computer, even before the printing press, there were international corporations with impressive networks spanning continents. The velocity of information was much different in those days, but the goals of the network haven't changed—to get important information to the concerned parties as quickly as possible and enable people to collaborate at a distance. Many of the problems and concerns which arise in the modern Internet already existed in the twelfth century: Security and encryption, network failures, baud rate (or gallop rate), common carrier versus private network, data format (written or spoken, English or French), gateways to other networks, and viruses (Bubonic plague, etc.) were all of importance back then as now, and one could look back even further. Their solutions may be of little current interest, but the similarities show that our concerns go beyond merely implementing the technology du jour and can give us a benchmark for judging our solutions.

If the Internet exists to support communication in an organization, what are the current requirements of this communication, and how do current solutions stack up against these requirements? There are two essential characteristics of the modern corporate network (as opposed to twelfth- or early twentieth-century corporate networks) really mandating a move to XML. The first is the incredible increase in the velocity of information, and the second is a shift from a dumb network linking information processing humans to a smart network where information is as likely (or more likely) to be processed by a computer as by a human. We will examine each of these in turn.

1.5 | The Velocity of Information

It was perfectly acceptable in the slow-paced days of the early nineteenth century for troops on the fringes of empires to continue fighting wars months after peace treaties had been signed, simply because it could take that long for word to spread; nowadays information travels at the speed of light and must be accessible any time, any place, anywhere. In particular, this means information must be able to find you and be presented to you in as meaningful a way as possible.

To do this, the network not only needs to know how to find you, but it must also have some idea of the importance of the information it is passing around and of the equipment you have at hand. In the old days, importance was determined by a secretary and presentation meant a sheet of paper with ink on it. Now few secretaries remain, so the network, or some components, must be able to examine and partly understand messages. The equipment at hand might still be paper, but it is more likely a workstation, a laptop, a PDA, a beeper, or even an audio response unit over the telephone. The variety of possible equipment means it must be possible to present the same message in a variety of formats.

1.6 | Into the Smart Network

While humans communicate with words, companies communicate with documents. Contracts, SEC filings, advertisements, memos, purchase orders, all of these are documents an organization uses to communicate both with other organizations and internally with itself.

Premodern networks communicated only among humans, and in the early computer age it was pretty obvious which nodes in the communication system were humans and which were not. No accounting program was likely to pass itself off as human. In corporations, computer usage was confined mostly to database and transactional applications.

However, as the power of computers increases, computers become capable of more flexible tasks. We will soon see computerized agents afloat in the corporate network becoming more and more central to a corporation's ability to respond quickly and accurately to changing circumstances. These agents will receive and process orders and invoices, schedule appointments, and perform other complex tasks integrated with humans. Their sophistication is limited only by their ability to understand and manipulate the information presented to them, in turn limited by our ability to program them.

The existence of these agents is inevitably driven by the increasing velocity, and amount, of information. Smaller decisions may no longer be delayable until a human can examine information; people may need to search through huge amounts of information and require agents to help sift it down to a manageable amount. In many cases there is a tremendous time savings if humans can pass information directly to their computers. For example, if an e-mail contains a meeting proposal, the proposed time should be checked automatically against the recipient's current schedule. Other kinds of interesting information, such as the biographies of the participants, should also be readily at hand. A decision to have the meeting should automatically start travel arrangements. Alternatively, incoming documents, such as SEC document filings, will be handled first by computers, then later by humans, who may then request further handling from computers, as well as sending the information to other humans.

Documents have traditionally been only human-readable; they have been used exclusively to pass information among the human participants of a corporation's networks. With the increase in computer power and performance, this view is too limited. For computers to do their tasks, they need to understand much the same information as the humans. Most document technologies, such as word processors, developed by and for humans, result in documents that are "illegible" to computers. Computers require large-scale artificial intelligence front ends to understand these, making agents difficult to write. Any document technology that bridges the gap between the human structures and the kinds of structure computerized agents need to act on will become strategically important. XML bridges the gap.

1.7 | Current Approaches— Can the Web Help?

Recently two approaches to distributed technologies, hypertext (represented by HTML) and object-oriented programming (represented by Java), have collided to provide the technological substrate for the current World Wide Web architecture. Unfortunately they have collided just where they are most incompatible. HTML is reasonably useful for displaying hyperlinked information to humans, while Java, an object-oriented language in the style of C++, functions well for controlling computers. But they don't talk to each other. Let's examine each.

1.7.1 *HTML*

Hypertext Markup Language (HTML), first developed in 1989 by Tim Berners-Lee at CERN and since extended in both a standard and ad hoc fashion by numerous programmers and researchers around the world, is the undisputed lingua franca of the Web and has introduced the concept of distributed hypertext to people around the globe. Despite this success, the language started out with simple goals; in many ways it is a paradigmatic example of a prototype too quickly made into a product.

We stated at the beginning of this book that HTML is an SGML application. SGML applications can and do have a wide variety of intended purposes; the purpose of HTML is to enable the transmission and display of hypertext documents across a network. (A hypertext document is a document which contains explicit links to other documents. On a command from the user, such as a mouse click, a computer can retrieve and display these other documents. Although many documents contain links to other documents, such as footnotes, hypertext is different because the links can be automatically, and immediately, traversed by a computer.) Unlike the majority of SGML applications, it is not suitable for representing the structure of the information contained in the document for purposes other than display. A typical HTML document (we will deal with exceptions later) is a string of text separated by *tags* (Figure 1–1). For the most part, the text specifies *what* to display, while the tags specify *how* to display it. There are additional tags to specify placement of pictures and tags to specify hyperlinks. An HTML document is like a standard Word Processing (WP) document with links added. WP documents are also strings separated by tags, except that the tags are usually unreadable control characters. In both cases the tags specify the layout of the document—where pieces of text and graphics are to be placed, which font to use, what size, color, and so on. In essence, HTML and WP documents are specifications for how to draw a picture on a screen or piece of paper for viewing by a human. HTML provides the additional functionality of hyperlinking to automatically retrieve other documents when requested by the user.

```
<!DOCTYPE HTML PUBLIC "+//ISBN 82-7640-037::WWW//DTD
HTML//EN//2.0" "html.dtd">
<HTML>
<HEAD>
<TITLE>Sane Corporation: How to Contact us</TITLE>
```

Figure 1-1   HTML Fragment

However this picture-oriented view of documents is very limited. Any number of perfectly reasonable tasks are difficult to impossible:

- Automatically find all the section titles in a document. This appears like an easy task, but HTML's heading tags are identified in authors' minds with a particular appearance, used wherever the desired text appearance is desired. Collecting all the H1, H2, and so on, tags in a document may retrieve all the section headings but might gather a lot more lines as well. In addition, font tags can also be used for sections.
- Automatically number document sections. Doing this requires solving the previous problem.
- Break a document into its constituent parts for storage in a database. As with finding section headings, HTML gives little idea of the document structure; there is no obvious way to break it up.
- Radically reformat the document for other purposes besides Web browsing. For example, a document might be part of a book or magazine as well as be displayed on-line.
- Hand a document, or part of a document, such as a schedule or purchase order to a specialized agent for further processing. This kind of capability is particularly useful for business forms.

- Specify in a systematic way what kind of link a URL points to, that is, how does it fit into the document at hand.
- Instantly change the way a particular item of information is displayed every place it occurs among your documents—without changing a single document.

The basic point of these examples is to show that HTML is good for little beyond its original purpose of showing a particular picture to humans on a particular type of screen. This makes HTML a very brittle format, particularly when one considers the large scaffolding necessary to support this particular task in an industrial setting.

HTML is particularly bad at communicating information to computational agents. While humans can communicate by sending HTML, humans and computers can barely communicate through the use of HTML forms; it is ludicrous to consider computational agents sending each other HTML documents as a means of communicating—they wouldn't know what to do besides draw a picture.

1.7.2 *Java*

The Java programming language, developed by James Gosling and his team at Sun Microsystems, is a fairly standard object-oriented programming language with a couple of very interesting features, making it ideal for developing computer programs to be delivered over the Web.

In object-oriented programming, the application is composed of many objects sending each other messages. Similar objects are organized in groups called *classes*. Each class accepts a specific group of messages. To create objects in a class that accept other messages, a *subclass* can be created with some additional messages. In most object-oriented languages, including Java, each message is handled by a chunk of computer code called a *method* (essentially a function), and sending a message is called *method invocation*. The contents of a message is a combination of program values, strings, references to other objects, and so on, corresponding to the values the method is expecting. For example, an e-mail object would have methods to retrieve senders, receivers, and contents. A multimedia e-mail would have additional methods to handle the different kinds of media it could contain.

What makes Java so interesting for Internet applications are

- Its use of a byte-code interpreter, allowing the same program code to be run on any workstation in the network, and

- Its run-time linker, allowing a client to dynamically load classes from anywhere on the network to create new objects.

Extensions to the basic language allow objects to invoke methods on objects residing on remote servers.

What interests us here is the manner in which Java objects communicate—by method invocation. As with other OO languages, the Java world is divided up into objects, and each object belongs to a class. The class defines a set of messages that member objects are able to receive and process. Method invocations in Java, as in C++, are similar to procedure calls in more traditional languages. Figure 1–2 gives a tiny example of a Java class.

Just as HTML is an acceptable means of communicating among humans using browsers, but lousy for communicating with computer programs, method invocation is a good means for software objects to communicate among themselves but lousy for communicating with or among humans, even if they are professional programmers. Just as it would be ludicrous for objects to communicate by passing HTML, it is equally ludicrous for humans to communicate by method invocation with binary data. Humans don't reach into each other's heads to manipulate objects when they communicate.

```
class HelloWorldClass {
  String message;
  public static void main(String [] args){
    HelloWorldClass instance = new HelloWorldClass("hello
world");
    instance.method();
  }
  public HelloWorldClass(String msg){
    message = msg;
  }
  public void method(){
    System.out.println(message);
  }
}
```

Figure 1–2   Java

1.8 | Where the Web Needs Help

The core problem of the current set of Web technologies is a lack of closure. HTML is acceptable for displaying information to humans, but not to computational agents. Method invocation [either Java, or the industry-standard Common Object Request Broker Architecture (CORBA), which is extending into the Internet with the IIOP protocol] provides a mechanism for fairly fine-grained communication among computational objects, but not among humans.

Each of these technologies is effective for communicating among a subset of the participants in the Internet, but none is capable of handling all of them. Handling the mismatches among them is a major programming effort, as each, to some degree, requires reinventing the wheel. These incompatibilities remain a major impediment. In a sense, we are in the position of application development before the invention of the database, when each application kept its own files and passing information among them was very difficult.

There is, however, one technology out there which has the possibility of bridging the gap between humans and computers. This is XML (and its parent SGML), designed to encode information in ways compatible to both man and machine. To really see how this works, though, we need to reconsider the meaning of a document.

1.9 | Beyond the Traditional Document

Documents are traditionally viewed in information systems as pictures shown to the user at the leaves of the network. Communication with users is through these pictures, which are not directly treatable by machine, and communication among programs is through means incomprehensible to humans (i.e., HTML versus Java). This relegates humans to receptive leaves and reduces their ability to impact the total system. And yet, the same information is being passed around in two incompatible forms (again, HTML and Java). By unifying how we pass information to humans with how we pass information to computational agents, we can remove humans from the periphery of the network and place them in the center.

We can unify these diverse technologies by viewing documents as *intentional* messages sent by agents (human or computational) out into the world to have some effect. In some cases, the desired effect is merely to convey information. In others it is to purchase goods and services, gather people together to meet, schedule production, and the like. From this perspective, sending the memo, document, or method invocation, *is* the action of offering, requesting, or informing, and not just a reflection of it, with the actual event done entirely behind the scenes in software. These messages can be passed among any parties in the network, as well as stored and later referenced.

This view of communication has its origin in *speech act theory*, first suggested by the English philosopher John Austin in his book *How to Do Things with Words* and later extended by the American philosopher, John Searle. More recently speech act theory has been influential in a number of areas of computer science, particularly artificial intelligence and groupware. The basic idea is a break with traditional logic, which views speech as only making statements about what is true or false in the world, and adopt a more active view where statements, themselves, can actually do things. The classic example is wedding vows. Once the couple has said "I do," they are married; two small statements said in the right context have changed the couple's status in the world and created a whole new set of rights and obligations. There are a variety of speech acts, such as promising, offering, requesting, and informing. We are less interested here in the exact list than in the viewpoint.

As we can see, our documents already behave as speech acts, but our computer systems only support this in the most tortured fashion. The goal of the next section is to begin to show how to implement this richer concept of document.

1.10 | Toward the Active Document

We can view documents as coming in three levels of structure:

1. Unformatted, or very loosely structured.
   Examples of such a document include e-mail and pure images. The structure is understood only by a human reader through his or her knowledge of grammar or the picture presented. There is little information for a computer to manipulate. They are extensions of older kinds of communications such as talking and drawing; they are perfect when humans communicate informally. E-mail can convey a certain amount of structure through the use of indentation; however it is limited through reliance on a single font. E-mail will normally

have the underlying structure of the human language it is written in, easily understood by human recipients willing to read it.

2. Formatted documents.

    These are typically word processed documents or forms. The presentation of the document is well specified, so the appropriate computer program can correctly display this document, but no more than that. Such documents are extensions of traditional print media, which themselves extended unformatted text with visual cues to aid readers. Unlike e-mail, formatted text can convey many visual cues using color, point size, pictures, and so on. Word processed documents, however, are very much like pictures, so the recipient can understand some of the structure without reading. The processing instructions tell the computer how to paint the picture of the document (formatting some text as centered, bold, 14 point, helvetica) but don't say what the picture means (a chapter title). This makes formatted documents extremely difficult for computers to understand beyond display, especially when the same instruction string (i.e., identical formatting) can mean different things in different places. HTML essentially belongs in this category.

3. Structured documents.

    These are documents where the document itself contains enough added information for either a computer or a human to easily understand the underlying structure. For this to be possible,

    ■ The markup should use names that are *semantically significant*, meaning they designate what something *is* (such as title, section, part, etc.), rather than how to display it as a picture (bold, helvetica, centered, etc.). Although a computer doesn't care what labels are given to markup, the humans programming the computer do. We can distinguish the semantics into two types, the *abstract* semantics, given by the element type name, and the *operational* semantics, which is what the program does with the information. Formatting information for printing is one kind of operational semantics, often derived from the abstract semantics (for example, we may associate the formatting semantics "24 pt. helvetica, centered" from the fact that the abstract semantics specifies a "Chapter Title").

■ The markup used must delineate the logical structure of the document, so a *book* element contains a *title* followed by one or more *chapters*, each containing some number of *paragraphs* and *figures*, and so on.

■ The markup must be *grammatical.* This means there is a set of rules available specifying how elements relate to each other, which elements can contain other ones, and what order they come in. Otherwise there is no way for the computer (and its users) to be sure that the title comes first in a book, and that chapters cannot, themselves, contain books.

Using this kind of hierarchical structure makes it possible for a computer to parse the pieces of a document and process them. The document becomes one large data structure, with these tags identifying each piece and what composes it. These structured documents subsume the two other types, as minimal markup could just indicate a string of ASCII text, or the markup terms could expressly indicate presentation format.

Address as unformatted text

```
Matthew Fuchs
110 Some St.
Anytown, CA 91100


{\rtf1\ansi\ansicpg1252\uc1
\deff0\deflang1033\deflangfe1033{\fonttbl{\f0\fro-
man\fcharset0\fprq2{\*\panose 02020603050405020304}Times
New Roman;}{\f16\froman\fcharset238\fprq2 Times New Roman
CE;}{\f17\froman\fcharset204\fprq2 Times New Roman Cyr;}
{\f19\froman\fcharset161\fprq2 Times New Roman
Greek;}{\f20\froman\fcharset162\fprq2 Times New Roman
Tur;}{\f21\froman\fcharset186\fprq2 Times New Roman Bal-
tic;}}{\col-
ortbl;\red0\green0\blue0;\red0\green0\blue255;\red0\green
255\blue255;
\red0\green255\blue0;\red255\green0\blue255;\red255\green
0\blue0;\red255\green255\blue0;\red255\green255\blue255;\
red0\green0\blue128;\red0\green128\blue128;\red0\green128
\blue0;\red128\green0\blue128;\red128\green0\blue0;\red12
8\green128\blue0;
\red128\green128\blue128;\red192\green192\blue192;}{\styl
esheet{\nowidctlpar\widctlpar\adjustright \fs20\cgrid
\snext0 Normal;}{\*\cs10 \additive Default Paragraph
Font;}}{\info{\title Matthew Fuchs}{\author matthew
fuchs}{\operator matthew fuchs}
{\crea-
tim\yr1998\mo1\dy22\hr2\min23}{\revtim\yr1998\mo1\dy22\hr
2\min24}{\version1}{\edmins1}{\nofpages1}{\nofwords0}{\no
fchars0}{\*\company   }{\nofcharsws0}{\vern71}}\widowc-
trl\ftnbj\aenddoc\form-
shade\viewkind4\viewscale100\pgbrdrhead\pgbrdrfoot \fet0
\sectd \linex0\endnhere\sectdefaultcl {\*\pnseclvl1\pnu-
crm\pnstart1\pnindent720\pnhang{\pntxta
.}}{\*\pnseclvl2\pnu-
cltr\pnstart1\pnindent720\pnhang{\pntxta
.}}{\*\pnseclvl3\pndec\pnstart1\pnindent720\pnhang{\pntxt
a .}}{\*\pnseclvl4
```

Figure 1–3   Document Taxonomy —The Three Levels of Structure

---

Address as formatted text in RTF

```
\pnlcltr\pnstart1\pnindent720\pnhang{\pntxta
)}}{\*\pnseclvl5\pndec\pnstart1\pnindent720\pnhang{\pntxt
b (}{\pntxta
)}}{\*\pnseclvl6\pnlcltr\pnstart1\pnindent720\pnhang{\pnt
xtb (}{\pntxta
)}}{\*\pnseclvl7\pnlcrm\pnstart1\pnindent720\pnhang{\pntx
tb (}
{\pntxta
)}}{\*\pnseclvl8\pnlcltr\pnstart1\pnindent720\pnhang{\pnt
xtb (}{\pntxta
)}}{\*\pnseclvl9\pnlcrm\pnstart1\pnindent720\pnhang{\pntx
tb (}{\pntxta )}}\pard\plain \nowidctlpar\widctlpar\
adjustright \fs20\cgrid {Matthew Fuchs
\par 110 Some St.
\par Anytown CA, 91100
\par }}
```

Address as structured text - XML

```
<address>
<name>Matthew Fuchs</name>
<street>110 Some St.</street>
<state>CA</state><zip>91100</zip>
</address>
```

Figure 1–3 Document Taxonomy *(continued)*—The Three Levels of

It is only the last type, structured documents, which can really function as general intentional messages among humans and computers. There are some significant differences between these messages and, say, e-mail messages:

- They contain a significant amount of structure. A fair amount of explicit structure is necessary for messages to be manipulated in any meaningful way by computer systems. Although hope for AI springs eternal, the systems available in the near term can only take advantage of the most obvious implicit structure.

- The structure conforms to a publicly available grammar. This way, any party can retrieve a description of the message syntax and parse it. Without such a grammar, it is impossible to agree on what is a correct document.

- The receiver is free to apply his own set of operational semantics to the message.

- The message may contain or reference more than one type of abstract semantics. Each abstract semantic type corresponds to a subdocument whose structure is interpreted separately by the receiving application. For example, an announcement of a meeting may contain an agenda for that meeting. The announcement would be the containing structure but the agenda would have its own structure which could be interpreted independently by the receiver's software.

A good example of these, in fact, are computer programs, which are highly structured documents humans use to communicate with computers and with each other (if subsequent programmers are included). The structure is partly for the benefit of humans, since the final program is always the same object code. The public availability of the grammar permits the development of compilers, pretty printers, revision control systems, and other development tools. Each one of these tools has a different semantics for the information—compilers see it as instructions for generating object code while pretty printers or class browsers see it as formatting instructions.

Programming languages, however, are large and complex beasts. They are also too highly structured to be really useful for communications among humans. Our goal is to develop far more manageable languages corresponding to the kinds of things your organization does.

1.11 | Down to the Nitty-Gritty

In the course of its business, a corporation may deal with a variety of different document types—purchase orders, memos, legal documents, and the like. Each of these represents a separate minilanguage the corporation must be able to understand, each with a different grammar and semantics.

It is not possible to escape this multilingual environment; your corporation speaks several dialects already. However, to keep order among these dialects, they should be defined so that the same software tools can be applied to all of them regardless of domain. This is accomplished through the use of a single metagrammar system for defining all the languages. This means that "under the hood" they all look the same; a metagrammar is essentially a grammar for defining grammars.

We now have the outline of a multilayer applications architecture. The components are

- The metagrammar itself. This is the system used to define the grammars for the various languages. In this book we will use one called XML because it has shown itself to be ideal for communication among humans and computers.
- The particular language definition for documents in the problem domain. In XML jargon, this is called a Document Type Definition (DTD). For our approach to work, this grammar must be *public*, so that all the applications which need access to it can find it.
- A particular document conforming to the language.
- A parser which, when given a DTD, can parse conforming documents. The parser recognizes the structural elements of the document and makes them available to the application which processes them.

- One of several potential applications which can work on the output of the parser. Each application applies a separate semantics to the parsed document, as discussed above.
- All the resources of the Internet.

These elements together form the kernel of the XML Internet architecture. We will show how all these pieces fit together through a small example. To do this we will discuss the core elements of XML and information markup; a more thorough tutorial on all of XML is coming up soon.

1.12 | What Do We Do with Documents?

Once we accept the fact that documents are the communication medium of the corporation, and the Internet is the channel by which they are passed around, our next step is to show how we do things with documents.

In the old world we wrote documents, we read them, we filed (or threw) them away, we sent them around, and occasionally we looked through our files and retrieved them. Sometimes we even took different actions based on the contents of the documents. Now we need to look at a wider repertoire of operations and create document-centric business applications by combining them. Some of these have been performed previously by computers; others were performed by the humans using the documents. Now we need to make them all explicit in order to let our computers do them as well.

There are 11 basic operations we will discuss here. We will list them briefly and then describe them at greater length.

- Search through a document or a set of documents.
- Retrieve either from a database or through the Internet.

- Store a document in a database or in files.
- Transform a document from one document type to another.
- Link information in one document to information in another document, or even in the same one.
- Send/receive a document to/from another "agent" on the network.
- Compare two or more documents, or pieces from within a single document.
- Import/export documents between XML and some other format, such as Microsoft's Rich Text Format (RTF).
- Interpret a document as if it were a program.
- Define a DTD or document language.
- Create a document either individually (using an editor) or automatically through an application.

While discussing these operations, we will refer to a small, but universally known, example: the organization chart (org-chart). The org-chart, which lists the employees of the corporation and chain of command, is fairly ubiquitous. In this scenario, which is intentionally kept simple and general, Widget Co. already has an internet with employee home pages on-line. They now wish to place the corporate org-chart on-line, with links to all the home pages. Employees, of course, will also want to be able to include the org-chart information in their own pages or to link to appropriate locations in it.

Figure 1–4 gives a short example DTD for an org-chart, Figure 1–5 shows the same DTD in a graphic version generated with Near & Far Designer, and Figure 1–6 describes a very small organization using our org-chart DTD. For the sake of clarity (and brevity) we have exploited an SGML feature and defined element types with common context models together. In XML, each element type is defined separately, leading, in this case, to a much larger DTD. It is not necessary for the reader to understand the DTD in detail at this point. We provide a microtutorial in the following section which will enable you to identify the portions of it we reference in subsequent sections and all discussion in this chapter is at a functional rather than syntactic level. This DTD is simple but still adequate for expressing basic organizational information. We will see that this baseline structure can be extended in any number of ways depending on the particularities of the implementation for a specific company. Elaborations and augmentation of this DTD can be constructed so that those additions and elaborations will be systematically derived from the base DTD. A base DTD often serves as the vehicle for interchange information between organizations, each of which has developed its own more specialized applications for internal use.

```
<!ELEMENT business-unit (name,address,officer,
  description,business-unit*)>
<!ELEMENT (name|address|position|phone|email)
  (#PCDATA)>
<!ELEMENT officer (employee,(officer|employee)*)>
<!ELEMENT employee (name,address,position,phone,
  email,home-page?,responsibilities)>
<!ELEMENT (responsibilities|description)
  (htext|essay)>
<!ELEMENT home-page EMPTY>
<!ELEMENT essay (title,section+)>
<!ELEMENT title (#PCDATA)>
<!ELEMENT section (title?, p+)>
<!ELEMENT htext (#PCDATA|a)*>
<!ELEMENT p (htext|ul|ol)*>
<!ELEMENT a (#PCDATA)>
<!ELEMENT (ul|ol) (li+)>
<!ELEMENT li (htext)>
<!ATTLIST (a|home-page) href CDATA #REQUIRED>
<!ATTLIST (phone|email)
  visibility (internal|external) "internal">
<!ATTLIST address
  visibility (internal|external) "external"
  location (hq|other) "other">
```

Figure 1–4 Org-Chart DTD

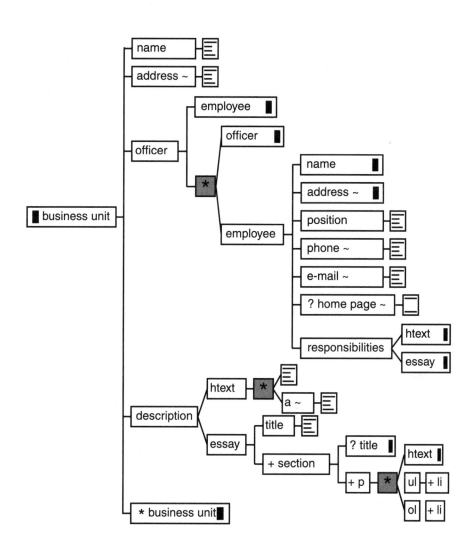

Figure 1–5 Org-Chart DTD—Graphic View

```
<business-unit>
<name>Sales</name><address>Main HQ</address>
<officer><name>John Bialystock</name>
<address>Corner Office</address><position>EVP</position>
<phone>951-555-1212</phone>....
</officer>
<description>They sell stuff</description>
  <business-unit> <!-- children -->
  <name>Consumer Sales</name>
  <officer><name>Alan Chuzzlewitz</name></officer>
  <address>In the Booneys</address>
  ...
  </business-unit>
</business-unit>
```

Figure 1–6 An Organization and Its Org-Chart

1.13 | DTDs and Content Specifications—A Short Excursion

A structured document is composed of a tree of elements. Each element can contain subelements or data. The entire document, such as a book, is a single element containing smaller elements, such as chapters, and they contain even smaller ones, down to the individual characters of the book's text.

The placement of the elements in this large, even enormous, tree is scarcely random—chapters cannot contain books, nor can footnotes contain chapters. Determining whether or not a document is a valid book requires rules stating which elements (if any) can go in other elements.

These rules create Book, a language for books, with its own grammar for generating or parsing books. While an English sentence has a noun, a verb, and an optional direct object, a sentence of Book may have a title, a list of chapters, and optional appendices.

As XML is traditionally used for documents, an XML grammar for a language such as Book is called a Document Type Definition, or DTD. The rule in a DTD which describes each structural component is called an element type declaration; the rule has a left-hand side, which names the element type being defined, and a right-hand side, called a content specification, which specifies the valid subelements. A DTD corresponding to the small book tree is in Figure 1–7.

```
<!ELEMENT book (front-matter, chapter+, index?)>
<!ELEMENT front-matter (title, author, dedication)>
<!ELEMENT title (#PCDATA)>
<!ELEMENT author (#PCDATA)>
<!ELEMENT dedication (#PCDATA)>
<!ELEMENT chapter (title, paragraph+)>
<!ATTLIST chapter revision CDATA #REQUIRED>
<!ELEMENT paragraph (#PCDATA)>
<!ELEMENT index (entry+)>
<!ELEMENT entry (phrase, location+)>
<!ELEMENT phrase EMPTY>
<!ATTLIST phrase text CDATA #REQUIRED>
<!ELEMENT location EMPTY>
<!ATTLIST location pageno CDATA #REQUIRED>
```

Figure 1–7   Book DTD

The exact anatomy of an actual element type declaration in a DTD is as follows:

- The opening string "<!ELEMENT" specifying this will be an element type declaration.
- The name of the element type being defined.
- The content specification specifying the subelement. An element can either
  - Be empty. This requires a content specification of EMPTY.
  - Contain only character data. This requires a content specification of #PCDATA (Parsed Character Data).

- ■ Contain only other elements.
- ■ Contain mixed content, meaning both character data and other elements.
- ■ A closing ">".

In the actual XML document, the document tree can only be implicit; the document is just a string of characters. The hierarchical structure is created through the use of markup specifying the beginning and ending of each element. So the book element, for example, starts with the *start-tag* <book> and ends with the *end-tag* </book>; the chapter element with <chapter> and </chapter>.

```
<book>
<front-matter>
<title>Something about the Internet</title>
<author>John Doe</author>
<dedication>To my loving wife and adoring children
</dedication>
<chapter revision = "10"><title>Isn't the Internet Wonder-
ful</title>
<paragraph>What could be as wonderful as the Internet?
Look how the
whole world is abuzz!  And what's at the middle of it all?
XML!</paragraph>
<paragraph>... more good stuff on XML ...</paragraph>
... more paragraphs ...
</chapter>
<chapter revision = "5"><title>HTML, or the Ways of our
Ancestors</title>
<paragraph>HTML is the primitive hypertext format which
helped spark
the Web</paragraph>...
</chapter>
<index>
<entry><phrase text="xml"><location pageno = "1"><location
pageno =
"2"></entry>...
</index>
</book>
```

Figure 1–8   XML Markup

The final XML concept we will need are attributes. Attributes allow one to annotate elements with additional information. Attributes are placed inside the element's start tag, as in Figure 1–9, where the chapter tag has a "revision" attribute. Attributes are defined by another type of DTD declaration, the ATTLIST. For the sake of brevity the syntax of an ATTLIST declaration is not described here but an example of an ATTLIST is shown in Figure 1–10.

```
<chapter revision="10">
```

Figure 1–9   Attributes Modify Elements

```
<!ATTLIST chapter revision NUMBER #REQUIRED>
```

Figure 1–10   ATTLIST

1.13.1 *Search*

Whether represented in XML or not, your documents are part of the greater corporate resources. And wherever there are data there is a need to search them. Queries on unstructured documents are limited in complexity to keyword search or string matching. It is possible to determine proximity of different phrases, but nothing as specific as:

- The first sentence in the third paragraph of the last chapter. This type of query is essential to any kind of group editing.
- All the meetings mentioned in memos to the president of Wild Widgets, Inc.
- All the lines Mercutio says to Romeo in *Romeo and Juliet.*

In the org-chart example, we might want to find out:

■ For whom does employee X work? (Alternatively, does employee X work under employee Y?)

■ How many employees work under X? What are their names?

■ What department does X work in? (Alternatively, who is in charge of X's department?)

```
<business-unit>
<name>Sales</name><address>Main HQ</address>
<officer><name>John Bialystock</name>
<address>Corner Office</address><position>EVP</position>
<phone>951-555-1212</phone>....
</officer>
<description>They sell stuff</description>
  <business-unit> <!-- children -->
  <name>Consumer Sales</name>
  <officer><name>Alan Chuzzlewitz</name></officer>
  <address>In the Booneys</address>
  ...
  </business-unit>
</business-unit>
```

Figure 1–11   Answering the Query "Who does Alan Chuzzlewitz work for?"

These kinds of queries are traditionally performed against databases, not documents, and the current Web effectively separates the information to be displayed from the information to be queried, thereby requiring two or more technologies: HTML for display, forms for canned queries provided by the server, and possibly a Java interface. Suppose a client receives the org-chart in HTML. Some questions, such as the name of an employee's supervisors might be simple to answer from looking at the screen, but others, such as how many people are in a particular department, are time-consuming to calculate solely from searching by hand. If the answers to these questions are not explicitly placed in the document, then either an HTML form or Java applet must perform the query. However, if the query is not one of a standard few, the user will need to know the database schema to compose the query and have general access to the database to perform it. As it is hard to anticipate all possible queries, it is quite likely that some desirable functionality is simply unimplemented.

If the org-chart is structured, however, many queries can be processed directly against the document. The information to display conforms to the same "schema" as the information to be queried. The same query can be processed either by the client or the server; the server need not implement all possible queries or make available all resources. A client can make queries against the org-chart by traversing the document, either up or down, without any server processing, except to return additional documents. Of course, the org-chart for a large multinational corporation would be several megabytes, but there are ways to divide up the document to require only portions of it.

Some of the queries possible with structured documents seem to require advanced AI technology not easily available to many companies, but that's not the case. AI is necessary when the document's structure provides no assistance to the query engine. This is particularly true when the document is just natural language. In a structured document, the markup is designed to highlight the structure by putting the semantics directly into the syntax, so the complexity of analysis is reduced to manageable levels. There is an upper limit to the amount of structure that can easily be imposed on a document intended for human consumption, but one of the nice aspects of XML is the ability to mix both structured and unstructured information, so a string of text with no explicit markup could also contain a chunk of highly structured information, such as a mention of a meeting in a paragraph of text.

1.13.2 *Retrieve*

Retrieval is closely linked to search but remains a separate, occasionally complex, activity. Both database and XML worlds share the concept (sometimes ignored for efficiency) that any particular piece of information should be stored only once, no matter how many other pieces it is linked to. Any particular document may be composed of a number of pieces to be (re)assembled for the finished product.

As an example, consider retrieving a form letter sent to a client. No copy of the letter itself may exist on-line, it was present in your system only for the few moments it took for it to be automatically composed and sent to the printer. Nevertheless, your system maintains a program or other skeleton which indicates how the various pieces can be reconstructed. The query "find me the letters sent to the Widget Corp. on June 23" may result in a number of records which are used, in turn, to retrieve the various pieces composing the actual letters.

Even where there is also a scanned version of the document stored locally, having access to the marked-up version remains important. It is more difficult to manipulate either the scanned version or a text version generated through Optical Character Recognition (OCR) than to manipulate the marked-up original. The marked-up version provides all the advantages of the structural search mentioned above, while the OCR version is no better than e-mail.

In the case of the org-chart, we must consider the potential size of the document. The complete document could comprise several megabytes of storage. Although the storage cannot be avoided, the time to load, format, and display the document for each retrieval can be controlled; only as much of the document should be loaded as is necessary.

With the org-chart we can deal with size issues by dividing the total document hierarchically. The topmost "hub" document contains only the upper echelons of the corporation. Departments and other subordinate entities are stored separately and only retrieved as required. Because the DTD defines both the entire organization and each department as a *business entity*, each department can exist as either an independent document or as part of the larger document. A particular retrieval might access only a particular office of a department, rather than the entire document. This can be implemented either directly by the document management system (in which case it should be transparent to the user), or by extending the DTD to explicitly describe how the pieces fit together, a subject which will be explored further in the section on hyperlinking.

1.13.3 *Store*

Storing a document is the obvious flipside of retrieval, but these are not just mirror operations. When retrieving a document, various pieces are assembled. When storing a document, it is broken up again. How to do this is not obvious: the seams among the original pieces may no longer be evident or may be inappropriate (if it is a document received from elsewhere, the original pieces may not exist locally). The simplest solution is to store the whole document in one chunk, but this can have drawbacks.

If you consider the document part of your corporate information resources on a par with more traditional forms of data, then the document must be stored in a way which makes it easy to search and otherwise manipulate. Our ability to do this is vastly increased by using a database. However, it must always be possible to resurrect the original document from its dissected form. So we need to retain a skeleton of the original document indicating where the various pieces have been placed. This could be automatic in some databases, but if not, must be done explicitly.

One example of the flexibility of information markup is the possibility to create a DTD for documents which describe how to break up other documents, which can be transmitted with the original document. This could be particularly useful if certain pieces are just "boilerplate" or are time-sensitive and should always be regenerated on the fly.

1.13.4 *Send/Receive*

Sending and receiving documents are analogous to storing and retrieving, as the storage system can be seen as just another agent. In practical terms, however, they are quite different. When sending or receiving, we are quite possibly sending documents over the network, so it is important to determine just what to send and how to package it so the document can be reconstructed on the other side.

In our scenario, changes in the org-chart can trigger memos to be sent to partners and employees, probably via e-mail.

Of course, sending the document as raw XML may not serve the needs of the recipient. If the org-chart uses a standard DTD, known to the recipient, then they can use their existing software, but if not, the sender must either send it with the document, or inform the receiver where to look for it.

In an internet, some of this problem can be mitigated by ensuring that standard organizational entities are present at all locations. Another approach is through standardizing on an XML MIME type. MIME allows the creation of multipart e-mail messages. XML MIME messages can contain all the pieces, such as entities, necessary for reassembling a document. Defining all possible pieces as URLs ensures that the recipient can eventually find everything necessary.

Beyond reconstructing a document, the other interesting question for the recipient is deciding what to do with an incoming document. It can simply be routed for display to a human, or it can be manipulated by an automated agent and stored in a database, or otherwise acted upon. For example, an incoming purchase order can be printed in a less automated organization or automatically processed to produce the corresponding work orders in a more sophisticated one.

1.13.5 *Import/Export*

It is unfortunate that not all information is encoded in some form of XML. Therefore it is occasionally, sometimes even frequently, necessary to convert between XML and some other format. Very common is conversion between XML and some word processing format, such as RTF or Postscript. Another issue is the exact mechanics of storage and retrieval—exporting from XML to a database format and importing back in again.

Importing and exporting may not be necessary for our org-chart unless we need to import it initially if it is in a database or project management software before we convert it to XML.

There are other uses for import and export. An important one is electronic commerce—converting between a rich internal XML format and a narrower EDI format, such as EDIFACT or ASC X12, both international standards, but very limited to fixed format fields—sufficient, perhaps for encoding a transmission, but not for internal use.

1.13.6 *Type Transformation*

Type transformation means converting a document of one type (i.e., conforming to a particular document type definition) to one or more new documents conforming to one or more DTDs. Transformation usually takes place when you put your information to some kind of use.

The most common form of transformation is converting a document encoded with high-level information markup to one with low-level presentation markup as preparation for final delivery to a bit-mapped display or printer. In the current Web world, the low-level presentation markup of choice appears to be HTML, and there are both public domain and for-profit tools for converting from a private DTD to HTML. If your company needs to deliver information in more than one format, such as for internal publication, manuals, instructional guides, and on-line documentation, as well as on the Web, you may need to convert from your private DTD to several other, more presentation-oriented DTDs.

Sometimes this can have more than one layer. In the case of the org-chart, conversion to an HTML page is an obvious start, but what should that HTML page look like? HTML lends itself well to a text-based version, perhaps with embedded lists but cannot easily handle a more graphical representation, such as a real chart. A graphical chart, such as corporations love to distribute after reorganization, would be very useful. The direct conversion from an org-chart document to a graphic, though, is not so obvious. However the org-chart is really a Directed Acyclic Graph, or DAG (like a tree, but a node can have more than one parent), and it is straightforward to convert from an org-chart to a different DTD for describing DAGs, such as in Figure 1–12 to 1–14. Since many kinds of structures (such as book contents) can be represented as DAGs, software to convert a DAG DTD to HTML or a graphic image would be very useful. Many documents can be transduced to a DAG, so the hard work of converting a DAG to a display format is spread over each of these, and transforming from any initial format to a DAG is much easier than going straight to display in one step.

Instance of Org Chart

```
<business-unit><name>Operations</name>
  ...
  <business-unit><name>North America</name>
    ...
    <business-unit><name>Northeast</name>
    </business-unit>...
  </business-unit>
  <business-unit><name>Asia</name>
    ...
    <business-unit><name>Japan</name>....
    </business-unit>
  </business-unit>
</business-unit>
```

Figure 1–12   Transformation

```
Org Chart as tree
<tree>
<node name = "Operations>
<children>
<node name = "North America">
<children>
<node name = "Northeast">...
</children>
</node>
<node name = "Asia">
<children><node name = "Japan">
...</children>
</node>
</node>
</tree>
```

Figure 1–13

```
Org Chart as Directed Graph
<directed-graph>
<nodelist>
<node name = "Operations>
<node name = "North America">
<node name = "Northeast">...
<node name = "Asia">
<node name = "Japan">
</nodelist>
<edges>
<edge tail = "Operations" head = "North America">
<edge tail = "Operations" head = "Asia">
<edge tail = "North America" head = "Northeast">
<edge tail = "Asia" head = "Japan">
...
</edges>
```

Figure 1–14

Type transformation also becomes important when you start to truly integrate documents with your corporation's workflow processes. An incoming purchase order may converted internally into several work orders sent to various departments. Other documents, such as for scheduling and reporting, may be combined into a single document, with only abstracts remaining from each. In our org-chart example, we might want to generate memos for each person describing their position and responsibilities. Later in the book we'll explore some of the issues around the relationship between XML and the commercial workflow systems which are beginning to generate interest. We confine ourselves here to making the observation that the actual work which gets accomplished by a workflow is the transduction of information objects, that is, the transformation of knowledge into products and services. XML offers the most precise way to describe and create information objects and to make those objects available to process-oriented workflow software. It is therefore critical that your workflow software does not force you to use a proprietary and limited document data representation or, worse still, to lock your workflow data into program code.

1.13.7 *Hyperlinking*

One of the important capabilities provided by hypermedia is the ability to hyperlink arbitrary pieces of information. In hypermedia terminology, these pieces of information are called the *anchors* of the hyperlink. As hyperlinks are an essential way to express relationships among objects in your domain, you want a technology that expresses all the ones important to you.

Different implementations of hyperlinking lead to different capabilities, however. The WWW, for example, has a very limited model. It requires all hyperlinks to be placed explicitly in the source document, and all hyperlinks to a particular location in the destination document require an explicitly named anchor in that document. This means all hyperlinks are unidirectional pointers from an HTML document to either a complete object (such as another HTML page, a

Java applet, or graphic) or the interior of another HTML document. This limitation does not exist for XML.

XML can support far more general models of linking. One of the most complete implementations of linking is found in HyTime, a companion standard to SGML (much of which will probably become part of XML over time). In HyTime, a link may have any number of anchors, each filling a particular role. As these roles are not limited to *source* and *destination*, they can describe far more complex relationships than HTML links. XML has a baseline of hyperlinking functionality that is less sophisticated than HyTime but is still far richer than HTML.

The link element itself can be stored either in one of the anchors or in a separate document. Once the link element is physically separated from its anchors, the anchors no longer need to be XML documents. In XML we can use links in one document to talk about relationships among other documents. For example, a user's manual could link a program, sample input, and sample output together, each residing in a separate file. By giving this particular kind of relationship a name, such as `test run`, we can treat them as a class, so we can, for example, find all the test runs, or substitute C++ test runs for Cobol test runs.

At its most fundamental level, an org-chart specifies the manager-employee links among people. Our example DTD specifies the organizational hierarchy with individual home pages as anchors. An employee's home page (were that to be in a DTD with the appropriate markup) could, in turn link back to the employee's entry in the org-chart document. A complete corporate reorganization can be reflected by changing a single document, the org-chart. (This assumes links from home pages are followed at query time. If pages are cached, then a program would need to perform a pass through the home pages to bring everything up to date.) No one would need to go through the laborious process of editing everyone's home page, possibly introducing errors on each one.

1.13.8 *Compare*

Comparing two documents can be a very difficult, but sometimes necessary, task. At the limit, it is just as difficult as comparing two programs to determine if they will have the same output, but it is often much simpler than that. Also, comparisons may need to be made only between sections of documents, as opposed to whole documents.

In many cases comparisons will be among different versions of the same document. The most common example of this is in revision control systems, such as are commonly used in software development. In these systems, members of a group working on a common set of documents can "check out" and "check in" documents. Whenever a revised version of a document is checked in, all the changes from the old to the new versions are recorded. In this way it is always possible to revert to a previous version of any document. As another example, by comparing before and after versions of the org-chart, we can determine who was hired, who was fired, who was promoted, and who changed areas. Similar comparisons can be used to determine editing changes. In the new field of electronic commerce, rival vendors will make bids and proposals. If these are documents conforming to the same DTD (or architecture, as will be explained later), the two bids can be compared automatically.

Comparisons which do not exhaustively compare the entire documents exist in combination with searching, as the areas to compare first need to be found.

1.13.9 *Interpret*

So far we have discussed many operations which can be performed on documents but have not yet discussed the operations that documents can perform on our information systems, or rather, the actions performed once the documents are understood, or interpreted. From this perspective, we can see a document as instructions for another program which will interpret it.

In the area of publishing, a document is normally interpreted as instructions to some kind of formatting engine, and the result of interpreting the document is a book. In a way, this subsumes our other operations, since they have all required having a document present to drive some process, so we have discussed many different ways of interpreting an org-chart. This is one of the great strengths of XML—the ability to apply a variety of different semantics to the same information according to the different ways it is needed.

However, there are applications where the document is treated more closely to a program. Forms are a very good example of this. In HTML, forms are just a set of data entry fields with optional labels. Each field corresponds to some piece of data the server requires of the client, but (as usual) it is not obvious to the client's program what these data are. Therefore it is always necessary for a human to interpret the displayed fields and enter the information.

If, however, there is a DTD describing the kind of information in the domain, a form can be a specification for exactly which data items it requires. A style sheet could display this to a human with a series of blank fields, but a local computational agent could also read the form, understand what information is requested, immediately retrieve it from a database without requiring any human intervention, and return the filled-in form to the server. Medical insurance forms are an important example of this. Once the kinds of information requested in insurance forms is standardized in a DTD, applications at the service provider's facilities can automatically fill in forms sent by insurance companies from the database. Where these applications do not exist, the insurance company can provide an applet to help a human perform the task manually. The two cases can be mixed, if there are questions of access rights to certain values, with an application filling in some and leaving the rest to a human.

1.13.10   *Define*

Data are not useful until they are structured and structure cannot exist until they are defined. The task of structuring corporate data has always been challenging, requiring specialized skills and knowledge. It has also always been acknowledged that a poor execution of that task may introduce expensive inefficiencies into the processing of data and can have an adverse impact on many aspects of business operations. For this reason a great deal of attention has been devoted to the science of structuring data: Countless Ph.D.s have been hired for work in this area, great competing schools of philosophy have sprung into existence, and an ocean of ink has been spilled in books on this subject.

The SGML community has devoted a great deal of energy to developing sound techniques for structuring your documents. This has been inherited by XML. The basic unit of document structure is, of course, the DTD. As in database design, creating a DTD is often an extended exercise in domain analysis, that is, the analysis of your business operations as it relates to your data needs. We'll discuss this later in the book and we'll point to some of the major reference works.

In addition to the techniques that have been developed, often called "document analysis," SGML is unique in having developed a large number of DTDs specific to various types of information (for example, technical publishing, software documentation, semiconductor data, aircraft maintenance, chemistry). It is often the case that you will be able to start from one of these public DTDs and, not infrequently, you may find that the existing work is sufficient for your needs.

Also parallel to the database world, sophisticated tools exist to help you design or modify DTDs.

The org-chart DTD presented here is deliberately small, for pedagogical reasons. Actually, a great deal of work is done in XML with such small, simple DTDs—often a little structure may go a long way.

One of the most interesting developments in this area is the growing unification of database and XML design concepts. Object-oriented databases seem to be particularly suited for representing document types and the incentive for doing so has become compelling as SGML becomes more and more essential for defining and circulating information in the electronic age.

1.13.11 *Create*

Once database schemas have been developed it is, of course, necessary to capture the data which will be stored in the database. Database Management Systems (DBMSs) typically provide a variety of tools, such as form builders, for this purpose. Form interfaces on the Web, that is, HTML forms, have begun to replace an older generation of client/server tools. The underlying objective of such tools is to present the data schema to users of the database in a way which shields the user from the complexity of the actual representation of the data in the database. The analogue to this in the XML world is the XML editor (currently adapted from existing SGML editors), a kind of form interface which adapts to the particular requirements of any DTD applied to it. The XML world is actually better off than the traditional database world in that there is only one schema language which is used to define document structures while database vendors each have their own schema language. Any XML editor can be used with any DTD.

There are other ways to create XML documents. Another advantage XML enjoys over databases is that XML documents can be created in any text editor. Many people, for example, use emacs to create XML. While the sophisticated SGML editors that are available are the easiest way to create XML documents, the fact that any user on any computing platform has the ability to create XML ensures that the technology is accessible to everyone.

Many documents, and probably most documents in the near future, are automatically generated by software from databases or in reaction to different events. (Many of these documents will be ephemeral responses to structured database queries and can't compete with humans on artistic merit. They are documents nonetheless.) Now that there are new Internet protocols based on XML, such as the Channel Definition Format proposed by Microsoft, the day is fast approaching when documents will routinely be exchanged unseen by human eyes.

With the advent of automatic document generation, on the one hand, and the development of smarter software on the other, we reach a point where computers and humans can communicate among themselves using a common language.

1.14 | Conclusion

This chapter has had two goals. The first has been to "take the high ground" in explaining XML almost from first principles by exposing its foundations and showing how it addresses the inescapable problems built into the current architecture of the Web. We hope from this you will better understand where generic markup, as exemplified by SGML and XML, differ from specific markup languages, such as HTML, and why the latter is inherently limited in its expressibility. We also hope you will appreciate how SGML can enable far more sophisticated distributed information systems, working in conjunction with applications, whether Java or Cobol.

Assuming we had accomplished the first goal, our second was to give a perspective on how to use documents based on a number of fundamental behaviors that present a kind of taxonomy of document handling. In the age of the electronic document, document-centric applications will be complex, multistage affairs. Categorizing these stages into a finite set of behaviors gives you, the Internet document engineer, a set of tools you can use in building these applications.

The chapters that follow will be much less concerned with such lofty concerns and much more interested in getting down and dirty with real software and problems to show how these different behaviors work in practice. At the end you will be able to join them together to create real Internet applications.

XML, Data, and Documents

This chapter examines XML in depth as a document description metalanguage and relates its capabilities in describing textual data to the construction of Internet applications. The relationship of XML to SGML and HTML is explained and a technical précis of SGML, the parent of XML, is presented. The goals of XML, the differences between it and SGML, and the two levels of XML compliance, well-formedness, and validity are laid out. The concept of data-centered Internet application design with XML is introduced and an examination of the advantages in applying XML and data-centered design to Internet document applications concludes the chapter.

2.1 | XML—What It Is, What It Does, SGML Ancestry

The eXtensible Markup Language (XML) is a subset of an international standard, Standard Generalized Markup Language (SGML) which is widely used in certain high-end areas of information management and publishing. One may also say that XML is greatly informed by our collective experience with HTML. HTML is an application of SGML, a rendition-oriented markup language which has an SGML DTD. It is useful to understand a bit of the evolutionary process which has brought all this about, both because it helps one to understand what XML is and does and also because designers, at the time this is being written, must select from tools and methodologies which might appertain uniquely to SGML, HTML, or XML.

We briefly discussed HTML and its failings as an Internet application substrata in the first chapter and will assume that readers who need a larger introduction to this topic will be able to pick up one of the many references on the topic. This work is not intended as a comprehensive source on SGML either but we think it will be worthwhile at this point to give a thumbnail description of SGML as a document metalanguage. Most of the concepts and vocabulary are shared by XML; for many it will be important to know where the differences between the two lie. Our concise SGML description may be tough sledding for some but bear in mind that the concepts will be developed and illustrated throughout the book and can be firmly acquired through repetition and practical application.

2.1.1 SGML Essential Description

1. SGML is an international standard, ISO (International Standards Organization) 8879. [XML and HTML are recommendations of the World Wide Web Consortium (W3C).]

2. SGML is a language for describing languages that represent documents; it is not, as commonly assumed, a language for representing documents or a superset from which HTML is taken. This language can readily be read and understood by human beings, but it is also a formally specified language which can be processed by computer programs. While any number of languages can be designed with SGML, they all must obey the syntax rules of SGML. The common syntax of SGML languages enables well-designed SGML implementations to read and process any SGML language.

3. An SGML language is defined in a Document Type Definition (DTD). There is also an SGML declaration which provides parameters needed in processing the document such as the identification of its character set. A document which is marked-up according to the low-level information in the SGML declaration and the language definition in the DTD is called a document instance.

4. An SGML document includes an SGML declaration, DTD, and a document instance. The SGML declaration is most often implicit; that is, there is one that your SGML program will use if you don't include your own. The DTD is not always included with its instance, but it normally must at least be explicitly referenced. An instance without a DTD is equivalent to a scrap of text in an unknown language. If the instance were also without an SGML declaration, it would be as if that language were in some sort of code where we could neither recognize individual letters or word separations. The SGML declaration and DTD together give SGML the unique property of being self-describing.

    The reader will have noticed that in SGML the term "document" has a precise, technical definition. Yet the word "document" is also an everyday and imprecise term. One thing we have learned from the Web is that a document is not just something which ends up on a bound set of 8 1/2-by-11 paper pages. In fact, the technical response of SGML to the question, What is a document?, proves to be the most inclusive and comprehensive response possible. Some of our thoughts on the different levels of self-description in documents were discussed in the first chapter and we have also broached the concept that the document metaphor may be useful for very undocumentlike things such as application frameworks and agent communication.

5. The DTD defines the types of elements that can be used in the document and the possible relationships among those elements. An element can be thought of as a kind of container for each distinct thing in the document. It is up to the person who creates the DTD to decide exactly what "things" are. For example, things could be paragraphs and headings. A document instance has a preferred hierarchy in which there are two kinds of relationships between elements: parent-child and peer-to-peer. In a parent-child relationship the child is contained by the parent. For example, a list might contain individual bulleted items. The entire list is a container which contains items. In SGML terms the list is the parent and the items are its children. The list item elements, in turn, could also be parents, containing, say, paragraph elements. In a peer-to-peer relationship, a group of elements have the same parent. For example, a memo header element could contain the peer elements to, from, date, and subject. The set of possible hierarchical relationships among elements is fully described in the DTD. Other relationships are represented by cross-references among elements using attributes.

6. Attributes may be declared for elements. Attributes are information which is "attached" to the element but not part of its content. The "content" of an element is the part of the document instance inside the element. One can think of attributes as element level "metadata," meaning that they are data which are about the data (content). A common use of attributes is to hyperlink elements, that is, to express nonhierarchical relationships between elements by adding addressing metadata.

7. The names of element types and attributes are made up by the DTD designers and declared in the DTD. In the best case these names will be based on the common terminology of the enterprise and will therefore be easy to understand and use. In the document instance, element markers are put directly into the text, surrounding the text which is contained by the element. An element marker is called a tag and it is most often distinguished from the text itself by being surrounded by angle brackets. One type of tag, the start-tag, indicates the start of an element and another type of tag, most often a backslash following the left angle bracket, indicates the end of the element. You are probably familiar with tagging if you have ever viewed the HTML source code of a document while surfing the Web. Attributes are written after the element type name within the angle brackets. SGML DTDs and instances can be read and written by human beings using any text editor but they can also be processed by computer programs.

8. The storage of an SGML document may be distributed over multiple virtual objects called "entities". They are connected by "entity references" which are indirect system independent pointers to the actual physical storage of the object. SGML does not assume any particular storage medium (such as files) and can readily use a single

storage object for multiple SGML documents. Entities can contain text and markup or binary data such as graphic files. A special kind of entity, the parameter entity, can contain DTD components. Parameter entities are most often used to modularize DTDs by grouping sets of related components into distinct entities.

2.1.2   *The XML Subset and HTML*

The SGML standard has been around since 1986. During most of this time SGML-based systems have remained the reserve of large corporations that can afford the high initial investment required to implement an SGML-based documentation process (or that have been forced to do so in order to comply with government or industry policy). In recent years, as SGML authoring and document management tools have improved and the advantages of SGML authoring systems have become clear, SGML has become the format of choice for large mission-critical applications in many sectors of industry and commerce. Automobile and airplane manufacturers have adopted SGML for their maintenance documentation, insurance companies for their policy proposals, and computer companies for software documentation.

To meet the mission-critical needs of such a diverse set of sophisticated users, SGML is necessarily extremely flexible and therefore complex. This complexity of full SGML is a serious limitation for its adoption in full-scale applications to be used by a large number of non-expert users over the Web, on the Internet, or on corporate intranets.

HTML, HyperText Markup Language addresses this problem. It was designed specifically to enable documents to be published on the World Wide Web. It defines a fixed set of element types (version 3.2 of HTML has 70) that let you describe simple (i.e., not very structured) documents containing headings, paragraphs, lists, illustrations, and so forth. One of the principal advantages of HTML as a document type for the Web is its built-in support for hypertext and multimedia, enabling the construction of easy and intuitive user interfaces for accessing published information. This user interface is implemented in browsers that are now the universal application on desktops.

However, the rapid (and often hectic) development of HTML, from the initial 1.0 version to the current 4.0 version, has meant that it has become overburdened with dozens of interesting but often incompatible inventions from different interested parties, primarily browser vendors. As an increasing number of companies are deploying intranets within their organizations, the Web now serves as the interface for a variety of information systems. Databases with an HTML front end, mail archives, handbooks, or shopping catalogs are some examples. However, these possess a much richer internal structure than can be represented in HTML. Information always gets lost in the conversion to Web documents. While the occasional author isn't affected by this limitation, it's preventing the Web from being used as a platform for information exchange on a large scale. It has become evident that many new applications require a more robust and flexible infrastructure than is possible with HTML.

What is required is a way of providing the richness of SGML, while at the same time providing the ease of use of HTML for publishing and accessing these documents on-line.

XML aims to bridge the gap between SGML and HTML. It is a fully compatible simplified subset of SGML that removes a large number of the more complex and sometimes less-used features which made SGML difficult and expensive to implement. The formal definition of XML fits onto 23 printed pages and 7 pages of appendices. This is often compared to the 664 pages of Charles F. Goldfarb's *The SGML Handbook* but it must be noted that *The SGML Handbook* is an annotation of the standard and partly a tutorial, not just the text of the standard. Even with this reservation, it is perhaps salient to note that the 30 pages of the XML recommendation have been sufficient for several people to produce XML parsers whereas a person setting out to write an SGML parser will definitely need *The SGML Hand-*

book with its fine elucidation of the many complexities in the standard. XML is based on a simpler, less flexible model that will make writing programs to handle XML much easier than for full SGML and promises also to make it easier for authors to produce documents for many different output media, whether printed paper, on-line help, or the World Wide Web.

The design goals for XML, from Clause 1.1 of the recommendation, are

- XML shall be straightforwardly usable over the Internet.
- XML shall support a wide variety of applications.
- XML shall be compatible with SGML.
- It shall be easy to write programs which process XML documents.
- The number of optional features in XML is to be kept to the absolute minimum, ideally zero.
- XML documents should be human-legible and reasonably clear.
- The XML design should be prepared quickly.
- The design of XML shall be formal and concise.
- XML documents shall be easy to create.
- Terseness in XML markup is of minimal importance.

2.1.3   *How XML Simplifies SGML*

A lot of SGML was thrown out in getting down to the essential core covered by XML. Some of these features will be essential to some and such users will continue to use SGML. A list of the major stuff that didn't make it and why is was there in the first place follows, in an approximate and highly subjective order of importance.

1. No tag minimization
    OMITTAG, SHORTTAG, DATATAG, RANK, SHORTREF, and USEMAP are all eliminated as are

content model minimization parameters. These all had something to do with allowing markup to be inferred by the parser in order to reduce the amount of work needed to markup documents and/or the volume of markup. Basically nothing can be left to the imagination of the parser any longer: Start- and end-tags must always be present, attribute names must always be present, attribute values must always be quoted.

2. No SGML declaration

    There are two, almost identical, SGML declarations that describe all XML documents but since they are fixed there is no reason to include one with an XML document. The SGML declaration allows markup delimiters and name characters to be defined, charsets to be declared, quantities and capacities to be passed to the parser, and optional features to be turned on or off. In XML the markup delimiters are fixed and the names are case-sensitive and the character set is UNICODE, quantities and capacities are either unlimited or at any rate cannot be limited by a user declaration and there are no optional features.

3. Empty element syntax changed

    Tags for SGML elements declared as EMPTY may or may not be syntactically different from start tags of elements that do have content. It is therefore not possible to tell if an empty element is actually a nonempty element with a missing end tag without reference to the DTD. XML enforces the use of a distinct syntax for empty elements to enable DTD-less processing: a slash precedes the closing angle bracket.

4. Mixed content models restricted

    An element type has mixed content when elements of that type may contain character data, optionally interspersed with child elements. Mixed content models must be optional, repeatable ORs, with the character data (#PCDATA) being declared first. In effect, this says that a character is both legal and actually character data anywhere in mixed content. SGML is less restrictive to the DTD designer but allows many situations where it is difficult for the parser to distinguish between white space separating markup and other types of characters which are significant and difficult for the author to understand mixed content errors. This issue is explored in more depth later in the book.

5. Inclusions and exclusions disallowed

Inclusions and exclusions modify the allowable subtree of an element type. An inclusion says that a particular element type can occur in the content of the element type it is declared in or in the content of any descendants. An exclusion excludes an element type from the content of the element type it is declared in and in the content of any descendants. Inclusions and exclusions can be combined to include or exclude something in only a section of a subtree. As an example let us say that we have paragraphs and paragraphs can contain footnote references and we have footnotes which can contain paragraphs. We don't wish to allow footnotes to contain footnote references so in SGML we put a footnote reference exclusion on a footnote. When a paragraph appears in the subtree of a footnote element, the footnote reference exclusion will apply it even though the content model for the paragraph allows footnote references. What to do in XML? Probably we must make a new type of paragraph just for footnotes so we can disallow footnote references.

6. AND (&) content model groups eliminated

   Another kind of shorthand is an AND can always be expanded into an OR of all the combinations of elements in the AND expression. However this expansion generates n! combinations, where n is the number of elements. Since the parser actually does do this expansion, users should be discouraged from abusing AND expressions. In XML they are discouraged by not having them at all.

7. Name groups eliminated

   Name groups allow the definition of multiple elements or their attributes with a single declaration. The lack of them in XML slightly increases the size of DTDs but more importantly eliminates one of the common ways to introduce organization and modularity into DTDs.

8. Elimination of attribute types

   NAME, NAMES, NUMBER, NUMBERS, NUTOKEN, NUTOKENS are tokenized attribute types. They are subsumed by NMTOKEN and NMTOKENS which is what must be used in XML. The relatively weak type checking provided by these attribute types is not general enough for the range of XML applications which are being developed.

9. Comments simplified

   Among a number of changes the most significant is that markup declarations cannot contain embedded comments.

10. Marked sections simplified

    The most important change is that marked sections can be only CDATA sections in the document instance and be used to unconditionally escape character data which would be recognized as markup. SGML allows marked sections to be used to include or ignore marked portions of the document instance.

11. Entities simplified

The most significant among many changes are the elimination of internal and external CDATA and SDATA entities. Typed external entities SDATA ("specific character data entity") and CDATA (character) are disallowed in XML. NDATA must be used for any external entity. Disallowed SDATA internal entities must be replaced with UNICODE numeric character references and disallowed internal CDATA entities must be made into external NDATA entities.

12. LINK, SUBDOC, and CONCUR nixed

These three SGML features were designed, respectively, to associate operational semantics, change DTDs during processing, and support concurrent markup. They have been less widely implemented. Namespaces may take XML back into this direction and are discussed later.

13. No RCDATA or CDATA declared content

These declared content types specify character data and disallow nested elements and elements and entities, respectively. The primary advantage in using them is to avoid the inconvenience of escaping markup delimiters that are actually character data.

14. Elimination of #CURRENT and #CONREF declared values for attributes

These are directives to the parser concerning attribute values. An example of a situation where #CONREF could be useful is shown in a later chapter but in general #CURRENT and #CONREF are very rarely used.

2.1.4 *Valid versus Well-Formed XML*

XML is particularly suitable for Web applications because of its ability to handle documents without the need to know the structure model (the DTD) that was used to create these documents, if a DTD was in fact used. XML does not remove the possibility of including the DTD with the document or necessarily do away with the advantage of having the DTD in many circumstances. Moreover, there are applications for which the DTD will absolutely be required to process the document. But with all these caveats we may still say that XML enables DTD-less document processing which, judging for HTML's success, is an important subset of Internet applications.

The ability to handle a document without a DTD was introduced to SGML with the WebSGML Adaptations annex. When the Web-SGML Adaptations are not used, a document must be distributed in its complete form, and it must fully comply with the DTD that was used to create it. This is not really a constraint in industrial projects where SGML documents are often mission critical and, in any case, created, edited, and managed through well-defined procedures on secure intranets. But such use is an impediment when publishing documents on the Internet at large, where possible users on the client side have no way to know the DTD used to create these documents.

The XML recommendation describes two levels of conformance: valid and well formed. Valid XML files are those which have a Document Type Definition (DTD) and adhere to it. Valid XML must also be well formed. Well-formed XML files can be used without a DTD, but they must follow some simple rules to enable a browser to parse the file correctly (so that it can apply your style sheet, enable linking, etc.). Well-formedness is defined in Clause 2.1 of the recommendation very succinctly:

A textual object is a well-formed XML document if

1. Taken as a whole, it matches the production labeled document.
2. It meets all the well-formedness constraints given this specification.
3. Each of its parsed entities is *well-formed*.

Document
[1] document ::= prolog element Misc*
Matching the document production implies that

1. It contains one or more elements.
2. There is exactly one element, called the *root*, or document element, no part of which appears in the content of any other element. For all other elements, if the start-tag is in the content of another element, the end-tag is in the content of the same element. More simply stated, the elements, delimited by start- and end-tags, nest properly within each other.

As a consequence of this, for each nonroot element C in the document, there is one other element P in the document such that C is in the content of P but is not in the content of any other element that is in the content of P. P is referred to as the *parent* of C, and C as a *child* of P.

We refer the reader to the recommendation itself for the full expansion of the document production but do note that there are a number of syntactical and other details which make this requirement, if not complex, at least nontrivial. The well-formed constraints, from version 1.0 of the recommendation, are as follows:

- If an internal DTD subset is included in the document, parameter-entity references can occur only where markup declarations can occur, not within markup declarations.
- The name in an element's end tag must match the element type in the start tag.
- No attribute name may appear more than once in the same start tag or empty element end tag.
- Attribute values cannot contain direct or indirect entity references to external entities.
- The replacement text of any entity referred to directly or indirectly in an attribute value (other than <) must not contain a <.
- Characters referred to using character references must be legal according to the nonterminal Char.
- Entities with the exception of amp, lt, gt, apos, and quot must be declared in some circumstances (see the recommendation for full details).
- An entity reference must not contain the name of an unparsed entity. Unparsed entities may be referred to only in attribute values declared to be of type ENTITY or ENTITIES.
- A parsed entity must not contain a recursive reference to itself, either directly or indirectly.
- Parameter-entity references may appear only in the DTD.

There are 18 additional checks specific to valid documents but this number does not really give an idea of relative difficulty of verifying a document's well-formedness versus its validity. Based on the experience of people who have written XML parsers and applications, it is a difference in the order of magnitude range. In effect there are really only two viable strategies for building a robust XML application in a reasonable amount of time: either to base it on well-formedness or, if it requires adherence to the DTD, to build it around an existing XML parser written by an expert. We will see in subsequent chapters that even just adhering to the well-formedness requirements can be onerous enough.

2.2 | XML and Data-Driven Architecture

In Chapter 1 we enunciated the guiding principles of intranet construction: build outward from the data, data which represent the business knowledge of our enterprise. This is the same principle which IS departments have used to deliver a consistent payback for more than 25 years of experience with databases. XML extends those principles to the enterprise data which have heretofore been untapped in documents and extend the document metaphor to serve the data description needs of a wide range of application interfaces (either human to computer program or computer program to computer program).

One of our architectural goals is to enable the construction of a heterogeneous system, a system which can integrate components regardless of vendor origin or their internal design. The rate of change, the rapidity of evolution, and the continual emergence of standards and quasi-standards are probably unprecedented and the Internet application designer is either trembling in his boots or has his head firmly buried in the sand. A data-centered, flexible, heterogeneous design is a design which can roll with the changes, shedding the losing technologies and taking advantage of new opportunities. XML's emphasis on unchaining the enterprise from vendor dependence could not be better suited for this new environment. Early attempts at document-oriented groupware have been process- rather than data-centered, imposing business model paradigms which quickly became obsolete as rapid technological change upended the business models, altered expectations, and also led to the creation of a new range of business services. These applications were designed to take advantage of the shift to client/server and the network server model. They have been left behind as work has shifted back to the client and the interaction between the server and client has grown rich and complex. We are looking at another major shift when server services become distributed throughout the network and communication is governed by the distributed object model. Our architecture is our recipe for survival: rapid development, lightweight applications, exposed and structured interfaces, and the preservation of long-term value accomplished by pushing that value into the data themselves.

At this juncture we have at least an outline of the characteristics of those data and perhaps a bit of an insight into how we might be able to set up, process, and manage those data to build a data-centered heterogeneous information architecture. We would like to develop that insight a little more before proceeding in the following chapters to the mechanics. The next section looks at how XML's data model applied to documents enables new approaches and capabilities in the areas of Internet document creation, delivery, and management.

2.3 | XML and Documents

Documents—document creation, distribution, and management—are among the most important Internet applications, especially in the intranet context where the costs of information gathering and sharing have a major impact on the bottom line. These types of applications are also SGML's traditional base and the starting point for XML. We will therefore conclude this chapter with an examination of how XML changes the complexion of Internet document applications.

2.3.1 *Using XML to Deliver Large and Complex Documents Efficiently*

XML allows documents to be defined, created, stored, and retrieved hierarchically. For an example of what might be possible, consider that a set contains books, books contain front matter, body, and back matter, body contains chapters, chapters contain sections, sections contain subsections, and so forth. By comparison, word processing formats, PDF, and HTML have no general capability for defining or otherwise dealing with hierarchical document components. It is possible to create an XML document delivery system which uses hierarchical subdivisions as retrieval units. Either the user can select the information unit that makes the most sense or the system can be set up to select a default retrieval unit which optimizes network traffic. For example, suppose that our on-line documents consist of repair manuals for automobiles (this is a popular example both because it is familiar to most people and because it is, in fact, a major real-world use of SGML). Such manuals are usually divided into chapters for each subsystem. Most of the time, however, the person doing the repairs only needs information on a specific component, for example, how to replace the fuel filter in the fuel system. So in this case it would be most efficient to design the system to retrieve small sections of component information by default.

Word processing formats, PDF, and HTML have no general capability for defining or otherwise dealing with hierarchical document components. The "HTML solution" to the "chunking" of information into network-efficient components is to handcraft smaller-sized pages and to manually insert (and maintain) hyperlinks between the pages. XML does this automatically, is maintainable, and suitable for high-volume production.

On-demand hierarchical retrieval may use a table-of-contents type interface to allow the user to select the desired information unit or may isolate the desired information through a hierarchy-sensitive full-text search or, often, may do both. Shrink-wrapped Internet application software which enables hierarchical-based retrieval of XML data includes such products as Open Text's LiveLink and INSO's DynaWeb, and Inforium's LivePage. Some products offer the option of either translating XML documents to HTML on the fly for delivery to any HTML browser or delivering XML directly to a client equipped with XML viewing software.

2.3.2 *Taming the Chaos*

We talk a bit about HTML in this section. The current version of HTML (4.0) is an SGML application which makes use of some SGML facilities not in the XML subset. We will talk about SGML when referring specifically to the HTML recommendation and XML when we are speaking on a conceptual level.

HTML is the de facto standard for the delivery of information on both the Internet and intranets. Within the latter it is necessary to promulgate some standards to ensure that all pages can be viewed properly by all users, that all related software will work properly (examples: searching, cataloging, document management), and that there is some consistency among pages. Furthermore, these qualities must be preserved over time even as there is constant change in the technology. After all, an intranet is a tool for streamlining business, not a playground for HTML hackers!

We learned in the previous section that XML allows for the hierarchical definition of document structure and we also learned that HTML, even though it is an application of SGML, is deficient in this respect. Some readers may have noted that the div element is sometimes used (albeit improperly with respect to its original intent) to create XML-like containers for HTML. In fact, div, the attribute class, cascading style sheets, and other changes in HTML clearly indicate that it is, of necessity, "rediscovering" its SGML roots as it is deployed in demanding intranet environments. The problem with such contortions of HTML is that they are contortions and do not compare favorably with clean, complete XML implementations which are correct from first principles. HTML does not inherit all the possible virtues of SGML simply by being an application of it; SGML gives one the flexibility to choose one's objectives. You can do a bad language design in SGML or XML—you can even hang yourself just as thoroughly as with any other approach. HTML obviously succeeded in its objectives but the designers did not choose to make a great deal of use of SGML's power to express hierarchy. It still benefits from SGML's ability to state unambiguously what the rules are and to validate the adherence of any document to those rules.

SGML provides clear standards for clean, supportable HTML. There are SGML DTDs for HTML which have been approved by the W3C and SGML conformity is the official policy of the W3C and is publicly supported by most of the major players in the marketplace.

HTML conformance to SGML is one side of the story. The other is that many organizations will find that it is worthwhile to use an application of SGML or XML other than HTML to store their intranet documents. Let us illustrate this with a real-world example. A company produced a large volume of documentation for an intranet where the browsing technology was incapable of displaying tables. This could have been, say, HTML 1.0, although in this case it was not. Although there was in fact a very large amount of tabular information, all tables were converted to a very primitive tabbed representation. Within a year HTML tables began to appear and the tabbed tables looked, and still look, ridiculous by current standards. Could this wasted effort have been avoided? Yes! Easily! The key is to represent the data according to the organization of information in the documents, not according to the limitations of the current viewing technology. Complex tables can readily be represented in XML (we'll devote some attention to this topic in a later chapter, in fact). It would have been a fairly simple matter to translate XML-encoded tables to the tabbed format required by the original browser and, without changing the source data at all, to change the output to HTML tables when that technology became available. The increasingly popular use of HTML framesets is another case in point, having brought another cycle of redesign and reorganization to many Web sites. It is simple to modify the transformation process which creates HTML from XML to use the XML document's organization to distribute content into different frames. The subject of XML transformation will be explored in depth later in the book.

Several versions of HTML have faltered in the marketplace. The most notable example was HTML 3.0 which was actually withdrawn and replaced by HTML 3.2. If you are going to make HTML your corporate standard, you'd better think long and hard about which HTML that is going to be. For many organizations a more stable approach will be to create standards around XML. Then you'll be set to ride whatever HTML wave comes along next.

2.3.3 *Production of Multiple Information Products from a Single Source*

Paper documents show no signs of becoming obsolete and it is often the case that you want both publishing quality paper output and an on-line version of the same document. XML is well suited for these kinds of requirements because it is capable of representing documents in a truly application-independent way. Other approaches tend to favor the type of application they were designed for initially even if it may be possible to produce other types of output through a translation process. In general, the objectives and means of effectively communicating information on paper and on-line are profoundly different. We may be able to convert the formatting in a word processor document to HTML but we cannot change the way we organize our ideas for presentation in the Web medium. We cannot even deal well with variant text where one phrase is intended for on-line use ("Click here to…") and another for paper. Likewise, while we can finally get a fairly decent printout of a Web page from our HTML browser, we cannot change the fact that the pages were not designed for a paper-based presentation.

Those who are unfamiliar with XML often have difficulty seeing possibilities which, to the XML-initiated, are obvious. For example, a well-defined body of information might be reused in many different formats (a magazine article, an article in an encyclopedia, a Web page, an on-demand fax report, a chapter in a book) and may be presented in other contexts (for example, a text about an artist may be used in a history book, a museum display, and a book on painting). While the information may be general purpose, it tends to get "locked in" to a particular use when created in an application-specific format.

2.3.4 *Reuse and Preservation*

Document markup languages created with XML can be very simple and very specific to a particular task or they can be made very general. The objective of the former is "lightness," a quick implementation, and quick processing. The objective of the general markup system is reuse and preservation.

- *Reuse* means that we are readily able to formulate new uses of the information including uses not envisioned when the document was created.
- *Preservation* means that the documents retain their usefulness over time instead of becoming obsolete as soon as the tools change.

The key to both of these properties is to create documents rich in content markup and structure. For example, most documents in the past were created without a formalized system for indicating that one piece of information was related to another piece of information either in the same or in a different document. Today we call that a hyperlink and it is considered an essential part of an information system. There are SGML documents that were created in the foggy past that did preserve such relationships even though the then-current set of display tools may not have supported hyperlinks. The application designers put it into the DTD because it was an intrinsic property of the information. Today those documents are readily translated into fully hyperlinked HTML. The information of long-term value was preserved; it survived into the next generation of tools.

Today, thousands of documents are being created in HTML which support only single, unidirectional hyperlinks. It is certain that browsers will eventually support a much richer set of relations between information nodes. There are XML documents which were created in the past and SGML documents being created today which encoded the fact that one piece of information may be related to many other pieces of information. These documents will preserve their information over the long term while the HTML documents will not. A lot of the time that is OK; lots of documents are, in fact, not of long-term value. When they are likely to retain value over time, XML pays.

What is the rate of change of technologies, tools, and fundamental paradigms in document technology? Let's look at some of the major waves over just the last ten years:

- Mainframe composition, typesetting codes
- Desktop publishing (DTP) on workstations
- Client/server document management
- DTP on PCs, style sheets, and layout in word processors
- Web, hand-coded HTML conversion
- Web-based document management
- Web publishing, HTML style sheets, and layout control
- Intranet document management and information management, information databases

Give or take some, we are probably seeing very big shifts in document technology every two years and near general obsolescence of a new technology in about four years. Wow! The rate of change is clearly not slowing down.

All XML documents adhere to XML's syntax rules. Any XML document, regardless of the particular application which was used to create it, can be read and processed by numerous XML systems. While it is nearly unthinkable to attempt to convert documents from a ten-year-old, obsolete typesetting or word processing format to something more current, ten-year-old XML documents can be handled readily by more powerful tools than those which existed when they were created. It is also easier to later modify XML documents to add new information or structure to them. You can add a room or a second story to a house which is well constructed with a good foundation and carefully designed subsystems with room for expansion.

2.3.5 *Information Interchange Standards*

Government procurements typically require adherence to applicable standards and SGML, the sole international, nonproprietary standard for document representation, is frequently the mandated standard for documentation. XML, as a recommendation of the W3C, a consortium of member organizations, does not have that same status. But since all XML documents, both valid and merely well-formed are also SGML documents they can satisfy government procurement requirements.

But would you still use XML anyway, without the incentive of a government contract? In fact, many industries have adopted standards for information delivery around SGML (it is still too early for industrywide adaptations of XML). Typically, suppliers are mandated to deliver documentation to the procuring organization in SGML conforming to a DTD or DTDs which have been developed by industry consortiums.

Often these initiatives are international in scope. For example, a great deal of work has been undertaken in the aviation, automotive, and semiconductor industries, to name a few. For instance, electronic component manufacturers, including Intel, National Semiconductor, Texas Instruments, Philips, IBM, HP, and Hitachi, have created an SGML standard for the creation and interchange of databook information. The newspaper industry has developed an SGML standard known as UTF (Universal Text Format) which is used for the delivery of information from news agencies to newspapers.

SGML and XML guarantee the long-term viability of the information delivered and do not lock the procurer into a particular vendor's documentation system. The DTD itself is a kind of subcontract which specifies to the supplier what information must be supplied and how that information must be organized. The supplier has the advantage of having clear, verifiable specifications and the procurer also has the advantage of being able to programmatically test conformance of the documents to the mandated DTD.

2.3.6 *Cost of Production*

Organizations which produce a lot of documents typically seek to maintain high-quality standards and consistency while reducing production costs. A simple form of automation is to impose standards for formatting and organization on authors so that the amount of work which is required to go from raw input to a finished product is reduced. In addition to written guidelines, authors are often required to use word processor style sheets with a given set of styles. Style templates have the desirable side effect of causing authors to spent a lot less time wrestling with the word processor and its formatting capabilities.

XML can be used for similar purposes and can be much more powerful than style sheets. Since XML specifies the relationships between elements, SGML or XML editors can guide the author in structuring the document correctly. While it is rare for an author to produce a document which rigorously adheres to a style sheet, one can only produce an XML document which doesn't follow the DTD by explicitly requesting that document validation be turned off!

For example, a glossary entry is required to have a short reference title, a long title, one or more paragraphs of explanatory text in a special glossary style, and a final line with the words "See also" and references to other glossary entries. A word processor style sheet will typically provide special styles for the short title, long title, glossary paragraphs, and "See also" references. It may or may not provide auto-text for the words "See also." There is no guarantee that the author will use those styles and if the author does use them, no guarantee that they will be used in right sequence. The author may also insert unwanted additional spacing or formatting which looks OK on the screen but are inconsistent with the stylebook. An XML editor, on the other hand, can require that the author create each of the required elements in the expected order. Moreover, XML editors will typically "put in" any required elements, allowing the author to simply fill in the text. The editor may also be able to check to see that the "See also" references actually point at actual glossary references.

Since XML documents can, unlike word processor documents, be rather easily processed by computer programs, it is possible to automate document production in other ways, ways in which people who have only worked with word processors or desktop publishing tools will have difficulty imagining. It is very common to customize the generation of indexes, tables or lists, and glossaries or to validate hyperlinks or cross-references or to produce data for databases or to add data from databases, just to name a few of the more common processes. We have seen publishing processes which took weeks of tedious, manual work reduced to a few keystrokes and a couple of minutes of computer time thanks to an hour's worth of programming to process XML documents.

2.3.7 *Safety, Regulatory, and Other Legal Documentation Requirements*

XML is the only technology which exists for creating rigorously structured documents and it provides a means for validating that such documents contain everything they are required to contain. In this kind of application, one can think of XML as a templating facility, similar to a database form or wizards found in some word processors. For example, suppose our intranet is used to provide operations information in a nuclear power plant. In the interests of decreasing the likelihood of a meltdown, standards have been developed which ensure that all information is comprehensive, accurate, replete with all appropriate warnings, and rigorously consistent in format. It's clearly a task which is made easier with XML. XML will allow you to express what the information requirements are, make the entering of that rigorously structured information easier, and ensure that everything required is there.

2.3.8 *Advanced Hypertext*

XML and SGML have a basic "built-in" facility for hyperlinking but it is a sufficiently rich notation to permit the definition of virtually any hyperlinking systems. HyTime is a companion standard to SGML which provides standardized techniques for applying SGML to the full range of hyperlinking capabilities. XML has its own companion recommendation under development, eXtensible Linking Language (XLL) which also specifies advanced hypertext capabilities. HyTime is not incompatible with XML but it does have a much broader agenda than just hypertext. XLL is not incompatible with

SGML but is primarily targeted at improving the hypertext capabilities of the World Wide Web.

The key to XML's ability to express the fullest possible range of hyperlinking is the fact that XML documents have a structure and named element types and attributes. We can use these properties, in addition to the simple source and destination model, to express many different types of relationships between objects in a document. A hyperlink may be an XML element itself and so can be typed, numbered, made conditional, or have other specific behaviors attached to it. Imagine, for example, that links are typed by areas of interest, say finance, marketing, engineering. In order to reduce "link clutter" or simply to provide more information to the prospective user of a hyperlinked document, hyperlinks can be color-coded or perhaps only activated on the user's request.

Even if the target output format is HTML and hyperlink anchor addresses are translated into URLs, it is still often useful to use some of XML's expressive power for a variety of ends including automatic generation of hyperlinks, validation of hyperlinks, and independence from continually evolving HTML hyperlinking standards. Any XML element can be converted into a hyperlink source or destination anchor, with unique identifiers generated automatically. You simply maintain the logical content of your documents and you get the management of hypertext at no extra charge.

2.3.9 | *Collaborative Authoring?*

XML allows documents to be either physically or logically broken up into chunks which can be parceled out among a group of authors. The XML structure, as expressed in the DTD, ensures that the parts can be joined back together. This is the most primitive model for collaborative authoring; XML permits a high degree of refinement of this concept. SGML-based software exists which allows checkin/checkout and revision control on SGML elements.

2.3.10 *Advanced Information Management—Connecting Databases*

In constructing a Database Management System (DBMS) the analyst develops a formal model of the information and the relationships between pieces of information. This approach and skill set carry over well to XML system design. Often they overlap as the strengths of DBMS for managing data and strengths of XML for describing documents are combined.

- Relational Database Management Systems (RDBMSs) are a good fit with SGML or XML when there is a large amount of metadata associated with units of structured information, often consisting of dependencies which are identified by key words or a numbering system
- Object-oriented databases may work well with SGML or XML in situations where the document components naturally fit the object paradigm. Such systems are characteristically organized around modules of information which are categorized by an abstract model of a particular domain's knowledge base and may also be richer in multimedia content.

XML is generally compatible with any storage system, including DBMS and file systems because the XML document can be a virtual container made up of parts whose actual physical location is specified by entity declarations.

XML and SGML Tools

I n this chapter we describe various categories of tools available for creating XML Internet applications and discuss the strategies for using them effectively. The evolution of XML tools is explored and we predict the course of tool development over the next several years. The applicability of SGML tools to XML development is touched on throughout the chapter.

3.1 | Tool Information Sources

Because there are so many new developments in XML we are not going to make any attempt to list all the tools out there or provide their URLs. All you need to do is check out the following sources.

3.1.1 *The SGML/XML Web Page (http://www.sil.org/sgml/sgml.html)*

This is the one place on the WWW to go for information about all the latest and greatest in the world of XML and SGML—not just tools. It is comprehensive, accurate, up to date, and searchable. The *SGML/XML on the Web Page* is the work of Robin Cover. He has our undying gratitude for his inestimable contribution to the development of XML.

3.1.2 *The Whirlwind Guide to SGML & XML Tools and Vendors (http://www.infotek.no/sgmltool/guide.htm)*

For more than five years the SGML/XML community has relied on Steve Pepper's Web site for the most reliable directory of tools, vendors, and service providers. The site is meticulously organized by category and includes full contact information and active links.

3.1.3 *SGML Buyer's Guide (ISBN 0-13-681511-1)*

This book is the definitive guide to choosing the right XML and SGML products and services. It was created with the full cooperation of the SGML/XML industry organizations, vendors, and service providers. In its nearly 1,200 pages are thorough discussions of selection criteria for all XML and SGML tool categories and subcategories, with descriptions of the tools themselves and their vendors. The accompanying CD-ROM has freeware (45 programs) and trialware from scores of suppliers—including the leading names in software—some available nowhere else.

3.2 | Evolution of SGML and XML Tools

A tool, in the broadest sense, is anything used to carry out a task more efficiently than would be possible without the tool. There are many tools which can be employed in the construction of XML Internet applications including software which may be ancillary to the actual application or integrated into it, data architectures (most often specific DTDs), and even specific concepts and knowledge.

A commercial market for SGML tools has existed for over ten years and the tools themselves have advanced considerably in maturity and robustness over the last several years. Major software companies such as Adobe, Corel, Microsoft, Oracle, and Xerox have entered the fray, signaling the entry of the technology into the mainstream. XML tools with the release of the W3C proposed recommendation in December 1997 would at best be in their infancy if it were not for the fact that XML is a subset of SGML. Most SGML tools can be adapted for use of XML with only moderate difficulty. Some SGML tool vendors released XML-capable versions of their SGML tools prior to the recommendation's attaining proposal status and many have announced XML-specific products for the near term.

On the other hand, SGML tools have been predominately publishing oriented and also preceded the Internet. Some SGML tools have added Internet-specific capabilities but more is needed as XML takes its place as a core Internet technology. Figure 3–1 illustrates what we see as the evolution of XML tools from the mature SGML technology which does things such as support dynamic table-of-contents (TOC), region-based search and retrieval, advanced hypertext, and style sheets to pure XML technology designed to do all the former and also support desktop applications, distributed objects, agents, and eCommerce.

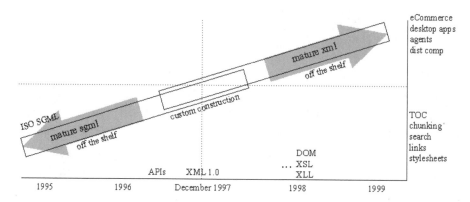

Figure 3–1   Evolution of XML Tools

This book was completed shortly after the release of XML 1.0 as a proposed recommendation, a piece of information which is important to know in order to understand the context of the remainder of the chapter. Of course, we have done our best here and throughout the book to focus on underlying concepts, albeit with a practical leaning, of lasting value. That approach is most difficult to sustain in this chapter but we will try to indicate the principles behind the use of certain tools and also the direction development will take in the next few years. When we talk about what is here now, however, we will tend to focus more on SGML rather than XML tools.

Of course, December 1997 is the birth month of XML and the point from which tool developers have had a stable definition of the language to work from. Serious work on the recommendation had been going on for at least a year so we have actually had preliminary versions of parsers and other tools as well as modified SGML tools appearing before December.

Several important developments still in the works will influence the timing and direction of tool development. In 1997 major Internet players like Microsoft and Netscape announced their support for XML as a core Internet standard but specific plans for XML development were restrained. In January 1998 Microsoft confirmed that XML will be added as one of the input/output formats of Word, Excel, PowerPoint, and Access. Clearly this is going to have a huge effect on the pace of XML tool development. Work is underway to provide a common interface to the many XML parsers which have been developed which will probably coalesce in early 1998. The Document Object Model (DOM) will standardize these efforts into an object data model and abstract interface to document components. We have created a trial implementation of the DOM using one of the new XML parsers in an application developed in this book. The DOM along with a linking standard (XLL) and a style sheet and transformation standard (XSL) will probably take a more solid form toward the end of 1998 and are already being tested in trial implementations of new tools.

3.3 | Software

3.3.1 *Parsers*

Every XML system, however small, has a parser somewhere. An XML parser is a computer program or part of a program that can process a document instance to validate conformance to the DTD or well-formedness. A valid document according to the DTD must be well-formed so just checking for well-formedness implies either that the parser has a less rigorous validation mode or that it is a less capable parser. An XML parser capable of validating a document is a "validating parser." All stand alone XML parsers are currently validating but many parsers built into applications may be limited to checking well-formedness. An SGML validating parser differs slightly in that it may not have the option of checking for well-formedness. Parsers are used in stand alone utility programs to find errors in the markup of a document or DTD and to produce a normalized version of a document for easier postprocessing with other programs. Parsers are also at the core of XML and SGML tools such as editors, browsers, programming languages, converters, and SG/XML databases. The parser solves the problem of how to get at all the parts of an XML document so the application designer can get on with the interesting things to be done with those parts. For purposes other than validation, an SGML parser that supports the Web SGML Annex can parse any XML document.

Both commercial and public domain parsers are available. There are at least eight XML parsers of recent vintage, four written in Java, one in C, one in TCL, one in Perl, and one in JavaScript. In addition, SP, the most recent and most complete SGML parser, has been modified to validate XML. SP is written in C++ and was expressly designed by its author, James Clark, to be readily integrated into applications. sgmls is an older SGML parser derived from the original ARCSGML parser written by SGML's inventor Charles Goldfarb, also maintained and enhanced by James Clark. All of the aforementioned parsers are available in the public domain.

With these parsers it is possible (not just theoretically—it has been done) to set up a zero-cost XML production shop. While expensive tools, like love and money, are nice to have, DTDs and XML instances can be created with any editor. The correctness of the markup can be verified with a validating parser and the parser output can be used with a free programming language like Perl to produce any output desired. The repository of documents can be searched with sgrep. While in a corporate intranet setting the availability of a zero-cost setup may not be of great direct importance, it is still definitely important as it is one of the major conditions necessary to ensure the continued evolution of the technology.

3.3.2 *Programming Languages*

Almost all of the XML programming languages are Application Programming Interfaces (API) designed to provide XML processing capability within Java, C++, C, and other languages. Another approach is to create a language expressly for XML document handling. The primary reasons for having a special-purpose language is to make programming easier for someone with knowledge of the domain and without a lot of programming expertise or to simply make an experienced programmer more efficient.

XML programming languages are document manipulation languages. Each individual element of a document can be accessed by the programmer; those elements can be changed, reordered, tested, and discarded according to the needs of whatever process has been defined. The programmer has complete access to the hierarchy of the document and the attributes of each element. He or she can decide to indent the first paragraph of a second bulleted item and italicize the second paragraph of a third bulleted item, for example. Complex page formatting commonly requires such fine-grained decisions, as well as much more complicated ones, and these can be easily accomplished with XML programming.

These languages all have SGML origins. An XML-specific, UNICODE-capable version of Balise has been released. Other languages include DSSSL, Omnimark, and CoST, the latter being freeware. Figure 3–2 will give the reader a bit of the flavor of programming in an SGML language, Omnimark in this case. This fragment is part of a program which takes an SGML document and translates it to a mixed HTML and XML document. Omnimark programs define actions which take place each time an SGML element of a specified type is encountered in the document being processed. The actions begin with the element statement which is flush to the left margin in the example. Processing can be conditional based on the value of the elements, attributes, or parentage or many other types of conditions.

Omnimark is "Englishlike." Elements are processed with ELEMENT rules, attributes are accessed with the ATTRIBUTE keyword, one tests to see if the parent of element LI is OL with the statement "element li when parent is ol."

```
element emph
    put text "<em>%c</em>"
element italic
    put text "<i>%c</i>"
element underlin
    put text "<em>%c</em>"
element il
    put text "</Pre></Ordeexam>" when previous is ordeexam
    activate first-ordeexam
    do when ATTRIBUTE mark is SPECIFIED
        do when ATTRIBUTE mark is equal ""
            put text "%c"
        else when ATTRIBUTE mark isnt equal UL "NOTE:"
              and ATTRIBUTE mark isnt equal UL "EXAMPLE:"
            put text "<ul>%c</ul>%n"
        else
            put text "<dl><dt><b>%v(mark)</b></dt>%c</dl>"
        done
    else
        put text "<ul>%c</ul>%n"
    done
element ol
    put text "</Pre></Ordeexam>" when previous is ordeexam
    activate first-ordeexam
    put text "<ol>%c</ol>"
element li when parent is ol
    put text "</Pre></Ordeexam>" when previous is ordeexam
    activate first-ordeexam
    put text "<li>%c</li>"
element li when parent is il
    local stream listmark
    set buffer listmark to ATTRIBUTE mark of parent
    put text "</Pre></Ordeexam>" when previous is ordeexam
    activate first-ordeexam
```

Figure 3-2

Document Style Semantics and Specification Language (DSSSL) is a companion international standard to SGML which describes a general SGML transformation language. It is implemented in the public domain program JADE (JAmes DSSSL Engine, for James Clark the developer). DSSSL is not noted for the ease of use of languages like Omnimark but it is noted for its comprehensive approach to the problem of document transformation. Moreover, back ends have been written for JADE for transformations to RTF, TeX, HTML, SGML-to-SGML, and an SGML flow object tree (that is, a standard representation of an SGML document as a tree from which a layout program could produce a formatted document).

It takes effort to learn an XML API even if one is quite fluent in its programming language. Some effort is also involved in learning an SGML programming language and also some expense in most cases. Is it always necessary? No. Perl, in particular, but also C, C++, and other languages can be and are used for many relatively simple tasks. Perl is the favored language for this sort of thing because of its superb pattern matching capabilities and its conciseness, as we will illustrate in the next few chapters.

3.3.3 *Browsers*

Microsoft's Internet Explorer 4 was the first major browser to come out with some XML capabilities, albeit restricted to the processing of their Channel Definition Format language. The ability to display XML using style sheets will not be far behind. Grif has an authoring tool/browser which displays XML using CSS which we discuss later in the book.

There are XML Java applets which can be used with Internet Explorer and Netscape browsers. JUMBO [Java Universal (Molecular | Markup) Browser] (Figure 3–3), developed by Peter Murray-Rust, displays the XML-based Chemical Markup Language (CML).

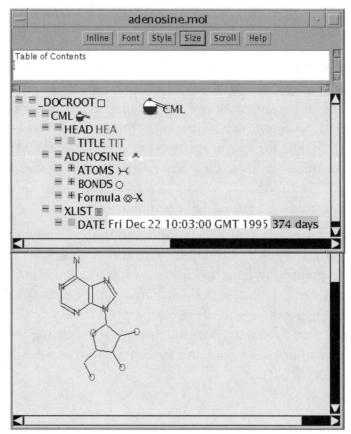

Figure 3–3   JUMBO—An XML Viewing Applet

DataChannel's PaxSyntactica (Figure 3–4) is another special-purpose JAVA applet-based XML browser. It displays Microsoft's Channel Definition Format (CDF), an XML language which enables Web broadcasters to set up push channels.

A number of SGML browsers have been around for some time. SGML browsers typically have very similar capabilities to HTML browsers with respect to the way information is displayed and their support for graphics, tables, lists, and multimedia. HTML Forms are not supported in current SGML browsers. No SGML browser cur-

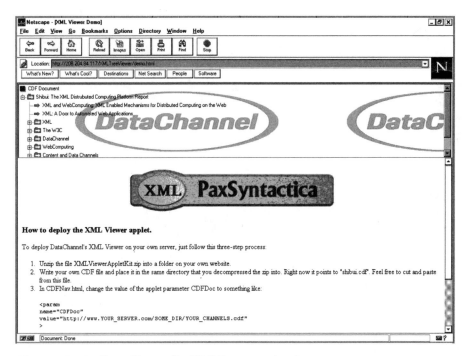

Figure 3–4 DataChannel's CDF Browser Applet

rently supports Java, JavaScript, or ActiveX although some of them have the capability to initiate local applications; some are OLE-capable and some have some interactive capabilities through private scripting languages.

SGML browsers have capabilities which HTML browsers do not have. The most common is that they use the document structure to automatically generate an expandable/collapsible hypertext table of contents. Expandable refers to the ability, when looking at a view which shows only higher-level headings, to click on a heading and see the subheading "beneath" it. Collapsible is the reverse process—the ability to click on an expanded view, causing the subheadings to be removed for easier viewing of the higher-level headings. The entire document itself may be expandable and collapsible by allowing text within selected subsections to be viewed or hidden at will. SGML browsers can reveal or hide SGML tags in-line and can often display a tree view of the document structure using the tags. Attributes are typically displayed by bringing up the SGML tagged view and clicking on tags themselves to reveal their "contents." Some SGML browsers implement HyTime and other hyperlinking schemes, allowing for different types of hyperlinks unavailable in HTML such as one-to-many and bidirectional links and links which point at other links. Figures 3–5, and 3–6 show the Panorama browser from Softquad. Figure 3–7 illustrates its one-to-many hyperlink capability.

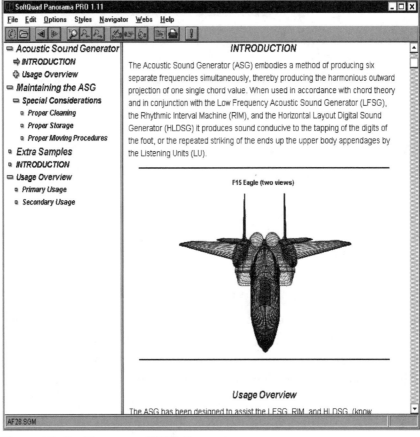

Figure 3–5   Panorama SGML Browser
The expanding TOC can be seen on the left-hand side.

Some browsers require that documents be converted from SGML to a binary format for more efficient rendering by the software. In general, this will be at worst an inconvenience for a fairly static collection of material but it may be unacceptable if the data change frequently or if documents are composed on the fly from SGML fragments.

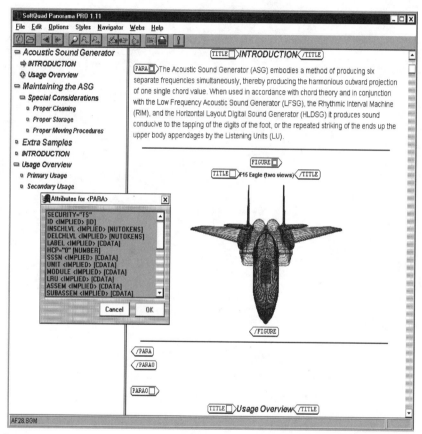

Figure 3–6   Panorama SGML Browser with SGML Structure Exposed
We have changed modes to "Show tags" and can now see the underlying SGML structure and have also exposed the attributes for the PARA tag revealing the metadata for that element.

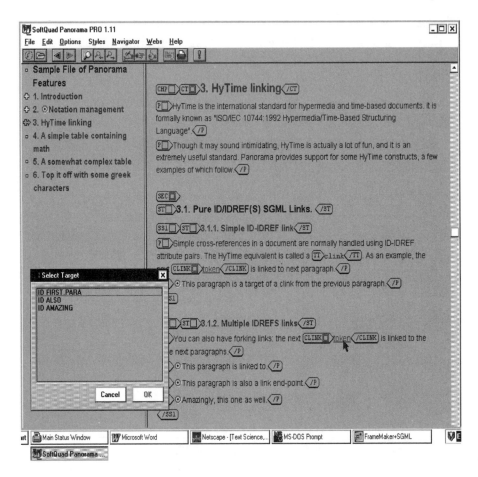

Figure 3–7   Panorama SGML Browser with HyTime Links
We have clicked on the CLINK text "token," a one-to-many hyperlink and are presented with three possible destinations.

Another important issue is the efficiency with which the browser works in a client/server environment. One of the advantages of SGML we discussed in the previous chapter is its ability to deliver sections of documents based on the document architecture. However, this is only an advantage when the browser and the server software are capable of retrieving and delivering chunks.

HTTPD can be used on the server side to deliver SGML text to an SGML browser, but SGML-specific functions such as retrieving entities or document chunks must be implemented by SGML-specific server-side software. Often such software may work with HTTPD through CGI or an equivalent extension.

SGML browsers have not made much headway in the marketplace against the HTML browsers in the Internet world although they have done well in other types of applications such as electronic books on CD-ROM. Even dedicated SGML shops often convert their SGML into HTML for delivery over the network to the desktop. Technical problems made the early SGML browsers hard to implement in an Internet environment. Pre-WebSGML browsers cannot display an SGML document without reference to the DTD so a way has to exist to find and retrieve the DTD over the network. Ditto for other entities. New standards had to be developed to address these kinds of problems. (These issues are discussed at length in our chapter on SGML e-mail.) Full SGML was too complex to build applets for it or to jazz it up with JavaScript. It was largely frustration at the limits of HTML coupled with the complexities of full SGML in the Internet browsing environment that led to the development of XML.

3.3.4 *Search Engines*

There aren't any XML-specific search engines but search engines that have been designed to work with SGML will work better with XML. Indexing algorithms can't handle things like SGML tag omission but handle well-formed (fully-tagged) XML very well.

SGML search engines are typically full-text search tools with the additional capability that they can restrict queries based on SGML structure. SGML searches provide an additional way to add precision to search operations. An Internet search application could present the ability to form ad hoc queries on arbitrary SGML elements if the users of the system are likely to know the element type set or, more commonly, they may provide a preconfigured set of queries which take advantage of SGML structure but eliminate the need for the user to know anything about it.

An example of an SGML-capable search engine is Open Text's Live Link. Open Text also happens to be one of the popular general search engines on the Web, though the majority of its users are unaware of its SGML capabilities. Figure 3–8 shows Open Text's "Power Search" page on the Web with multiple within (container) fields for increasing precision. On the right-hand side we can see that we can restrict searches to summaries, titles, first headings, URLs, and any combination of any or all of these. Unfortunately, the usefulness of this feature can be limited by the existence of "tag-salad," that is, improperly structured HTML which makes it difficult or impossible to identify containers. Intranets can really leverage this kind of capability by enforcing HTML standards and by using XML.

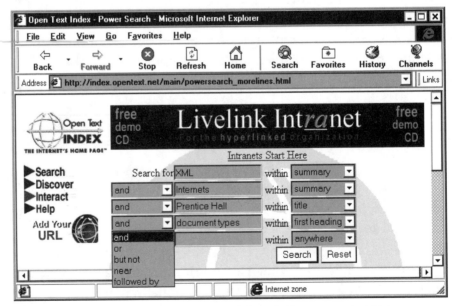

Figure 3–8   Open Text's SGML-based Search Engine on the Web

SGML search engines often also function as SGML fragment retrieval engines since they are able to isolate regions out of larger SGML documents in the course of performing structure-based searches.

Search engines can find matches among hundreds of thousands of documents quickly because they build indices where they can look up phrases quickly. A simpler approach which can be used for small document sets is to go through each document one by one looking for matches. A public domain program, sgrep, does this and also has SGML-structured search facilities. It is possible to create a simple SGML search tool on internets by installing this program on the server and providing a CGI script to execute it on demand. An extensive tutorial on sgrep is presented later in the book.

3.3.5 *Document and Component Management*

Document management is usually some form of a database with special features designed expressly for the storage, modification, and retrieval of documents. Among the more common and important of such features are checkin/checkout and revision control, In the context of XML, the difference between a document management system and component management is that the latter would have the possibility of handling fragments, data at a finer level of granularity, than the document.

XML-specific tools in this area are not yet in the marketplace but like search engines XML should work as well as fully-tagged SGML with existing systems. SGML document and component management systems have been implemented in most flavors of database technology: relational, object relational, and object oriented. RDBMS products may get you some mileage out of your investment in current database technology. Object-oriented databases are the wave of the future, especially as database technology coalesces with distributed object standards (a technique for putting services or programs on the network comparable to the way HTML pages are currently distributed) in Web/intranet environments. XML can fit in well with object-oriented concepts and it would be quite plausible to put a CORBA (a standard for distributed objects) wrapper around intelligent text objects based on XML.

3.3.6 *Authoring*

Most vendors of SGML authoring software have announced that they will be releasing XML-capable versions of their products. The changes required to support XML are relatively minor and overall the situation is improved for SGML editor vendors by XML. The burden of supporting some of the more arcane complexities of SGML fell on the editor vendors to a disproportionate degree.

XML opens the possibility of new approaches to authoring. For example, one of the major advantages of an SGML editor is that the DTD is used to guide the author in a correctly structured and formatted document. The document is "correct by construction" because the DTD has been checked as it is created. Documents, such as XML documents, that conform to the WebSGML Annex, are not required to have DTDs. This opens the possibility of generating the DTD dynamically as the document instance is being created. Figure 3–9 shows GRIF's Symposia being used to edit a well-formed document—new elements can be added at will. A DTD can, however, be read in to provide the user with the opportunity to chose from a list of element type names and associated attribute lists. This is shown in the figure in the Add Custom Tag panel. The user may also ask Symposia to scan a document and to create a simple DTD (every content model is ANY). Symposia provides a What-You-See-Is-What-You-Get (WYSIWYG) interface and uses Cascading Style Sheets (CSS) to format the document.

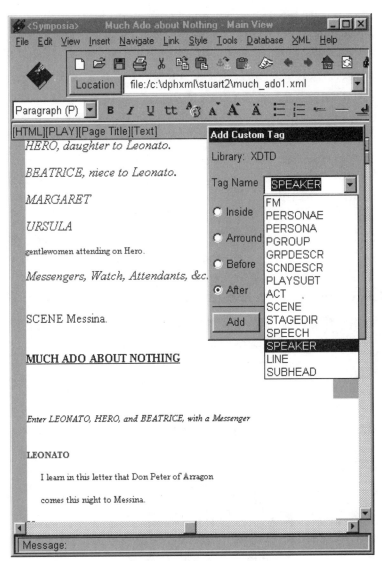

Figure 3–9 DTD Generation in GRIF's Symposia

Just as SGML is a not a language but a metalanguage, SGML editors are really metaeditors, not editors. It is not until a DTD is added and, usually, presentation instructions specific to the DTD, that the editor does something useful. This makes the SGML editor astonishingly flexible. But flexibility almost always demands a trade-off of performance or efficiency for a specific task or both. One can always obtain better results by constructing a custom editor for a specific language rather than customizing a metaeditor for that language. In many situations those better results may not be worth the additional cost which should be weighed over the long term. XML lowers those costs while reaching out for a much broader market. It is therefore no surprise that among the first XML editors is a tool which creates Microsoft CDF format XML files, shown in Figure 3–10.

We continue in this section with a review of the many approaches to authoring—creating SGML and XML documents. We will spend much of our time addressing the situation of a publications environment where traditional word processing and desktop publishing are in use. For these prospective users of XML technology the bad news is that they cannot continue doing whatever they are doing and expect

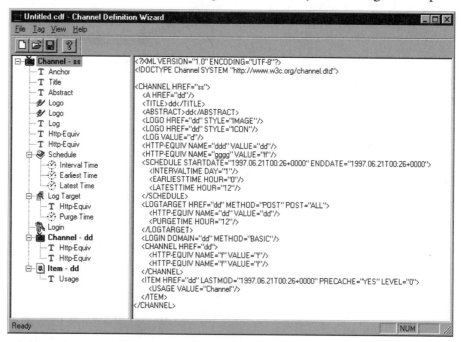

Figure 3–10   Microsoft's CDF Generator

to get XML out of it. The good news is that many of the tools with which they are familiar offer SGML capabilities. The danger here is in assuming that the best choice will be the one that involves using those tools that are most familiar.

As elsewhere in this chapter we talk about "XML" Tools when we know today that the tools we are talking about are SGML-based. We remind the reader that we always use XML unless we are pointing out something that is and will remain something applicable only to full SGML.

3.3.6.1   Native XML Editors

It always seems easier to keep doing things the same way, but consider this: XML editors, once they are set up properly, are easy to use. In fact, they are much easier than word processors such as Microsoft Word. If you are footing the bill for your publications department, you'll be glad to know that when you make your authors switch to an XML editor that you'll see productivity go up and in fairly short time at that. And that isn't even the reason for using an XML editor. The reason is that the quality of documents that come out will be higher and costs and problems at every step down the line will be lower.

Not that there isn't a down side. Although prices are dropping rapidly, XML editors remain mostly premium-priced tools. Because of the abstraction of dealing with a metaeditor, it always seems difficult to set up an XML editor. Setup of an SGML editor often requires an understanding of the SGML declaration so the newbie will find him- or herself struggling to understand terminology like "Reference Concrete Syntax" on day one. The editor must know where to find public entities so on day two one learns about "Public Entity Catalogs." There is no getting around the fact that you have to understand something about XML to use a general-purpose XML metaeditor; for some authors it is unlike anything they have ever seen before. Finally, while we will hold to our contention that XML editors are overall much simpler than Microsoft Word, Word is surely a widely used, robust, carefully designed product which cannot be matched in smoothness by the much smaller scale efforts of the traditional XML vendors.

Three categories of native XML editors may be discerned: high-end publishing systems, WYSIWYG or partially WYSIWYG editors which are roughly comparable to word processors, and non-WYSI-WYG or structure-oriented editors.

Publishing Systems

These are the XML cousins of desktop publishing tools such as Interleaf. They will have extensive support for producing high-quality paper documents from the XML source as well as other extended features for publishing automation. An example of this kind of tool is the Adept Publisher from ArborText.

WYSIWYG or Partial WYSIWYG Editors

WYSIWYG (What You See Is What You Get) has slightly different meanings in the word processing and XML worlds. In the former, it means that what you see on the screen is what you will see on paper, implying a process whose objective is to produce paper copy. XML makes no assumptions about the output medium. XML WYSIWYG mainly means that a style sheet may be used to cause on-screen formatting to be applied to particular elements so the structure of the document may be seen from the appearance of the text rather than just the tags. Some editors try harder than others to seem like word processors which is why I've given this category a range from full to partial WYSIWYG. An example of this kind of tool is Softquad's Author/Editor and Grif's MaXimal, with Grif being on "full" end of the scale with strong support for page-based layout and Softquad on the "partial" end.

Structure Editors

Structure editors make no pretense of being WYSIWYG word processors; they accentuate the fact that you are creating a structured document in all its naked XMLness. They could be as full featured as the

WYSIWYG editors but tend not to be, having less in the way of support for paper output among other things, and fall on the lower end of the price scale. The PSGML emacs mode is an example of this genre. PSGML makes no bones about XML structure, displaying the nested element view on the left-hand side and the content of elements in boxes emphasizing the idea of containment. The right-hand side shows the style sheet editor, where we are creating a formatting association for the COMPCLOS element which will be used in printing the document.

3.3.6.2   Hybrid DTP and XML

Desktop Publishing (DTP) tool vendors have had an advantage in the XML business in that their tools have always encouraged writers to think in a more structured way and their internal markup languages have some strong similarities to XML. It has therefore been possible to adapt their products to support XML. One such product, FrameMaker+SGML, maintains the document in an internal format which is extremely close to XML. Although, unfortunately, "extremely close" still leaves a sometimes irritating gap; in most cases one can import and export valid XML without difficulty, although it does not at this writing perform well-formedness checks. The author works both in WYSIWYG and structural modes, with one window displaying the paper-page, print-ready view of the document and another window showing the XML structure. Elements can be directly moved and manipulated in the structure window and when one does so the WYSIWYG view will be updated immediately. Likewise, the author can type text in the WYSIWYG window but the text will actually be entered in XML elements and the structure view will immediately be updated. The advantage of this genre of tools is that the full paper output capabilities of the original tool are preserved as are the essential look and feel of the non-XML product. As sort of a way to introduce XML painlessly to your writers, just remove their copy of Frame and swap in FrameMaker+SGML. Figure 3–11 provides a look at the Frame+SGML interface. In the figure we are using the GLOSSARY definitions from the DocBook DTD with the structure view showing the element in use and the Elements showing what elements may be added in the current context of a PARA inside a GLOSDEF.

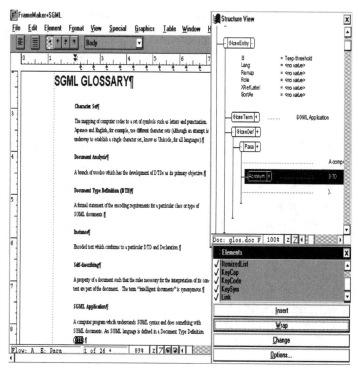

Figure 3–11   FrameMaker+SGML

3.3.6.3   Word Processor-based Environments

XML editors may be integrated into a word processor, the reason being to give authors a familiar interface with expanded capabilities which are the same as applied with DTP. Examples of this category include Corel WordPerfect and the MS Word-based, plug-in editors such as Near & Far Author from Microstar. These are among the lowest-cost editors.

3.3.6.4 Word Processors Which Can Read and Write XML

Would you like to keep using Microsoft Word exactly the way you always have, without changing a thing, and then hit the Save As XML button and have it all come out just right? Well, there is a product from Microsoft, SGML Author, which is more or less supposed to do exactly that—down to the Save As SGML button. But there *is* a catch. More than one. You have to use styles as if your life depended on it. Mess up and your XML will be messed up. If your XML does get messed up, you'll get a bunch of messages which are ten times more incomprehensible than you'd get from a vanilla XML editor because they are the messages from an XML editor which are buried somewhere beneath the word/style interface you are using. Styles do not nest beyond the possibility of having character styles within paragraph styles so one has to resort to various tricks to map word processor documents into even relatively "flat" DTDs. For example, you may find yourself having to simulate a hierarchy by making dozens of style names like second-paragraph-inside-first-bulletlistitem-inside-last-numberedlistitem. And finally, the tool which actually converts between Word and XML is designed to be easy to use at the cost of not having enough flexibility to enable you to specify any and all mappings between the two formats.

We can give three recommendations to increase the chances of success with this tool.

1. Be prepared to tweak both your Word template and your XML DTD in order to get around some of the weaknesses of the translator. As many degrees of freedom as possible are needed!

2. Seriously consider converting to XML in two steps. The first step would use SGML Author and have as its target a very simple DTD designed expressly to work with the Word template. The second step is to take the XML from the first step and transform it into the "real" XML using one of the languages described in the section on XML Programming.

3. Do not plan on foisting all of this on the authors without adequate support. Productivity will be higher if a document administrator who is thoroughly trained in XML is on hand to decipher error messages and debug conversion problems.

3.3.6.5   Text Editors

It seems that only programmers still prefer to use text editors, that is, editors, like Notepad or emacs which edit only plain text without formatting. Yet, it should not be forgotten that XML can be edited very well, thank-you, with any text editor. So, while lots of slick tools exist to make the job easier, you can be sure that you will never find yourself unable to edit an XML file for lack of a particular tool. For those who do prefer to use emacs there is a major mode for SGML, psgml. An XML parser should be run on documents produced by a text editor to confirm validity. Documents which "look OK" but are not valid may not be processed as expected by other applications.

3.3.7 *Conversion, Capture, and Export of XML*

This section deals with creating XML by programmatic means: by mass conversion of existing documents and by "capturing" XML from non-XML sources.

3.3.7.1   Legacy Conversion

Legacy, as in the legal sense of the word, is what someone left you. The difference is that this is the kind of legacy you don't want to get if you can help it. Typically, one is confronted with a mishmash of documents, in a mishmash of formats, which you want somehow to get into XML all at once.

This isn't an authoring job; it's a conversion problem since the most efficient way to go about it is usually to write computer programs to do as much of the work as possible before handing the stuff over to some editorial grunts (an unlovely word for an unlovely task, but an important task which requires fanatical attention to detail and a good understanding of the objectives of the process) to do quality assurance and cleanup. There are companies that specialize in this kind of work and since it's a one-time thing it often makes sense to hire someone to do this. One should be prepared to not expect miracles; it is difficult and sometimes impossible to go from documents which were created with little or no concept of structure to pristinely structured XML documents. Unfortunately, some companies conclude that XML isn't cost-effective after the legacy conversion phase. In fact they have only seen the very least XML can do for them while incurring the highest cost XML will ever demand of them. We therefore recommend that when prototyping an XML system, be sure to include new material created from scratch as well as legacy data in order to get a balanced view of the eventual outcome.

3.3.7.2   Capture and Export of XML

When XML is created, one creates both markup and content. The markup is the structural framework of the document. An XML editor expects the document author to be able to create the structural framework while providing the content unless the DTD is so restrictive that there are no choices to be made about the framework. Most XML editors will infer all the elements needed in the document and present the user with a complete but empty document with each field ready to fill in. This type of document is a "form." The underlying concept in HTML forms and in database forms is identical.

An HTML form or a database form may have optional fields. These can be mapped to an OR in a content model of a DTD. A particular response in a form may cause a second form to appear which requests additional information. This might be equivalent to the selection between elements with different children in an XML editor. The point is that the information gathering process of forms can be captured in a DTD and mapped to a document instance.

It follows from this that an XML editor can replace an HTML form or a database form. The opposite may also be true; other form presentation tools may be used to capture XML, and it is sometimes effective to do that. A simpler form interface such as the HTML form may be an easier tool to use for simple data entry. But we will want to have the data in XML so we can easily search it and process it later.

We will develop this concept in a form-to-XML Internet application in later chapters.

When forms get extremely complex, the process of capturing XML becomes negotiation. We will also develop concepts of negotiation in an application later in the book.

All information humans create and use has some or many kinds of underlying structure. If the structure is regular, it is usually straightforward to map it into an XML representation. Database content organized in relational, object-oriented, or other schema types can be exported to XML for interchange and for processing with XML tools. This can be done with other types of applications as well; for example, Microsoft has announced their intention to provide XML export from Word, Access, PowerPoint, and Excel. This is another way XML data are created.

XML exported from databases and other structured information tools often conforms to a DTD which is designed to very closely match the internal data format of the tool which exported it. It may not be a very useful form for subsequent processing. In this case it is common to do one or more XML-XML transformations in order to get into a structure which is compatible with the intended application. An XML programming language is the type of tool most often used in this situation. Although this might seem like a lot of trouble, it is smart to make no assumptions about the eventual use of the exported XML and therefore to keep it as simple as possible.

3.3.8 *DTD Design Tools*

XML DTD syntax involves four statement types, each with its own syntax rules and many possible parameters (although only a small subset will suffice for most DTDs). Content models, the notation used for expressing the arrangement of possible elements which may be contained by the parent element, are encoded using a notation derived from regular expression syntax from computer science. And that is the easy part. The hard part is forming all those DTD statements into a coherent, efficient, elegant, usable, maintainable, and extensible document architecture. The number of element types needed in a document architecture is sometimes quite large; HTML, a "simple" SGML language, started out as "just a few tags" and has expanded to "quite a few"—the latest HTML DTD is some 60 pages long (comments included) and still growing.

Fortunately, there are several tools on the market which can be very helpful to the DTD designer. One, Microstar's Near & Far, is a graphic design tool for constructing, manipulating, viewing, and documenting DTDs. Element types are presented as boxes which can be moved around on the screen and connected in expandable and collapsible tree structures to form parent and child relationships. Special types of connectors visually represent whether an element type or element type group (full SGML only!) is repeatable and/or optional. Attribute definitions for element types may be viewed by clicking on element type boxes.

This category of tool allows the novice to create correct DTDs without mastering every detail of the syntax and gives any user the ability to understand the structure of the architecture at a glance. The reader will probably find this to be the case for the Glossary fragment from the DocBook DTD shown in Figure 3–12 using Near & Far. Compare this presentation to the text version in Figure 3–13.

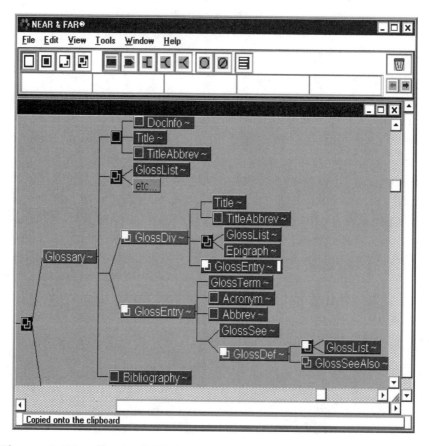

Figure 3–12   Graphic DTD Tool
Shows the element structure of the Glossary fragment from the DocBook DTD. Attribute definitions are displayed for each element type in a separate window on demand.

```
<!--
.................................................. -->
<!-- Glossary
.................................................. -->
<![ %glossary.content.module; [
<![ %glossary.module; [
<!ENTITY % local.glossary.attrib "">
<!ELEMENT Glossary - O ((%bookcomponent.title.content;)?,
(%component.mix;)*, (GlossDiv+ | GlossEntry+),
Bibliography?)>
<!ATTLIST Glossary%common.attrib;
%local.glossary.attrib;>
<!--end of glossary.module-->]]>
<![ %glossdiv.module; [
<!ENTITY % local.glossdiv.attrib "">
<!ELEMENT GlossDiv - O ((%sect.title.content;), (%compo-
nent.mix;)*,
GlossEntry+)>
<!ATTLIST GlossDiv%common.attrib;
 %local.glossdiv.attrib;>
<!--end of glossdiv.module-->]]>
<!--end of glossary.content.module-->]]>
<!-- GlossList ...................... -->
<![ %glosslist.module; [
<!ENTITY % local.glosslist.attrib "">
<!ELEMENT GlossList - - (GlossEntry+)>
<!ATTLIST GlossList%common.attrib;
%local.glosslist.attrib;>
<!--end of glosslist.module-->]]>
<![ %glossentry.content.module; [
<![ %glossentry.module; [
<!ENTITY % local.glossentry.attrib "">
<!ELEMENT GlossEntry - O (GlossTerm, Acronym?, Abbrev?,
  (GlossSee|GlossDef+))>
```

Figure 3–13   Text Version of Glossary DTD Fragment

```
<!ATTLIST GlossEntry      --SortAs: alternate sort string for
automatically
     alphabetized set of glossary entries--
SortAsCDATA#IMPLIED
%common.attrib;
%local.glossentry.attrib;>
<!--end of glossentry.module-->]]>
<!--ELEMENT GlossTerm (defined in the Inlines section,
below)-->
<![ %glossdef.module; [
<!ENTITY % local.glossdef.attrib "">
<!ELEMENT GlossDef - O ((%glossdef.mix;)+, GlossSeeAlso*)>
<!ATTLIST GlossDef
--Subject: one or more subject area keywords for searching--
SubjectCDATA#IMPLIED
%common.attrib;
%local.glossdef.attrib;>
<!--end of glossdef.module-->]]>
<![ %glosssee.module; [
<!ENTITY % local.glosssee.attrib "">
<!ELEMENT GlossSee - O ((%para.char.mix;)+)>
<!ATTLIST GlossSee
--OtherTerm: link to GlossEntry of real term to look up--
OtherTermIDREF#CONREF
%common.attrib;
%local.glosssee.attrib;>
<!--end of glosssee.module-->]]>
<![ %glossseealso.module; [
<!ENTITY % local.glossseealso.attrib "">
<!ELEMENT GlossSeeAlso - O ((%para.char.mix;)+)>
<!ATTLIST GlossSeeAlso
--OtherTerm: link to GlossEntry of related term--
OtherTermIDREF#CONREF
%common.attrib;
%local.glossseealso.attrib;>
<!--end of glossseealso.module-->]]>
<!--end of glossentry.content.module-->]]>
```

Figure 3–13   *(continued)* Text Version of Glossary DTD Fragment

Near & Far is a sophisticated design tool. Less sophisticated and less expensive (including free) tools exist which provide a formatted view of the DTD. These are useful for understanding the document structure and perhaps also for documentation purposes. One public domain tool, DTD2HTML, converts a DTD to a formatted view in HTML.

FRED, from OCLC, offers an alternative or perhaps complementary way to approach DTD design. FRED, available as a free on-line service, will generate a DTD from marked-up document instances. This could very useful in creating a DTD for a legacy document set. One could take a representative sample of the documents, mark up all the elements that occur in the whole set and, voila, FRED will create a (probably rough) DTD sufficient to encompass all of the documents input to it.

3.3.9 *Down Conversion from XML*

XML is often used to represent information which will be delivered to the user in either non-XML form or in an XML form that is different from the one used to store the document. Until we have an XML browser on everyone's desktop, a common scenario will be to translate the XML, on the server, to HTML, which may be either SGML-compliant or *HTML du Jour*, as the nonstandard variants of HTML are sometimes called. There is a third possibility which we'll call XML+HTML. XML is converted into XML with embedded HTML. HTML browsers will ignore the unrecognized tags and display the HTML parts of the document but the XML structures, names, attributes, and containment will remain available to client-side Java scripts. Of course, HTML is not the only possible output format: Word processor or desktop publishing formats, for printing and editing, are also common. We also see postscript, PDF, proprietary formats used for CD-ROM production, proprietary typesetting languages, and multimedia/virtual reality scripting languages.

Translation from XML to HTML may be performed "on-demand," that is, when the user requests a page, or it may be done off-line. The translation process is generally extremely simple and quick due to the family relationship between HTML and other XML languages, so on-demand translation is usually not unreasonable overhead for the server. The mapping between XML and HTML may be accomplished through a style sheet or may be accomplished through a script written in either an XML programming language or, with a little more effort, any server-side programming language such as Perl or C.

NSO's DynaWeb and Open Text's Live Link Server are two complete solutions to XML delivery in HTML. They both translate to HTML on-demand, using a style sheet mapping, and run off of HTTPD. These products also offer automatic HTML TOC generation from XML, and XML structure-sensitive search capabilities. Omnimark's Omnimark language and AIS's Balise are full-featured SGML programming languages which are also designed to run off HTTPD and can perform complex transformations and interface to an SQL database.

The primary advantages of performing XML to HTML translation on-demand are

1. Ability to deliver "chunks" of data based on XML-structure without deciding beforehand how to break down the document into HTML pages.
2. A single repository instead of parallel HTML and XML, saving disk space and perhaps avoiding update problems.
3. Dynamic composition of documents from XML source and possibly out of OR with data from databases.

Off-line conversion of XML to HTML has the advantage of not requiring any special server process, which may reduce cost as well as server load.

Conversion from XML to other output formats can be accomplished with a variety of tools or by using a programming language. The latter possibility is discussed in the section SGML Programming Languages. Most of the WYSIWYG authoring tools discussed in the Authoring section have "round-trip" capabilities; that is, not only can you go from, say Word to XML, but you can also get from XML to Word.

Many XML translation products use style sheets to give the user a familiar way to specify some output mapping of XML. Work that had been underway for a number of years to standardize this process has recently come to fruition in the passage of Internal Standard 10179, Document Style, Semantic and Specification Language (DSSSL). A public domain reference application called Jade which will output RTF (Microsoft Word format) or HTML from an DSSSL script is available.

3.3.10   *HyTime*

XML is quite good at providing a syntax for document representation but it has nothing to say about what the document might be used for. You need a a specific language to do that such as HTML. It was discovered after some time that people were continually reinventing the wheel: creating XML languages which do the same thing but call those things by different names. This has been at least in part the impetus behind HyTime, a companion international standard to SGML, which codifies a set of common behaviors having to do with hypermedia. HyTime preserves the ability of the language creator to create his or her own element type names but provides a mechanism for indicating that a particular element or attribute conforms to one of the codified common behaviors. For example, HyTime provides several different types of hyperlinks including aggregate, bidirectional, and indirect links and provides markup-based methods for referencing objects by temporal and spatial position.

Parts of HyTime have been implemented in some XML browsers, databases, and other XML applications. A HyTime engine is a processor which can interpret XML documents with HyTime behaviors, providing the set of services defined in the HyTime standard. A commercial HyTime engine has been implemented by TechnoTeacher. HyTime is a modular standard. It may be of interest to those constructing Internet applications who simply want to support a richer hypertext paradigm. On the other end of the scale, HyTime can be used to implement the state of the art in hypertextual, hypermedia, interactive, dynamic intranets.

There are a number of companion standards to HyTime which further specify the application domain to which HyTime may be applied. For example, Topic Mapping uses HyTime's link behaviors to define a standard way to support arbitrary, typed relations (mappings) between pieces of information in a repository. One could say that Topic Mapping provides a way to say "why" one piece of information is linked to another, a new way of dealing with intranet infoglut which is possible due to the mechanism and concepts implicit in the XML view of information.

Although HyTime and Topic Mapping were originally full-SGML-related standards, they do not have any syntax requirements which would render them incompatible with XML. Some of the concepts in HyTime overlap with work being done in the XML language recommendation on namespaces and in XLL, XML linking. At the present time HyTime is stable, being an approved international standard, albeit with a relatively (to the Web!) small user community.

3.4 | DTDs as Development Resources

Some DTDs have had decades (in person-years) of work put into them. Usually the organizations and individuals that create DTDs are eager for them to be used as widely as possible so a huge corpus is available from which one can borrow and learn. A DTD, or possibly more than one, is the contract between the components of an Internet application. Even though we will show how to design applications which do not actually use the DTD during processing, we will always provide a DTD for all the types of documents we process. (An excellent resource on this topic is "Structuring XML Documents" by David Megginson, also in the Charles F. Goldfarb series.)

It appears from our early experience that XML DTDs will be quite different from SGML DTDs. SGML DTDs have been oriented toward technical publishing and usually contain a great deal of support for layout. Most SGML DTDs are very large. The Internet application-oriented DTDs of XML have less to do with documents and are more data oriented. Some examples of XML DTDs are:

- Channel Definition Format (CDF)

  Channel Definition Format is a language that permits a Web publisher to describe frequently updated collections of information, or channels enabling automatic delivery to compatible Web clients.

- Open Software Description (OSD)

  OSD describes software components, including their versions, underlying structure, relationships to other components, and dependencies. Software packages that are described using OSD can be delivered automatically through "push" technology.

- Mathematical Markup Language (MathML)

  MathML describes mathematical notation, capturing both its structure and content. The goal of MathML is to enable mathematics to be served, received, and processed on the Web, just as HTML has enabled this functionality for text. MathML is a W3C project.

- Web Interface Definition Language (WIDL)

WIDL, used in the WebMethods Web Automation Toolkit, describes resources of the World Wide Web in order to enable automation of all interactions with HTML/XML documents and forms. The WIDL DTD is presented on the following pages.

```
<!ELEMENT WIDL ( SERVICE | BINDING )* >
<!ATTLIST WIDL
        NAME       CDATA    #IMPLIED
        VERSION (1.0 | 2.0 | ...) "2.0"
        TEMPLATE   CDATA    #IMPLIED
        BASEURL    CDATA    #IMPLIED
        OBJMODEL (wmdom | ...) "wmdom"  >
<!ELEMENT SERVICE EMPTY>
<!ATTLIST SERVICE
        NAME       CDATA    #REQUIRED
        URL        CDATA    #REQUIRED
        METHOD (Get | Post) "Get"
        INPUT      CDATA    #IMPLIED
        OUTPUT     CDATA    #IMPLIED
        AUTHUSER   CDATA    #IMPLIED
        AUTHPASS   CDATA    #IMPLIED
        TIMEOUT    CDATA    #IMPLIED
        RETRIES    CDATA    #IMPLIED >
<!ELEMENT BINDING ( VARIABLE | CONDITION | REGION )* >
<!ATTLIST BINDING
        NAME       CDATA    #REQUIRED
        TYPE (Input | Output) "Output">
<!ELEMENT VARIABLE EMPTY>
<!ATTLIST VARIABLE
        NAME       CDATA    #REQUIRED
        FORMNAME   CDATA    #IMPLIED
        TYPE (String | String[] | String[][]) "String"
        USAGE (Default | Header | Internal) "Function"
        REFERENCE CDATA    #IMPLIED
        VALUE      CDATA    #IMPLIED
        MASK       CDATA    #IMPLIED
        NULLOK              #BOOLEAN >
<!ELEMENT CONDITION EMPTY>
```

Figure 3–14

```
<!ATTLIST CONDITION
      TYPE   (Success | Failure | Retry) "Success"
      REF         CDATA    #REQUIRED
      MATCH       CDATA    #REQUIRED
      REBIND      CDATA    #IMPLIED
      SERVICE     CDATA    #IMPLIED
      REASONREF   CDATA    #IMPLIED
      REASONTEXT  CDATA    #IMPLIED
      WAIT        CDATA    #IMPLIED
      RETRIES     CDATA    #IMPLIED >
<!ELEMENT REGION EMPTY>
<!ATTLIST REGION
      NAME        CDATA    #REQUIRED
      START       CDATA    #REQUIRED
      END         CDATA    #REQUIRED >
```

Figure 3–14   (continued)

Part Two

Perl and XML

The Desperate Perl Hacker and Internet Applications: Overview

4

T his chapter briefly describes the "Desperate Perl Hacker" and his or her relation to XML and the applications implemented by the Desperate Perl Hackers in the following chapters, including the specific XML functionality required to implement these applications, and the software components which are used. The operation of the entire system is diagrammed and explained at a high level.

4.1 | Apropos of Perl and the Desperate Perl Hacker

I still think that by leaving the behavior hanging around outside in CGI's, we return to the messy spaghetti days. CGI's, I start to think, look a bit like a surgeon who, instead of neatly tucking all the organs into the abdominal cavity and stitching it shut, leaves all the entrails and organs and intestines hanging outside for all to see! Yuck!

from the Internet

Yes, in fact, Internet application construction can be messy, as our commentator so graphically describes. But our hasty surgeon seems to get the job done, the patients walk out alive, and his skills are very much in demand. From a pedagogical point of view his surgical techniques are very useful as one sees how it is done and how everything works.

This is the main objective of the next several chapters—to build everything from the ground up and to leave nothing to the imagination. The applications that are developed are complete, do something useful, are easy to understand, and bring up many of the key issues in XML-based Internet design. Perl is the language of choice here because it is easy to understand and incredibly concise. In other places we will discuss using higher-level tools and more robust construction techniques but we will have less opportunity to unpeel all of the details.

Which is not to disdain Perl or the construction techniques presented in these chapters because the Desperate Perl Hacker with solid data-centric XML Internet application design skills is very much in demand. The reason he is desperate is because he is everybody's hero, the programmer called on to make everything work in the face of impossible requirements and deadlines.

4.1.1   *Java Versus Perl*

For the record, Java does have many advantages over Perl for XML Internet construction:

1. Internal character set compatibility (UNICODE)
2. Object model of programming (somewhat supported by Perl 5, though)
3. Network support
4. Compatibility with distributed object standards such as CORBA
5. Security model
6. Tools such as JCC (Java Compiler Compiler)
7. Support for RMI (Remote Method Invocation)

8. Byte code program distribution (and machine code compilation on some platforms) versus source-only for Perl
9. Widespread use for client-side scripting
10. Universal availability of the run-time platform
11. Database standards compatibility (JDB)
12. Transaction management compatibility
13. Availability of several XML APIs and tools written in Java

Quite a lot but we should remember, as Bill Gates has said, that Java is just a language and one that is beginning to show some weaknesses as well. With Perl we say that there is always more than one way to do anything and this applies to almost every item on this list of Java strengths. And Perl has the four 5-to-1 points on its side:

1. Accessible to 5 times as many programmers
2. Development time 5 times faster
3. Footprint 5 times smaller
4. Performance 5 times faster

Of course, quibblers can and will quibble on the exact ratio. In fact the languages are not competitive any more than Perl and C or C++ have been competitive. Each has an important domain of suitable applications and the experienced programmer will choose the language best suited to the task at hand.

4.1.2 *Perl and XML Compliance*

> At the time that this book went to press, Larry Wall, the creator of Perl, announced the commencement of a project to fully support XML in Perl. So we are pleased to say that the following comments will be obsolete in the not too distant future. Of course they will continue to apply to Perl 4 and 5 and hence to the code presented in this text. Nonetheless, this section is filled with great wisdom and timeless insight like every other section of our book.

There is actually some question as to whether Perl can be used in a fully compliant manner with XML. Of course, Perl has been widely used for years with SGML, a much more complex standard, and the applications presented here argue for the use of Perl with XML with all the persuasiveness of running code. Nonetheless, the XML standard will not bless an application with compliancy unless it meets one of two levels of requirements: either be able to verify well-formedness or validation. One of the reasons for XML's existence is to lower SGML's bar for compliance and full functionality (no SGML application ever supported everything) in order to make lighter weight processing and application construction possible and to promote interoperability among applications. So it is highly desirable that Perl applications be fully XML compliant even if they never were that with SGML.

The bad news can be summed up in one word: UNICODE. The standard states: "All XML processors must accept the UTF-8 and UTF-16 encodings of 10646." 10646 is now synonymous with UNICODE and UTF-16 is the 16-bit UNICODE character encoding. Perl is not designed to handle double-byte characters and Perl regular expressions are next to impossible to write for double-byte characters. Perl applications will therefore never qualify as XML processors according to the standard.

Perl applications should attempt nonetheless to conform to the well-formedness prescriptions if for no other reason than the basic requirement of well-formedness, proper element nesting, is precisely what is required to ensure that programs work correctly. However, there are many other well-formedness constraints related to entity handling, CDATA sections, and the internal DTD subset where the Desperate Perl Hacker will be sorely tempted to cut corners and will succumb to that temptation most of the time. We have pointed out these kinds of problems wherever they occur in our application. Nothing swept under the rug here.

One of the goals of XML, as declared in the standard itself, was that "It shall be easy to write programs which process XML documents."

To some of us that meant that respectability was about to be bestowed on the Desperate Perl Hacker by making Perl's natural capabilities the minimal baseline for XML conformance. It turned out that this clause was subject to varied interpretation. Instead of "easy" meaning that the Desperate Perl Hacker with a sufficient supply of Jolt Cola could churn something out, it was most commonly taken to mean that a computer science graduate student could write an XML parser in a weekend. Once people sat down and started to write parsers it became two weeks and by the time they had dotted all their i's it was more like two months. In consequence, current thinking is that "easy" means that an application programmer can take a parser or XML API written by our poor graduate student and, shielded from whatever complexities might exist in low-level processing of XML, construct a robust component architecture.

So where does that leave Perl vis-à-vis XML? Right where it is right now—still the language of choice for a myriad of applications, still the quickest way from here to there when quick really matters. And still a great language for teaching the nitty-gritty of XML data design and programming.

4.2 | System Components

4.2.1 *Applications*

4.2.1.1   Customer Service System

1. Customer Communication Bulletin Board

    Customers and support staff can engage in threaded, news-style discussions and information can be posted under a variety of topic headings.

2. Customer Information Database

    Customer and sales lead contact information.

4.2.2   *Functionality*

1. Editing of XML documents
2. Importing into XML format
3. Structured-based search
4. Retrieval of XML documents and document fragments
5. Transformation of XML into HTML
6. Browsing of XML documents

4.2.3   *Software*

1. Symposia XML Editor/Browser
2. XMLForms Form to XML Engine
3. XML Bulletin Board
4. SGREP XML Search Engine
5. DPHXML XML Parser
6. DPHXML XML Transformation Engine

4.3 | System Operation

Figure 4–1 shows an information system with two types of input. The first is a customer database containing essential information about clients. Information is entered directly using an XML editor or through an HTML forms interface. The forms interface data are based on an engine, XMLForms, which transform them to XML using the same DTD as the XML editor. The other type of input is a bulletin board system which uses XML to store its messages. The user interface is HTML form-based and the transformation to XML is accomplished using the internal engine of the bulletin board. The DTD for the bulletin board XML is different from the DTD for the customer information. We will see that we use the DTDs for guiding input when we use an XML editor and do not use them in any other place, at least in the formal sense. One could say that we use the DTD informally in that it is the known structure of the document type or an implicit DTD which governs the generation and search and retrieval of data.

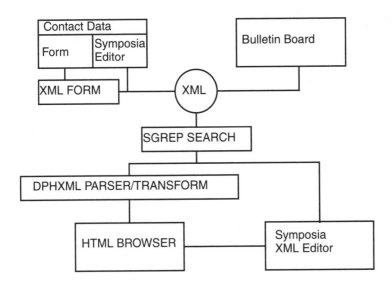

Figure 4–1 Architecture

The choice of a bulletin board and a customer database is in part an accidental combination although one could imagine easily enough this combination fulfilling the needs of a customer service organization. The bulletin board might be provided externally to allow customers to ask support questions or discuss issues related to products and the customer database might be used internally to record essential support information about each customer. There could be situations where an employee would want to search in both sets of data; suppose he or she wanted to know all the customers using a certain product and all the comments mentioning that product in the last month. The SGREP search engine would easily enable us to do this.

Results of queries, that is, documents matching the query parameters, can be delivered to the user in two different ways. The first is to transform the document or document fragment into HTML using the DPHXML parser and a transformation engine particular to the document type. The second is to deliver the document directly to a tool capable of rendering an XML document, in this case the Grif Symposia XML editor.

An XML Bulletin Board

The operation, data notations, and code relating to the treatment of the data for a Web-based bulletin board are described in this chapter. The bulletin board uses HTML and HTML forms for the delivery and collection of data and XML for the storage of messages and organizational data such as user identification and state information. Many points are considered in data design, with options from the most elementary implementations of XML to the use of object-oriented typing mechanisms. SGML and XML data notations are compared. Code fragments which illustrate a very basic use of XML as a groupware data notation are explained.

5.1 | Overview

Bulletin boards were one of the first applications which linked together heterogeneous sets of users using computers and telephone lines. Bulletin boards were based on proprietary data storage schemes and have a wide variety of interfaces and special features specific to a given application or user community. Much of the usage of bulletin boards has migrated over to news on both the Internet and intranets. News has a standard protocol (NNTP) and servers and clients have been highly optimized and become fairly rich in powerful features over the years and news readers are now embedded within Web browsers.

Then why have we chosen to write a Web/XML-based bulletin board? Bulletin boards continue, in fact, to exist because they address specific needs of a community of users who are not optimally served by standard news. There are a large number of other types of applications in other categories, falling today under the general rubric of "groupware" which essentially enables people to organize their work and their thoughts collectively and collaboratively. We therefore think it is useful to provide a code base for building applications of this nature.

The bulletin board has a simple password access mechanism, primarily to ensure that each user is identified by his or her chosen name when messages are posted. Once the user's identity has been established, the user ID is passed back to the server at each operation through values tacked on to the end of a URL. Once admittance to the bulletin board has been obtained, the user is presented with a list of topics. The creation of topic categories is restricted to the person designated as the system administrator as is the ability to modify passwords and perform other housekeeping operations. Figure 5–1 shows a screen shot of a topic board.

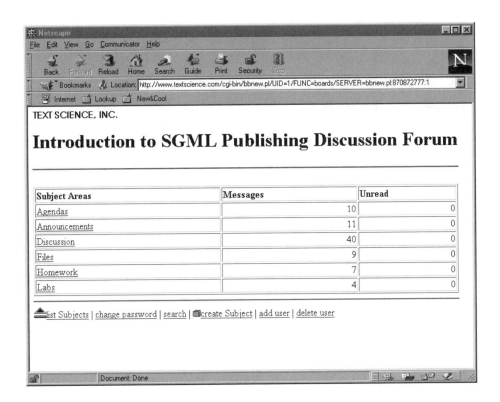

Figure 5–1 XML Bulletin Board Topic

When a topic is selected the user will be presented with the threaded discussion list for that topic, as illustrated in Figure 5–2.

The threaded discussion list shows the status, title, submittor, and date for each message. A response is indented below the message to which it responds. The user can "hide" any message, in effect, deleting it from view either when it is read or at any time the user desires. We are therefore required to maintain an individual state for every user which makes this application much closer to groupware than news. When the user clicks on the title of a message he or she will see the message body as shown in Figure 5–3.

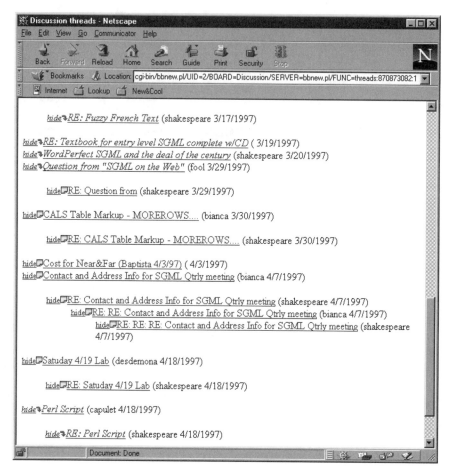

Figure 5-2   XML Bulletin Board Threaded Discussion

The user may reply to the message by clicking on an icon at the bottom of the page. An HTML text box will be presented to the user with the text of the message to which he or she is responding quoted at the top. The user may add their own text, including XML or HTML (entered in plain text mode) although this interface happens to require that XML or HTML be surrounded with a special tag <RAW>...</RAW>. (The default behavior is to encode the brackets which start the tags as character entities, preventing the browser from interpreting any markup as anything but plain text.)

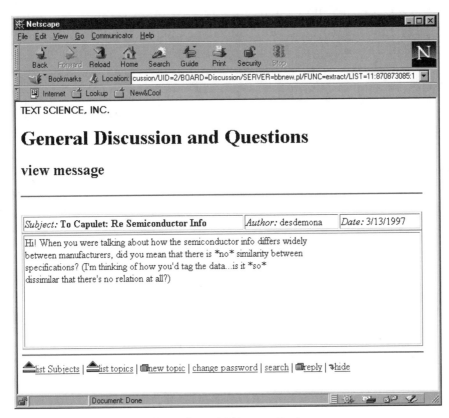

Figure 5–3   XML Bulletin Board Message Body

The entire interface is done in HTML and may be used with browsers capable of displaying only HTML 3.2. XML is used behind the scenes, as we will see the next section.

5.2 | XML Document Types

5.2.1 *Messages*

Each message posted to the bulletin board is stored as an individual XML document. Messages are linked to their parents (the message that is being responded to, if any), and their children (messages which have responded to the current message) through the use of numeric fields containing message identifiers assigned by the software. The other fields are what one would expect: author, subject, time, message body, and the raw element, which, as described above, separates body text which is to be interpreted as XML or HTML. The DTD for messages is shown in Figure 5–4 and a document instance is shown in Figure 5–5.

```
<!Element Record      (Head, Body)>
<!Element Head        (ID, Parent, Children, Author,
                       Subject, Time)>
<!Element Body        (#PCDATA | Raw)*>
<!Element ID          (#PCDATA)>
<!Element Parent      (#PCDATA)>
<!Element Children    (#PCDATA)>
<!Element Author      (#PCDATA)>
<!Element Subject     (#PCDATA)>
<!Element Time        (#PCDATA)>
<!Element Raw ANY>
```

Figure 5–4   Message DTD

```
<RECORD><HEAD><ID>8</ID><PARENT>0</PARENT>
<CHILDREN>9,10</CHILDREN><AUTHOR>desdemona</AUTHOR>
<SUBJECT>Pictures on these Soup Labels</SUB-
JECT><TIME>858115582</TIME></HEAD><BODY>Well, I haven't
figured out yet how to address the many graphic images on
these here Soup Labels. Pretty pictures of asparagus,
etc....is there a line we can draw between what is text-
oriented (the ingredients, the nutrition info, etc.) and
what seems to make more sense to be printed first on the
labels (such as the recipe pictures--even the middle part
of the label)? Or are folks adding .gif references to han-
dle the images?</BODY></RECORD>
```

Figure 5–5   XML Representation of a Message

There are a few things worthy of notice in the DTD.

■ It is short and very simple.
   SGML has, by and large, been a technology used for

extremely complex documents. This will not be the case for a very large number of XML documents. It is clear that there is nothing difficult about handling this document type, little advantage to be gained from choosing a proprietary, non-XML syntax, and great advantages in having a notation which is standard, well formed, and easy to understand.

- Although links exist between documents but we have chosen not to use XML link syntax.
  Instead we simply specify the ID within the ID element and the references within the PARENT and CHILDREN elements. One could very well argue that using an XML link would make the relationships standard and also be supported by standard tools supporting XML link syntax. The fact that multiple links are represented within the CHILDREN element using a private syntax (comma separation) can be criticized with some justice. The point is that these are choices which the system designer makes and these choices will often fall somewhere on the line between expediency and conformity with external systems. It's the 80/20 rule: We have consciously chosen to get the bigger part of the benefit of XML, the 80 percent, and haven't gone all the way. Let the purist cringe.

- No use has been made of attributes.
  There is at least a place where they would have made a lot of sense. Within the TIME element we have used a particular format for storing the time value. It would have been sensible to indicate the format used with an attribute. The application will simply assume that this particular format is the only one used.

- BODY has mixed content model which allows characters and RAW elements to be mixed. Mixed content models are restricted in XML to optional repeatable OR groups with #PCDATA coming first, a simplification which has eliminated a host of complexities which could arise in SGML.

- RECORD instances do not have the XML declaration and are therefore simply well formed.

  We will not actually use the DTD except in those cases where we choose to edit instances with an XML-aware editor.

5.2.2 *Password Document*

Security was not a concern in this project, user names and passwords serving primarily to uniquely identify each user when he or she posts a message. Therefore, login information is kept using the simple XML markup scheme in Figure 5–6 and Figure 5–7.

```
<!Element UserDB (Header, Record*)>
<!Element Header (UID)>
<!Element UID    (#PCDATA)>
<!Element Record (UName, PassWd, EMail, UID)>
<!Element UName  (#PCDATA)>
<!Element PassWd (#PCDATA)>
<!Element EMail  (#PCDATA)>
```

Figure 5–6   Password File DTD

```
<USERDB><HEADER><UID>4</UID></HEADER>
<RECORD><UNAME>shakespeare</UNAME>
<PASSWD>swr</PASSWD>
<EMAIL>michael@grif.fr</EMAIL><UID>1</UID></RECORD>
<RECORD><UNAME>fool</UNAME><PASSWD></PASSWD>
<EMAIL></EMAIL><UID>2</UID></RECORD>
<RECORD><UNAME>lear</UNAME><PASSWD></PASSWD>
<EMAIL></EMAIL><UID>3</UID></RECORD>
</USERDB>
```

Figure 5–7   XML Representation of a Password List

In order to simplify the software which reads and writes the user records, every field (element) is required although, as seen in Figure 5–7, there isn't always data content. (#PCDATA is always zero or more characters.) The facilities in XML alone for checking the validity of data is very limited. (The SGML Extended Facilities in ISO/

IEC 10744 offer complete datatyping.) We are able to say that there must be an e-mail element but we are not able, in the DTD, to describe what kind of data must go in it or even to prevent it from being empty. XML requires this level of validation to be performed by the application. Certain DTDs will include validity checks within attribute values. For example, the data representation in Figure 5–8 could have been used to tell an application to check that a valid password may be required:

```
<!Element PassWd (#PCDATA)>
<!Attlist PassWd validck (none|any|rigor) "none">
```

Figure 5–8   DTD Fragment with Validity Check

The attribute validck may take the value none, meaning that a password is not required; any, meaning that any nonnull password will be accepted; or rigor, meaning that the password should conform to the "rigorous" rule for passwords, for example, that it must be at least eight characters and have at least one uppercase letter, one lowercase letter, and one number. This example does not indicate how the validck attribute would be set for each record but we might suppose, for example, that it would be a property of the type of user or environment. If we simply wanted to indicate that the password value be checked in every case for documents based on this particular DTD, we could use a fixed attribute value as shown in Figure 5–9.

```
<!Element PassWd (#PCDATA)>
<!Attlist PassWd validck CDATA #FIXED "rigor">
```

Figure 5–9   DTD Fragment with Fixed Attribute for Validity

Fixed attributes are not coded in the document instance since they are "fixed." The application knows that the attribute is intrinsically present each time the element PassWd is used and that its value is "rigor." How does the application know? It must read the DTD. And here we have the crux of the most important design decision that must be taken in building an XML system: Does the application read the DTD and use it to guide processing? If the answer is no, one cannot take advantage of fixed attributes or even default attribute values as shown in Figure 5–9. Either every needed attribute value is included in the document instance each time an element with that attribute is used or the behavior is hardcoded into the application as shown in Figure 5–10.

```
# plogin.pl
# 10-22-95 Revision 2 Gene Kan
#          Added newuser confirmation.
# 03-02-97 Revision 3 Michael Leventhal
#          Comment out confirm new user.
...
#  remove ability of users to self register
#  uncomment next line to allow and delete the
#  following line
#  { print "Content-type: text/html\n\n";
#  &confirmnewuser (%CGI); }
   { print "Content-type: text/html\n\n";
      &denyuser ($CGI{"UNAME"}); }
```

Figure 5–10 What Happens When Behavior Is Hardcoded into the Application?

Here is our claim to fame: You can find dozens of books which will show you how to program properly but how many books will show you hacking at its ugliest! New user confirmation could have been encoded as a property of the data within, say, a fixed attribute of the record. A program which is DTD-aware can be written to either confirm new users if the attribute indicates that this is the appropriate behavior for the document type or not confirm them for another document type. We do not have to change our source code and we do not even have to change our data; we just change a parameter in our data schema. Figure 5–11 shows how the above program segment might look if we had added the capability to process the DTD:

```
if ((&attrValue(&elementType('RECORD'),
     'confirmUser') eq "yes") {
       &confirmnewuser (%CGI);    }
else { &denyuser ($CGI{"UNAME"}); }
```

Figure 5–11 DTD-Driven Behavior

5.2.2.1 A Little Digression on Advanced Approaches to Data Design

Although we are wandering far from our Desperate Perl Hacker's (henceforth to be known affectionately as the DPH) little program, we are just a stone's throw from understanding architectures and the mother of all SGML architectures, HyTime. So let us plunge ahead a little further and the reader will see the range of design choices laid out before him or her.

Architectures simply group element type and attribute list declarations together and put them into a form so it is easy to assign characteristics of that architecture to parts of DTDs. For example, suppose that we were to say that our password validity check and our confirmed new user behavior was to be thought of as standard attributes for program behavior related to Registration. We would like to use these standard Registration-related attributes with any number of DTDs which have user registration-related elements. What we are really after is the ability to write one standard library which has functions that are invoked whenever we use a registration architecture. The reader with some familiarity with object-oriented programming will recognize the architecture as a sort of class definition mechanism and our standard library as a set of methods. They will also recognize the objective of such a system is to promote code reuse while allowing standard (architecture-derived) and situation-specific (parts of the DTD not derived from the architecture) processing to be performed. Figure 5–12 illustrates this by creating an architecture DTD (called a meta-DTD) and modifying our original DTD to reference this base DTD:

```
<?XML version="1.0"?>
<!DocType Registration [
<!Element Access (Any)>
<!AttList Access
      exposure (system | user) "user"
      validate (none|numeric|any|passwd) "none">]>
```

Figure 5–12 Registration Architecture Prolog with Meta-DTD

The exposure and validate attributes will be associated with elements that are declared to be of type "Access." The exposure attribute indicates whether Access is an element which is exposed to the user or if it is reserved for system use. The validate attribute specifies different types of checking which could be performed on the contents of the Access element when it is entered or provided by the application; none means no checking is to be performed; numeric means that we must make sure it is a numeric data; any means that we check to see that some value has been entered; and passwd means that we apply rules specific to passwords. Now we can write a set of generic methods which can be applied to any DTD which uses the Registration architecture, as shown in Figure 5–13.

```
<!Element UserDB (Header, Record*)>
<!Element Header (UID)>
<!Element UID     (#PCDATA)>
<!AttList UID
      exposure (system | user) "system"
      validate (none|numeric|any|passwd) "numeric"
      Registration NAME #FIXED "access">
<!Element Record (UName, PassWd, EMail, UID)>
<!Element UName   (#PCDATA)>
<!AttList UName
      exposure (system | user) "system"
      validate (none|numeric|any|passwd) "any"
      Registration NAME #FIXED "access">
<!Element PassWd (#PCDATA)>
<!AttList PassWd
      exposure (system | user) "user"
      validate (none|numeric|any|passwd) "passwd"
      Registration NAME #FIXED "access">
<!Element EMail   (#PCDATA)>
<!AttList EMail
      exposure (system | user) "user"
      validate (none|numeric|any|passwd) "none"
      Registration NAME #FIXED "access">
```

Figure 5–13   Password File DTD Using Registration Architecture

When we want to indicate that an element is derived from the "Access" form in the Registration architecture, we use a fixed attribute with the name of the architecture and a value which indicates the element form "Access." We can declare any attributes specified in the architecture DTD for that element type: exposure and validate in this case. Hypothetically, an architecture processing engine exists which validates that the attributes defined by the element form are included. Our "confirmuser" logic would be implemented-based on the exposure attribute value: If it is "system," an attempt to create a new user value will be denied since only the system is permitted to do that and if it is user, we will execute the confirm routine.

Now we can understand what HyTime is. HyTime is a set of architectures designed to define a set of data descriptions useful in the processing of hypermedia documents including applications which must perform actions according to some time constraints. HyTime is therefore theoretically appropriate for all Web-based applications. To fulfill this tall order a total of seven major architectural components have been described, of which three are base behaviors appropriate to nearly any on-line document type and four are directed toward more esoteric operations involving geometry and time. A HyTime application would consist of an engine, written in some programming language which provides services to implement the three base behaviors and perhaps some or all of the optional ones. The system builder would add whatever application-specific processing is required to the HyTime library of functions or methods. HyTime has suffered from being both a little overly abstract and a lot overly ambitious. Nonetheless, it can be of considerable value for anyone building Internet applications today to have a look at the data definitions described by HyTime, as a rather thorough job has been done in dealing with common problems in hyperlinking and data validation.

On the other hand, our DPH, like many a harried designer, perhaps had thoughts of HyTime and architectures cross his mind once or twice but went ahead and hammered out some quick and dirty data definitions, the last of which we now present.

5.2.3 *User State Documents*

We will continue our policy to hide nothing since the messy parts of our system are at least as instructive as the better-done bits. The User State document, which holds information such as which messages each user of the board has or hasn't read, cannot be represented in XML, although it is acceptable SGML. It will be valuable to understand why. Let's first look at Figure 5–14, which shows the DTD.

```
<!Element UsrState  o o   (Perm?, Groups?,
                          (Board, Board)*)>
<!Element Perm        - -   (#PCDATA)>
<!Element Groups      - -   (#PCDATA)>
<!Element Board       - -   (Pointers | Junked)>
<!AttList Board Name CDATA #REQUIRED>
<!Element Pointers    - -   (#PCDATA)>
<!Element Junked      - -   (#PCDATA)>
```

Figure 5–14   User State DTD

The reader who is not familiar with SGML will perhaps be perplexed by the pair of "o"s and the pairs of dashes following the element type names. This is quite usual in SGML DTDs where one has the possibility to specify that either the start and or the end tag is optional for any particular element type. The "o" means "can omit" and the dash means "cannot omit" and the first value is for the start tag and the second value is for the end tag. If a tag is permitted to be omitted, and is omitted the SGML parser must "infer" the existence of the missing tag in order to correctly parse the document. Figure 5–15 shows an example.

```
<!DocType x [
<!Element x   - -   (a, b)>
<!Element a   o o   (#PCDATA)>
<!Element b   o o   (#PCDATA)>]>
<x>This is data for element A
<b>This is data for element B</x>
```

Figure 5–15   Tag Omission

The parser will have no trouble recognizing that the string "This is data for element A" is the content of element "a" because the DTD says that an "a" element must begin after the "x" start tag and must end right before the beginning of the "b" tag, which is present. Equally, the parser has no difficulty recognizing the end of the "b" element because it must come before the "x" end tag. Figure 5–16 shows an alternative case.

```
<!DocType x [
<!Element x  - -  ((a, b) | (c, d))>
<!Element a  o o  (#PCDATA)>
<!Element b  o o  (#PCDATA)>]>
<!Element c  o o  (#PCDATA)>
<!Element d  o o  (#PCDATA)>]>
<x>This is data for element A
<b>This is data for element B</x>
```

Figure 5–16   Tag Omission Requiring Lookahead

A human being finds this quite simple, reasoning that the "This is data for element A" must be the content of element "a" because the following element is "b," meaning that the first content model in the OR group is the one being used. In fact, the parser cannot solve this problem because it is forbidden to look ahead to the next token which, in this case, would be "b." Each state must be unambiguous without knowing what the next token is. (This is a restriction in SGML carried over into XML for reasons of compatibility. It was felt at the time that the SGML standard was written that lookahead would be too computationally expensive. There are indeed some who doubt the wisdom of that position in today's powerful computing environments.)

We require the ability to omit the start and end tags of the UsrState element because our actual file does not have a UsrState element. At the same time even simply well-formed XML documents must always have a root element, a container for the document, so we must have the document container provided by the UsrState element. The trick works in SGML because of the possibility of omitting the tags but not in XML which, in the interests of avoiding the complications of tag omission described above, simply disallows the feature.

Let's look at a document instance in Figure 5–17.

```
<PERM>R</PERM>
<GROUPS>Announcements</GROUPS>
<BOARD name="Announcements">
<POINTERS>1-11</POINTERS></BOARD>
<BOARD name="Announcements">
<JUNKED>6</JUNKED></BOARD>
<BOARD name="Homework">
<POINTERS>1-7</POINTERS></BOARD>
<BOARD name="Homework"><JUNKED>0</JUNKED></BOARD>
<BOARD name="Discussion">
<POINTERS>1-40</POINTERS></BOARD>
<BOARD name="Discussion">
<JUNKED>0</JUNKED></BOARD>
<BOARD name="Labs">
<POINTERS>1-4</POINTERS></BOARD>
<BOARD name="Labs"><JUNKED>0</JUNKED></BOARD>
<BOARD name="Files">
<POINTERS>1-9</POINTERS></BOARD>
<BOARD name="Files"><JUNKED>0</JUNKED></BOARD>
<BOARD name="Agendas">
<POINTERS>1-10</POINTERS></BOARD>
<BOARD name="Agendas"><JUNKED>0</JUNKED></BOARD>
```

Figure 5–17   User State Document Instance

There is one state document for each active user, named and referenced using the user ID as the key which is modified as the user alters his or her state by reading or discarding messages. This enables us to maintain a personal view of each board for each individual user. Each board is identified by its name in the Name attribute field of the Board tag and the messages read are kept track of in the content of the Pointers element. The messages removed from the user's view are recorded in the content of the Junked element which, the reader will have noticed, is a child element of a second Board element, all the Board elements coming in pairs. There are two points to note here. The first is that it isn't a particularly good design. Pointers and Junked elements should simply be children of a single Board element for each individual Board.

We can see the DPH's desperate mind at work here. Since he eschewed the use of an XML parser...because he was desperate, he did not have an easy way to verify when scanning the file that the parent of the element after Pointers was still Board, since he uses regular expressions which treat the file as a linear string. He simplified his regular expression by repeating the Board element around Junked.

The second thing to notice and reflect on is that fact that SGML cannot represent the grammar of this construction exactly. An exact grammatical representation would be able to say that each pair of Board elements have the same value for the Name attribute and the first occurrence of Board contains a Pointers element and the second contains a Junked element. SGML doesn't really need this capability because in SGML one would normally make the Name value an attribute of the parent element Board. But, since we are hacking, the closest we can come is to say that Board elements do indeed come in pairs, that any Board element is required to have a Name attribute, and that each Board element must contain either a Pointers or a Junked element. In fact, our application depends on the more rigid structure being adhered to but the only place this more rigid structure is expressed is in the code itself. If another application were to have write access to the User State document, the system would probably break.

One of our reviewers felt that we indulged in a little too much self-flagellation here and suggested that we either fix the problem we have described or fake it. We pass in silence on the latter alternative. We could fix the problem but since we're desperate perl hackers there never is time to fix something that already sort of works. But more importantly we know that many hackers out there will reach a point where they feel they have the jist of XML and will not master the (seemingly) minutia. And they will get bitten. Thus we happily flagellate ourselves if the reader will glean from this discussion two grave lessons:

- XML and SGML are not all-powerful type-defining mechanisms. There are many things that you might want to do and cannot.

- You are better off confining your document-type definition to what XML/SGML can do to ensure system robustness. The DTD is your contract between applications.

The User State documents and the Password documents are updated fairly frequently, differing fundamentally from the Message file which could be written just once. "Could" because we happened to choose to record the children in the Message and this requires the document to be updated each time a child is added. Since our system is file-based we must, of course, do a lot of reading, seeking, and overwriting of document files. Although Perl has facilities such as file locks, this is not extremely robust when compared to the persistent storage capabilities of database applications. (And, as will be seen in the next section, we were not very respectful of safe programming practices. The DPH loves to live on the edge.) There are good reasons to design real-world applications like the bulletin board around a database. At the same time, databases, particularly relational databases, lack the expressive power of XML and its text-specific capabilities. Object-oriented databases are more expressive although they are not necessarily more text-oriented. We'll see in later sections that the strength of XML is the easy way with which we are able to go from our repository representation to applications which manipulate it as a structured text document or display it. The trade-off that we often make is between the solidity of nontext oriented but tried and true methods of data storage and organization and the fluid, text-centric, quick, easy to manipulate XML approach. Often, we are not necessarily forced to make that trade-off because the database vendors are quickly jumping into the XML business, providing the best of both worlds.

5.3 | Reading and Writing XML in the Bulletin Board

The implementation of logic specific to the functionality of the bulletin board which does not touch on the subject of XML is not within the scope of this book. In fact, even the code which does read and write XML data is of little interest. Once we've understood how to process simple, notparsed XML in Perl there is little left to learn. XML used in this way is just a data notation which is just slightly more difficult to handle than other data notations which could be designed with the idea in mind that they would be parsed with a regular expression, line-oriented scanner.

On the other hand, it will be useful to get an idea of the progression of approaches from the low end to the high end. This first part concentrates on the very lowest end, where XML markup is basically treated as a field separator, to the higher part of the low end where we actually do hierarchical decomposition and perform some context-sensitive operations based on our position in the parse tree. The last two parts use more rigorous approaches. XML applications will run the gamut and we think it is important to educate the system designer about all the possibilities…and consequences of their choices.

5.3.1 *Writing Messages*

The writemessage subroutine is shown in Figure 5–18.

The message markup and content are simply hard-coded in a print statement. The content of each element is read from an associative array which was created when the message was extracted from the form used to capture it. The associative array uses one little notational trick which helps to keep the data organized: the use of multiple field keys that make it appear that an actual hierarchical data structure corresponding to the DTD is being maintained. For example:

$record{"HEAD","AUTHOR"}

which appears to specify the content of the AUTHOR child of HEAD but is in fact hashing into a normal single-level associative array. If the message has a parent, the ID of the current message is added to the list of children, using a comma-delineated syntax, and the routine is invoked again on the parent.

```perl
sub writemessage
{
local (%record, $updating) = @_;
local (*OFP);

if (open (OFP, "+>". $glob_topdir . $glob_blackboarddir .
    $glob_argv{"BOARD"} .$glob_expdle .
    $record{"HEAD", "ID"}))
{
  print OFP ("<RECORD><HEAD><ID>", $record{"HEAD", "ID"},
     "</ID>","<PARENT>", $record{"HEAD", "PARENT"},
     "</PARENT>", "<CHILDREN>", $record{"HEAD", "CHILDREN"},
     "</CHILDREN>", "<AUTHOR>", $record{"HEAD", "AUTHOR"},
     "</AUTHOR>", "<SUBJECT>", $record{"HEAD", "SUBJECT"},
     "</SUBJECT>", "<TIME>", time, "</TIME>",
     "</HEAD>\n<BODY>", $record{"BODY"},
     "</BODY></RECORD>\n");
  close (OFP);
}
if (!$updating && $record{"HEAD", "PARENT"} &&
    !&extractmessage ($record{"HEAD", "PARENT"}))
{
  $glob_record{"HEAD", "CHILDREN"} .= "," .
     $record{"HEAD", "ID"};
  $glob_record{"HEAD", "CHILDREN"} =~ s/^,//;
  &writemessage (%glob_record, 1);
}

}
```

Figure 5–18 writemessage Subroutine

5.3.2 *Reading Messages*

The extractmessage subroutine is listed in Figure 5–19.

The message file is read in and scanned for the RECORD start and end tags, with everything between the two being stored in recordstring. The HEAD and BODY sections are likewise scanned and extracted from recordstring and each element is found in the respective sections of the document and stored in the associative array described in the previous section.

```
sub extractmessage
{
local ($recordnumber) = shift (@_);
local ($recordstring, $head, $body, %record);
local (*IFP);

if (!open (IFP, $glob_topdir . $glob_blackboarddir .
    $glob_argv{"BOARD"}  . $glob_expdle . $recordnumber))
{
  &HTML ("TEXT",
         "extractmessage: could not open file for
$recordnumber.$EOL");
  return 1;
}
while (1)

{
  while (<IFP>)
    { if ($_ =~ m/<RECORD/) { last; } }
  $recordstring = $_;
  while ($_ && !($_ =~ m/<\/RECORD>/))
    { $_ = <IFP>; $recordstring .= $_; }
  if (!$_ || (($recordstring =~ m/<ID>([^<]*)<\/ID>/) &&
             ($1 == $recordnumber)))
    { last; }
  }
```

Figure 5–19 ExtractMessage Subroutine (Sheet 1 of 2)

```
$head = &extractfromstr ($recordstring,
                 "<HEAD>", "<\/HEAD>");
$body = &extractfromstr ($recordstring,
                 "<BODY>", "<\/BODY>");
$record{"HEAD", "ID"} = &extractfromstr ($head,
                 "<ID>", "</ID>");
$record{"HEAD", "PARENT"} = &extractfromstr ($head,
                 "<PARENT>", "</PARENT>");
$record{"HEAD", "CHILDREN"} = &extractfromstr ($head,
                 "<CHILDREN>","</CHILDREN>");
$record{"HEAD", "SUBJECT"} = &extractfromstr ($head,
                 "<SUBJECT>","</SUBJECT>");
$record{"HEAD", "TIME"} = &extractfromstr ($head,
                 "<TIME>", "</TIME>");
$record{"HEAD", "AUTHOR"} = &extractfromstr ($head,
                 "<AUTHOR>", "</AUTHOR>");
$record{"BODY"} = $body;

%glob_record = %record;
close (IFP);

if (!$record{"HEAD", "ID"})
{ return 1; }
else { return 0; } }
```

Figure 5–19   ExtractMessage Subroutine (Sheet 2 of 2)

The extractfromstr subroutine uses the Perl string library to extract the content of the elements using the start and end tags as substring delimiters, demonstrated in Figure 5–20.

```
sub extractfromstr
{
local ($string, $openstr, $closestr) = @_;
local ($pos);

return (substr ($string, $pos = index ($string, $openstr,
0)
        + length ($openstr), rindex ($string, $closestr,
        length ($string)) - $pos));

}
```

Figure 5–20   extractfromstr Subroutine

5.3.3 *Password and User State Documents*

The techniques used to read and write password and user state data are identical to those used for message data and do not need further elaboration.

5.3.4 *Transformation from XML to HTML*

We have shown how XML documents are written. The data used in the XML documents such as the message content is provided through HTML forms and placed into the data structures shown with CGI routines. These are topics covered in works on HTML and CGI and will not be discussed here. The next chapter will discuss a template approach for transforming HTML form data into XML.

We have also shown how XML documents are read. The data content extracted from the XML documents is saved in data structures and written out as HTML. We have written our own library of HTML-specific routines which can be found on the CD-ROM and we also note that several more current ones are available in the public domain. Chapter 8 will describe a general-purpose tool written in Perl for performing transformations between XML and HTML or other notations.

An XML Contact Database

Chapter

6

A n application for collecting customer contact data is illustrated in this chapter. The application is very similar to the kind of thing currently done with light databases such as Access. This chapter shows how to do it using more Web-centric technology the XML way. Two approaches are illustrated, one using an HTML form as the primary user interface and the other built around an XML editor. A programming template for converting HTML form data to XML is presented, as is a tutorial on the use of cascading style sheets with XML.

6.1 | Overview

The Contact database stores information relating to clients and prospects and is designed for the use of marketing and other business-related functions. We capture the information required through some

155

convenient interface and store that information as XML-encoded records. Once we have the records in XML we can display them over the Web, perform structured searches on them, and perform other operations such as generating mailing labels and performing marketing analyses. As with other projects of this nature, standard database technology is our competitor with respect to implementation alternatives but we think we can decisively prove that for simple applications such as this the format should be highly compatible with the main vehicle of dissemination of the information, the Web. The development time for such a system compares very favorably to the effort required to, for example, implement an Access database without even including the special tools and development that would be necessary to make the Access database available on the Web.

We have taken two entirely different approaches to capturing the data. The systems can exist in parallel and there could be justification for having both in place but our main goal in demonstrating both is pedagogical. The first uses an HTML form to collect the information and then transform the form data into XML. The second uses a Web-enabled XML editor, GRIF's Symposia, to create the XML fields directly. The GRIF editor is included on the CD-ROM accompanying the book. The main advantage of the first approach is that no knowledge of XML is required and the interface is one which has become familiar to everyone. The major advantage of the second approach is that no transformation of the data is required, i.e., no CGI programming is required, and the entry of data is more flexible.

Figure 6–1 and Figure 6–2 show the HTML form for creating a new record in the Contact database.

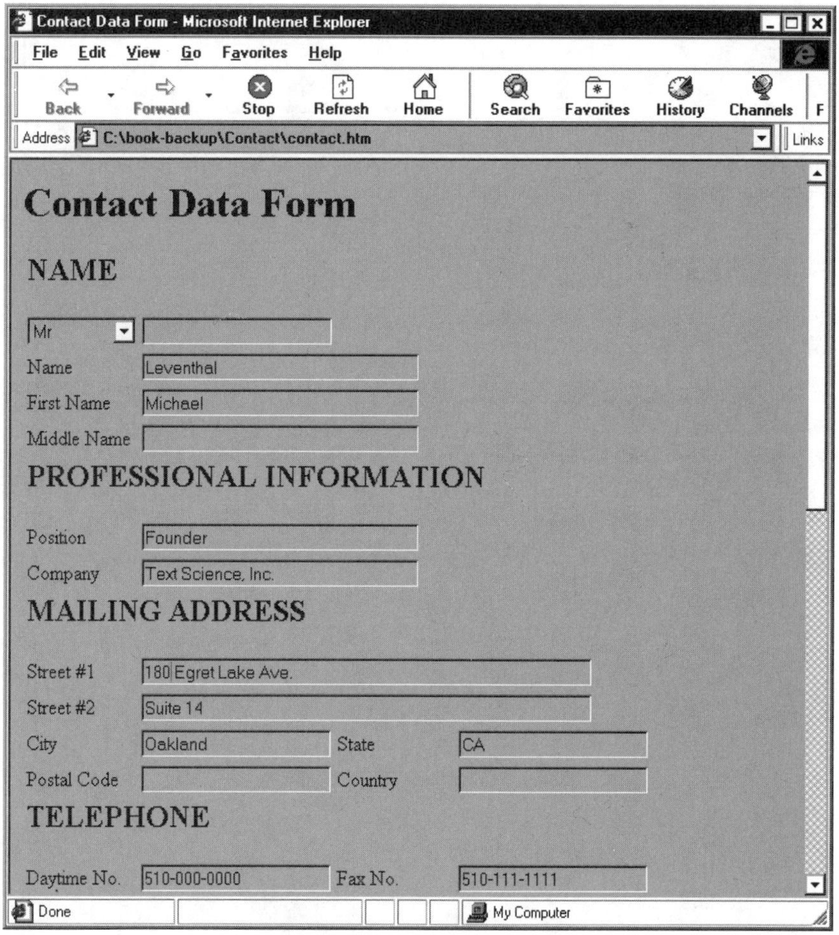

Figure 6–1   Contact Database Form

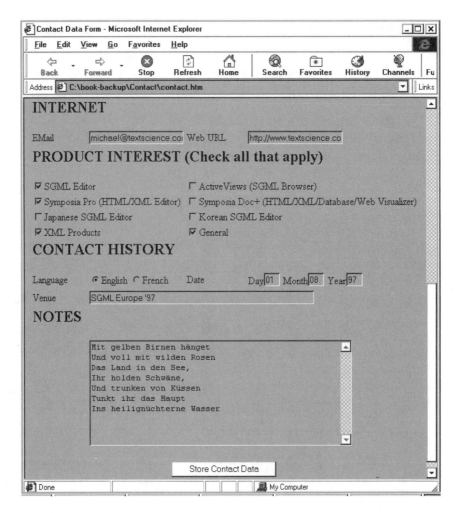

Figure 6–2   Contact Database Form (Second Page)

6.2 | XML Data Formats

There are two interesting points to be noted about the DTD shown in Figure 6–3. The first is that it violates the XML's nonbinding recommendation for interoperability in the ATTLIST for Product. The recommendation for interoperability pertains to the ability of older SGML parsers to support optional facilities of SGML on which XML relies. SGML once forbade the repetition of enumerated attribute type values within a single ATTLIST (in this case the values YES and NO) in order to allow a certain type of minimization where the attribute value could appear without the attribute name. Standard SGML practice has been to use NUMBER attribute values and to let a value of "0" represent NO and a value of "1" represent YES, as shown in Figure 6–4. Typically a parameter entity would be used to indicate more clearly the intent of the DTD author.

```
<!Element ContactRec    (Name, Company, Address,
                         Product, Contacts)>
<!Element Name          (Honorific?, First,
                         Middle?, Last)>
<!Element Company       (JobTitle?, CompanyName)>
<!Element Address       (Street+, City, Region?,
                         PostCode, Country, Phone,
                         Internet)>
<!Element Product       Empty>
<!AttList Product
         SGMLEditor        (Yes|No) #REQUIRED
         SGMLEditorKorean  (Yes|No) #REQUIRED
         SGMLEditorJapanese (Yes|No) #REQUIRED
         ActiveViews       (Yes|No) #REQUIRED
         SymposiaPro       (Yes|No) #REQUIRED
         SymposiaDocPlus   (Yes|No) #REQUIRED
         XMLProducts       (Yes|No) #REQUIRED
         General           (Yes|No) #REQUIRED>
<!Element Contacts      (Language, History)>
<!Element Honorific     (#PCDATA)>
<!AttList Honorific
         Title (Mr|Ms|Mrs|Miss|Dr|Professor|
M|Mme|Mlle|SeeContent) "SeeContent">
```

Figure 6–3   Contact DTD (Sheet I of 2)

```
<!Element First        (#PCDATA)>
<!Element Middle       (#PCDATA)>
<!Element Last         (#PCDATA)>
<!Element JobTitle     (#PCDATA)>
<!Element CompanyName  (#PCDATA)>
<!Element Street       (#PCDATA)>
<!Element City         (#PCDATA)>
<!Element Region       (#PCDATA)>
<!Element PostCode     (#PCDATA)>
<!Element Country      (#PCDATA)>
<!Element Phone        (DayTime, Fax?)>
<!Element Internet     (Email, Web)>
<!Element Language      EMPTY>
<!AttList Language
          Preference  (English|French) "English">
<!Element History      (Events+)>
<!Element DayTime      (#PCDATA)>
<!Element Fax          (#PCDATA)>
<!Element Email        (#PCDATA)>
<!Element Web          (#PCDATA)>


<!Element Events       (Date, Venue, Notes)>
<!Element Date         (Day, Month, Year)>
<!Element Venue        (#PCDATA)>
<!Element Notes        (#PCDATA)>
<!Element Day          (#PCDATA)>
<!Element Month        (#PCDATA)>
<!Element Year         (#PCDATA)>
```

Figure 6–3   Contact DTD (Sheet 2 of 2)

```
<!ENTITY % yesorno "NUMBER" >

<!AttList SGMLEditor %yesorno; '0'>
```

Figure 6–4   An Ugly Little Workaround in SGML

The second point of interest concerns the HONORIFIC element type. What we want to say is that it is one of the items on the enumerated attribute list or it is an honorific we didn't think of which is specified as the element data content. We will ignore the content (which could be zero characters) if the value SeeContent is provided, either by default or explicitly.

The element would then be encoded as either

> *<Honorific Title="Professor"></Honorific>*

or

> *<Honorific>Admiral</Honorific>*

or

> *<Honorific Title="Professor"/>*

The latter syntax allows the parser, in the absence of a DTD, to recognize that the element is empty without scanning to the end tag of the parent element.

Note: SGML users may recognize this as a work-around for XML's lack of SGML's CONREF facility.

6.3 | Reading and Writing XML in the Customer Database

6.3.1 *XMLForms*

XMLForms is a process and a set of programs for developing an application which takes HTML form data and converts them to XML through CGI. There is quite a bit of variability in the details of such a system, rendering it difficult to come up with a seamless approach. It is very likely that a seamless approach would not be conceptually or mechanically any simpler. With XML forms it is possible to develop the input process in a few hours and the framework provided does eliminate the necessity of dealing with the intricacies of CGI. We will walk through the entire process for the Contact database.

We have already completed our first task which is to perform an analysis of our data requirements, the result of which is expressed by the DTD shown in the prior section. In fact, the DTD is not strictly necessary for any part of the implementation of XML Forms, although it is extremely useful as an implicit specification of the steps needed to implement our data model. It is also strongly recommended that the XML data which are generated by XML Forms be validated with an XML parser. A DTD is required for validation. Since the XML is generated dynamically, we may even wish to build automatic validation of the results with a parser. This is not shown for this particular project.

Once our data model is in place we need to create the HTML form which will capture the content stored in the XML document instances. The markup for our Contact database form is shown in Figure 6–5.

```
<!DOCTYPE HTML PUBLIC "-//W3C//DTD HTML 3.2 Final//EN" >
<HTML VERSION="-//IETF//DTD HTML 3.2//EN">
<head><title>Contact Data Form</title><body>
<FORM METHOD="POST"
ACTION="http://www.textscience.com/cgi-bin/contact.pl">
<h1>Contact Data Form</h1>
<table><tr><td colspan=4><h2>NAME</h2></td></tr>
<tr><td colspan=1><SELECT NAME="honor">
<OPTION VALUE="seecont" selected>None or -&gt;</OPTION>
<OPTION>Mr</OPTION><OPTION>Ms</OPTION><OPTION>Mrs</OPTION>
<OPTION>Miss</OPTION><OPTION>Dr</OPTION>
<OPTION>Professor</OPTION><OPTION>M</OPTION>
<OPTION>Mme</OPTION><OPTION>Mlle</OPTION></SELECT></td>
<td colspan=3><INPUT TYPE="text" NAME="hcontent" SIZE="20" MAX
LENGTH="100"></td></tr>
<tr><td colspan=1>Name</td><td colspan=3><INPUT TYPE="text"
NAME="last" SIZE="30" MAXLENGTH="100"></td></tr>
<tr><td colspan=1>First Name</td><td colspan=3><INPUT
```

Figure 6–5   Contact Database HTML Form Markup (Sheet 1 of 3)

```
TYPE="text" NAME="first" SIZE="30" MAXLENGTH="100"></td></tr>
<tr><td colspan=1>Middle Name</td><td colspan=3><INPUT
TYPE="text" NAME="middle" SIZE="30" MAXLENGTH="100"></td></tr>
<tr><td colspan=4><h2>PROFESSIONAL INFORMATION</h2></td></tr>
<tr><td colspan=1>Position</td><td colspan=3><INPUT TYPE="text"
NAME="jobtitle" SIZE="30" MAXLENGTH="100"></td></tr>
<tr><td colspan=1>Company</td><td colspan=3><INPUT TYPE="text"
NAME="company" SIZE="30" MAXLENGTH="100"></td></tr>
<tr><td colspan=4><h2>MAILING ADDRESS</h2></td></tr>
<tr><td colspan=1>Street #1</td><td colspan=3><INPUT
TYPE="text" NAME="street1" SIZE="50" MAXLENGTH="100"></td></tr>
<tr><td colspan=1>Street #2</td><td colspan=3><INPUT
TYPE="text" NAME="street2" SIZE="50" MAXLENGTH="100"></td></tr>
<tr><td>City</td><td><INPUT TYPE="text" NAME="city" SIZE="20"
MAXLENGTH="100"></td>
<td>State</td><td><INPUT TYPE="text" NAME="region" SIZE="20"
MAXLENGTH="100"></td></tr>
<tr><td>Postal Code</td><td><INPUT TYPE="text" NAME="postcode"
SIZE="20" MAXLENGTH="100"></td>
<td>Country</td><td><INPUT TYPE="text" NAME="country"
SIZE="20" MAXLENGTH="100"></td></tr>
<tr><td colspan=4><h2>TELEPHONE</h2></td></tr>
<tr><td>Daytime No.</td><td><INPUT TYPE="text" NAME="daytime"
SIZE="20" MAXLENGTH="100"></td>
<td>Fax No.</td><td><INPUT TYPE="text" NAME="fax" SIZE="20"
MAXLENGTH="100"></td></tr>
<tr><td colspan=4><h2>INTERNET</h2></td></tr>
<tr><td>EMail</td><td><INPUT TYPE="text" NAME="email"
SIZE="20" MAXLENGTH="100"></td>
<td>Web URL</td><td><INPUT TYPE="text" NAME="web" SIZE="20"
MAXLENGTH="100"></td></tr>
<tr><td colspan=4><h2>PRODUCT INTEREST (Check all that
apply)</h2></td></tr>
<tr><td colspan=2><input type="checkbox" name="ed"
value="checked">SGML Editor</td>
<td colspan=2><input type="checkbox" name="av"
value="checked">ActiveViews (SGML Browser)</td></tr>
<tr><td colspan=2><input type="checkbox" name="sp"
value="checked">Symposia Pro (HTML/XML Editor)</td>
<td colspan=2><input type="checkbox" name="sdp"
value="checked">Symposia Doc+ (HTML/XML/Database/Web Visual-
izer)</td></tr>
```

Figure 6–5   Contact Database HTML Form Markup (Sheet 2 of 3)

```
<tr><td colspan=2><input type="checkbox" name="jed"
value="checked">Japanese SGML Editor</td>
<td colspan=2><input type="checkbox" name="ked"
value="checked">Korean SGML Editor</td></tr>
<tr><td colspan=2><input type="checkbox" name="xml"
value="checked">XML Products</td>
<td colspan=2><input type="checkbox" name="general"
value="checked">General</td></tr>
<tr><td colspan=4><h2>CONTACT HISTORY</h2></td></tr>
<tr><td colspan=1>Language</td>
<td colspan=1><input type="radio" name="lang" value="English"
checked>English
<input type="radio" name="lang" value="French">French</td>
<td colspan=1>Date</td>
<td colspan=1>Day<INPUT TYPE="text" NAME="day" SIZE="2" MAX-
LENGTH="2">

Month<INPUT TYPE="text" NAME="month" SIZE="2" MAXLENGTH="2">
Year<INPUT TYPE="text" NAME="year" SIZE="2" MAXLENGTH="2"></
td></tr>
<tr><td colspan=1>Venue</td>
<td colspan=3><INPUT TYPE="text" NAME="venue" SIZE="50" MAX-
LENGTH="100"></td></tr>
<tr><td colspan=4><h2>NOTES</h2></td></tr>
<tr><td colspan=1></td><td colspan=3><TEXTAREA NAME="comment"
ROWS=10" COLS="50"></TEXTAREA><p>
<tr><td colspan=4 align=center><INPUT TYPE="submit"
value="Store Contact Data"></td></tr></table>
</form></body></html>
```

Figure 6–5   Contact Database HTML Form Markup (Sheet 3 of 3)

An HTML form does not in itself bring in its wake any revelations but it is of interest to note the correspondence between its mechanisms of data organization and the DTD. For the most part, the hierarchical structure of the DTD is reflected in the visual organization of the document; <H1> headings usually correspond to the major components of a ContactRec, for example, NAME with NAME, PROFESSIONAL INFO with COMPANY, and so on. Many a conversion effort which takes documents in some legacy format such as word processor files and puts them into formally structured SGML is based on the fact that humans need structure to process information and have always used various indicators of structure such as typography, itemizing, enumerating, and so forth.

The evolution of such concepts is an interesting study in itself although unfortunately not within the scope of this book. For example, many languages such as Arabic and Chinese have had until recently little or no idea of punctuation. An Arabic book before this century typically consisted of one extremely long sentence (and Europeans think they invented stream of consciousness writing!). Which is not to say that Arabic books contain no structure but that all the structural markers are imbedded in the words themselves and only in the words. There is a lot of repetition in Arabic writing due to this fact with the odd consequence that repetition is accepted as a device of potentially sublime beauty in that language while every English-speaking writer is exhorted from the first day he or she puts pen to paper to avoid it at all costs.

SGML simply insists on making those "natural" structures consistently intelligible to the computer which is given the thankless task of processing the document in some way.

We have a rather hard time in an HTML form handling a repeating structure. For example, in the DTD we have indicated that more than one contact event may be recorded but in the form we allow for only one. There are a number of ways we could go about addressing this problem. We could have a special form (and corresponding server-side function) for adding new event records. We could use D/dynamic (big or little D/d depending on whether you are a partisan of Netscape or Microsoft) HTML to implement some kind of client-side application which could gather multiple events before sending it off the server. We could have more fields in our form. We'll see in the next section though that using an interface based on the XML editing paradigm avoids this problem entirely.

Closely related to the problem of repeating data is the problem of representing optional data such as a middle name and a region. Ordinary HTML does not give a choice; we must present the optional field and perhaps indicate to the user that it is not required. Or we have the options mentioned above of a more complex multiple-form process or the dynamic HTML route. And again we point out that this problem, intrinsic to the nature of data itself, can be approached in a completely different fashion with a different type of interface tool.

Attribute list specifications for the honorific, product interest, and language preference are represented with a drop list, checkboxes, and radio buttons, respectively. In effect, HTML forms have exact equivalents to the attribute constructions used in the DTD. The same difficulty that existed in the DTD with the lack of CONREF also exists in the form: We have no way to indicate that the value is either provided by the user as an element or field content or selected from the attribute value list/drop list.

We must now write a CGI program which will run on the server and use the values collected in the form to write an XML file conforming to our DTD. We begin this task with the program template XMLFORM. First Figure 6–6 will give a pseudocode outline of what XMLFORM does.

1. Initialize application- and environment-specific variables
2. Create unique new record name
   The record name is generated from an application variable to which an incrementing counter is suffixed.
3. Read CGI parameters
   CGI parameters are copied into variables using routines generated by the form2sub utility.
4. Write XML document using CGI parameters
   Using the variables created in the previous step, this step may require custom logic, depending on the complexity of the application.
5. Send confirmation to the user
   This step is required by CGI.

Figure 6–6   Outline of XMLFORM in Pseudocode

The complete program template for XMLFORM is given in Figure 6–6.

```perl
#!/usr/bin/perl
#######################################################
# xmlform.tp -  This is a perl template file,        #
#               meaning that it provides the frame-  #
#               work for an application which        #
#               converts HTML form data to XML.     #
#                                                    #
# Here are the steps to turn this into a working     #
# application:                                       #
#                                                    #
# 1 Create an HTML form which captures the info      #
# 2 Run form2sub.pl on your form to extract NAME     #
#   fields into variables you can manipulate.        #
# 3 Create an template XML file with all the         #
#   elements in place but without content.  You      #
#   should be able to do this easily using an XML    #
#   editor with your DTD, if you have a DTD and an   #
#   XML editor.                                      #
#   See the next step if you have optional elements  #
#   or attributes.                                   #
# 4 Modify form2sub.pl where needed to support       #
#   programming logic related to optional elements   #
#   or attributes or to support any operation where  #
#   you don't map straight from the form field to    #
#   to element content.                              #
# 5 Wrap a print statement around the XML file from  #
#   step 3, putting the variables from step 4 in     #
#   place for element content.  Implement any        #
#   programming logic in the print statement(s)      #
#   in conformity with step 4.  Output should be     #
#   written to the file DOC.                         #
# 6 Insert the result of steps 4 and 5 into this     #
#   template or use require statements.              #
# 7 Set the 3 user defined variables in this file    #
#   and make sure you followed the naming convention #
#   explained below for the routine produced in step #
#   5 or change the subroutine variable.             #
```

Figure 6–7   XMLFORM Program Template (Sheet 1 of 5)

```
# 8 Buy Internet Design with SGML and XML if the 7     #
#   steps above don't seem straightforward because     #
#   once you see how it is done it is EASY!             #
#                                                       #
# Copyright Matthew Fuchs, Michael Leventhal, and       #
# David Lewis, published in Designing XML Internet       #
# Applications, Prentice-Hall, 1998.  Permission        #
# for unrestricted use as long as the authors are       #
# credited.                                             #
#########################################################
# Set the following three variables
$appName = "contact";
$userDir = "/aimweb/homets/Contact/";
$myURL = "http://www.textscience.com";
# make sure that you name your XML output subroutine
# according the following pattern or modify the
# variable to agree with your subroutine name
$outputXML = $appName."2XML";
#-------------------------------------------------------#


# This section of the code creates the file name which will
# be used in the format $appNameNUMBER.xml where NUMBER is
# the largest number appended to application name found in
# directory incremented by one.
$largest = 0;
opendir (dirhandle, $userDir);
while ($_ = readdir (dirhandle))
{
  if ($_ =~ m/^$appName(\d+)\.xml/)
  {
    if ($1 > $largest)
    { $largest = $1; }
  }
}
closedir (dirhandle);
$largest++;
$fileName = $appName.$largest.".xml";
#-------------------------------------------------------#
```

Figure 6–7   XMLFORM Program Template (Sheet 2 of 5)

```
&ReadParse;
foreach $atype (sort (keys %in)) {
  $atype =~ tr/A-Z/a-z/;
  eval &$atype;
}
unless (open(DOC,">$userDir$fileName")) {
  print "Failure to open $userDir$fileName\n"; }
&$outputXML;
close DOC;
&respond;
#----------------------------------------------------------#

# Insert output of form2sub.pl after modification contain-
ing
# subroutines which assign CGI form fields to variables or
# use require or use to include
# insert subroutines HERE:
#----------------------------------------------------------#

# Insert $outputXML.pl routine which you have written to
# output XML statements using variables as content from
# form2sub.pl subroutines or use require or use to include
# insert subroutine HERE:

#----------------------------------------------------------#
# This routine sends something back to the user and could
# be replaced with whatever is desired.
sub respond {
print "content-type: text/html\n
<HTML><HEAD><TITLE>FORM TO XML RESPONSE</TITLE>
</HEAD><BODY><BODYTEXT>
<H1>FORM TO XML RESPONSE</H1>
<TABLE BORDER=1><TR><TD>
<P>Your Data was transformed to XML and written successful
to $fileName.</P>
<P><A HREF=\"$myURL/$appName.htm\">Click here to enter new
contact data.</A>
</P></TD></TR></TABLE></BODYTEXT></BODY></HTML>";
}
#----------------------------------------------------------#
```

Figure 6-7   XMLFORM Program Template (Sheet 3 of 5)

```
# Keep the following CGI utility subroutines
# Note that these are officially out of date and may be
# replaced with a more current version
#


# Perl Routines to Manipulate CGI input
# S.E.Brenner@bioc.cam.ac.uk
# $Header: /people/seb1005/http/cgi-bin/RCS/cgi-lib.pl,v
1.2 1994/01/10 15:05:40 seb1005 Exp $
#


# Copyright 1993 Steven E. Brenner
# Unpublished work.
# Permission granted to use and modify this library so
long as the
# copyright above is maintained, modifications are docu-
mented, and
# credit is given for any use of the library.
# ReadParse
# Reads in GET or POST data, converts it to unescaped text,
and puts
# one key=value in each member of the list "@in"
# Also creates key/value pairs in %in, using '\0' to sepa-
rate multiple
# selections
# If a variable-glob parameter (e.g., *cgi_input) is
passed to ReadParse,
# information is stored there, rather than in $in, @in,
and %in.
sub ReadParse {
  if (@_) {
    local (*in) = @_;
  }
  local ($i, $loc, $key, $val);
  # Read in text
```

Figure 6–7   XMLFORM Program Template (Sheet 4 of 5)

```
  if ($ENV{'REQUEST_METHOD'} eq "GET") {
    $in = $ENV{'QUERY_STRING'};
  } elsif ($ENV{'REQUEST_METHOD'} eq "POST") {
    for ($i = 0; $i < $ENV{'CONTENT_LENGTH'}; $i++) {
      $in .= getc;
    }
  }
  @in = split(/&/,$in);
  foreach $i (0 .. $#in) {
    # Convert plus's to spaces
    $in[$i] =~ s/\+/ /g;
    # Convert %XX from hex numbers to alphanumeric
    $in[$i] =~ s/%(..)/pack("c",hex($1))/ge;
    # Split into key and value.
    $loc = index($in[$i],"=");
    $key = substr($in[$i],0,$loc);
    $val = substr($in[$i],$loc+1);
    $in{$key} .= '\0' if (defined($in{$key})); # \0 is the
multiple separator
    $in{$key} .= $val;
  }
  return 1; # just for fun
}
# END OF FILE
#-------------------------------------------------------#
```

Figure 6-7   XMLFORM Program Template (Sheet 5 of 5)

The CGI parameters are parsed by S.E. Brenner's ReadParse routine, which, as noted in the source file, could be replaced by a more current routine such as Lincoln Stein's CGI.pm package. Compatibility with Perl 4 is one reason we have not updated it. However, ReadParse puts the parameters in an associative array of "parameter name," "parameter value" pairs. To simplify subsequent programming we store each value in a variable bearing the name of the form input field. We generate a file of subroutines, one for each variable, which set the variable using the utility form2sub which is outlined in Figure 6–8 and listed in Figure 6–9.

1. Scan HTML form for INPUT, TEXTAREA, or SELECT start tags.
2. When one of the tags in the step above is found, scan for a NAME parameter before the end of the tag.
3. If the NAME attribute value hasn't already been scanned (it could be repeated in error or for a radio button), store it for subsequent checks and write a subroutine which assigns the CGI parameter to the value of the NAME attribute, using the value of NAME attribute for the actual name of the subroutine.

Figure 6–8   form2sub Pseudocode

```
#!/usr/bin/perl
########################################################
# form2sub.pl - This utility takes an HTML form        #
#               file on standard input and writes      #
#               one subroutine on standard output      #
#               for each INPUT, TEXTAREA, or SELECT     #
#               element using its NAME attribute        #
#               value for the sub-routine name and      #
#               also for a mapping to a variable        #
#               which hold the value extracted by       #
#                GGI.                                   #
#                                                   #
# <INPUT ... NAME = "x" ...> or                        #
# <TEXTAREA ... NAME = "x" ...> or                     #
# <SELECT ... NAME = "x" ...>                          #
#           writes                                     #
# sub x {                                              #
#   $x = $in{"$atype"};                                #
# }                                                    #
#                                                      #
# This program is invoked by                           #
# perl form2sub.pl < formFile.htm > outputFile.pl      #
# Perl 4 and Perl 5 compatible.                        #
#                                                      #
# Copyright Matthew Fuchs, Michael Leventhal, and      #
# David Lewis, published in Designing XML Internet     #
# Applications, Prentice-Hall, 1998.  Permission       #
# for unrestricted use as long as the authors are      #
# credited.                                            #
########################################################
```

Figure 6–9   form2sub.pl (Sheet 1 of 2)

```
undef($/);
$file = <>;
$file =~ s/\n//g;
while ($file =~ /(<INPUT|<TEXTAREA|<SELECT)/i)
{
  $file = $';
  $file =~ />/;
  $tag = $`;
  $file = $';
  $tag =~ /NAME *= *\" *([^\"]*)\"/i;
  $field = $1;
  $field =~ tr/A-Z/a-z/;
  if ($noduplicate{"$field"} ne "n") {
    $noduplicate{"$field"} = "n";
    $output .= "sub $field \{ \n  \$$field =
\$in\{\"\$atype\"\};\n\}\n";
  }
}

print
"##########################################################
#                                                        #
# file generated by form2sub.pl, extracting HTML form    #
# fields to create subroutines which assign CGI vari-     #
# bles to variable names for inclusion in xmlforms.pl.    #
#                                                        #
# Copyright Matthew Fuchs, Michael Leventhal, and        #
# David Lewis, published in Designing XML Internet        #
# Applications, Prentice-Hall, 1998.  Permission          #
# for unrestricted use as long as the authors are        #
# credited.                                              #
##########################################################\n
\n";
print $output;
```

Figure 6–9   form2sub.pl (Sheet 2 of 2)

The result of running form2sub on the Contact HTML form is shown in Figure 6–10.

```
############################################################
#                                                          #
# file generated by form2sub.pl, extracting HTML form      #
# fields to create subroutines which assign CGI vari-       #
# bles to variable names for inclusion in xmlforms.pl.      #
#                                                          #
# Copyright Matthew Fuchs, Michael Leventhal, and           #
# David Lewis, published in Designing XML Internet          #
# Applications, Prentice-Hall, 1998.  Permission            #
# for unrestricted use as long as the authors are           #
# credited.                                                 #
############################################################

sub honor {
  $honor = $in{"$atype"}; }
sub hcontent {
  $hcontent = $in{"$atype"}; }
sub last {
  $last = $in{"$atype"}; }
sub first {
  $first = $in{"$atype"}; }
sub middle {
  $middle = $in{"$atype"}; }
sub jobtitle {
  $jobtitle = $in{"$atype"}; }
sub company {
  $company = $in{"$atype"}; }
sub street1 {
  $street1 = $in{"$atype"}; }
sub street2 {
  $street2 = $in{"$atype"}; }
sub honor {
  $honor = $in{"$atype"}; }
sub hcontent {
  $hcontent = $in{"$atype"}; }
sub last {
  $last = $in{"$atype"}; }
sub first {
  $first = $in{"$atype"}; }
```

Figure 6-10   Output of form2sub Run on Contact HTML Form
(Sheet I of 3)

```
sub middle {
  $middle = $in{"$atype"}; }
sub jobtitle {
  $jobtitle = $in{"$atype"}; }
sub company {
  $company = $in{"$atype"}; }
sub street1 {
  $street1 = $in{"$atype"}; }
sub street2 {
  $street2 = $in{"$atype"}; }
sub city {
  $city = $in{"$atype"}; }
sub region {
  $region = $in{"$atype"}; }
sub postcode {
  $postcode = $in{"$atype"}; }
sub country {
  $country = $in{"$atype"}; }

sub daytime {
  $daytime = $in{"$atype"}; }
sub fax {
  $fax = $in{"$atype"}; }
sub email {
  $email = $in{"$atype"}; }
sub web {
  $web = $in{"$atype"}; }
sub ed {
  $ed = $in{"$atype"}; }
sub av {
  $av = $in{"$atype"}; }sub sp {
  $sp = $in{"$atype"}; }
sub sdp {
  $sdp = $in{"$atype"}; }
sub jed {
  $jed = $in{"$atype"}; }
sub ked {
  $ked = $in{"$atype"}; }
sub xml {
  $xml = $in{"$atype"}; }
```

Figure 6–10   Output of form2sub Run on Contact HTML Form
(Sheet 2 of 3)

```
sub general {
  $general = $in{"$atype"}; }
sub lang {
  $lang = $in{"$atype"}; }
sub day {
  $day = $in{"$atype"}; }
sub month {
  $month = $in{"$atype"}; }
sub year {
  $year = $in{"$atype"}; }
sub venue {
  $venue = $in{"$atype"}; }
sub comment {
  $comment = $in{"$atype"}; }
```

Figure 6–10   Output of form2sub Run on Contact HTML Form
(Sheet 3 of 3)

The use of subroutines to perform the variable assignment allows the user to loop through the associative array of CGI values and set each variable with just three lines of application independent code as shown in Figure 6–11.

```
foreach $atype (sort (keys %in)) {
  $atype =~ tr/A-Z/a-z/;
  eval &$atype;
}
```

Figure 6–11   Using Eval to Set CGI Variables

The NAME value of the CGI parameter is set lowercase to avoid case mismatches and eval is used to invoke the generated function using the NAME value in the $atype variable as the name of the function. The output of form2sub is either inserted right into the template file or included through the Perl require or use mechanism.

The final task is to write the subroutine which will actually take the CGI variables and create the XML document instance. One way to do this would be to use an XML editor to create a document instance where in place of actual element content one inserts the variable names extracted from the HTML form and to put a print statement and subroutine block around the document. For a simple DTD with no optional elements this could be done in a couple of minutes. Our DTD is only slightly more complex. The process is outlined in Figure 6–12 and the program code is listed in Figure 6–13

1. Write an XML document to the output with form variables for element content and attributes.
2. For optional elements and attributes or for other situations involving parsing of form data, write additional Perl code to perform the necessary transformation to XML.

Figure 6–12   Pseudocode for Contact2XML

```
#######################################################
# contact2xml.pl - This subroutine writes out an XML #
#                  file conformant with the          #
#                  ContactRec DTD using variables    #
#                  from the contact HTML form        #
#                  extracted by xmlform.pl CGI code  #
#                  and the output of form2sub.pl run #
#                  on the contact HTML form.         #
#                                                    #
# Copyright Matthew Fuchs, Michael Leventhal, and    #
# David Lewis, published in Designing XML Internet   #
# David Lewis, published in Internet Design with     #
# Applications, Prentice-Hall, 1998.  Permission     #
# for unrestricted use as long as the authors are    #
# credited.                                          #
#######################################################
sub contact2XML {
print DOC "<!xml version=\"1.0\">

<!DOCTYPE ContactRec SYSTEM \"contact.dtd\">
```

Figure 6–13   Contact2XML Subroutine (Sheet 1 of 3)

```
<ContactRec>
<Name>\n";
if ($honor ne "seecont") {
  print DOC "<Honorific Title=\"$honor\"></Honorific>\n"; }
elsif ($honor eq "seecont" && $hcontent ne "") {
  print DOC "<Honorific Title=\"SeeContent\">$hcontent
  </Honorific>\n"; }
print DOC "<First>$first</First>";
if ($middle ne "") {
  print DOC "<Middle>$middle</Middle>"; }
print DOC "<Last>$last</Last>
</Name>
<Company>\n";
if ($jobtitle ne "") {
  print DOC "<JobTitle>$jobtitle</JobTitle>\n"; }
print DOC "<CompanyName>$company</CompanyName>
</Company>
<Address>
<Street>$street1</Street>\n";
if ($street2 ne "") {
  print DOC "<Street>$street2</Street>\n"; }
print DOC "<City>$city</City>\n";
if ($region ne "") {
  print DOC "<Region>$region</Region>\n"; }
print DOC "<PostCode>$postcode</PostCode>
<Country>$country</Country>
<Phone>
<DayTime>$daytime</DayTime>\n";
if ($fax ne "") {
  print DOC "<Fax>$fax</Fax>\n"; }
print DOC "</Phone>
<Internet>
<Email>$email</Email>
<Web>$web</Web>
</Internet>
</Address>
<Product ";
if ($ed eq "checked")    { print DOC "SGMLEditor=\"Yes\" "; }
else                     { print DOC "SGMLEditor=\"No\" "; }
if ($av eq "checked")    { print DOC "ActiveViews=\"Yes\" "; }
else                     { print DOC "ActiveViews=\"No\" "; }
```

Figure 6–13   Contact2XML Subroutine (Sheet 2 of 3)

```
if ($sp eq "checked")    { print DOC "SymposiaPro=\"Yes\" "; }
else                     { print DOC "SymposiaPro=\"No\" "; }
if ($sdp eq "checked")   { print DOC
                            "SymposiaDocPlus=\"Yes\" "; }
else                     { print DOC
                            "SymposiaDocPlus=\"No\" "; }
if ($jed eq "checked")   { print DOC
                            "SGMLEditorJapanese=\"Yes\" "; }
else                     { print DOC
                            "SGMLEditorJapanese=\"No\" "; }
if ($ked eq "checked")   { print DOC
                            "SGMLEditorKorean=\"Yes\" "; }
else                     { print DOC
                            "SGMLEditorKorean=\"No\" "; }
if ($xml eq "checked")   { print DOC "XMLProducts=\"Yes\" ";
}
else                     { print DOC "XMLProducts=\"No\" "; }
if ($general eq "checked") { print DOC "General=\"Yes\"/>";
}
else                      { print DOC "General=\"No\"/>\n"; }
print DOC "<Contacts>
<Language Preference=\"$lang\"/>
<History>
<Events>
<Date>
<Day>$day</Day><Month>$month</Month><Year>$year</Year>
</Date>
<Venue>$venue</Venue>
<Notes>$comment</Notes>
</Events>
</History>
</Contacts>
</ContactRec>";
}
```

Figure 6–13 Contact2XML Subroutine (Sheet 3 of 3)

Everything is rather straightforward, leaving us for once with little to say. We note that optional elements are handled by testing to see if any content has been entered by the user into the field. The CONREF construction works similarly; we test to see if the list item seecont for the honorific field was selected and if it was a test to see if there is actually any content or not. We convert checkbox values for the Product attributes to yes or no by testing the value of the checkbox field. The reader should not have difficulty imagining that more complex operations could easily be constructed although we have covered most of mappings possible between the form paradigm and XML.

It is sometimes desirable to simplify things for the user while making things a bit more difficult for the programmer. For example, in our form we require the user to enter the date in three fields: day, month, and year. These fields correspond precisely to the breakup of information in the DTD. We could decide to have a single date field and to break the field into the components with programming logic, as shown in Figure 6–14.

```
$datecontent =~ /(.*)\/(.*)\/(.*)/;
$day   = $1;
$month = $2;
$year  = $3;
```

Figure 6–14   Letting the Processor Do the Work: Date Example

Of course, if the user does not adhere to the format expected by the processing program the data cannot be interpreted properly. This is the problem in a nutshell, in fact it is the whole of the problem we alluded to earlier in the conversion from approximate human-centered conventions for structuring to ones that can be processed reliably by computers. There is a simple quantitative way to approach the problem. You simply estimate the amount of labor that would be saved by simplifying the data entry and balance that against the labor cost of fixing all the errors that result from your simplification. It is most often the case that something between forcing the user to cope with all the structure and not requiring the user to do any wins—the happy middle ground. A concept has evolved around this observation of having "authoring" DTDs designed to capture information and "upstream" DTDs for the use and enjoyment of computer programs that put the information to work. However, in our simple project the data are simple and the programmer is left with plenty of time for sitting in cafes and other essential activities proper to a dignified life.

The reader can also imagine the relative simplicity of performing an equivalent transformation on the client side with d/Dynamic HTML, offering the advantage of offloading the computational work from the server to the client and perhaps allowing a more interactive approach to the creation of the data. We will see this in our project on negotiation and Java.

We conclude this section with a document instance created by our XMLFORM contact application, shown in Figure 6–15.

```
<!xml version="1.0">
<!DOCTYPE ContactRec SYSTEM "ContactRec.dtd">
<ContactRec>
<Name>
<Honorific Title="Mr"></Honorific>
<First>David</First><Last>Lewis</Last>
</Name>
<Company>
<JobTitle>Principal Webmaster</JobTitle>

<CompanyName>Lewis Systems</CompanyName>
</Company>
<Address>
<Street>2600 Wilson Boulevard</Street>
<City>San Tabisco</City>
<Region>CA</Region>
<PostCode>94583</PostCode>
<Country>US</Country>
<Phone>
<DayTime>415-000-0000</DayTime>
</Phone>
<Internet>
<Email>drlewi1@lewis.com</Email>
<Web>http://www.lewis.com</Web>
```

Figure 6–15   Contact Document Produced by XMLFORM (Sheet 1 of 2)

```
</Internet>
</Address>
<Product SGMLEditor="Yes" ActiveViews="Yes"
SymposiaPro="Yes"
SymposiaDocPlus="Yes" SGMLEditorJapanese="No"
SGMLEditorKorean="No" XMLProducts="Yes" General="No"/>
<Contacts>
<Language Preference="English"/>
<History>
<Events>
<Date>
<Day>01</Day><Month>04</Month><Year>96</Year>
</Date>
<Venue>SGML '96</Venue>
<Notes>Send Evaluation Software</Notes>
</Events>
</History>
</Contacts>
</ContactRec>
```

Figure 6–15   Contact Document Produced by XMLFORM (Sheet 2 of 2)

6.3.2 *Using an XML Editor and CSS to Create Contact Database Records*

Let's take a look at what is involved in replacing our HTML form and XMLFORMS with Grif's Symposia, an XML Editor which can read and write XML documents on the Web.

As discussed in Chapter 3, a number of approaches have been taken by the vendors of SGML and XML editing products with respect to the extent that they emulate WYSIWYG word processors or emphasize the structure of the document and the underlying constructs in the markup language. Grif's products are decidedly on the WYSIWYG end of the spectrum. The WYSIWYG document presentation is specified with a formatting language known as P (Presentation) language in their SGML Editor and the Cascading Style Sheets (CSS) language in Symposia. CSS is a Web standard and Symposia is a Web-centric application offering not only XML, CSS, and connectivity to the Web but also HTML editing. Symposia is a well-formed XML document editor, which is to say that while it can read a DTD to capture element names and attributes in order to make them available in the editing environment, it does not enforce document structure as expressed in the content model of each element. In our application we will begin with a complete document template containing all the elements we wish to use so we do not have a strong need for structure validation. A well-formed editor could also be used in certain circumstances where the structure must be validated. For example, Microsoft's Notepad continues to be a popular tool for creating HTML files although it does nothing except allow the user to enter text. Notepad users will periodically check their work in the Web browser which provides a kind of validation (in the case where the interest of the user is purely in the presentation of the document on the screen in a particular browser). Likewise, a user of a well-formed document editor can always validate his or her work with one of XML parsers mentioned in Chapter 3. There are also applications of XML which, like HTML, have no further objective than the pleasing display of the document. Symposia may be used to verify the application of CSS commands in this type of application.

Before proceeding to a discussion of our implementation of the XML editor approach to data entry in our Contact database application, we would like to give the reader some background in CSS. Readers already familiar with CSS can skip ahead to the next section.

6.3.2.1   Introduction to CSS and a CSS Tutorial

Cascading Style Sheets (CSS) is a style sheet mechanism specifically developed to meet the needs of Web designers and users. HTML provides only very limited possibilities for the formatting and positioning of text, and the few mechanisms that are provided (such as the FONT element, or the ALIGN attribute) are a somewhat cumbersome solution that mixes structure and presentation with content. What was required for HTML was a real style sheet language that provided far greater control over documentation in a way that was independent of document content. CSS style sheets provide that mechanism and can be used to set fonts, colors, white space, and many other presentational aspects of a document. It is possible for several documents to share the same style sheet, enabling you to maintain consistent presentation within a collection of related documents without having to modify each document separately.

Welcomed by many Web page designers who have been demanding a way to improve and standardize the display of their documents, CSS potentially represents a far more important development with regard to XML, as it is currently the *only* way to specify document formatting for XML documents.

About Cascading Style Sheets

The term "cascading" refers to the fact that more than one style sheet can influence the presentation of a single document simultaneously. A style sheet can "import" style rules from one or more generic, or corporate, style sheets as well as define additional or alternative style rules locally. In addition, the user can specify an additional style sheet to use for consulting documents. CSS includes a mechanism to resolve conflicts that may arise between the different style sheets using a series of relative weights for each style rule.

A CSS style sheet can either be stored within the document itself, or within a separate text file which is referenced (in the case of HTML) using the LINK element. As we will see later, a different method for referencing style sheets has been proposed for XML.

About Styles, Selectors, and Declarations

A style sheet contains one or more style rules. Each style rule consists of a selector and a declaration.

The selector identifies the part(s) of the document to which the style rule is to be applied. The declaration is a list of one or more style properties and their corresponding values. The syntax of a simple style rule is thus

> *selector { property1: value1 ; property2:value2 ; ... propertyn:value-n}*

The selector is separated from the declaration with a space. A colon (:) is used to separate a property from its corresponding value and a semicolon (;) is used to separate property/value pairs from each other. The declaration (that is, the entire list of property/value pairs) is enclosed in curly brackets ({}).

Selectors

A selector can be one of several types. A *simple selector* indicates the name of an element type, such as P, H1, or LI. For example;

> *P {text-align:center}*

A *class selector* defines a name for a group of style declarations and may or may not have an associated element type. A class name begins with a period (.). It is good practice to name classes according to their function rather than their appearance.

For example,

> *P.WARNING {text-color:red; font-size:large; text-decoration:bold}*

> *.IMPORTANT {text-color:red}*

In the above examples, P.WARNING creates a class .WARNING for use with the P element and .IMPORTANT creates a class .IMPORTANT whose style rules may be applied to any element.

In HTML, the CLASS attribute is used to indicate the class of an element. In the case of the example given above, only paragraph elements with the CLASS="WARNING" attribute defined will be formatted accordingly, as here:

> *<P CLASS="WARNING">Don't Look Down!</P>*

An *ID selector* specifies a unique reference for a style rule and can be used to define styles on a per element basis. This selector type should be used sparingly due to its inherent limitations (an ID selector can be applied only once in a document). An ID selector is assigned using the indicator "#" to precede a name. For example,

#abc123 {border:solid red}

A *contextual selector* is a list of two or more simple selectors separated by spaces, such as: P STRONG.

The style rule is applied to the last element in the list only when it is enclosed within the element(s) specified earlier in the list. In the above example, the style rule will only be applied to STRONG elements that appear within P elements.

According to the rules of cascading order, contextual selectors take precedence over simple selectors.

Declarations

The declaration is made up of one or more property/value pairs. A colon (:) is used to separate a property from its corresponding value.

A *style property* is the aspect of the selector that is to be modified by the style rule. For example, color, margin, or font.

The *value* part of the declaration assigns a value to the style property. For example, for the color property, possible values might be red or #191970.

Grouping

You can group several selectors together with a single style declaration in order to avoid repeating the same statements for different parts of the same document. For example, you could change all the headings in a document with the following style rule:

H1, H2, H3, H4, H5, H6 { color : blue; font-family: sans-serif }

Pseudoclasses and Pseudoelements

Pseudoclasses and pseudoelements are special "classes" and "elements" that refer to subparts of elements. A predefined set of pseudoelements and pseudoclasses forms part of the CSS standard. Examples include the first letter of a paragraph ("first-letter"), or hypertext links that have already been followed ("visited") or that are active ("active").

A colon (:) is used to separate the name of the pseudoclass or pseudo-element from the name of the selector, as in the following examples:

> *P:first-letter { font-size: 125% }*
>
> *A:active { color: blue; font-size: 125% }*
>
> *A:visited { color: green; font-size: 85% }*

A Thespian Example

The following steps illustrate the use of a CSS style sheet for an XML document (an extract from the Shakespeare play *Much Ado about Nothing*).

Step 1: The Document Source

The portion of the original text is shown in Figure 6–16.

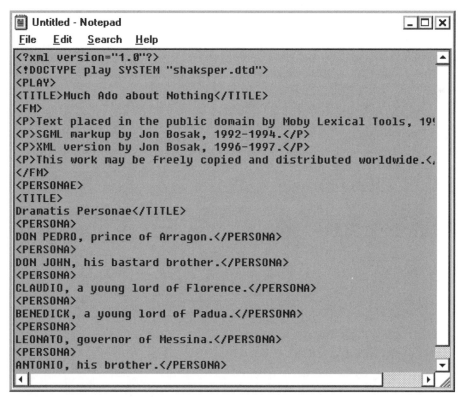

Figure 6–16 XML Fragment of *Much Ado About Nothing*

Step 2: Define Style Sheet Rules

As mentioned above, the style rules for a document can be stored either within the document itself, or within a separate text file. In this example, we will save the style sheet as a separate file, **shaksper.css**, so that it can be easily applied to other Shakespeare plays that we might like to publish.

You can create the style sheet manually using your favorite text editor, as in Figure 6–17.

Alternatively, you can create the style sheet using an editor that supports CSS, such as Symposia, as in Figure 6–18.

```
shaksper.css                              _ □ ✕
PLAY { background-color : white }
FM { font-style : italic;
      font-size : 14;
      color : #400040;
      text-align : right }
SPEAKER { font-weight : bold;
          color : #ff0080 }
LINE { color : #800040;
       left : 15 }
PERSONA { font-style : italic;
          font-size : -1 }
PERSONAE { color : #800040 }
SCNDESCR { margin-top : 30;
           font-size : 18;
           color : #0000a0;
           height : 20 }
STAGEDIR { font-weight : bold;
           font-style : italic;
           height : 20 }
PLAYSUBT { font-weight : bold;
           font-size : 16;
           text-decoration : underline;
           height : 20 }
SPEECH { margin-top : 5 }
```

Figure 6–17   CSS file for *Much Ado About Nothing*

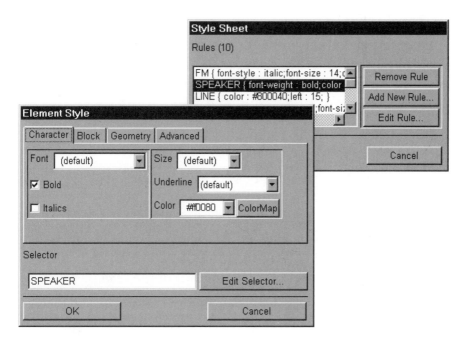

Figure 6–18 Interactive CSS Development with Grif's Symposia

Step 3: Link the Style Sheet to the Document

At the time of writing, there is not yet a standardized method for linking an XML document with a style sheet. This subject forms part of the work currently in progress by the W3C in the area of stylesheets.

The method we will use in this example is therefore based on a draft proposal for style sheet linking in XML which consists of inserting an XML processing instruction **<?XML-stylesheet?>** at the top of the document. The processing instruction has two required attributes, *type* and *href*, which specify, respectively, the type of style sheet and its address. In our example, we therefore need to add the following line to our XML document:

<?XML-stylesheet type="text/css" href="shaksper.css"?>

Symposia supports this XML style sheet linking mechanism and inserts the processing instruction for you automatically when you specify an external style sheet using the create new style sheet/external command.

Step 4: Publish the Document and Its Style Sheet

Once the style sheet is linked to the document, it can be published. When opened in an XML browser (or in this case, Symposia), the style rules are applied to the different XML elements in the document as shown in Figure 6–19.

Limitations of CSS for Complex Applications

Although CSS style sheets can be very effective for improving the presentation of HTML documents, the CSS1 standard has a number of important omissions which can limit the effectiveness of CSS style sheets for more complex applications. The following list, taken from Jon Bosak's document "Overview: XML, HTML, and all that," describes just a few of the major limitations of the CSS standard.

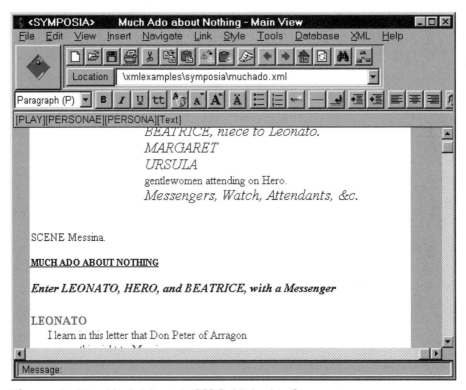

Figure 6–19   *Much Ado* with CSS Published in Symposia

- CSS cannot grab an item (such as a chapter title) from one place and use it again in another place (such as a page header).
- CSS has no concept of sibling relationships. For example, it is impossible to write a CSS style sheet that will render every other paragraph in bold.
- CSS is not a programming language; it does not support decision structures and cannot be extended by the style sheet designer.
- CSS cannot calculate quantities or store variables. This means, at the very least, that it cannot store commonly used parameters in one location that is easy to update.
- CSS cannot generate text (page numbers, etc.)
- CSS uses a simple box-oriented formatting model that works for current Web browsers but will not extend to more advanced applications of the markup, such as multiple-column sets.
- CSS is oriented toward Western languages and assumes a horizontal writing direction.

It is for these reasons that a new W3C project has been chartered with the goal of defining a simplified version of the DSSSL standard, Extensible Style Language (XSL). XSL promises to provide far more layout and document presentation features than CSS and is a more comprehensive approach to stylesheets and, generally, the transformation of XML. This topic is discussed in briefly in Chapters 7 and 8 but as work on XSL is in the early phases we cannot give a great deal of practical guidance at this point in time.

What is clear, however, is that the limitations of CSS1 do represent a serious hindrance for its use in the more complex types of applications that are possible with XML. As the following section shows, even for a somewhat simple XML application, the CSS standard needs to acquire a certain number of essential features if it is realize its full potential.

6.3.2.2   Creating the Equivalent of XMLForm with CSS and an XML Editor

Let us now see what we can do with our Contact database application. One of our objectives is to avoid spending time developing a CGI script and form interface simply to enable users to enter contact information. A second objective is to allow more flexible entry of information. For example, in our HTML form we were only able to allow the user to enter a single contact event. With an XML editor we will be able to enter multiple contact events as long as that is permitted by our DTD.

Although complicated to implement, the HTML form-based interface described earlier did provide many user-friendly features that made things easier for the user, such as the ability to select from a predetermined list of options, or the possibility to select or deselect different options, as appropriate.

To provide an equivalent level of "comfort," we need to provide a predefined document template in which all the user has to do is fill in the required data. Using the DTD as our guide, we can produce a document instance that contains all required document elements. Without a style sheet, however, this template is not of great value. The authoring tool has no indication on how to render the document and, at best, could only display the document as a list of tags. We need to be able to indicate to users what information to insert where without displaying these tags. Our only means to do this is using our style sheet.

With the HTML form, it was possible to simply label each input zone with some text. Unfortunately, the CSS standard does not provide a means of displaying predefined text before or after an element. This seemingly essential style sheet feature was apparently left out of CSS1 because of the inherent difficulty of implementing this feature in today's Web browsers (which by the time you read these words will of course already be yesterday's Web browsers). Structure-based editor/browsers such as Symposia, or indeed the thoroughbred XML structured editors to come, would have no problem implementing this type of feature, if it were allowed for in the CSS standard.

The only viable solution for the moment seems to be to provide default text content for each data field that is then replaced by the user as he or she enters the information in the page, as in Figure 6–20.

This layout is still not very satisfactory, however. We can of course improve the layout of the page using our style sheet to highlight certain elements and group related items together, as in Figure 6–21.

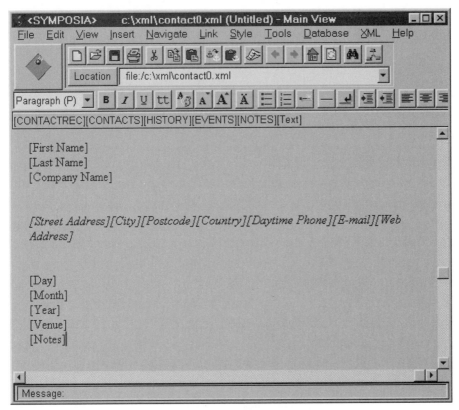

Figure 6–20   XML Editor Template without CSS

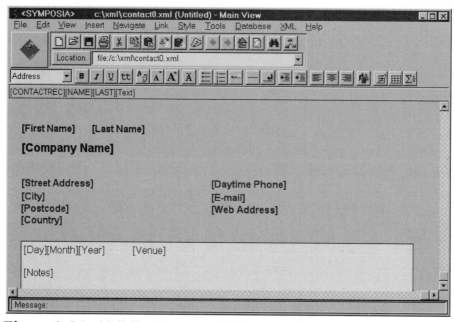

Figure 6–21   XML Template with CSS Presentation

Using the style sheet, we can achieve quite a pleasing presentation for our data entry screen. However there are two elements which we cannot display in this same way: *Product* and *Language*. These two elements are empty elements and have no content. If you recall, the Product element provides a number of optional attributes to indicate the contact's interest in the company's different products (the value of each attribute is "Yes" or "No," accordingly. The Language element provides the attribute "Preference" which can exhibit the values "English" or "French" and for which the default value is "English," indicating that any communication with or documentation sent to the contact should be in English. One way around this problem, although not very elegant, would be to specify a background image for each element using the style rule:

Product {background-image:image.gif}

Using our authoring tool, we would then be able to select the element by clicking on the image and pulling up a list of the element's attributes for modification, as illustrated in Figure 6–22.

Of course, we are still left with the problem that using CSS, it is not possible to display the attribute names or values for an element in the document itself. In our example, it would have been nice to be able to pull up the list of attributes for the Product element, supply a value for each attribute, and then see these changes appear in the document (display some text or an image to indicate which products the contact was interested in, for example). Nor does CSS provide the possibility to apply conditional style rules based on an element's attribute values (one might imagine a different image to be displayed for "Yes" or for "No" values).

Although CSS does have certain limitations, it has the virtue of simplicity at least to the extent to which it demands programming skill. At this point, the alternative, DSSSL, remains a tool reserved for those with a substantial grasp of programming concepts. It may happen that DSSSL is as sufficiently simplified as XSL is to become accessible to page designers but it may also happen that CSS will undergo the small improvements needed to make it useful for most XML applications.

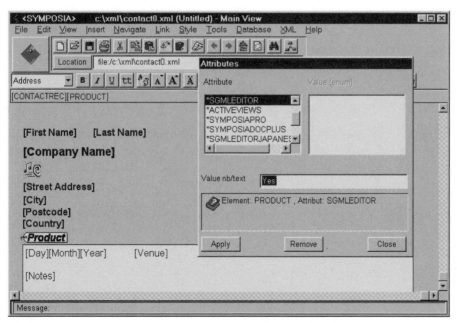

Figure 6–22   Improved XML Template with CSS Presentation

Structure-based search

The theory and techniques of searching and retrieving XML are examined in this chapter and an application is presented which provides both an application-specific and general interface to an XML search engine. An exhaustive tutorial and reference to the query language are provided. Several XML design issues are discussed in the course of the presentation including metadata, tables, math, and white space.

7.1 | Overview: Structure- and Property-Driven Search

We would like to be able to find records in our bulletin board and Contact database based on properties of those records. For example, in our bulletin board we might want to find all the messages written by one author or dealing with a certain subject or containing a particular word or phrase in the message body. In the Contact database we may wish to find all records which were entered at a particular trade

197

show or where the customer expressed interest in a specific product. In fact, we may not be interested in actually retrieving records; it may be sufficient to simply see the resulting list generated by our query. For example, I may need a list of all customers in Germany. I should be able to generate this list with a simple query without looking at the actual records of customers from Germany.

The bulletin board already has an interface to message summaries which can be navigated to retrieve any message. This interface is based on a model of interaction, the threaded discussion. Of course, the number of messages may be large and, in any case, the user will want to individualize his or her view of the discussion space by contracting threads and deleting messages. An important function of the search tool will therefore be to provide a means of rapid archival reference. It is also an alternate view of the discussion space for the user who does not find the threaded discussion metaphor congenial. For example, discussions in separate threads may overlap the same topics. A well-aimed query may render this more readily apparent than a perusal of the thread list.

The XML records which are to be searched from the Contact database and the bulletin board will be stored and searched on the server. The software which searches through the XML repository is a public domain tool called sgrep. sgrep is invoked on the server by a CGI script which forms the query in sgrep's query language and also tells sgrep where to search and what type of results to return. The CGI script is triggered by HTML forms which present an XML record query interface to the user. While three HTML query forms are available to the user, each one invokes the same CGI script. The first two query forms are designed to be specific to a particular DTD and eliminate the need for the user to know either sgrep or XML. The third query form is designed for the power user and allows the user who has both knowledge of the DTD of the target documents and sgrep's region expression language to issue queries directly to the server.

The first query form is designed to support queries to the bulletin board, allowing the user to specify up to three search strings within various structural elements of the bulletin board message listed in a select list. When the user issues a query a results list will be returned to the user containing

- a new query form, so the user can refine his or her query
- the actual text of the query generated by the CGI program and input to sgrep
- a table of results showing each file in which a match was made and the text in the structural element in which the containing string (or wildcard) was found

The user can download the file by clicking on the file name or icon. Our intranet supports the transformation of XML to HTML for downloads to an HTML browser or the direct download of XML files. The transformation process will be discussed in the next chapter.

Figure 7–1 shows the results list generated by searching the bulletin board for the word "JAVA" within the XML element `<subject>`.

Figure 7–1   Query Form for Bulletin Board Messages

The second query form is designed to support queries to the contact database. The DTD for contact records is considerably more complex than the bulletin board message DTD and the query form reflects this. There are more fields which may be selected in the structure element select list and up to four `containing` clauses which may be ORed together. In addition, a checklist is used to allow the users to query on the empty PRODUCT elements attribute list.

Figure 7–2 shows the results list generated by searching the contact database records containing the word "Microsoft" in the `<company>` element or in which the contact has interest in "XML Products."

The last query panel provides a general interface to sgrep which can be used to issue any query in the sgrep language and to search within any repository. One of four query types may be selected including sgrep region expressions, plain full-text queries, HTML-specific searches, and raw searches that search both in the text and the markup. Several

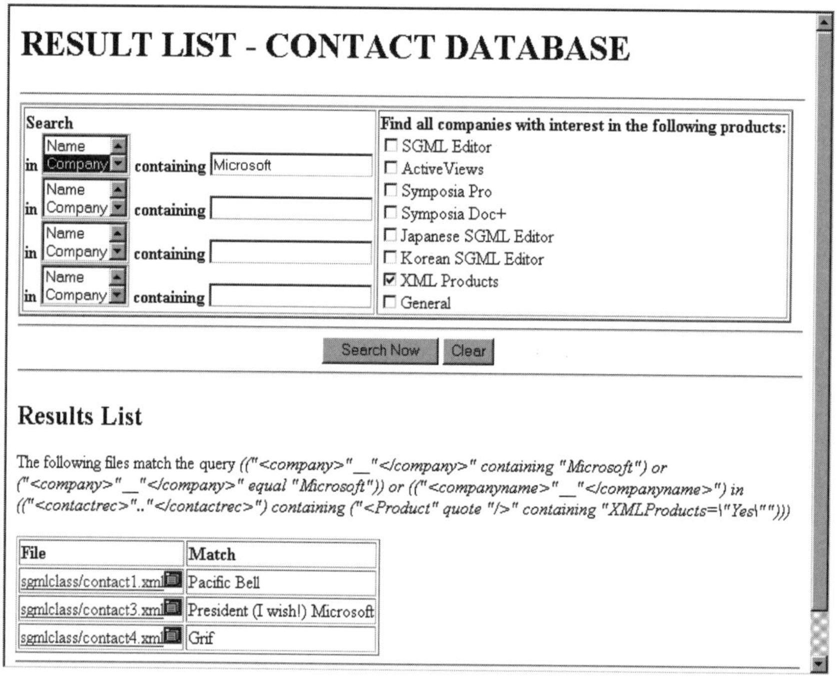

Figure 7–2   Query Form for Contact Database

SGREP GENERAL QUERY RESULTS LIST - SEARCH XML OR HTML

Enter a Search String or Region Expression:

```
(("<Notes>"_"</Notes>") in
(("<ContactRec>"_"</ContactRec>")
containing ((("<Last>"_"</Last>")
containing "Lewis") or
```

| Search Now | Clear |

Simple phrase	
Region expression	in	Web Pages	
		Bulletin Board	

Do

Results List

The following files match the query (("<Notes>"_"</Notes>") in (("<ContactRec>"_"</ContactRec>") containing ((("<Last>"_"</Last>") containing "Lewis") or (("<Last>"_"</Last>") equal "Lewis"))))

File	Match
sgmlclass/contact1.xml	Send Evaluation Software

Figure 7–3   sgrep General Query Form

known repositories may be selected in the repository select list or a new repository can be specified in the adjacent input field.

Figure 7–3 shows the results of issuing a complex query to the bulletin board repository requesting the contents of <Notes> elements to be displayed when the <ContactRec> contains the word "Lewis" in the <Last> element.

7.1.1   *Search Tools in Internet Applications*

Today there is little need to demonstrate the key role played by a search facility in the Internet as all of us are familiar with the wonderful utility of the various search engines on the World Wide Web. Anyone who has used a search engine on the World Wide Web is also aware that a search engine can be a very coarse sieve for the information seeker, either failing to return the particular documents we are seeking because the particular phrases we have queried are not used in the desired documents and are returning so many irrelevant documents that we have difficulty finding what we want in the results. Formally, these are problems with relevance and precision. Relevance is a measure of the value of each item in the result set to the person searching for information. Precision measures the proportion of relevant documents among all documents returned. In university environments where the bulk of research and experimentation in information retrieval was conducted until recently, the problem of quantifying the essentially subjective measures of relevance and precision was a major challenge. In an intranet environment the situation is different; it is often quite straightforward to quantify the efficiency of a worker performing routine tasks day in and day out. For example, search engines are now being used by workers performing "help desk" or telephone support functions. The search tool used in this kind of situation must deliver extremely high relevance and precision. One way to improve relevance and precision is to allow the user to form more exact queries; most search engines permit, for example, the use of boolean operators such as AND and OR between phrases. The actual improvement in relevance and precision from this approach is not definitively known and may be less than commonly supposed but in any case it has been observed that users seldom use complex queries. In a high-pressure position in customer support it is even more unlikely that the user will be able to formulate complex queries yielding precise result sets.

In an intranet environment an enterprise is much better able to characterize the documents which will be searched and to set standards which can increase the relevance and precision of searches. More effort may go into the preparation of documents and in the overall engineering of the information system but this additional effort is recouped by the increased productivity of the information consumers. More precise searching saves each user time and sometimes produces better solutions to the problems. If, for example, the document being searched is the yellow pages, the large number of users cost-justifies a great deal of effort in improving search effectiveness even if the gain in productivity is slight. The concerns of information producers must be balanced against concerns of readers, bearing in mind that documents are written once (perhaps frequently revised, though) but can be read many, many times. This is the fundamental motivation for this chapter and one of the major motivations for putting XML on the Web.

Most search engines, including all the search engines on the World Wide Web are full-text, that is, they index every word in every document in the corpus. Keyword-based systems which only search on the values entered in a keyword field associated with each document preceded full-text and are still relatively popular in their modern incarnation in document management systems. A keyword-based system has the advantage of allowing the person who wrote the document to appropriately classify it according to whatever taxonomy makes the most sense within a particular enterprise. For example, it would be difficult to know what phrases would retrieve the last State of the Union address but keywords such as "government," "speech," and even "State of the Union" would quickly yield the desired document. This is an example of one way of putting additional effort into creation of information that can increase reader productivity. Document management systems make use of keyword-based search by providing special fields for document properties such as the subject, date of creation, author, and so forth which can be used to increase relevance and precision. Keyword-based search is often combined with full-text search, albeit often without the assistance of high-speed indices.

XML can be used to combine the strengths of keyword and full-text search while providing a way to integrate the architecting and production of documents with the capabilities of the search engine.

1. Generic identifiers (element type names) can be used to classify documents or portions of documents. For

example, one could have element types such as SPEECH, REPAIR_MANUAL, ANNUAL_REPORT, and so forth.

2. Element attributes can provide the type of data used by document management systems such as the author, date of composition, revision information, and additional search parameters. All this stuff is collectively known as the document metadata.

3. XML supports a completely different kind of search which can often be very effective in increasing relevance and precision: context sensitive. A context-sensitive search uses XML's containment and hierarchy to allow searches to be specified in a specific context in an SGML subtree. For example, suppose someone wants to find an illustration of how to install a fuel filter with figures that have descriptive captions. The following query (written in a pseudolanguage) might be submitted: *SEARCH in CAPTION in FIGURE for "fuel pump."*

Figure 14: Fuel Pump

```
<figure>
<caption>Fuel Pump</caption>
<graphic fileref="ff_install"/>
</figure>
```

4. Unlike a document management system metadata may be associated with any element or any subtree in an XML document and may be combined with a context-sensitive search. Let's take a look at an extended example. Suppose a user is searching for pricing information on ABEC-3 bearings and further that such information is saved in tables with a metadata attribute of PRICING and further metadata attributes for the cells contained in the subtree of the table.

Table 7.1 contains the information we are searching for. The actual SGML markup used to represent this table in the preparation of this book is shown in Figure 7–4. The markup is based on the CALS table DTD subset supported by Adobe's Frame+SGML editor. (We will discuss CALS tables at greater length later in the chapter.) This table is represented in the figure as a tree with the attribute metadata included in the tree in the small font adjacent to the element name.

Type	Single Price	Volume Price (1000)
ABEC-1	0.75	400
ABEC-3	1.25	625
ABEC-5	3.00	2,100

Table 7.1   Bearings

```
<table colsep = "1" tabletype="pricing" frame = "all" rowsep
= "1">
<tgroup cols = "3" colsep = "1" rowsep = "1">
<colspec colname = "type" colnum = "1" colwidth = "1.00in">
<colspec colname = "unitprice" colnum = "2" colwidth =
"1.00in">
<colspec colname = "lotprice" colnum = "3" colwidth =
"1.20in">
<tbody>
<row rowsep = "1">
<entry colname = "type">Type</entry>
<entry colname = "unitprice">Single Price</entry>
<entry colname = "lotprice">Volume Price (1000)</entry>
</row>
<row rowsep = "1">
<entry colname = "type">ABEC-1</entry>
<entry colname = "unitprice">0.75</entry>
<entry colname = "lotprice">400</entry>
</row>
<row rowsep = "1">
<entry colname = "type">ABEC-3</entry>
<entry colname = "unitprice">1.25</entry>
<entry colname = "lotprice">625</entry>
</row>
<row rowsep = "0">
<entry colname = "type">ABEC-5</entry>
<entry colname = "unitprice">3.00</entry>
<entry colname = "lotprice">2100</entry>
</row>
</tbody>
</tgroup>
</table>
```

Figure 7–4   CALS Representation of Bearing Table

A query which could be used to combine searching in metadata and context sensitivity is shown below. The query is written in pseudolanguage but is similar to languages proposed for XML style-sheet languages and the DOM (Document Object Model).

The query requests return of a row element inside a `pricing` table. It further specifies that row by saying that it must have an `entry` element with a `colname` of "type" and must have element content matching the string "ABEC-3."

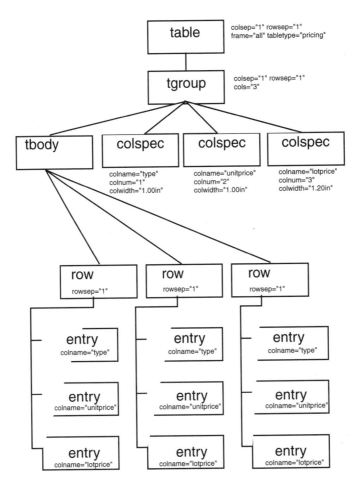

Figure 7–5 Price Table Document Tree

```
retrieve ROW
   containing ENTRY with ATTRIBUTE colname="type"
      containing "ABEC-3"
   in TABLE with ATTRIBUTE TABLETYPE="pricing"
```

Figure 7–6 Metadata Query

XML search typically implies the support of subtree retrieval. This is not the case with most full-text search engines which may not support any retrieval capability at all, relying on the existence of some mechanism to fetch entire documents. Our structure-capable application should be capable of returning the following subtree shown in Figure 7–7 in response to the query.

Figure 7–8 shows the result of the retrieval operation graphically as a subtree.

```
<row rowsep = "1">
<entry colname = "type">ABEC-3</entry>
<entry colname = "unitprice">1.25</entry>
<entry colname = "lotprice">625</entry>
</row>
```

Figure 7–7   XML Query Fragment Retrieval

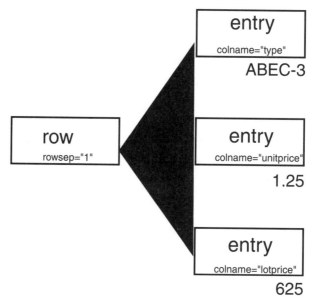

Figure 7–8   Query Results

An important point to understand is that the additional search capabilities provided by XML flow naturally out of XML's data-centrism. Once the design work has been done up front, the documents which are created will automatically have everything in them needed to support an advanced XML search engine. Even if an advanced XML search engine is not used, a very significant benefit can be realized simply by assuring the automatic population of the parameters put in a document management system or keyword search tool through the enforcement mechanism of the DTD.

In the course of the above discussion we have touched on two points which fall outside the discussion of XML search but which are nonetheless interesting. In keeping with the spirit of meandering where the discussion may lead us, we will leave the main thread for a bit to talk about attributes, elements, and metadata and table representation. Those lacking a peripatetic sensibility will wish to skip the next two sections for the time being.

7.1.1.1   Attributes and Elements and Metadata

Every student of XML will eventually find him- or herself confused about when to create a new container element as opposed to adding some additional information as attribute data of existing elements. The underlying philosophical question is addressed by learning to identify the metadata role of attributes. This leads us to briefly consider metadata about metadata, a new application area in which some exciting XML work is happening.

The general theory of elements and attributes goes like this.

The name of an element type is the noun which fills in the blank in the following question:
The content of this element IS A _____.

If it is an empty element, the question could be altered slightly to something like
The function of this element IS TO _____.

Attributes are the adjectives which fill out the answer to the IS A question or they may be the answer to any question one might not need to pose about the element other than the IS A question. For example, I have a list of prices in various currencies:

696 U.S. Dollars 990 Swiss Francs

I ask myself the question: what is "696"? Answer: It is the U.S. dollar price. I ask what is 990 and the answer is: the Swiss franc price. So my noun and hence my generic identifier is price and U.S. dollar and Swiss franc are adjectives, that is, attributes. So my markup is

```
<price units="us">696</price> and <price units="ch">990</price>
```

The element type name and the attributes are both information about the content and are properly both considered metadata of the content. We simply must distinguish between the IS A function of the element type name and the other functions of the attribute data. This IS A question is the most fundamental property of the data and should not be subject to too much evolution; other properties of the data, on the other hand, may change rather often and will be driven by the type of applications we build around the data.

In legacy analysis we create DTDs from existing documents. The basic technique is to go through as much material as possible and identify all the places where you have a distinct answer to the IS A question and then work out some rules for the relationships between IS A objects (nesting and sequence and perhaps hyperlinking relationships). What one usually finds is that like the little boy who never tires of asking questions, one can continue to find IS A objects for as long as one cares to look for them. So we add another question: X IS A fool, but do I care? The problem with this approach is that you will always be wrong; sometimes you will say yes and will, in fact, never care, and sometimes you will say no and find you care a lot once you thought you had finished your first million or so documents. This is why SGML consultants enjoy expensive vacations in tropical paradises at your expense; their experience and good instincts can lessen some of these inevitable travails.

It is usually productive to lessen the number of IS A objects for the same reasons that we try to abstract functionality in code. We write less of it, it is more reusable, and we are better able to understand the workings of our system and to pass that knowledge on to others. The code analogy is perhaps a good way to think generally about element names and attributes; they correspond nicely to function type names and arguments. The way that we often combine two similar elements is to add an attribute which distinguishes one from the other in the same way that we might add an extra argument to the argument list.

We often run into a nasty practical problem: Many nonconforming SGML and XML tools do not do a good job of handling attributes or don't actually handle them at all. Shocking! But true. We will see this very problem in this chapter as our search engine is among these. One solution is to dump whatever processor you are using which is an entirely good idea except that you and I know that there are many situations where you will simply look for a quick way to hack your way through it just this once. So we might use the fact that since there really isn't any difference between the element type name and the attributes—it is all metadata—we can make everything into elements. So we might have

```
<price><us>696</us></price>
```

   or

```
<price><us/>696</price>
```

   or even shameless agglutination

```
<priceus>696</priceus><pricech>990</pricech>.
```

While we are talking about agglutination and IS A relationships, perhaps we are at a good juncture to add a word about namespaces. This is something that has been discussed exhaustively by those working on the XML standard although no consensus on it was reached for version 1.0. The idea with namespaces is basically to enable you to be able to relate IS A objects to IS A relationships or, in object-oriented terms, to establish a class hierarchy. Or we should say rather that this is what we and some others think that namespaces should do but a consensus is still lacking. The current proposal simply allows for element and attribute names to be prefixed with name and a colon. The purpose of the namespace:' syntax and any behavior that should be associated with that syntax is currently undefined. With that caveat we proceed to give an example of namespaces as we see them.

We have a price which has two different roles in a document. In the one case it is a text-entry field such as that which would be used in an HTML form; it requires input validation to ensure that the user enters a whole number and a two-digit decimal value preceded by a decimal point.

The second price is a cell within a spreadsheet. In addition to validating the value entered by the user the entry has properties unique to a spreadsheet cell in terms of its display, ability to be calculated or used in calculations, and relationship to other cells in the spreadsheet.

In either case we could mark up the data as follows:

```
<price units="us">18.99</price>
```

But to distinguish between the two applications of price we can make everything explicit with

```
<input:price units="us">18.99</input:price>
```

and

```
<cell:price units="us">18.99</input:price>
```

We have observed that the element type name and the element's attribute values are both metadata. But the justification for a special syntax for the IS A relationship of an element name is the same justification for a special syntax for the element type name itself: It is the primary piece of metainformation for the data. Some have advocated, however, consigning the namespace identification to an attribute. Some further advocate using architectural form attributes (see Chapter 5) to enable the namespaces to be affixed without cluttering up the element instance markup. Finally some are not so enamored of the whole concept and propose limiting the application of namespaces to "disambiguating duplicate element type names." This might apply to our example, although we would argue that the underlying reason for needing unambiguousness is the existence of implicit class hierarchies in XML application architectures.

There are, in principle, an infinite number of data relationships other than the IS A relationship. Resource Discovery Framework (RDF) is a new standard related to XML which attempts to provide a formal mechanism for declaring and applying these relationships. Metadata is treated as named property/value sets, declared in XML, and applied to data through namespaces. In our exploration of attributes and elements and metadata we end up looking again at property-driven search since one of the major objectives of RDF is to enable "resource discovery," that is, searching for data using properties defined in a consistent way on the Web.

7.1.1.2 Tables (and Math)

In our discussion of XML structured search we happened to use the example of search within a table. The markup of tables is a very important topic for publishing applications and, in consequence, an area where a great deal of thought and attention have been devoted since SGML's earliest days.

At one time it was felt by some that it was impossible to arrive at a satisfactory general markup language for tables. They argued that tables were the product of a specific, visually oriented layout design within a space of known dimensions and therefore should be represented electronically by images rather than rendered dynamically from markup. Many early SGML tools displayed only tables which had been prepared as graphic images. The U.S. Department of Defense (DoD) did not accept this position and sponsored the development of a markup model for tables known today as "CALS tables." CALS is the acronym for a DoD program under which this and many other founding works related to SGML were undertaken. Apparently the DoD is taking the hard line on the increase in the number of acronyms since, rather than changing the acronym to reflect new program objectives the letters have been retained and the words changed —three times! The end result is that no one is quite sure what CALS stands for anymore.

Even if the meaning of "CALS" is a mystery, CALS tables have been a great success. The CALS table model is sufficient to encode just about any table ever laid out on paper. Most SGML display tools have a CALS table rendering built in. The CALS table model is very extensive and no vendor, to our knowledge, has implemented 100 percent of the specification so one must be aware of what subset of CALS a particular vendor supports and also be alert to possible interoperability problems between tools.

Other table models have been created since CALS, HTML tables being the most notable, but CALS remains the most comprehensive.

Despite the success of CALS, there is little reason for disappointment with the results. One of the goals of generalized markup is to avoid layout-specific information in the data which would restrict output of those data in various mediums and formats. The CALS model does not require one to represent every detail of the layout but it does require one to establish the geometric relationships between the cells in the table. What isn't specified is calculated at rendering time. The CALS model does permit one to specify just about every detail of the layout if one so chooses with a very large set of attributes. This enables one to be sure of getting exactly the layout desired. From the perspective of wild-eyed generalized markup fanatics this is at best a partial success. After all, underlying the concept of a table is a set of relationships among data items. In theory there should be a way to represent those data and those relationships independent of their visual presentation.

There have been some small accomplishments along these lines. Some SGML tool vendors, motivated by the desire to support multiple table models, have created mappings between the layout-oriented table models and their abstract table models on which they base a rendering. In practice, however, every aspect of this has proven to be difficult. Just rendering the tables from a layout-oriented model is difficult enough.

The SGML DTD of one of the CALS table variants is shown in Figure 7–9. The SGML-specific features of the DTD include the use of tag omission, exclusions, and attribute types such as NMTOKEN and NUMBER not supported in XML. Exclusions are a mechanism for excluding certain elements from occurring as children of the entire subtree of an element. For example, the statement

```
-(table)
```

in the element definition for table forbids the nesting of TABLE elements inside another TABLE.

```
<!ELEMENT table - - (%titles;, tgroup+) -(table)>
<!ATTLIST table
        tabstyle NMTOKEN #IMPLIED
        tocentry %yesorno; "1"
        shortentry %yesorno; #IMPLIED
        frame (top|bottom|topbot|all|sides|none) #IMPLIED
        colsep %yesorno; #IMPLIED
        rowsep %yesorno; #IMPLIED
        orient (port | land) #IMPLIED
        pgwide %yesorno; #IMPLIED
        %bodyatt;
        %secur;>
        %secur;>
```

Figure 7–9   CALS Table DTD

```
<!ELEMENT tgroup - o (colspec*, spanspec*, thead?, tfoot?,
                       tbody)>
<!ATTLIST tgroup
          cols NUMBER #REQUIRED
          tgroupstyle NMTOKEN #IMPLIED
          colsep %yesorno; #IMPLIED
          rowsep %yesorno; #IMPLIED
          align (left|right|center|justify|char) "left"
          charoff NUTOKEN "50"
          char CDATA ""
          %secur;>
<!ELEMENT colspec- o EMPTY>
<!ATTLIST colspec
          colnum NUMBER #IMPLIED
          colname NMTOKEN #IMPLIED
          align (left|right|center|justify|char) #IMPLIED
          charoff NUTOKEN #IMPLIED
          char CDATA #IMPLIED
          colwidth CDATA #IMPLIED
          colsep %yesorno; #IMPLIED
          rowsep %yesorno; #IMPLIED>
<!ELEMENT spanspec - o EMPTY>
<!ATTLIST spanspec
          namest NMTOKEN #REQUIRED
          nameend NMTOKEN #REQUIRED
          spanname NMTOKEN #REQUIRED
          align (left|right|center|justify|char) "center"
          charoff NUTOKEN #IMPLIED
          char CDATA #IMPLIED
          colsep %yesorno; #IMPLIED
          rowsep %yesorno; #IMPLIED>
<!ELEMENT (thead | tfoot) - o(colspec*, row+) -(entrytbl)>
<!ATTLIST thead
          valign (top|middle|bottom) "bottom"
          %secur;>
<!ATTLIST tfoot
          valign (top|middle|bottom) "top"
<!ELEMENT tbody - o (row+)>
<!ATTLIST tbody
          valign (top|middle|bottom) "top"
          %secur;>
```

Figure 7-9   CALS Table DTD *(continued)*

```
<!ELEMENT row - o (entry | entrytbl)+>
<!ATTLIST row
          rowsep %yesorno; #IMPLIED
          %secur;>
<!ELEMENT entry - o ((para | %spcpara;)+ | %paracon;)>
<!ATTLIST entry
          colname NMTOKEN #IMPLIED
          spanname NMTOKEN #IMPLIED
          morerows NUMBER "0"
          colsep %yesorno; #IMPLIED
          rowsep %yesorno; #IMPLIED
          rotate %yesorno; "0"
          valign (top|bottom|middle) "top"
          align (left|right|center|justify|char) #IMPLIED
          charoff NUTOKEN #IMPLIED
          char CDATA #IMPLIED
          %secur;>
```

Figure 7–9   CALS Table DTD *continued*

CALS tables are composed of TGROUPs, sections of a table governed by a set of column definitions. COLSPECs are the column definitions and SPANSECs are definitions of spans across multiple columns. Figure 7–10 shows the column and span layout for a table containing two TGROUPs.

The TGROUP contains a TBODY, the body of the table, and optionally one THEAD or table header and one TFOOT or table footer. One use of special header and footer sections is to enable the same header and/or footer information to be repeated on each page for a table that spans several pages without having to know in advance the exact layout of the table. The three table sections each contain ROWs and the ROWs contain either ENTRY, table cells, or ENTRYTBL, a subtable inside a cell. Figure 7–10 shows the table illustrated in Figure 7–11 with rows of table cells defined for each of the TGROUPs and is followed with the document fragment containing the complete SGML markup of the table.

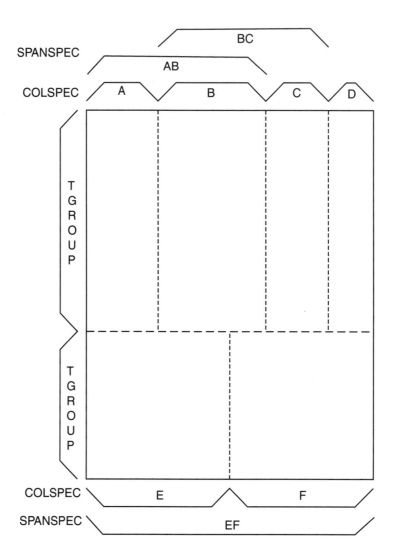

Figure 7–10   CALS Table Organization

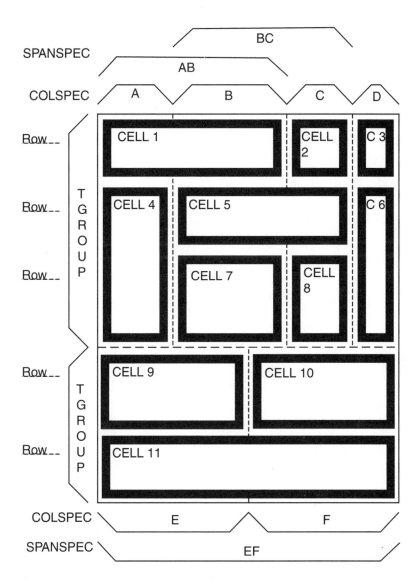

Figure 7-11 Cell Layout in CALS Tables

```
<TABLE>
<TITLE>A TABLE WITH SPANS</TITLE>
<TGROUP COLS="4">
<COLSPEC COLNUM="1" COLNAME="A" COLWIDTH="1in">
<COLSPEC COLNUM="2" COLNAME="B" COLWIDTH="1.6in">
<COLSPEC COLNUM="3" COLNAME="C" COLWIDTH="1in">
<COLSPEC COLNUM="4" COLNAME="D" COLWIDTH="0.8in">
<SPANSPEC SPANNAME="AB" NAMEST="A" NAMEEND="B">
<SPANSPEC SPANNAME="BC" NAMEST="B" NAMEEND="C">
<!-- BODY -->
<TBODY>
<ROW>
<ENTRY SPANNAME="AB">CELL 1</ENTRY>
<ENTRY COLNAME="C">CELL 2</ENTRY>
<ENTRY COLNAME="D">C3</ENTRY>
</ROW>
<ROW>
<ENTRY COLNAME="A" MOREROWS="1">CELL 4</ENTRY>
<ENTRY SPANNAME="BC">CELL 5</ENTRY>
<ENTRY COLNAME="D" MOREROWS="1">C6</ENTRY>
</ROW>
<ROW>
<ENTRY COLNAME="B">CELL 7</ENTRY>
<ENTRY COLNAME="C">CELL 8</ENTRY>
</ROW>
</TBODY>
</TGROUP>
<TGROUP COLS="2">
<COLSPEC COLNUM="1" COLNAME="E" COLWIDTH="2.2in">
<COLSPEC COLNUM="2" COLNAME="F" COLWIDTH="2.2in">
<SPANSPEC SPANNAME="EF" NAMEST="E" NAMEEND="F">
<!-- BODY -->
<TBODY>
<ROW>
<ENTRY COLNAME="E">CELL 9</ENTRY>
<ENTRY COLNAME="F">CELL 10</ENTRY>
</ROW>
<ROW>
<ENTRY SPANNAME="EF">CELL 11</ENTRY>
</ROW>
</TBODY></TGROUP>
</TABLE>
```

Figure 7–12   CALS Table Instance

The table cells that begin in the second row in columns A and D have the MOREROWS attribute set to "1" which means that they will a have a vertical span to the bottom of the third row. Because columns A and D in the third row have a vertical straddle from row two, we only have table cells defined in that row for columns B and D. All table cells on the same row will have the same horizontal scan line along the bottom of the cell unless a MOREROWS value pushes the horizontal scan line on a particular cell to match that of lower rows. The row height cannot be specified: Each cell will be at least as tall as is needed in order to accommodate the data within it when the table is rendered.

Many attributes are available to control the rendering of the table. Attributes may be repeated at several levels in the table subtree; the rule is that the attribute at lower levels in the tree overrides an attribute already set at a higher level. For example, colsep set to "0" in the TABLE element will cause the omission of a column separator everywhere in the table. But if we had colsep="1" in our second TGROUP in the table instance shown in Figure 7–12, the column separator would be present for all the table cells in that TGROUP. FRAME, COLSEP, ROWSEP, PGWIDE, and ORIENT control table and cell boundaries, sizing, and orientation; ALIGN, CHAROFF, CHAR, ROTATE, and VALIGN control the presentation of data within cells; and several other attributes either are related to the definition of columns and spans or are general attributes.

Let's consider some of the alternatives to the layout-oriented CALS table DTD. First we will propose an encoding system for the pricing table example discussed earlier which uses just one element, PRICE. We are able to treat this simple table as a two-dimensional matrix where the only pieces of information needed to place the data in a table cell with the matrix are the X and Y coordinates, in this case the item value and the quantity value. We include this information as attribute information. We do not need any explicit containment relationships in order to establish the relationships between data items.

The DTD fragment and the complete markup for the table are shown below in Figure 7–13.

```
<!ELEMENT price (#PCDATA)>
<!ATTLIST price
          item CDATA #IMPLIED
          quantity (unit|lot) #REQUIRED>

<price item="ABEC-1" quantity="unit">0.75</price>
<price item="ABEC-1" quantity="lot">400</price>
<price item="ABEC-3" quantity="unit">1.25</price>
<price item="ABEC-3" quantity="lot">625</price>
<price item="ABEC-5" quantity="unit">3.00</price>
<price item="ABEC-5" quantity="lot">2100</price>
```

Figure 7–13   A Stable with Just One Element Type

How might we be able to output a table looking like the formatted example shown earlier from this kind of markup? Here is where we return to the subject of this chapter: search. The key is to query the data so that the data are retrieved in the sequence required for table construction. The following query shown in Figure 7–14 is written in pseudolanguage.

```
foreach (sort (retrieve PRICE) on ATTRIBUTE ITEM)
    write COL1 with ATTRIBUTE ITEM
    write COL2 if ATTRIBUTE quantity eq "unit" with CONTENT
    write COL3 if ATTRIBUTE quantity eq "lot" with CONTENT
```

Figure 7–14   Using an XML Query to Generate a Table

The query retrieves all PRICE elements and sorts them on the value of the attribute ITEM, ensuring that records belonging to the same row will be grouped together. We then go through the records one by one, writing the value of the ITEM attribute (ABEC-1, ABEC-3, etc.) in the first column, the single price, identified by an attribute QUANTITY with a value of "unit" in the second column, and the volume price, identified by its QUANTITY "lot," in the third column.

We do not state how the actual formatting of the table is affected. We could assume some sort of stylesheet which is able to general table formatting to the entire output and to associate column specific formatting to the COL1, COL2, and COL3 objects used in the query statement. This approach is consistent with the techniques used in DSSSL and in the XSL style sheet language derived from DSSSL. XSL consists of a series of patterns or queries and actions which together constitute construction rules. Patterns select XML elements to which flow objects are applied by the actions resulting in the construction of a flow object tree expression, that is, output. Flow objects may be thought of as style sheet rules. Figure 7–15 shows the components of XSL-based XML transformation.

Transformations of this nature are currently most often approached with a procedural language with capabilities specific to XML. We will discuss this at length in the next chapter.

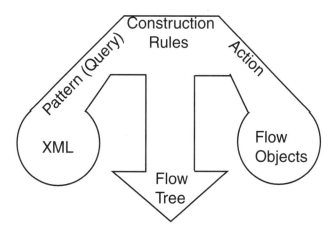

Figure 7–15 XSL Transformation

We conclude this section with an alternative markup of our example table shown in Figure 7–16. This markup also uses just a single element but uses linking rather than property-based search to connect related pieces of information into a table. In fact, the table is a linked list structure where each cell is connected to the next cell both in the adjacent column and the adjacent row.

```
<!ELEMENT cell (#PCDATA)>
<!ATTLIST cell
          id ID #REQUIRED
          nextcol IDREF #IMPLIED
          nextrow IDREF #IMPLIED>

<cell id="tp001" nextcol="tp002" nextrow="tp004">Type</
cell>
<cell id="tp002" nextcol="tp003" nextrow="tp005">0.75</
cell>
<cell id="tp003" nextrow="tp006">400</cell>
<cell id="tp004" nextcol="tp005" nextrow="tp007">Single
Price</cell>
<cell id="tp005" nextcol="tp006" nextrow="tp008">1.25</
cell>
<cell id="tp006" nextrow="tp009">625</cell>
<cell id="tp007" nextcol="tp008">Volume Price</cell>
<cell id="tp008" nextcol="tp009">3.00</cell>
<cell id="tp009">2100</cell>
```

Figure 7–16   A Table of Linked Elements

Many of the issues in the representation of mathematics are similar to those which come up for tables. The ability to represent mathematics is extremely important for publishing applications of XML and SGML and markup schemes tend to fall somewhere on a plane with visualness and content-orientedness being the x and y axes. Mathematics is a bit more of an imbroglio for several reasons:

- TeX. It is a visually-oriented markup system and is in extremely widespread use.
- New mathematical notations are continually being invented.

- No comprehensive DTD for math equivalent to CALS for tables.

- Less need to be able to apply text, structure, and property-driven search techniques to mathematical data.

It is therefore common for SGML systems to support the display of math using TeX or in some cases to not support SGML math markup at all. The higher-end SGML editors do support math markup and are usually limited to a vendor's own markup system or one of the less-than-comprehensive public math DTDs. In order to give the reader some idea of math markup Figure 7–17 shows an equation using the Euromath DTD.

$$H(\sigma) = \int_{0}^{+\infty} e^{-\alpha} h(t) dt$$

```
<math>
    <Textual>H(&sigma;) = </Textual>
    <int.cst>
        <l.part.a>
            <IntSym>
            <Lower.bd><Textual>0</Textual></Lower.bd>
            <Upper.bd><Textual>+&infin;</Textual></Upper.bd>
        </l.part.a>
        <Integrnd>
            <subscr.d>
                <Main><Textual>e<Textual></Main>
                <supscr><Textual>-&sigma;t</Textual>
            </supscr>
            </subscr.d>
            <Textual>h(t) dt</Textual>
        </Integrnd>
    </int.cst>
</math>
```

Figure 7–17 Math using the EuroMath DTD

7.2 | sgrep's Query Language

In our Internet application we have chosen to use sgrep as our search engine. sgrep takes it name from the popular UNIX file search utility grep with the addition of the prefix "s" for "structured." sgrep was written by Pekka Kilpeläinen and Jani Jaakkola at the University of Helsinki, Finland and is distributed under the GNU General Public License. The GNU license says, essentially, that the software (including source code) is free, may be used freely, and must remain free, that is, it cannot be sold and cannot be sold after being modified. It is written in C and has been ported to a number of UNIX platforms.

sgrep does full-text search but it does not use an index; files are searched for matches one by one. While sgrep is incredibly fast at what it does, it is not suitable for very large corpora. Unlike some versions of grep, sgrep does not support regular expressions for search phrases. Despite these limitations sgrep is a very useful tool and good vehicle for illustrating the use of XML-based searching in Internet applications. sgrep's source code has been included on the CD-ROM but it is outside the scope of this book to look into its design. We will, however, thoroughly examine the sgrep query language with a focus on its use with XML. Once we have explored the query language we will discuss the construction of a Web-based interface tailored for our application.

We have somewhat simplified our presentation of sgrep in focusing on its use with XML and the practical aspects of constructing a system with it. For the sake of precision and correctness we would like to emphasize that sgrep works on a precisely defined and general set (or lists) of regions and that the arguments and results of any sgrep operator are set (or lists) of regions. The one exception to this is "join" whose first argument is integer rather than a set of regions.

We also would like to emphasize to the reader that sgrep is not XML-aware or XML-smart. This makes sgrep useful for querying document formats other than XML but the XML user must be careful to write sgrep queries that will match the markup used.

We will use the well-formed XML document shown in Figure 7–18 in many of the examples we discuss. This document is stored and accessed by sgrep as a file and will be referred to as file.xml in sgrep commands. When other files are used as examples their content are shown.

```
<?xml version="1.0"?>
<ContactRec>
<Name>
<First>Stuart</First><Last>Culshaw</Last>
</Name>
<Company>
<JobTitle>President (I wish!)</JobTitle>
<CompanyName>Microsoft</CompanyName>
</Company>
<Address>
<Street>Paradise Mansion</Street>
<Street>Big Street</Street>
<City>New York</City>
<Region>New York</Region>
<PostCode>12345</PostCode>
<Country>USA</Country>
<Phone>
<DayTime>123456789</DayTime>
<Fax>123456789</Fax>
</Phone>
<Internet>
<Email>me@mycompany.com</Email>
<Web>http://www.mycompany.com</Web>
</Internet>
</Address>
<Product SGMLEditor="Yes" ActiveViews="Yes" Sympo-
siaPro="Yes" SymposiaDocPlus="Yes" SGMLEditorJapanese="No"
SGMLEditorKorean="No" XMLProducts="No" General="No"/>
<Contacts>
<Language Preference="English"/>
<History>
<Events>
<Date>
<Day>07</Day><Month>12</Month><Year>97</Year>
</Date>
```

Figure 7–18   XML Document Used in sgrep Examples

```
<Venue>XML Intranet Tutorial SGML/XML '97</Venue>
<Notes>Ces messieurs concluaient contre les nouvelles
theories criminalistes; avec cette belle invention de
l'irresponsabilite dans certains cas pathologiques, il n'y
avait plus de criminels, il n'y avait que des malades.
</Notes>
</Events>
</History>
</Contacts>
</ContactRec>
```

Figure 7–18 XML document used in sgrep examples (*continued*)

There are 70 examples of sgrep queries annotated in detail below. The examples are comprehensive, covering every aspect of the query language. The presentation is also progressive, later examples will build on the understanding of region-based queries gained in earlier material. Many points about XML data representation, processing, and querying are developed wherever they are relevant to a particular example. For these reasons a careful reading of this section from beginning to end should be beneficial to the reader and, of course, experimentation with sgrep while reading this section would double that benefit.

COMMAND	`sgrep -e '"www"' *.xml`
OUTPUT	www
NOTES	-e 'expression' means read the expression (an sgrep query) from the command line. *.xml are the files to be searched, any file with an xml extension in the current directory in this case.
	We call this type of expression RAW because it searches both markup and data content for matches.

COMMAND	`sgrep -f exp *.xml`
OUTPUT	`www`
NOTES	-f filename means that the sgrep expression should be read from the named file. In this case the content of exp is: `"www"` (without single quotes).

COMMAND	1. `sgrep -e '"WWW"' *.xml` 2. `sgrep -i -e '"WWW"' *.xml`
OUTPUT	1. `no output` 2. `www`
NOTES	The first statement is case sensitive and fails to find a match. The -i makes the second statement case insensitive and therefore find a match.

COMMAND	`sgrep -i -l -e '"WWW"' *.xml`

OUTPUT	`------------- #1 file.xml: 3 (482,484 :`
	`482,484)`
	`www`

NOTES	–l generates the long output format. #1 ordinal number of the region file.xml name of file where the region starts 3 the length of the region in bytes (482, byte start position of region in the whole text ,484 : byte end position of region in the whole text 482, byte start position of region in the current file 484) byte end position of region in the current file

COMMAND	```sgrep -i -l -e '"WWW"' *.xml```

OUTPUT	```------------- #1 file.xml: 3 (482,484 :```
	```482,484)```
	```www```
	```------------- #2 file2.xml: 3 (1627,1629 :```
	```482,484)```
	```www```

NOTES	file2.xml is a copy of file.xml. We see that matches are reported in both files and that the first set of start and end byte positions in the second file includes the size in bytes of the first file.
COMMAND	```sgrep -i -o "%f\n" -e '"WWW"' *.xml```
OUTPUT	```file.xml``` ```file2.xml```
NOTES	-o is followed by the output specification. The output specification consists of text and sgrep variables. The command above shows the use of the %f filename variable. Each time a match is encountered the filename in which that match was found followed by a carriage return is output.

COMMAND	`sgrep -i -o "------------- %n %f: %l (%s,%e` `: %i,%j)\n%r\n" -e '"WWW"' *.xml`

OUTPUT	`------------- #1 file.xml: 3 (482,484 :`
	`482,484)`
	`www`
	`------------- #2 file2.xml: 3 (1627,1629 :`
	`482,484)`
	`www`

NOTES	This is the output statement used to produce the long format obtained with the -l option shown two examples back. Here is a table of the sgrep output variables: `%f` name of the file containing the start of the region `%s` start position of the region (files concatenated) `%e` end position of the region (files concatenated) `%l` length of the region in bytes `%i` start position of the region in the current file `%j` end position of the region in the current file `%r` text of the region `%n` ordinal number of the region
COMMAND	`sgrep -i -o "<tr><td>%f</td><td>%r</td></` `tr>\n" -e '"WWW"' *.xml`
OUTPUT	`<tr><td>file.xml</td><td>www</td></tr>` `<tr><td>file2.xml</td><td>www</td></tr>`
NOTES	An output statement which causes the results of the query to be output as an HTML fragment.

COMMAND	`sgrep -i -e '[(482,484)]' file.xml`
OUTPUT	www
NOTES	This uses a constant region list to extract text by its byte position in the file.
COMMAND	`sgrep -i -e '[(482,484) (976,991)]' file.xml`
OUTPUT	wwwirresponsabilite
NOTES	This query contains two constant region ranges in the list and extracts both. **Caution:** Constant regions have to be listed in increasing order of their start positions (and regions with the same start positions must be listed in strictly increasing order of their end positions).
COMMAND	`sgrep -i -e '[(472,494)]' file.xml`
OUTPUT	eb>http://www.mycompany
NOTES	The constant region list has been expanded by 10 characters on each side of the match on "www." It is usually desirable to do this in order to give the user some context around each match. For PHRASE and RAW searches we will perform two sgrep commands, the first to find the byte address of the match and the second to extract the match and some bytes on either side of the match.

COMMAND	`sgrep -i -l -e '"<postcode>".."</post-code>"' file.xml`
OUTPUT	`------------- #1 file.xml: 26 (310,335 : 310,335)` `<PostCode>12345</PostCode>`
NOTES	.. matches from the start of the start region to the end of the end region.

COMMAND	`sgrep -i -l -e '"<postcode>"_."</post-code>"' file.xml`
OUTPUT	`------------- #1 file.xml: 16 (320,335 : 320,335)` `12345</PostCode>`
NOTES	_. matches from the end of the start region to end of the end region.

COMMAND	`sgrep -i -l -e '"<postcode>"._"</post-code>"' file.xml`
OUTPUT	`------------- #1 file.xml: 15 (310,324 : 310,324)` `<PostCode>12345`
NOTES	._ matches from the start of the start region to the start of the end region.

COMMAND	```sgrep -i -l -e '"<postcode>"__"</post-code>"' file.xml```
OUTPUT	```------------ #1 file.xml: 5 (320,324 : 320,324)``` ```12345```
NOTES	__ matches from the end of the start region to the start of the end region.
COMMAND	```sgrep -i -e '"<company>"__"</company>"' file.xml```
OUTPUT	```<JobTitle>President (I wish!)</JobTitle>``` ```<CompanyName>Microsoft</CompanyName>```
NOTES	Regions may contain an XML subtree. This expression returns the company subtree.
COMMAND	```sgrep -i -l -e '"il n" .. "de"' file.xml```

OUTPUT	```------------ #1 file.xml: 20 (1027,1046 : 1027,1046)```
	 ```il n'y avait plus de```
	 ```------------ #2 file.xml: 19 (1060,1078 : 1060,1078)```
	 ```il n'y avait que de```

NOTES	Any string may be used to define a region. XML markup-based regions are nothing more than strings.

COMMAND	`sgrep -i -l -e '"<postcode>" quote "</post-code>"' file.xml`
OUTPUT	`------------- #1 file.xml: 26 (310,335 : 310,335)` `<PostCode>12345</PostCode>`
NOTES	Quote will work the same as .. except where regions overlap. The difference between the two is illustrated in the next two examples.

COMMAND	`sgrep -i -l -e '"1" quote "5"' file.xml`

OUTPUT	`------------- #1 file.xml: 310 (15,324 : 15,324)`
	`1.0">`
	`<ContactRec>`
	`<Name>`
	`<First>Stuart</First><Last>Culshaw</Last>`
	`</Name>`
	`<Company>`
	`<JobTitle>President (I wish!)</JobTitle>`
	`<CompanyName>Microsoft</CompanyName>`
	`</Company>`
	`<Address>`
	`<Street>Paradise Mansion</Street>`
	`<Street>Big Street</Street>`
	`<City>New York</City>`
	`<Region>New York</Region>`
	`<PostCode>12345`
	`------------- #2 file.xml: 5 (377,381 : 377,381)`
	`12345`
	`------------- #3 file.xml: 5 (402,406 : 402,406)`
	`12345`

NOTES

Quote matches from the first occurence of 1 to the first occurrence of 5, from the XML declaration to the post-code element. The command makes two other matches in DayTime and Fax Elements.

A match is not made in the PostCode element. Quote regions are nonnesting and nonoverlapping. The Post-Code match overlaps with match from the 1 in the declaration to the 5 in PostCode.

Quote needs to do thinks like match C comments where a begin comment nested inside a comment must be ignored. For example,

/* /* This is a C Comment. */

To match this comment we must ignore the second /*. The quote command

"/*" quote "*/"

does exactly that.

With well-formed XML quote will lead to incorrect results since it does not handle nested matches.

See the next example to see how .. operates on the same regions.

COMMAND	`sgrep -i -l -e '"1" .. "5"' file.xml`

OUTPUT	`------------- #1 file.xml: 5 (320,324 :`
	`320,324)`
	`12345`
	`------------- #2 file.xml: 5 (377,381 :`
	`377,381)`
	`12345`
	`------------- #3 file.xml: 5 (402,406 :`
	`402,406)`
	`12345`

NOTES	.. does not match the 1 in the XML declaration to the 5 in PostCode because there is a start region of 1 which is closer to the end region. The rules which sgrep follows in making a match are as follows:

- the start region must come before the end region

- the start region is not matched with an earlier end region

- the end region is not matched with any start region which comes after the matching start region

See the previous example to see how using quote instead of .. would change the results. For well-formed XML .. provides the correct results in cases where matches are nested.

COMMAND	```sgrep -i -l -e '"<a>" .. "</a>"' file3.xml```
	The content of file3 is a well-formed XML document with the following contents:
	```<a><a>data</a></a>```

OUTPUT	```------------ #1 file3.xml: 18 (0,17 : 0,17)```
	```<a><a>data</a></a>```
	```------------ #2 file3.xml: 11 (3,13 : 3,13)```
	```<a>data</a>```

NOTES	This command correctly handles the nested regions, as explained in greater detail in the example above. See the example below for the result of using quote instead of ..
COMMAND	```sgrep -i -l -e '"<a>" quote "</a>"' file3.xml```
	The content of file3 is a well-formed XML document with the following contents:
	```<a><a>data</a></a>```
OUTPUT	```------------ #1 file3.xml: 14 (0,13 : 0,13)``` ```<a><a>data</a>```
NOTES	This command does not correctly handle nested regions in well-formed XML documents. See the example above for the same example using .. and see the two examples before that for a more detailed explanation of the respective behaviors of quote and ..

COMMAND	`sgrep -i -l -e '"<postcode>"_quote "</post-code>"' file.xml`
OUTPUT	`------------- #1 file.xml: 16 (320,335 : 320,335)` `12345</PostCode>`
NOTES	_quote matches from the end of the start region to end of the end region.
COMMAND	`sgrep -i -l -e '"<postcode>"quote_"</post-code>"' file.xml`
OUTPUT	`------------- #1 file.xml: 15 (310,324 : 310,324)` `<PostCode>12345`
NOTES	quote_ matches from the start of the start region to the start of the end region.
COMMAND	`sgrep -i -l -e '"<postcode>"_quote_"</post-code>"' file.xml`
OUTPUT	`------------- #1 file.xml: 5 (320,324 : 320,324)` `12345`
NOTES	_quote_ matches from the end of the start region to the start of the end region.

COMMAND	`sgrep -i -1 -e '"X" in "XML"' file.xml`

OUTPUT	`------------ #1 file.xml: 1 (2,2 : 2,2)`
	`X`
	`------------ #2 file.xml: 1 (659,659 :`
	`659,659)`
	`X`
	`------------ #3 file.xml: 1 (822,822 :`
	`822,822)`
	`X`
	`------------ #4 file.xml: 1 (849,849 :`
	`849,849)`
	`X`

NOTES	in matches the first region if it is inside the second region.

COMMAND	`sgrep -i -1 -e '"X" not in "XML"' file.xml`

OUTPUT	`------------ #1 file.xml: 1 (400,400 :`
	`400,400)`
	`x`
	`------------ #2 file.xml: 1 (415,415 :`
	`415,415)`
	`x`

NOTES	not in matches the first region if it is not inside the second region. This command matches the FAX start and end tags.

COMMAND	`sgrep -i -l -e '"456" in ("<DayTime>".."</DayTime>")' file.xml`
OUTPUT	`------------- #1 file.xml: 3 (380,382 : 380,382)` `456`
NOTES	Parentheses may be used to group region expressions. This command matches a 456 in the content of the DayTime element.
COMMAND	`sgrep -i -l -e '"XML" not in ("<"..">")' file.xml`

OUTPUT	`------------- #1 file.xml: 3 (822,824 : 822,824)`
	`XML`
	`------------- #2 file.xml: 3 (849,851 : 849,851)`
	`XML`

NOTES	This command matches XML which does not occur inside of markup. This is the basis of the PHRASE search performed in our application. Without the "not in ("<"..">")" clause we perform a RAW search–both in markup and content. The reader will note that the use of < or > characters in the element content can wreak havoc on our results. This can be avoided by the use of the character entities > and <. This is illustrated in our example below.

COMMAND

```
1.  sgrep -i -l -e '"XML" not in ("<".."">")'
file4.xml
```

file4.xml contains:

```
<a>XML < XML + 1 > XML/2</a>
```

It is not a well-formed document because '<' is an illegal character in this context.

```
2.  sgrep -i -l -e '"XML" not in ("<".."">")'
file5.xml
```

file5.xml contains:

```
<a>XML &lt; XML + 1 > XML/2</a>
```

The '<' character in the element content in file4.xml has been replaced with the < character entity. file5.xml is a well-formed document.

OUTPUT

```
1.  ------------ #1 file4.xml: 3 (3,5 :
3,5)
     XML
    ------------ #2 file4.xml: 3 (19,21 :
19,21)
     XML
2.  ------------ #1 file5.xml: 3 (3,5 :
3,5)
     XML
    ------------ #2 file5.xml: 3 (12,14 :
12,14)
     XML
    ------------ #3 file5.xml: 3 (22,24 :
22,24)
     XML
```

NOTES

In the first example the word XML between the '<' and '>' is not caught because that section is treated as a region which is excluded. In the well-formed document it is recognized.

The example should help the reader to recognize one of the reasons for checking document well-formedness before attempting to process it.

COMMAND	`sgrep -i -l -e '"XML" not in "<".."">"'` `file.xml`

OUTPUT	`-------------- #1 file.xml: 18 (2,19 : 2,19)`
	`XML version="1.0">`
	`-------------- #2 file.xml: 31 (659,689 :`
	`659,689)`
	`XMLProducts="No" General="No"/>`
	`-------------- #3 file.xml: 50 (822,871 :`
	`822,871)`
	`XML Intranet Tutorial SGML/XML '97</Venue>`
	`<Notes>`
	`-------------- #4 file.xml: 15 (849,863 :`
	`849,863)`
	`XML '97</Venue>`

NOTES	Region expressions associate from left to right. The command is interpreted as `("XML" not in "<") .. ">"` Compare this to the result from the example before last.

COMMAND	`sgrep -i -l -e '("<a>"__"</a>") in`
	`(("<a>"__"</a>") in ("<a>"__"</a>"))'`
	`file7.xml`
	
	file7 is a well-formed XML document with the following contents:
	
	`<a>That <a>This <a>X</a> This</a> That</a>`

OUTPUT	`-------------- #1 file7.xml: 1 (19,19 :`
	`19,19)`
	`X`

NOTES	This command shows how sgrep can be used to uniquely identify data within in precise structural context (nesting).

COMMAND	```sgrep -i -l -e '("<Street>"__"</Street>") containing "Big"' file.xml```
OUTPUT	```------------- #1 file.xml: 10 (242,251 : 242,251) Big Street```
NOTES	containing matches those regions on the left hand side which contain the expression on the right hand side. The element STREET containing Big is returned but not the element STREET which does not contain Big.

Warning: containing regions cannot contain themselves ("strict" containment). This means that the above query will not match

<Street>Big</Street>

Another query with the 'equal' operator must be combined with an 'or" to include exact matches. The 'equal' and 'or' operators are described in later examples. |
COMMAND	```sgrep -i -l -e '("<Street>"__"</Street>") not containing "Big"' file.xml```
OUTPUT	```------------- #1 file.xml: 16 (208,223 : 208,223) Paradise Mansion```
NOTES	The command returns the STREET element which does not contain the substring Big.

COMMAND	`sgrep -i -l -e '(">"__"<") containing "www"' file.xml`
OUTPUT	`------------- #1 file.xml: 24 (475,498 : 475,498)` `http://www.mycompany.com`
NOTES	This command matches element content without knowledge of the element name. **Caution:** This query will fail, of course, if there are '<' characters inside PCDATA. However, XML permits the '<' character in its literal form only when used as a markup delimiter. As an ordinary character within PCDATA it must be escaped either by using a numeric character reference or the string <. This query, therefore, should work on XML documents. **Caution:** Performing this query on a mixed content container (that is, subelements mixed with PCDATA inside the containing element) will result in only the PCDATA being returned. The contained tags will be stripped out.

COMMAND	`sgrep -i -e '("<".."">")' file.xml`

OUTPUT	`<?xml version="1.0"?><ContactRec>`
	`<Name><First></First><Last></Last>`
	`</Name><Company><JobTitle></JobTitle>`
	`<CompanyName></CompanyName></Company>`
	`<Address><Street></Street><Street></`
	`Street><City></City><Region>`
	`</Region><PostCode></PostCode><Country>`
	`</Country><Phone><DayTime>`
	`</DayTime><Fax></Fax></Phone>`
	`<Internet><Email></Email><Web></Web>`
	`</Internet></Address><Product SGMLEdi-`
	`tor="Yes" ActiveViews="Yes" Sympo-`
	`siaPro="Yes" SymposiaDocPlus="Yes"`
	`SGMLEditorJapanese="No" SGMLEditorKore-`
	`an="No" XMLProducts="No" General="No"/`
	`><Contacts><Language Preference="English"/`
	`><History><Events><Date><Day></`
	`Day><Month></Month><Year></Year></`
	`Date><Venue></Venue><Notes></Notes></`
	`Events></History></Contacts></ContactRec>`

NOTES	This command matches all markup in the document.

COMMAND	`sgrep -i -e '("<".."">") not containing "</` `"' file.xml`

OUTPUT	`<?xml version="1.0"?><Contac-`
	`tRec><Name><First><Last><Company>`
	`<JobTitle><CompanyName><Address>`
	`<Street><Street><City><Region><PostCode>`
	`<Country><Phone><DayTime><Fax><Internet>`
	`<Email><Web><Product SGMLEditor="Yes" Ac-`
	`tiveViews="Yes" SymposiaPro="Yes" Sympo-`
	`siaDocPlus="Yes" SGMLEditorJapanese="No"`
	`SGMLEditorKorean="No" XMLPro ducts="No"`
	`General="No"/><Contacts>`
	`<Language Preference="English"/>`
	`<History><Events><Date><Day>`
	`<Month><Year><Venue><Notes>`

NOTES	This command matches all start tags, empty elements, and the declaration.

COMMAND	`sgrep -i -e '("<".."/>")' file.xml`

OUTPUT	`<Product SGMLEditor="Yes"`
	`ActiveViews="Yes" SymposiaPro="Yes"`
	`SymposiaDocPlus="Yes"`
	`SGMLEditorJapanese="No"`
	`SGMLEditorKorean="No" XMLProducts="No"`
	`General="No"/>`
	`<Language Preference="English"/>`

NOTES	This command matches XML EMPTY tags.

COMMAND	`sgrep -i -l -e '(("<"..">") not containing`
	`"</") in (("<".."</") containing "www")'`
	`file.xml`

OUTPUT	`------------- #1 file.xml: 5 (470,474 :`
	`470,474)`
	`<Web>`

NOTES	This command matches the start tag of an element containing a particular string.

COMMAND	`sgrep -i -l -e`
	`'("SymposiaPro"..("\""..\""))  in`
	`("<Product".."/>")' file.xml`

OUTPUT	`------------ #1 file.xml: 17 (573,589 :`
	`573,589)`
	`SymposiaPro="Yes"`

NOTES	This command matches a particular attribute and its value. A more correct but complex approach would be to use 'quote' and to restrict to only those characters "" characters that occur inside tags.

COMMAND	`sgrep -i -l -e '("<Notes>".."</Notes>" con-`
	`taining "criminels") equal ("<Notes>".."</`
	`Notes>" containing "bonheur")' file.xml`
	`sgrep -i -l -e '("<Notes>".."</Notes>" con-`
	`taining "criminels") equal ("<Notes>".."</`
	`Notes>" containing "malades")' file.xml`

OUTPUT	`1. no output`
	`2. ------------ #1 file.xml: 232 (865,1096`
	`: 865,1096)`
	`<Notes>Ces messieurs concluaient contre les`
	`nouvelles theories criminalistes; avec`
	`cette belle invention de l'irresponsabilite`
	`dans certains cas pathologiques, il n'y`
	`avait plus de criminels, il n'y avait que`
	`des malades.</Notes>`

NOTES	equal returns those regions which occur in the result of the expression on the left hand side and in the result of the expression on the right hand side.

COMMAND	`sgrep -i -l -e '("<Notes>".."</Notes>" con-`
	`taining "criminels") not equal`
	`("<Notes>".."</Notes>" containing "bon-`
	`heur")' file.xml`
	`sgrep -i -l -e '("<Notes>".."</Notes>" con-`
	`taining "criminels") not equal`
	`("<Notes>".."</Notes>" containing`
	`"malades")' file.xml`

OUTPUT	`1. ------------- #1 file.xml: 232 (865,1096`
	`: 865,1096)`
	`<Notes>Ces messieurs concluaient contre les`
	`nouvelles theories criminalistes; avec`
	`cette belle invention de l'irresponsabilite`
	`dans certains cas pathologiques, il n'y`
	`avait plus de criminels, il n'y avait que`
	`des malades.</Notes>`
	`2. no output`

NOTES	not equal returns those regions which occur in the result of the expression on the left-hand side but do not occur in the result of the expression on the right- hand side.

COMMAND	`sgrep -i -l -e '(">"__"<") containing` `("http" or "@")' file.xml`

OUTPUT	`------------- #1 file.xml: 16 (445,460 :`
	`445,460)`
	`me@mycompany.com`
	`------------- #2 file.xml: 24 (475,498 :`
	`475,498)`
	`http://www.mycompany.com`

NOTES	or matches regions matching either the right- or left-hand expression or both. This command shows a search for electronic addresses, e-mail, and/or web.

COMMAND	```sgrep -i -l -e '("<Date>".."</Date>") extracting ("<Month>".."</Month>")' file.xml```
OUTPUT	```------------ #1 file.xml: 20 (754,773 : 754,773) <Date> <Day>07</Day> ------------ #2 file.xml: 23 (791,813 : 791,813) <Year>97</Year> </Date>```
NOTES	extracting returns the regions created by removing any regions on the right-hand side from the region on the left hand-side.
	At this juncture it may be helpful to remind the reader of the statement made at the beginning of this section that sgrep actually works on sets or lists of regions. The "extracting" operation takes a list of regions as input and extracts or subtracts from this list all regions meeting the criteria for the right-hand side of the extract clause.
COMMAND	```sgrep -i -l -e '("<Date>".."</Date>") extracting [(754,773) (791,813)]' file.xml```
OUTPUT	```------------ #1 file.xml: 17 (774,790 : 774,790) <Month>12</Month>```
NOTES	Here a constant list is used to extract everything from the DATE element except the MONTH.

COMMAND
```
sgrep -i -l -e 'concat([(943,949)
(950,970)])' file.xml
sgrep -i -l -e 'concat([(943,948)
(950,970)])' file.xml
sgrep -i -l -e 'concat("belle " or
" invention")' file.xml
```

OUTPUT
```
1. ------------ #1 file.xml: 28 (943,970
: 943,970)
    avec cette belle invention
2. ------------ #1 file.xml: 6 (943,948 :
943,948)
     avec
   ------------ #2 file.xml: 21 (950,970
: 950,970)
    ette belle invention
3. ------------ #1 file.xml: 15 (955,969
: 955,969)
    belle invention
```

NOTES

concat concatenates overlapping or adjacent regions. In example 1 the two constant list regions are concatenated into a single region because they are adjacent. In the second example the regions are not concatenated because they are not adjacent.

The third example show the concat operation using string regions.

COMMAND	`sgrep -i -l -e 'inner("<a>".."</a>")'`
	`file3.xml`
	
	The content of file3 is a well-formed XML document with the following contents:
	
	`<a><a>data</a></a>`

OUTPUT	`------------ #1 file3.xml: 11 (3,13 :`
	`3,13)`
	`<a>data</a>`

NOTES	inner returns those regions in its argument set which do not contain any of the regions of the argument set, i.e., where A is a region it is equivalent to A not containing A. For the above example this expression would be `("<a>".."</a>")` not containing `("<a>".."</a>")` or, more abstractly, For any sgrep express E, "inner(E)" is equivalent to "E not containing E."

COMMAND	`sgrep -i -l -e '("<a>".."</a>") extracting`
	`inner("<a>".."</a>")' file8.xml`
	
	The content of file8 is a well-formed XML document with the following contents:
	
	`<a>This<a>data</a>That</a>`

OUTPUT	`------------ #1 file8.xml: 7 (0,6 : 0,6)`
	`<a>This`
	`------------ #2 file8.xml: 8 (18,25 :`
	`18,25)`
	`That</a>`

NOTES

This command extracts the inner region of element A, returning the regions on the left and right side which it is nested in. This command illustrates the basic idea for using sgrep queries to recursively process an XML document from the "inside out."

COMMAND

```
sgrep -i -l -e 'inner(">"__"<")' file8.xml
```

The content of file8 is a well-formed XML document with the following contents:

```
<a>This<a>data</a>That</a>
```

OUTPUT

```
------------- #1 file8.xml: 4 (3,6 : 3,6)
This
------------- #2 file8.xml: 4 (10,13 :
10,13)
data
------------- #3 file8.xml: 4 (18,21 :
18,21)
That
```

NOTES

This command shows a technique for extracting all element content from an XML file using inner. This expression is equivalent to '">"__"<"' on any well-formed XML file ('<' does not occur in PCDATA).

COMMAND   sgrep -i -1 -e 'inner(">"__"<")' file9.xml

The content of file9 is a well-formed XML document
with the following contents:

```
<doc>
<a>This</a>
<b>data</b>
<c>That</c>
</doc>
```

OUTPUT   -------------- #1 file9.xml: 1 (5,5 : 5,5)

-------------- #2 file9.xml: 4 (9,12 : 9,12)
This
-------------- #3 file9.xml: 1 (17,17 :
17,17)

-------------- #4 file9.xml: 4 (21,24 :
21,24)
data
-------------- #5 file9.xml: 1 (29,29 :
29,29)

-------------- #6 file9.xml: 4 (33,36 :
33,36)
That
-------------- #7 file9.xml: 1 (41,41 :
41,41)

NOTES   The purpose of this example is to draw the reader's attention to the issue of white space (spaces, tabs, and blank lines). sgrep identifies carriage returns after the DOC, A, B, and C tags as inner content of DOC.

If the element definition for DOC is

`<!ELEMENT DOC (A,B,C)>`

we can see that white space between elements was intended only to enhance readability of the document and is not significant to the document. However, if element declaration were:

`<!ELEMENT DOC (A | B | C | #PCDATA)*>`

the carriage returns may indeed be significant since they are #PCDATA like any other character.

SGML has relatively complicated rules for the treatment of white space; an attempt was made to simplify this in XML. First, an XML processor is required to pass all white space onto the application. A validating XML processor must specifically distinguish between white space and other characters in the element content. A special attribute xml:space with either a value of default or preserve may be placed on any element to indicate, respectively, whether the default processing mode of the processor should apply or if white space must always be preserved.

COMMAND	`sgrep -i -l -e 'inner(">"__"<") extracting "\n"'' file9.xml`
	
	The content of file9 is a well-formed XML document with the following contents:
	
	`<doc>`
	`<a>This</a>`
	`<b>data</b>`
	`<c>That</c>`
	`</doc>`

OUTPUT	`------------- #1 file9.xml: 4 (9,12 : 9,12)`
	`This`
	`------------ #2 file9.xml: 4 (21,24 :`
	`21,24)`
	`data`
	`------------ #3 file9.xml: 4 (33,36 :`
	`33,36)`
	`That`

NOTES	This sgrep command matches all data inside elements but removes regions consisting of carriage returns. See the previous example for a discussion of white space and XML.

COMMAND	```sgrep -i -l -e 'outer("<a>".."</a>")' file3.xml```

The content of file3 is a well-formed XML document with the following contents:

```
<a><a>data</a></a>
```

OUTPUT	```------------- #1 file3.xml: 18 (0,17 : 0,17)``` ```<a><a>data</a></a>```

NOTES	outer matches regions which do not contain themselves, i.e., where A is a region it is equivalent to A not in A. For the above example this expression would be `("<a>".."</a>")` not in `("<a>".."</a>")`. There are two regions `("<a>".."</a>")` in file3.xml, `"<a>data</a>"` and `"<a><a>data</a></a>"`. Only the second is matched as it is not contained by an A element.

COMMAND

```
sgrep -i -l -e 'join(1,"<a>".."</a>")'
filea.xml
sgrep -i -l -e 'join(2,"<a>".."</a>")'
filea.xml
sgrep -i -l -e 'join(3,"<a>".."</a>")'
filea.xml
sgrep -i -l -e 'join(4,"<a>".."</a>")'
filea.xml
```

The content of filea is a well-formed XML
document with the following contents:
```
<a>1</a>
<a>2</a>
<a>3</a>
```

OUTPUT

```
1.  ------------ #1 filea.xml: 8 (0,7 :
0,7)
    <a>1</a>
    ------------ #2 filea.xml: 8 (9,16 :
9,16)
    <a>2</a>
    ------------ #3 filea.xml: 8 (18,25 :
18,25)
    <a>3</a>
2.  ------------ #1 filea.xml: 17 (0,16 :
0,16)
    <a>1</a>
    <a>2</a>
    ------------ #2 filea.xml: 17 (9,25 :
9,25)
    <a>2</a>
    <a>3</a>
3.  ------------ #1 filea.xml: 26 (0,25 :
0,25)
    <a>1</a>
    <a>2</a>
    <a>3</a>
4.  no output
```

NOTES

join concatenates regions matching the second argument returning region sets which contain the number of regions given in the first argument. filea has the following concatenations of element A possible (the elements content is used to identify the instance and the number of elements concatenated together are shown in parentheses following the regions set): 1 (1), 2 (1), 3 (1), 12 (2), 23 (2), 123 (3). The first query returns the 3 sets of size 1, query 2 returns the 2 sets of size 2, query 3 returns the 1 set of size 3, and query 4 doesn't return anything because there are no sets of size 4.

See the example following the next example to see how to use join to express nearness conditions.

COMMAND	`sgrep -i -l -e chars file.xml`

OUTPUT	`------------- #1 file.xml: 1 (0,0 : 0,0)`
	`<`
	`------------- #2 file.xml: 1 (1,1 : 1,1)`
	`!`
	`... each character in the document is list-`
	`ed`

NOTES	This command will simply return each character in the file or each entire file if no output parameter is provided.

COMMAND	`sgrep -i -l -e '(">"__"<") containing`
	`((join(40,chars) containing "malade")`
	`containing "criminel")' file.xml`
	`sgrep -i -l -e '(">"__"<") containing`
	`((join(38,chars) containing "malade")`
	`containing "criminel")' file.xml`

OUTPUT	`1. ------------- #1 file.xml: 217 (872,1088`
	`: 872,1088)`
	`Ces messieurs concluaient contre`
	`les nouvelles theories  criminalistes;`
	`avec cette belle invention`
	`de l'irresponsabilite dans certains cas`
	`pathologiques, il n'y avait plus de`
	`criminels, il n'y avait que des malades.`
	`2. no output`

NOTES	A join on chars simply returns all sequences of characters of the specified length. The (join(40,chars)) containing "malade" returns those sequences that contain the word malade and the outer containing further reduces that set to those also containing the word criminel. The element content containing these regions is ultimately returned by the outermost containing region. This sgrep command returns elements where the word malade is within a proximity of 40 characters to the word criminel.
	The second example does not return any output because the malade is not within 38 characters of criminel.
	Proximity searches are used to improve relevance as a certain set of words can usually be identified which should be close to each other in a document on a subject with a distinct vocabulary.

COMMAND	```sgrep -i -l -e start *.xml```

OUTPUT	```------------- #1 file.xml: 1 (0,0 : 0,0)```
	 ```<```
	 ```------------- #2 file2.xml: 1 (1145,1145 :```
	 ```0,0)```
	 ```<```

NOTES	This command matches on the first character of each file.

COMMAND	`sgrep -i -l -e end *.xml`

OUTPUT	`------------ #1 file.xml: 1 (1144,1144 : 1144,1144)`
	
	`------------ #2 file2.xml: 1 (2289,2289 : 1144,1144)`

NOTES	This command matches on the last character of each file.

COMMAND	`sgrep -a -o "[[[%r]]]" -e '"This" or "That"' file8.xml`
	
	The content of file8 is a well-formed XML document with the following contents:
	
	`<a>This<a>data</a>That</a>`

OUTPUT	`<a>[[[This]]]<a>data</a>[[[That]]]</a>`
NOTES	-a parameter outputs matching regions formatted as requested with text interleaved.
COMMAND	`sgrep -C`
OUTPUT	`sgrep version 0.99 - search a file for structured pattern` `. . .`
NOTES	-C displays the copyright notice.

COMMAND	`sgrep -c -e '("<".."<">") not containing` `"<!"' file.xml`
OUTPUT	60
NOTES	-c parameter displays the count of the regions that match the express. No other output is displayed. This command counts all the tags in the document, excluding the XML declaration.

COMMAND	`sgrep -d -e '("<Month>".."</Month>")`
	`or("<Date>"__"</Date>")' file.xml`
	`sgrep -e '("<Month>".."</Month>")`
	`or("<Date>"__"</Date>")' file.xml`

OUTPUT	1.
	    `<Day>07</Day><Month>12</`
	`Month><Year>97</Year>`
	    `<Month>12</Month>`
	2.
	    `<Day>07</Day><Month>12</`
	`Month><Year>97</Year>`

NOTES	-d parameter causes matching regions to be displayed without merging nested or overlapping regions. In the first example both the region inside of the DATE element and the MONTH element region are displayed even though the MONTH element is contained in the DATE region. In the second example the -d parameter is not used and only the DATE element region is displayed. The -d parameter is always in effect if an output format is specified either through the -l long form or -O an -o output format expression whether or not it is requested in the command.

COMMAND	`sgrep -h`

OUTPUT	`Usage: sgrep <options> 'region expression'`
	`[<files...>]`
	`...`

NOTES	Displays help information.

COMMAND	`sgrep -N -e '"<Venue>".."</Venue>"'` `file.xml`
OUTPUT	`<Venue>XML Intranet Tutorial SGML/XML '97</` `Venue>`
NOTES	-N parameter overrides the default of adding a carriage return to the end of the output. A newline is not added after the last output region when -N is used.

COMMAND	`sgrep -n -p m4 -f sgml_macros -l -e`
	`'D6_ELEMS' file.xml`
	
	`sgml_macros is a macro file with the fol-`
	`lowing contents (these macros were written`
	`by the creators of sgrep, Jani Jaakkola and`
	`Pekka Kilpeläinen):`
	
	`define(ETAGO, "</" )`
	`define(MDO, "<!" )`
	`define(PIO, "<?" )`
	`define(STAGO, ("<" not in (ETAGO or MDO or`
	`PIO)) )`
	`define(TAGC, ">" )`
	`define(STAG, inner(STAGO .. TAGC) )`
	`define(ETAG, inner(ETAGO .. TAGC) )`
	`define(ELEMS,(STAG .. ETAG) )`
	`define(D1_ELEMS, outer(ELEMS) )`
	`define(D2_ELEMS, outer(ELEMS in D1_ELEMS) )`
	`define(D3_ELEMS, outer(ELEMS in D2_ELEMS) )`
	`define(D4_ELEMS, outer(ELEMS in D3_ELEMS) )`
	`define(D5_ELEMS, outer(ELEMS in D4_ELEMS) )`
	`define(D6_ELEMS, outer(ELEMS in D5_ELEMS) )`

OUTPUT

```
------------- #1 file.xml: 13 (761,773 :
761,773)
<Day>07</Day>
------------- #2 file.xml: 17 (774,790 :
774,790)
<Month>12</Month>
------------- #3 file.xml: 15 (791,805 :
791,805)
<Year>97</Year>
```

NOTES

-p parameter specifies a preprocessor to be applied to the region expression before sgrep evaluates it. In this example m4 is specified as the preprocessor and the -f parameter is used to specify a file of macros which will be used by m4 in preprocessing the file. m4, in fact, is used by default.

The example matches regions which are at nested 6 levels deep. All macros needed to expand the expression D6_ELEMS are shown. The basic idea is to take the outer of a match on elements 6 times until those elements nested this deeply have been completely unpeeled.

sgrep reads $HOME/.sgreprc or /usr/lib/sgreprc at start-up. These files may contain macros. -n parameter instructs sgrep not to read these files.

| *COMMAND* | ```
sgrep -P -p m4 -f sgml_macros -1 -e
'D6_ELEMS' file.xml
``` |
| *OUTPUT* | ```
outer((inner(("<" not in ("</"  or "<!"  or
"<?" ))  .. ">" )  .. inner("</"  .. ">" )
)  in outer((inner(("<" not in ("</"  or
"<!"  or "<?" ))  .. ">" )  .. inner("</"
.. ">" ) )  in outer((inner(("<" not in ("</
"  or "<!"  or "<?" ))  .. ">" )  .. in-
ner("</"  .. ">" ) )  in outer((inner(("<"
not in ("</"  or "<!" or "<?" ))  .. ">" )
.. inner("</"  .. ">" ) )  in outer((in-
ner(("<" not in ("</"  or "<!"  or "<?" ))
.. ">" )  .. inner("</"  .. ">" ) )  in out-
er((inner(("<" not in ("</"  or "<!"  or
"<?" ))  .. ">" )  .. inner("</"  .. ">" )
) ) ) ) ) ) )
``` |
| *NOTES* | -P parameter displays the preprocessed region expression without executing it. This example shows the expanded expression from the previous example using m4 macro expressions. |
| *COMMAND* | ```
sgrep -e '"<a>".."</a>"' filef.xml
fileg.xml
sgrep -S -e '"<a>".."</a>"' filef.xml
fileg.xml
```<br><br>filef.xml contains:<br><br>`<a>Here`<br><br>fileg.xml contains:<br><br>`There</a>` |
| *OUTPUT* | 1. no output
2. `<a>Here There</a>` |
```

NOTES	-S parameter causes sgrep to treat multiple input files as a continuous stream enabling matching across files. The first example is an sgrep expression without the -S parameter which does not match any region in the two input files. The second example does use the -S parameter and matches the region for element A which has the start tag in the first file and the end tag in the second file.
COMMAND	```sgrep -s -e '"<Language".."/>"' file.xml```
OUTPUT	```<Language Preference="English"/>```
NOTES	-s parameter causes the short form output format to be used: the text of the output region output without additional formatting and overlapping parts of regions are displayed only once. This is the default so the output will be the same in the absence of any formatting parameter.
COMMAND	```sgrep -t -e '"<Language".."/>"' file.xml```
OUTPUT	
NOTES	-t parameter displays statistics about time usage.

```
<Language Preference="English"/>
sgrep time usage       usr     sys    total
   parsing            0.00s   0.01s   0.01s
   acsearch           0.01s   0.00s   0.01s
   evaluating         0.00s   0.00s   0.00s
   output             0.00s   0.01s   0.01s
-------------------------------------------
 -
   total              0.01s   0.02s   0.03s

   preprocessor       0.12s   0.05s   0.17s
```

COMMAND	`sgrep -T -e '"<Language".."/>"' file.xml`
| OUTPUT | ```
<Language Preference="English"/>
Scanned 1 files, having total of 1K size
finding 3 phrases.
Operator tree size was 3, optimized 3
Output list size was 1 region.
Operations:
        containing:0        in:0    order:1
or:0      extracting:0    quote:0
 not containing:0    not in:0    inner:0    out-
er:0            concat:1    join:0
        equal:0    not equal:0
Memory:
 25K memory allocated, 0 realloc operations
 7 gc lists, 6 gc lists allocated
 7 gc blocks used, 5 gc blocks allocated.
 Longest list size was 2 regions.
 8K nest stack size, 0K inner tablesize
Things done:
 7 regions created, 8 gc lists scanned, 18
regions scanned
 0 sorts by start point, 0 sorts by end
point
 2 sorts optimized
``` |
| NOTES | -T parameter displays statistics about the execution of the program. |

COMMAND	`sgrep -V -e '"<Language".."/>"' file.xml`
OUTPUT	`sgrep version 0.99 compiled at May  5 1996`
NOTES	-V parameter displays program version information.
```

7.2.1 *A Web Interface to sgrep*

Three forms were developed to provide a Web-based user interface to sgrep. These forms were shown at the beginning of this chaper. Two are application-specific and the third provides a general-purpose interface. All three forms invoke the same CGI program. The markup of the three forms is shown in Figure 7–19.

```
<!DOCTYPE HTML PUBLIC "-//W3C/DTD HTML 3.2 Final//EN">
<HTML><HEAD><TITLE>SEARCH THE BULLETIN BOARD</TITLE></HEAD>
<BODY><BODYTEXT><H1>SEARCH THE BULLETIN BOARD</H1>
<FORM
ACTION="http://www.textscience.com/cgi-bin/queryx.pl"
METHOD="POST"><hr>
<INPUT TYPE="HIDDEN" NAME="INTERFACE" VALUE="BOARD">
<INPUT TYPE="HIDDEN" NAME="library" VALUE="board">
<INPUT TYPE="HIDDEN" NAME="region" VALUE="embedded">
<table border=2><tr><td>Search</b><br><b>in </b>
<select name="element1" size="2">
<option value="body" selected>Message Body</option>
<option value="author">Author</option>
<option value="subject">Subject</option>
</select><b> containing </b>
<input type="text" name="contain1" size="30"
maxlength="100"><br><b>in </b>
<select name="element2" size="2">
<option value="body" selected>Message Body</option>
<option value="author">Author</option>
<option value="subject">Subject</option>
</select><b> containing </b>
<input type="text" name="contain2" size="30"
maxlength="100"><br><b>in </b>
<select name="element3" size="2">
<option value="body" selected>Message Body</option>
<option value="author">Author</option>
<option value="subject">Subject</option></select>
<b> containing </b>
<input type="text" name="contain3" size="30"
maxlength="100"><td></tr></table>
```

Figure 7–19 Bulletin Board Form

```
<hr><center><INPUT TYPE="SUBMIT" VALUE="Search Now">
<INPUT TYPE="RESET" VALUE="Clear"></center><hr></FORM>
<hr><table width=\"100%\"><tr>
<td><A HREF="http://www.textscience.com/
qbboard.html">Query BBoard</A></td>
<td><A HREF="http://www.textscience.com/qcon-
tact.html">Query Contact</A></td>
<td><A HREF="http://www.textscience.com/qadhoc.html">Ad-
Hoc Query</A></td>
</tr></table></bodytext></body></html>
```

Figure 7–19 Bulletin Board Form (*continued*)

Three pieces of critical information will be passed to the CGI program queryx.pl:

- the type of interface which should be presented to the user (INTERFACE)
- the library (in effect, the subdirectory) to search (LIBRARY)
- the type of search to perform (REGION)

Four types of searches are supported:

- PHRASE text inside of markup
- EMBEDDED any sgrep region expression
- TITLE HTML specific, uses region expressions to search in HTML TITLE and H1, H2, and so on, elements.
- RAW text search with no special treatment of markup

The bulletin board form uses hidden input to set the INTERFACE, LIBRARY, and REGION to "board," "board," and "embedded," respectively. The query-form user is able to specify searches within several elements supported by bulletin board record format: BODY, AUTHOR, and SUBJECT and to specify a search string in an adjacent text input field. Up to three element-specific searches can be specified with the form sending the value of the element selected and the associated string to search for in the CGI variables (element1, contain1), (element2, contain2), and (element3, contain3). If more than one element-specific search is requested, the searches will be combined with an OR operator. The value '*' can be entered in the field for the search string to indicate that the program should return matches on any element of this type regardless of content. Note that this is not a real wild-card operator as it cannot be used within substrings. We will see how '*' is implemented when we examine the CGI program itself.

```
<!DOCTYPE HTML PUBLIC "-//W3C/DTD HTML 3.2 Final//EN">
<HTML>
<HEAD><TITLE>SEARCH THE CONTACT DATABASE</TITLE></HEAD>
<BODY><BODYTEXT><H1>SEARCH THE CONTACT DATABASE</H1>
<FORM
ACTION="http://www.textscience.com/cgi-bin/queryx.pl"
METHOD="POST"><hr>
<INPUT TYPE="HIDDEN" NAME="INTERFACE" VALUE="CONTACT">
<INPUT TYPE="HIDDEN" NAME="library" VALUE="contact">
<INPUT TYPE="HIDDEN" NAME="region" VALUE="embedded">
<table border=2><tr><td><b>Search</b><br><b>in </b>
<select name="element1" size="2">
<option value="name" selected>Name</option>
<option value="company">Company</option>
<option value="state">State</option>
<option value="country">Country</option>
<option value="venue">Venue</option>
<option value="notes">Notes</option>
<option value="month">Month</option>
<option value="year">Year</option>
</select><b> containing </b>
<input type="text" name="contain1" size="20"
maxlength="100"><br><b>in </b>
<select name="element2" size="2">
<option value="name" selected>Name</option>
<option value="company">Company</option>
<option value="state">State</option>
<option value="country">Country</option>
<option value="venue">Venue</option>
<option value="notes">Notes</option>
<option value="month">Month</option>
<option value="year">Year</option>
</select><b> containing </b>
```

Figure 7-20   Contact Database Form

```
<input type="text" name="contain2" size="20"
maxlength="100"><br><b>in </b>
<select name="element3" size="2">
<option value="name" selected>Name</option>
<option value="company">Company</option>
<option value="state">State</option>
<option value="country">Country</option>
<option value="venue">Venue</option>
<option value="notes">Notes</option>
<option value="month">Month</option>
<option value="year">Year</option>
</select><b> containing </b>
<input type="text" name="contain3" size="20"
maxlength="100"><br><b>in </b>
<select name="element4" size="2">
<option value="name" selected>Name</option>
<option value="company">Company</option>
<option value="state">State</option>
<option value="country">Country</option>
<option value="venue">Venue</option>
<option value="notes">Notes</option>
<option value="month">Month</option>
<option value="year">Year</option>
</select><b> containing </b>
<input type="text" name="contain4" size="20"
maxlength="100"></td>
<td><b>Find all companies with interest in the following
products:</b><br>
<input type="checkbox" name="ed" value="checked">SGML
Editor<br>
<input type="checkbox" name="av" value="checked">
ActiveViews<br>
<input type="checkbox" name="sp" value="checked">Symposia
Pro<br>
<input type="checkbox" name="sdp" value="checked">Symposia
Doc+<br>
<input type="checkbox" name="jed" value="checked">Japanese
SGML Editor<br>
<input type="checkbox" name="ked" value="checked">Korean
SGML Editor<br>
<input type="checkbox" name="xml" value="checked">XML
Products<br>
```

Figure 7–20 Contact Database Form *(continued)*

```
<input type="checkbox" name="general" value="checked">
General</td>
</tr></table>
<hr><center>
<INPUT TYPE="SUBMIT" VALUE="Search Now">
<INPUT TYPE="RESET" VALUE="Clear"></center>
</FORM>
<hr><table width=\"100%\"><tr>
<td><A HREF="http://www.textscience.com/
qbboard.html">Query BBoard</A></td>
<td><A HREF="http://www.textscience.com/qcon-
tact.html">Query Contact</A></td>
<td><A HREF="http://www.textscience.com/qadhoc.html">Ad-
Hoc Query</A></td>
</tr></table></bodytext></body></html>
```

Figure 7–20 Contact Database Form *(continued)*

The Contact database form listed in Figure 7–20 passes the values of INTERFACE, LIBRARY, and REGION (contact, contact, and embedded, respectively) to the CGI program through the use of hidden input fields, as the bulletin board form did. The DTD for the contact database records is much bigger than the bulletin board's so we provide up to four element/string pairs which are passed to the CGI application using the variables (element1, contain1), (element2, contain2), (element3, contain3), and (element4, contain4). The element types supported are NAME, COMPANY, STATE, COUNTRY, VENUE, NOTES, MONTH. Not all possible element types are supported; just those deemed important to users of this interface. As with the bulletin board, multiple element searches will be combined with an OR and the value '*' may be used to return any occurrence of a particular element. This interface also allows the user to match based on the attribute values coded in the PRODUCT element. Each attribute may have a value of yes or no. The user of the query form may indicate that he or she wants records returned which have yes values for any of the PRODUCT attributes by checking the checkbox next to the attribute name. Unique CGI variables are used for each PRODUCT attribute. PRODUCT attribute searches are combined with element content searches using the OR operator.

```
<!DOCTYPE HTML PUBLIC "-//W3C/DTD HTML 3.2 Final//EN">
<HTML><HEAD>
<TITLE>
sgrep GENERAL QUERY PANEL - SEARCH XML OR HTML</TITLE>
</HEAD><BODY><BODYTEXT>
<H1>sgrep GENERAL QUERY PANEL - SEARCH XML OR HTML</H1>
<H2>Enter a Search String or Region Expression:</H2>
<FORM
ACTION="http://www.textscience.com/cgi-bin/queryx.pl"
METHOD="POST">
<INPUT TYPE="HIDDEN" NAME="INTERFACE" VALUE="GENERAL">
<TABLE BORDER="BORDER">
<TR><TD><center><INPUT TYPE="SUBMIT" VALUE="Search Now">
<INPUT TYPE="RESET" VALUE="Clear"></center></TD>
<TD><textarea name="sstring" rows="4" cols="40">
</textarea>
</TD></TR>
<TR><TD><b>Do </b><select name="region" size=2>
<option value="phrase" selected>Simple phrase</option>
<option value="embedded">Region expression </option>
<option value="title">HTML title or H*</option>
<option value="raw">Raw</option>
</select><b> in </b></TD>
<td><select name="library" size=2>
<option value="html" selected>Web Pages</option>
<option value="board">Bulletin Board</option>
<option value="contact">Contact Repository</option>
<option value="other">Enter Repository Name -&gt;</option>
</select><input type="text" name="repository"></td>
</tr></TABLE>
</FORM>
<h2>Instructions</h2>
...
```

Figure 7–21   General Query Form

The general query form shown in Figure 7–21 requires that the user enter a valid sgrep expression which is passed to the CGI program in the variable SSTRING. The search type REGION is not preset as in the previous two forms but is explicitly selected by the user from among the four possibilities mentioned earlier. The INTERFACE CGI variable is hidden with a fixed value of general. The user may also select the LIBRARY: a select list provides the choices html, board, contact, and others. The CGI application will know where to find html, board, and contact repositories but in the case of the others the user is expected to provide an actual path which will be passed to the sgrep application through the CGI variable REPOSITORY.

Our general query interface and many others, including most everything currently on the Web, do not lack room for improvement. Among the possibilities,

- ability to browse and create storied queries and macros
- help for forming syntactically correct queries

In fact, Jaakkola and Kilpeläinen did create an X-windows tcl/tk application Sgtool, which purports to do just these two things. Looking at adapting their concepts to an Internet environment is on our own to-do list (along with many other things, sigh). An XML-specific query interface raises some other interesting possibilities. The query users are probably limited in their ability to query based on structure and property. They may not know the structures and properties of a given set of data or they simply may not remember the myriad details of particular sets of data or they may not even know what structures and properties are! Therefore we add to the wish list

- ability to explore structure of the data within the query interface and to use data models in query formation

Let's take a look at the CGI program which actually generates queries and returns a result list, queryx.pl.

Here is an outline of processing performed by the first section of the program followed by the code listing:

- Sets up variables for
  - files local to the server
  - returning the query form with the last query parameters to enable modification of the query
  - locating the search directory
- Prints the first part of the CGI response: a new query form for issuing subsequent queries if desired, using the interface specified in the INTERFACE CGI variable and with the last query parameters set
- Constructs the sgrep query expression

```perl
#!/usr/bin/perl
############################################################
#
# queryx.pl - CGI program for executing sgrep queries    #
#                                                         #
# INPUT (via POST METHOD)                                 #
#   sstring    : query (embedded only)                    #
#   region     : type of search                           #
#   library    : where to search                          #
#   INTERFACE : type of interface to return               #
#   element1,element2,element3,element4 : element         #
#     regions (board or contact only)                     #
#   contact1,contact2,contact3,contact4 : strings to      #
#     search for inside element regions above (board      #
#     or contact only)                                    #
#   ed,av,sp,sdp,jed,ked,xml,general : attributes for     #
#     PRODUCT element (contact only)                       #
#                                                         #
# OUTPUT                                                   #
#   RESULTS LIST FROM SEARCH                               #
#   Query Interface as requested in INTERFACE             #
```

Figure 7–22   Generating Queries, queryx.pl

```
#                                                          #
# Copyright Matthew Fuchs, Michael Leventhal, and David   #
# Lewis, published in Designing Internet XML              #
# Applications, Prentice-Hall, 1998.  Permission for      #
# unrestricted use as long as the authors are credited.   #
###########################################################
###############
# Set up stuff #
###############
# unset record separator (default newline).
undef($/);
# set server specific locations
$cgipath           = "http://www.textscience.com";
$webpath           = "/aimweb/homets/";
$boardpath         = "/aimweb/homets/cgi-bin/blackboard/";
$sgmlpath          = "/aimweb/homets/sgmlclass/";
$sgrep             = "/aimweb/homets/cgi-bin/sgrep";
# return header and HTML file no matter what happens
print &PrintHeader;
print
"<!DOCTYPE HTML PUBLIC \"-//IETF//DTD HTML 3.0//EN//\">";
# read in all the CGI variables into the $in array.
&ReadParse;
# set working variables for CGI input array
  # $searchfor will be null except for general query
$searchfor = $in{"sstring"};
  # type of search (phrase,embedded,title,raw)
$region    = $in{"region"};
  # where to search
$library   = $in{"library"};
  # which interface to return
$interface = $in{"INTERFACE"};
# set values that will used when in the form returned so
# that current values can be rewritten on output allowing
# user to refine the query
if    ($region eq "phrase")   { $phrase_sel =
"SELECTED";   }
elsif ($region eq "embedded") { $embedded_sel =
"SELECTED";}
elsif ($region eq "title")    { $title_sel = "SELECTED";   }
elsif ($region eq "raw")      { $raw_sel = "SELECTED";     }
```

Figure 7–22 Generating Queries, queryx.pl *(continued)*

```perl
# for location of search (library) set $searchfile - where
# to search, and $anchor - retrieval cgi to be executed
from
# results use by user, and current values of library for
# form to be returned
if ($library eq "html")
{
  $searchfile = $webpath."*.htm*";
  $anchor     = "";
  $html_sel   = "SELECTED";
}
elsif ($library eq "board")
{
  $searchfile = $boardpath."*.*";
  $anchor     = "cgi-bin/transrec.pl/";
  $board_sel  = "SELECTED";
}
elsif ($library eq "contact")
{
  $searchfile = $sgmlpath."*.xml";
  $anchor     = "cgi-bin/transcon.pl/";
  $contact_sel = "SELECTED";
}
elsif ($library eq "other")
{
  $searchfile = $in{"repository"}."/*.*";
  $anchor     = "";
  $other_sel  = "SELECTED";
}
else
{
  print "<p>Unrecognized library.</p>";
}
# set location of some temporary files we'll need
$outfile1 = $webpath."temp1/out1";
$outfile2 = $webpath."temp1/out2";
$outfile  = $webpath."temp1/out3";
# return requested interface with new query form
# containing current values and compose the sgrep
# search expression
if ($interface eq "GENERAL") {
  &PrintGeneral; }
```

Figure 7-22 Generating Queries, queryx.pl *(continued)*

```
elsif ($interface eq "BOARD") {
  &WriteBoardSearchfor;
  &PrintBoard; }
elsif ($interface eq "CONTACT") {
  &WriteContactSearchfor;
  &PrintContact; }
else {
  print "<p>Unrecognized interface type.</p>" }
```

Figure 7–22 Generating Queries, queryx.pl *(continued)*

Let's look at the subroutines invoked so far (Figures 7–23 thru 7–29):

```
# PrintHeader - Returns the magic line which tells
# WWW that we're an HTML document
sub PrintHeader {
  return "Content-type: text/html\n\n";
}
```

Figure 7–23   PrintHeader Subroutine

```
# ReadParse
Listed in Chapter 7
```

Figure 7–24   ReadParse Subroutine

```
# PrintGeneral
# Prints Query form for General Query Interface
sub PrintGeneral {
# $printsearch echos the full sgrep query
# must HTMLify it for correct display using
# entities for angle bracket and quotes
$printsearch = $searchfor;
$printsearch =~ s/"/&quot;/g;
$printsearch =~ s/</&lt;/g;
print "<HTML>
```

Figure 7–25   PrintGeneral Subroutine

```
<HEAD>
<TITLE>
sgrep GENERAL QUERY RESULTS LIST - SEARCH XML OR HTML
</TITLE>
</HEAD><BODY>
<BODYTEXT>
<H1>
sgrep GENERAL QUERY RESULTS LIST - SEARCH XML OR HTML
</H1><H2>
Enter a Search String or Region Expression:
</H2>
<FORM ACTION=\"$cgipath/cgi-bin/queryx.pl\"
METHOD=\"POST\">
<INPUT TYPE=\"HIDDEN\" NAME=\"INTERFACE\" VALUE=\
"GENERAL\">
<TABLE BORDER=\"BORDER\">
<TR><TD><center><INPUT TYPE=\"SUBMIT\" VALUE=\"Search
Now\">
<INPUT TYPE=\"RESET\" VALUE=\"Clear\"></center></TD>
<TD><textarea name=\"sstring\" rows=\"4\"
cols=\"40\">$searchfor</textarea></TD></TR>
<TR><TD><b>Do </b><select name=\"region\" size=2>
<option value=\"phrase\" $phrase_sel>Simple phrase</option>
<option value=\"embedded\" $embedded_sel>Region expression
</option>
<option value=\"title\" $title_sel>HTML title or H*</
option>
<option value=\"raw\" $raw_sel>Raw</option>
</select><b> in </b></TD>
<td><select name=\"library\" size=2>
<option value=\"html\" $html_sel>Web Pages</option>
<option value=\"board\" $board_sel>Bulletin Board</option>
<option value=\"contact\" $contact_sel>Contact Repository</
option>
<option value=\"other\" $other_sel>Enter Repository Name -
&gt;</option>
</select><input type=\"text\" name=\"repository\"></td>
</tr></TABLE>
</FORM>
<h2>Results List</h2>
<p>The following files match the query <i>$printsearch</
i></p>"; }
```

Figure 7-25 PrintGeneral Subroutine *(continued)*

WriteBoardSearchfor and WriteContactSearchfor will test to see which variables have values from the input form and set up a query expression accordingly.

```
# WriteBoardSearchfor
# write the sgrep expression for the bulletin board
# the bboard uses element1-3 and contain1-3 variables
sub WriteBoardSearchfor {
# $previous is a flag which tells us if we need an OR
# preceding
  $previous = 0;
# process if any value has been put in the input text area
#    i.e., contain1,2 or 3 isn't null
# searchfor is a simple Start Tag__Eng Tag containing
string
#    unless contains is '*' in which case we have no con-
tains
#    clause causing all to be elements to be returned
  if ($in{"contain1"} ne "") {
    $gi = $in{"element1"};
    $sel1{"$gi"} = "selected";
    if ($in{"contain1"} eq "*") {
      $searchfor = "(\"<$gi>\"__\"</$gi>\")"; }
    else {
      $searchfor = "((\"<$gi>\"__\"</$gi>\" containing
\"$in{'contain1'}\") or (\"<$gi>\"__\"</$gi>\" equal
\"$in{'contain1'}\"))"; }
    $previous = 1;
  }
  if ($in{"contain2"} ne "") {
    $gi = $in{"element2"};
    $sel2{"$gi"} = "selected";
    if ($previous) { $searchfor .= " or "; }
    if ($in{"contain2"} eq "*") {
      $searchfor .= "(\"<$gi>\"__\"</$gi>\")"; }
    else {
    $searchfor .= "((\"<$gi>\"__\"</$gi>\" containing
\"$in{'contain2'}\") or (\"<$gi>\"__\"</$gi>\" equal
\"$in{'contain2'}\"))"; }
    $previous = 1;
  }
```

Figure 7–26 WriteBoardSearchfor Subroutine

```
  if ($in{"contain3"} ne "") {
    $gi = $in{"element3"};
    $sel3{"$gi"} = "selected";
    if ($previous) { $searchfor .= " or "; }
    if ($in{"contain3"} eq "*") {
      $searchfor .= "(\"<$gi>\"__\"</$gi>\")"; }
    else {
      $searchfor .= "((\"<$gi>\"__\"</$gi>\" containing
\"$in{'contain3'}\") or (\"<$gi>\"__\"</$gi>\" equal
\"$in{'contain3'}\"))"; }
    $previous = 1;
  }
}
```

Figure 7–26 WriteBoardSearchfor Subroutine *(continued)*

The contact database includes checking for records with attributes set in the PRODUCT empty tag. We arbitrarily decided to return the company name in the match field and our query is consequently somewhat complex as we must extract the COMPANYNAME element out the CONTACTREC containing PRODUCT with the desired attribute set.

```
# WriteContactSearchfor
# write the sgrep expression for the contact database
# the contact database uses element1-4 and contain1-4
# variables
sub WriteContactSearchfor {
# $previous is a flag which tells us if we need an OR
# preceding
  $previous = 0;
# process if any value has been put in the input text area
#   i.e., contain1,2,3 or 4 isn't null
# searchfor is a simple Start Tag__Eng Tag containing string
#   unless contains is '*' in which case we have no contains
#   clause causing all to be elements to be returned
  if ($in{"contain1"} ne "") {
    $gi = $in{"element1"};
    $sel1{"$gi"} = "selected";
```

Figure 7–27 WriteContactSearchfor Subroutine

```
      if ($in{"contain1"} eq "*") {
    $searchfor = "(\"<$gi>\"__\"</$gi>\")"; }
  else {
    $searchfor = "((\"<$gi>\"__\"</$gi>\" containing
\"$in{'contain1'}\") or (\"<$gi>\"__\"</$gi>\" equal
\"$in{'contain1'}\"))"; }
  $previous = 1;
}
if ($in{"contain2"} ne "") {
  $gi = $in{"element2"};
  $sel2{"$gi"} = "selected";
  if ($previous) { $searchfor .= " or "; }
  if ($in{"contain2"} eq "*") {
    $searchfor .= "(\"<$gi>\"__\"</$gi>\")"; }
  else {
    $searchfor .= "((\"<$gi>\"__\"</$gi>\" containing
\"$in{'contain2'}\") or (\"<$gi>\"__\"</$gi>\" equal
\"$in{'contain1'}\"))"; }
  $previous = 1;
}
if ($in{"contain3"} ne "") {
  $gi = $in{"element3"};
  $sel3{"$gi"} = "selected";
  if ($previous) { $searchfor .= " or "; }
  if ($in{"contain3"} eq "*") {
    $searchfor .= "((\"<$gi>\"__\"</$gi>\")"; }
  else {
      $searchfor .= "(\"<$gi>\"__\"</$gi>\" containing
\"$in{'contain3'}\") or (\"<$gi>\"__\"</$gi>\" equal
\"$in{'contain3'}\"))"; }
  $previous = 1;
}
if ($in{"contain4"} ne "") {
  $gi = $in{"element4"};
  $sel4{"$gi"} = "selected";
  if ($previous) { $searchfor .= " or "; }
  if ($in{"contain4"} eq "*") {
    $searchfor .= "(\"<$gi>\"__\"</$gi>\")"; }
  else {
    $searchfor .= "((\"<$gi>\"__\"</$gi>\" containing
\"$in{'contain4'}\") or (\"<$gi>\"__\"</$gi>\" equal
```

Figure 7–27 WriteContactSearchfor Subroutine *(continued)*

```
\"$in{'contain4'}\"))";  }
   $previous = 1;
  }
# Query for on attributes in PRODUCT element.  If
# attribute is checked simply search in Product element
# for attributename="yes" BUT we want to return the
# company name in the match field so query is companyname
# in contractrec containing the desired attribute
  if ($in{"ed"} eq "checked") {
    $checked{"ed"} = "checked";
    if ($previous) { $searchfor .= " or "; }
    $searchfor .= "((\"<companyname>\"__\"
</companyname>\") in ((\"<contactrec>\"..\"
</contactrec>\") containing (\"<Product\" __ \"/>\"
containing \"SGMLEditor=\\\"Yes\\\"\")))";
    $previous = 1;
  }
  if ($in{"av"} eq "checked") {
    $checked{"av"} = "checked";
    if ($previous) { $searchfor .= " or "; }
    $searchfor .= "((\"<companyname>\"__\"
</companyname>\") in ((\"<contactrec>\"..\"
</contactrec>\") containing (\"<Product\" __ \"/>\"
containing \"ActiveViews=\\\"Yes\\\"\")))";
    $previous = 1;
  }
  if ($in{"sp"} eq "checked") {
    $checked{"sp"} = "checked";
    if ($previous) { $searchfor .= " or "; }
    $searchfor .= "((\"<companyname>\"__\"
</companyname>\") in ((\"<contactrec>\"..\"
</contactrec>\") containing (\"<Product\" __ \"/>\"
containing \"SymposiaPro=\\\"Yes\\\"\")))";
    $previous = 1;
  }
  if ($in{"sdp"} eq "checked") {
    $checked{"sdp"} = "checked";
    if ($previous) { $searchfor .= " or "; }
$searchfor .= "((\"<companyname>\"__\"</companyname>\") in
((\"<contactrec>\"..\"</contactrec>\") containing
(\"<Product\" __ \"/>\" containing
\"SymposiaDocPlus=\\\"Yes\\\"\")))";
```

Figure 7-27 WriteContactSearchfor Subroutine *(continued)*

```
      $previous = 1;
  }
  if ($in{"jed"} eq "checked") {
    $checked{"jed"} = "checked";
    if ($previous) { $searchfor .= " or "; }
    $searchfor .= "((\"<companyname>\"__\"</com-
panyname>\") in ((\"<contactrec>\"..\"</contactrec>\")
containing (\"<Product\" __ \"/>\" containing
\"SGMLEditorJapanese=\\\"Yes\\\"\")))";
    $previous = 1;
  }
  if ($in{"ked"} eq "checked") {
    $checked{"ked"} = "checked";
    if ($previous) { $searchfor .= " or "; }
    $searchfor .= "((\"<companyname>\"__\
"</companyname>\") in ((\"<contactrec>\"..\
"</contactrec>\") containing (\"<Product\" __ \"/>\"
containing \"SGMLEditorKorean=\\\"Yes\\\"\")))";
    $previous = 1;
  }
   if ($in{"xml"} eq "checked") {
    $checked{"xml"} = "checked";
    if ($previous) { $searchfor .= " or "; }
    $searchfor .= "((\"<companyname>\"__\
"</companyname>\") in ((\"<contactrec>\"..\
"</contactrec>\") containing (\"<Product\" __ \"/>\"
containing \"XMLProducts=\\\"Yes\\\"\")))";
    $previous = 1;
  }
 if ($in{"general"} eq "checked") {
    $checked{"general"} = "checked";
    if ($previous) { $searchfor .= " or "; }
    $searchfor .= "((\"<companyname>\"__\
"</companyname>\") in ((\"<contactrec>\"..\
"</contactrec>\") containing (\"<Product\" __ \"/>\"
containing \"General=\\\"Yes\\\"\")))";
    $previous = 1;
  }
}
```

Figure 7–27 WriteContactSearchfor Subroutine *(continued)*

```
# PrintBoard
# Prints Query form for Bulletin Board Interface
sub PrintBoard {
# $printsearch echos the full sgrep query
# must HTMLify it for correct display using
# entities for angle bracket and quotes
$printsearch = $searchfor;
$printsearch =~ s/"/&quot;/g;
$printsearch =~ s/</&lt;/g;
print "<HTML>
<HEAD>
<TITLE>
RESULTS LIST - SEARCH THE BULLETIN BOARD
</TITLE>
</HEAD><BODY>
<BODYTEXT>
<H1>
RESULTS LIST - SEARCH THE BULLETIN BOARD
</H1>
<FORM ACTION=\"$cgipath/cgi-bin/queryx.pl\" METHOD=\"POST\">
<hr>
<INPUT TYPE=\"HIDDEN\" NAME=\"INTERFACE\" VALUE=\"BOARD\">
<INPUT TYPE=\"HIDDEN\" NAME=\"library\" VALUE=\"board\">
<INPUT TYPE=\"HIDDEN\" NAME=\"region\" VALUE=\"embedded\">
<table border=2><tr>
<td>Search</b><br>
<b>in </b>
<select name=\"element1\" size=\"2\">
<option value=\"body\" $sel1{'body'}>Message Body</option>
<option value=\"author\" $sel1{'author'}>Author</option>
<option value=\"subject\" $sel1{'subject'}>Subject</option>
</select><b> containing </b>
<input type=\"text\" name=\"contain1\" size=\"30\"
maxlength=\"100\" value=\"$in{'contain1'}\"><br>
<b>in </b>
<select name=\"element2\" size=\"2\">
<option value=\"body\" $sel2{'body'}>Message Body</option>
<option value=\"author\" $sel2{'author'}>Author</option>
<option value=\"subject\" $sel2{'subject'}>Subject</option>
</select><b> containing </b>
<input type=\"text\" name=\"contain2\" size=\"30\"
maxlength=\"100\" value=\"$in{'contain2'}\"><br>
<b>in </b>
```

Figure 7–28   PrintBoard Subroutine

```
<select name=\"element3\" size=\"2\">
<option value=\"body\" $sel3{'body'}>Message Body</option>
<option value=\"author\" $sel3{'author'}>Author</option>
<option value=\"subject\" $sel3{'subject'}>Subject</
option></select><b> containing </b>
<input type=\"text\" name=\"contain3\" size=\"30\"
maxlength=\"100\" value=\"$in{'contain3'}\"><td>
</tr></table>
<hr><center>
<INPUT TYPE=\"SUBMIT\" VALUE=\"Search Now\">
<INPUT TYPE=\"RESET\" VALUE=\"Clear\"></center>
<hr>
</FORM>
<h2>Results List</h2>
<p>The following files match the query <i>$printsearch</i></
p>";
}
```

Figure 7–28 PrintBoard Subroutine *(continued)*

```
# PrintContact
# Prints Query form for Contact Database Interface
sub PrintContact {
# $printsearch echos the full sgrep query
# must HTMLify it for correct display using
# entities for angle bracket and quotes
$printsearch = $searchfor;
$printsearch =~ s/"/&quot;/g;
$printsearch =~ s/</&lt;/g;
print "<HTML>
<HEAD>
<TITLE>
RESULT LIST - CONTACT DATABASE
</TITLE>
</HEAD><BODY>
<BODYTEXT>
<H1>
RESULT LIST - CONTACT DATABASE
</H1>
<FORM ACTION=\"$cgipath/cgi-bin/queryx.pl\" METHOD=\"POST\">
<hr>
<INPUT TYPE=\"HIDDEN\" NAME=\"INTERFACE\" VALUE=\"CONTACT\">
```

Figure 7–29 PrintContact Subroutine

```
<INPUT TYPE=\"HIDDEN\" NAME=\"library\" VALUE=\"contact\">
<INPUT TYPE=\"HIDDEN\" NAME=\"region\" VALUE=\"embedded\">
<table border=2><tr>
<td><b>Search</b><br>
<b>in </b>
<select name=\"element1\" size=\"2\">
<option value=\"name\" $sel1{'name'}>Name</option>
<option value=\"company\" $sel1{'company'}>Company</option>
<option value=\"state\" $sel1{'state'}>State</option>
<option value=\"country\" $sel1{'country'}>Country</option>
<option value=\"venue\" $sel1{'venue'}>Venue</option>
<option value=\"notes\" $sel1{'notes'}>Notes</option>
<option value=\"month\" $sel1{'month'}>Month</option>
<option value=\"year\" $sel1{'year'}>Year</option>
</select><b> containing </b>
<input type=\"text\" name=\"contain1\" size=\"20\" max-
length=\"100\" value=\"$in{'contain1'}\"><br>
<b>in </b>
<select name=\"element2\" size=\"2\">
<option value=\"name\" $sel2{'name'}>Name</option>
<option value=\"company\" $sel2{'company'}>Company</option>
<option value=\"state\" $sel2{'state'}>State</option>
<option value=\"country\" $sel2{'country'}>Country</option>
<option value=\"venue\" $sel2{'venue'}>Venue</option>
<option value=\"notes\" $sel2{'notes'}>Notes</option>
<option value=\"month\" $sel2{'month'}>Month</option>
<option value=\"year\" $sel2{'year'}>Year</option>
</select><b> containing </b>
<input type=\"text\" name=\"contain2\" size=\"20\" max-
length=\"100\" value=\"$in{'contain2'}\"><br>
<b>in </b>
<select name=\"element3\" size=\"2\">
<option value=\"name\" $sel3{'name'}>Name</option>
<option value=\"company\" $sel3{'company'}>Company</option>
<option value=\"state\" $sel3{'state'}>State</option>
<option value=\"country\" $sel3{'country'}>Country</option>
<option value=\"venue\" $sel3{'venue'}>Venue</option>
<option value=\"notes\" $sel3{'notes'}>Notes</option>
<option value=\"month\" $sel3{'month'}>Month</option>
<option value=\"year\" $sel3{'year'}>Year</option>
</select><b> containing </b>
```

Figure 7–29 PrintContact Subroutine *(continued)*

```
<input type=\"text\" name=\"contain3\" size=\"20\"
maxlength=\"100\" value=\"$in{'contain3'}\"><br>
<b>in </b>
<select name=\"element4\" size=\"2\">
<option value=\"name\" $sel4{'name'}>Name</option>
<option value=\"company\" $sel4{'company'}>Company</option>
<option value=\"state\" $sel4{'state'}>State</option>
<option value=\"country\" $sel4{'country'}>Country</option>
<option value=\"venue\" $sel4{'venue'}>Venue</option>
<option value=\"notes\" $sel4{'notes'}>Notes</option>
<option value=\"month\" $sel4{'month'}>Month</option>
<option value=\"year\" $sel4{'year'}>Year</option>
</select><b> containing </b>
<input type=\"text\" name=\"contain4\" size=\"20\" max-
length=\"100\" value=\"$in{'contain4'}\"></td>
<td><b>Find all companies with interest in the following
products:</b><br>
<input type=\"checkbox\" name=\"ed\" value=\"checked\"
$checked{'ed'}>SGML Editor<br>
<input type=\"checkbox\" name=\"av\" value=\"checked\"
$checked{'av'}>ActiveViews<br>
<input type=\"checkbox\" name=\"sp\" value=\"checked\"
$checked{'sp'}>Symposia Pro<br>
<input type=\"checkbox\" name=\"sdp\" value=\"checked\"
$checked{'sdp'}>Symposia Doc+<br>
<input type=\"checkbox\" name=\"jed\" value=\"checked\"
$checked{'jed'}>Japanese SGML Editor<br>
<input type=\"checkbox\" name=\"ked\" value=\"checked\"
$checked{'ked'}>Korean SGML Editor<br>
<input type=\"checkbox\" name=\"xml\" value=\"checked\"
$checked{'xml'}>XML Products<br>
<input type=\"checkbox\" name=\"general\" value=\"checked\"
$checked{'general'}>General</td>
</tr></table>
<hr><center>
<INPUT TYPE=\"SUBMIT\" VALUE=\"Search Now\">
<INPUT TYPE=\"RESET\" VALUE=\"Clear\"></center>
<hr>
</FORM>
<h2>Results List</h2>
<p>The following files match the query <i>$printsearch</i>
</p>";
}
```

Figure 7–29 PrintContact Subroutine (cotinued)

Now we examine the final section in which the sgrep queries are actually modified and the results are manipulated into the desired output format (Figures 7–30 thru 7–34). The processing is different for each type of search— phrase, embedded, title, and raw—so we branch on the value of the $region variable. The final results will consist of a file name, match data, and hyperlinks to retrieve the file or invoke a transformation script formatted into an HTML table.

Phrase searching issues an sgrep expression which excludes results inside XML markup. We also want to display context around the match so we issue a second sgrep on each match using a constant list where we can specify the byte range to return based on the result returned by the first query.

```
###############################################
# execute searches and produce results list #
###############################################
# phrase search - search within markup
if ($region eq "phrase") {
# search inside markup is just search
# expression not in < >.  Assume use
# of entities for embedded <> and will
# search in CDATA.
# Do not output match, output filename
# and start and end position.
# Write result to temp file.
  system("$sgrep -n -i -o \"[f:%f][i:%i][l:%l]\" -p - -e
\'\"$searchfor\" not in (\"<\"..\">\")\' $searchfile >
$outfile1 2>&1");
# manipulate output in order to create
# constant list with 7 chars to either
# side of match for context
  if (open(FILE,"$outfile1")) {
    system("more $outfile1 > $cpfile 2>&1");
    $_ = <FILE>;
# loop through each match
# make an associate array of filename,
```

Figure 7–30   Phrase Search

```
# constant list pairs
    while (/\[f:([^\]]*)\]\[i:([^\]]*)\]\[l:([^\]]*)\]/) {
      $file = $1; $start = $2; $len = $3;
      $_ = $';
      $end = $start + $len + 6;
      if ($start > 6) { $start = $start - 7; }
      else { $start = 0; }
      $region = "($start,$end) ";
      $files{"$file"} .= $region; }
    close(FILE); }
  else {
    print "<dl><dt>ERROR</dt><DD>Unable to open results
file.</DD></dl></body></html>";
    exit;  }
# first pass switch to tell us whether we need
# to cat results with previous results or not
  $switch = 0;
# sort on filename and loop through associate array
# each time through do another sgrep on constant
# list to pull up match with context around it
  for each $searchfile (sort(keys %files)) {
    $searchfor = "[".$files{"$searchfile"}."]";
    if (!$switch) {
      $switch = 1;
# output is formatted with table markup for HTML output
# and hyperlinks to retrieval application.
      system("$sgrep -n -i -o \"<tr><td><A HREF=\\\
"$cgipath/$anchor%f\\\">%f</A><A HREF=\\\"$cgipath/
%f\\\"><IMG SRC=\\\"$cgipath/fichier.gif\\\"></A></
td><td>%r</td></tr>\" -p - -e \'$searchfor\' $searchfile >
$outfile 2>&1"); }
    else {
      system("$sgrep -n -i -o \"<tr><td><A HREF=\\\
"$cgipath/$anchor%f\\\">%f</A><A HREF=\\\"$cgipath/
%f\\\"><IMG SRC=\\\"$cgipath/fichier.gif\\\"></A></
td><td>%r</td></tr>\" -p - -e \'$searchfor\' $searchfile >
$outfile1 2>&1");
      system("cat $outfile $outfile1 > $outfile2");
      system("mv $outfile2 $outfile");
        } } }
```

Figure 7–30 Phrase Search *(continued)*

Embedded search is a complete sgrep expression so we have nothing to do but issue the sgrep command.

```
# embedded search - sgrep expression
# we just issue the sgrep statement formatted
# as an HTML table
elsif ($region eq "embedded") {
  system("$sgrep -n -i -o \"<tr><td><A HREF=\\\"$cgipath/
$anchor%f\\\">%f</A><A HREF=\\\"$cgipath/%f\\\"><IMG
SRC=\\\"$cgipath/fichier.gif\\\"></A></td><td>%r</td></
tr>\" -p - -e '$searchfor' $searchfile > $outfile 2>&1");
}
```

Figure 7–31   Embedded Search

Title search limits the search to content of HTML heading elements h1, h2, h3, and h4 or the TITLE element. An OR clause containing the search string is created and executed.

```
# title search - HTML title h1-h9
# simply create a big OR with each type of
# heading or title element
elsif ($region eq "title") {
  $searchexp = "((\"<h1>\" __ \"</h1>\") or (\"<h2>\" __
\"</h2>\") or (\"<h3>\" __ \"</h3>\") or (\"<h4>\" __ \"</
h4>\") or (\"<title>\" __ \"</title>\")) containing
\"$searchfor\"";
  system("$sgrep -n -i -o \"<tr><td><A HREF=\\\"$cgipath/
%f\\\">$anchor%f</A><A HREF=\\\"$cgipath/%f\\\"><IMG
SRC=\\\"$cgipath/fichier.gif\\\"></A></td><td>%r</td></
tr>\" -p - -e '$searchexp' $searchfile > $outfile 2>&1");
}
```

Figure 7–32   Title Search

Raw search is just like a phrase search except that it does not exclude markup.

```
# raw search - This works just like phrase search
# except we don't have the not <> clause to exclude
# markup
elsif ($region eq "raw") {
  system("$sgrep -n -i -o \"[f:%f][i:%i][l:%l]\" -p - -e
\'\"$searchfor\"\' $searchfile > $outfile1 2>&1");
  if (open(FILE,"$outfile1")) {
    $_ = <FILE>;
    while (/\[f:([^\]]*)\]\[i:([^\]]*)\]\[l:([^\]]*)\]/) {
      $file = $1; $start = $2; $len = $3;
      $_ = $';
      $end = $start + $len + 6;
      if ($start > 6) { $start = $start - 7; }
      else { $start = 0; }
      $region = "($start,$end) ";
      $files{"$file"} .= $region; }
    close(FILE); }
  $switch = 0;
  foreach $searchfile (sort(keys %files)) {
    $searchfor = "[".$files{"$searchfile"}."]";
    if (!$switch) {
      $switch = 1;
      system("$sgrep -n -i -o \"<tr><td><A HREF=\\\
"$cgipath/$anchor%f\\\">%f</A><A HREF=\\\"$cgipath/
%f\\\"><IMG SRC=\\\"$cgipath/fichier.gif\\\"></A></
td><td>%r</td></tr>\" -p - -e \'$searchfor\' $searchfile >
$outfile 2>&1"); }
    else {
      system("$sgrep -n -i -o \"<tr><td><A HREF=\\\
"$cgipath/$anchor%f\\\">%f</A><A HREF=\\\"$cgipath/
%f\\\"><IMG SRC=\\\"$cgipath/fichier.gif\\\"></A></
td><td>%r</td></tr>\" -p - -e \'$searchfor\' $searchfile >
$outfile1 2>&1");
      system("cat $outfile $outfile1 > $outfile2");
      system("mv $outfile2 $outfile");
        } } }
```

Figure 7–33   Raw Search

Finally, we form the HTML table with the results, output all, and conclude processing of the query.

```
# we shouldn't be here - type of search
# should be correctly identified - but
# try something anyway
else {
  system("$sgrep -n -i -o \"<tr><td><A HREF=\\\"$cgipath/
$anchor%f\\\">%f</A><A HREF=\\\"$cgipath/%f\\\"><IMG
SRC=\\\"$cgipath/fichier.gif\\\"></A></td><td>%r</td></
tr>\" -p - -e '\"$searchfor\"' $searchfile > $outfile
2>&1");
  print "<h2>ERROR: Unrecognized search type</h2>"; }
# output results inserted into HTML table structure
if (open(FILE,"$outfile")) {
  $result = <FILE>;
# get rid of server specific path info
  $result =~ s/\/aimweb\/homets\///g;
  print "<table border=\"border\"><tr><td><b>File</b></
td><td><b>Match</b></td></tr>$result</table>";
  close(FILE); }
else {
  print "<h2>No results file</h2>"; }
# finish HTML and done
print "<hr><table width=\"100%\"><tr>
<td><A HREF=\"$cgipath/qbboard.html\">Query BBoard</A></
td>
<td><A HREF=\"$cgipath/qcontact.html\">Query Contact</A></
td>
<td><A HREF=\"$cgipath/qadhoc.html\">Ad-Hoc Query</A></td>
</tr></table></body></html>";
```

Figure 7–34   Output Results List

Many kinds of reports can be produced by sgrep which are useful in their own right without further processing. For example, sgrep queries can give us the phone numbers or addresses of customers matching certain criteria.

We have seen that sgrep is a retrieval tool that is capable of extracting subtrees from documents. In fact, in this query interface we make little use of that capability. We can in principle extract subtrees and see the content in the results lists but in an HTML browser the XML elements will not be displayed meaningfully. We would either need to use an XML browser (and set up a style sheet as was shown in a description of CSS in an earlier chapter) or have a transformation capability either built into the output formatting provided by sgrep or supplied by a more sophisticated facility.

Therefore transformation is logically our next topic and, in fact, is the subject of our next chapter, the final chapter in our foray into the Desperate Perl Hacker's XML universe.

Type Transformation, Import, and Export

T his chapter delves into the subject of transformation of XML into output formats such as HTML and RTF. Some theoretical concerns in transformation are presented followed by a discussion of event stream, grove, and DSSSL-XSL-based transformations. The programming section of the chapter presents a Perl event stream transformation program consisting of a core stack-based well-formed parser and application-specific routines. The applications presented are XML to HTML transformations of the bulletin board and contact record document types and an XML to RTF transformation of the bulletin board document type. Algorithms are presented in the course of discussion for expanding the capabilities of the system presented to better handle element-in-context processing and to deal with delayed output and forward references.

8.1 | Overview

Type transformation is the main theme of this chapter although we will give one example of export and discuss the relationship between type transformation and import and export.

The process of transforming an unstructured document into a structured one entails going from a high entropy state (unordered and information-poor) to a low entropy state (highly structured and information-rich) through work applied in identifying and structuring the document's components (Figure 8–1). We call this process *import* although in the SGML literature it is most often called *up-translation*. Everything above the dotted line in our figure is a structured XML document or something equivalent in a low entropy state. A transformation between document types in low entropy states is what we call a *type transformation* and the SGML literature will most often call a *DTD-to-DTD conversion*. The final transformation process shown is one in which we go from a structured document type to an unstructured one and entails the loss of the organization contained in the document's structure. The SGML literature calls this *down-translation* and we call it *export*.

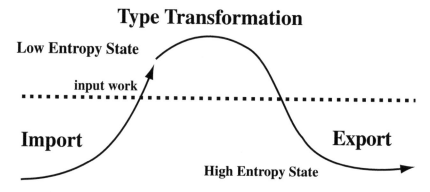

Figure 8–1   Energy State of Transformation Processes

8.1.1 *Import*

We do not cover import in this book despite the fact that up-translation has traditionally played a very significant role in SGML projects and has been both a major cost area for implementors and a major revenue area for service organizations. This stems from the fact that SGML was almost uniquely a publishing technology and every adopter of SGML had to either incorporate or transition from older systems. The most successful transitions usually involved a one-time conversion of existing documentation into SGML and a wholesale replacement of non-SGML tools with SGML-capable systems. There has been interest in approaches which would permit authors to continue to work with familiar tools such as Microsoft's Word and later convert their documents into SGML. Part of the problem with this approach is illustrated by our entropy diagram: Work must be input into the system in order to achieve a low-entropy state. The other aspect of the problem is that purely WYSIWYG tools permit and even encourage inconsistencies in the document formatting which may defeat all attempts to apply automated processes to the up-translation. Style sheets provide a partial remedy to these problems by capturing a higher level of organization in the initial authoring process and also by eliminating inconsistencies wherever styles are applied. In fact, the vigorous application of style sheets is the key to all successful up-translation processes and all the art and science that can be applied to the process is contained in a number of "tricks" which map between the style sheet and SGML markup paradigms.

The difference between the paradigms is, however, fundamental and inconsistencies can never be completely avoided. Up-translation has an overhead that increasing experience can lessen but never completely eliminate. The overhead usually consists of resources consumed in manually finding and correcting errors introduced by failures in the up-conversion process. Experientially we would place that overhead at between 20 and 10 percent of the overall production cost of a document (after authoring). This can be reduced to between

10 and 2 percent over time but this improvement also requires a large investment in programming resources to ameliorate the process and this investment is not counted in the overhead. Much depends on the discipline of the organization and the programming talent. Most organizations that have the wherewithal to succeed in this kind of process also have the wherewithal to set up a more efficient SGML-based authoring system. This state of affairs strongly favors the one-time conversion where total costs can be accurately predicated and the staff does not need to master an arcane set of skills for a process which will be a continuous drain on resources.

The reader may have noted that we have not made reference to XML in the above discussion. While there will be publishing-oriented organizations which may be interested in an import process from word processors to XML, this area will shift, percentage-wise, from a dominant sector of the SGML market to a minor sector of the XML market. XML software architectures will capture XML directly from the user or interchange XML with other software objects most of the time. Even for publishers the mainstreaming of XML technology will make it much easier to find the appropriate tools and dive into the direct production of XML documents. Coupled with the problematic nature of import processes, the subject does not have the same importance in a book on XML and internets that it has for SGML applications.

8.1.2 *Type Transformation*

Type transformation, on the other hand, will increase in importance as XML becomes a fundamental part of the Internet's infrastructure. One common use of type transformation in SGML is in an up-conversion where one gets from a high to low entropy state by discrete jumps from less to more structurally rich DTDs. This approach allows for better management of the complexity of the type transformation process. Smaller, incremental changes are easier to design, develop, and understand. Intermediate stages may be closer to new output requirements which arise, lessening the amount of work which will have to be done to create new type transformation filters. Finally, staged type transformation can yield the same benefits as multi-tier software architectures which insulate each layer from the operational details of the other layers. This stepped approach is illustrated conceptually in Figure 8–2.

SGML work does not involve a great deal of transformation between DTDs with the same entropy level. This was in part because SGML applications were not designed in the environment of the internet and distributed object architectures and therefore did not emphasize the dynamic interchange of processing information through structured documents. In addition, publishing applications have tended to generate very large DTDs for which a peer-to-peer transformation would be exceedingly complex.

The other side of the type transformation slope from low-entropy states to higher-entropy states bordering on export processes is very

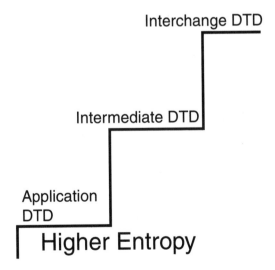

Figure 8–2 Discrete Type Transformation

commonly used to produce application-specific document markup from a more general and non-application-specific repository format. We include in this group the transformation of XML into HTML. Many SGML applications currently do this in order to deliver SGML document data on the Web. This will become much less commonplace once the Web browsers support XML and XML style sheets but since the total conversion of the marketplace to XML-capable browsers is still some time off, we feel this subject is worthy of some attention. Therefore the main contents of this chapter will be an in-depth examination of this process using a set of "roll-yer-own" tools written in Perl.

Our Perl tools have been implemented in the same spirit as the prior projects: We get the job done by knocking some stuff together quickly. If we were to put a fine point on things, we would probably insist that a type transformation process be DTD-driven throughout, both in the interpretation of the source document and in the writing and validation of the output. In fact our tools will be instance driven, dealing once again with well-formed instances and we will take advantage of the laxness of HTML browsers and eschew validation against a DTD on the output side. SGML languages such as Omnimark and Balise are capable of performing the more rigorous type transformation process and have other advantages besides. We will point these out as we go along as well as discuss some other approaches to type transformation.

Our project consists of taking our XML contact database and bulletin board records and providing on-demand conversion of these documents to HTML using a CGI script. The CGI script has a tiny built-in XML well-formed document parser which will provide a gentle introduction to that topic in preparation for our discussion in later chapters of applications constructed with SP and NXP.

The results of our type transformation scripts are shown in Figure 8–3 and 8–4. Figure 8–3 shows the HTML output of type transformation of a bulletin board message and Figure 8–4 the HTML output from the contact database.

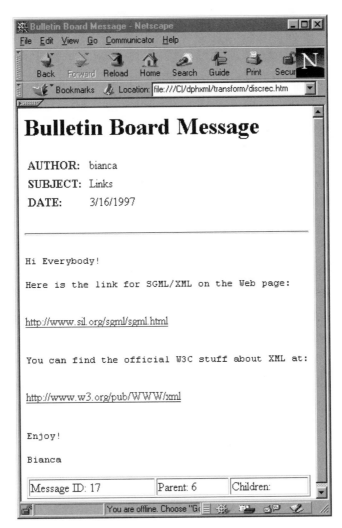

Figure 8–3 Transformed Bulletin Board Message

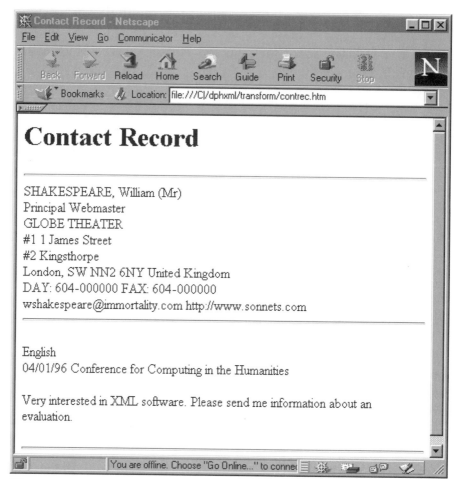

Figure 8–4   Transformed Contact Record

8.1.3 *Export*

Down-conversion or export processes have been extremely important primarily because of the need to produce documents for printing and will, for the foreseeable future, continue to be important for this reason. Of course, we have probably already arrived at the point where the quantity of information produced for on-line consumption exceeds the amount of printed material and are probably not far from the day when all printed material will be derived from on-line materials. Export processes will still exist but we will probably think of them more as style-sheet driven rather than programmatically specified. At the moment, however, rendering from XML is not so highly evolved that an understanding of the export process is superfluous. We therefore have also devoted some of this chapter to an export process whereby a bulletin board message is transformed to RTF, in this case using Microsoft Word as our print engine. The results of this process are shown in Figure 8–5.

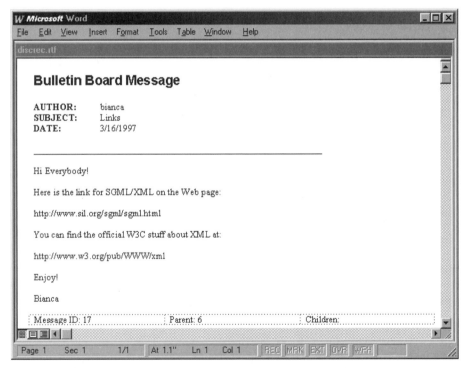

Figure 8–5   Bulletin Board Message Transformed to RTF

8.2 | Approaches to Transformation

8.2.1 *Event Stream*

Consider the following XML document:

```
<a type="question">Is <b>this <c/></b>the promised end?</a>
```

A parser processing this document from left to right "sees" the events shown in Table 8.1:

Sequence	Event	Token	Stack
1	Start-Tag	<a>	a
2	Attribute Name	type	a
3	Attribute Value	question	a
4	PCDATA	"Is "	a
5	Start-Tag	<b>	b < a
6	PCDATA	"this "	b < a
7	Empty-Element Tag	<c/>	b < a
8	End-Tag	</b>	a
9	PCDATA	"the promised end?"	a
10	End-Tag	</a>	

Table 8.1   Event Stream Processing

Table 8.1 actually fully describes the event stream parsing process which, in reality, does very little work beyond scanning—the lexical recognition of tokens. Parsing, the syntactic analysis of the document, consists of maintaining a stack showing the current element and all of its ancestors. Generation of the output of the transformation process, which we call *processing*, may make conditional decisions based on the value of this stack, commonly called the *element context*. An element with a specific context is called an *element-in-context*. Processing may also be based on many other types of conditions, such as

- attribute values

- data content

- sibling relationships between elements

- other types of tree-based relationships between element or element attributes and data content other than direct parentage

While an event stream processor can potentially be modified to support these types of conditions, it is basically not the correct programming infrastructure to do so to any significant extent. Transformation processes which make use of such conditions should be based on *groves*.

8.2.2 *Groves*

Grove is SGML terminology for a tree representing a document and its associated properties. The *grove of reference* is a grove containing every possible property of the document. In practice, considerable overhead may be required to construct the grove of reference so less comprehensive groves may be used. These less comprehensive groves are derived from the grove of reference using a kind of mapping known as a *grove plan*.

A pictorial representation of part of a grove for the SGML document below (Figure 8–6) is shown in Figure 8–7. The grove illustration was created by Henry S. Thompson of the Human Communication Research Centre of the University of Edinburgh.

```
<!doctype simp [
<!element simp o o (bit*)>
<!element bit - - (#PCDATA)>
<!attlist bit name id #required>
]>
<bit name="one">1</bit>
<bit name="two">2</bit>
```

Figure 8–6

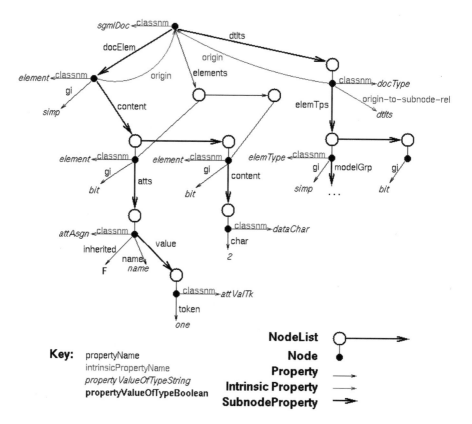

Figure 8–7

This is an SGML document which uses omitted-tag minimization. Nevertheless, the grove describes the complete abstract document, so on the left-hand side we have a node for the element `<b>simp</b>`, even though its tags were omitted. In the middle we have the two `<b>bit</b>` elements, whose tags were present. On the right-hand side we have a representation of the DTD.

In grove-based transformation a grove is first constructed and subsequent processing is accomplished by traversing the grove to evaluate conditions based on the document's properties.

Construction and traversal of a grove are the most efficient ways to implement procedures which need to process an element's children before the parent because the result of processing the children may change the results of processing the parent. This sort of thing is often implemented recursively. Consider the following depth-first program which prints the number of characters in each element (written in pseudocode).

```
process-element(ELEMENT)
CONTENT = LEFT-CONTENT .
          foreach CHILD
              process-element(ELEMENT)
              . RIGHT-CONTENT
          . RIGHT-CONTENT
  print ELEMENT len(CONTENT)
  return CONTENT
```

Figure 8–8

Executing

```
process-element(a)
```

on the document presented in Section 8.2.1 on event streams causes the processing shown in Table 8.2 to take place.

Execution Step	Scope	Output
process-element a	a	
"Is " .	a	
process-element b	a	
"this "	b	
process-element c	b	
print c len("")	c	c 0
return ""	c	
print b len("this ")	b	b 5
return "this "	b	
. "the promised end?"	a	
print a len("Is this the promised end?")	a	a 25
return "Is this the promised end?"	a	

Table 8.2   Recursive Processing

The event stream model can obtain the same results by saving the content of children and triggering processing off end-tag events when all children of the current element must have been processed. But this kind of processing quickly becomes complex and difficult to manage compared to the simplicity and elegance of recursive procedures on tree structures.

Although Omnimark, Balise, and several other SGML transformation languages do not formally use the concept of a grove or grove plan they are, in fact, based on tree construction and traversal and operate on fairly complete groves.

Groves provide the most complete framework for transformation programming. Groves may, however, consume substantial memory and processing time for their construction and processing compared to ultra-lightweight event-based processing.

8.2.3 *DSSSL/XSL Transformation*

DSSSL (Document Style and Semantic Specification Language) is a grove-based attempt to address the problem of transformation in a general and very comprehensive way. XSL (Extensible Style Sheet Language) will apply DSSSL concepts to the creation of a style sheet language for XML documents. While XSL is billed as a style sheet language, it inherits full transformation capabilities from DSSSL and is Turing-complete (meaning, speaking loosely, that it is a full programming language).

The XSL processor executes a series of rules which match patterns in the grove and assign actions to take place when a match is made. Those actions may generate output known as flow objects. The set of flow objects constitute a second tree which may be manipulated by device-specific media back ends to produce the transformation product. This process is illustrated in Figure 8–9. The illustrations in Figures 8–9 and 8–10 were created by Ingo Macherius.

Figure 8–10 presents a very small example of XSL style sheet code. The reader should note that XSL both supports the style specification of XML and also uses XML for its own language syntax. The XSL rule contains a pattern for identifying a portion of the grove, in this case, it matches the element type *warning*. Each time a warning element is matched, a *box* flow object is created which contains a *paragraph* with the specified font size and family, the text "Warning:" and the children of the object matched in the grove.

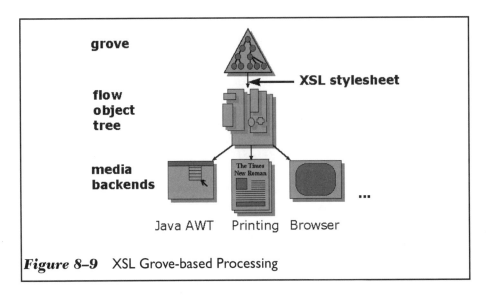

Figure 8–9   XSL Grove-based Processing

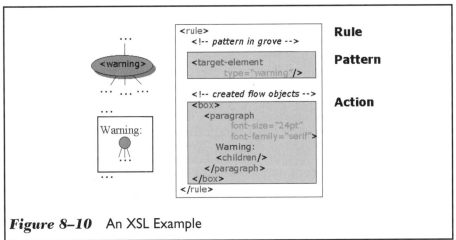

Figure 8–10   An XSL Example

8.3 | Event Stream Transformation with Perl

8.3.1 *Core Routine*

The core of all the transformation scripts discussed in this section is the module *transwf*. It may be run either as a CGI on the server or as a stand-alone program. Its basic behavior is to scan a well-formed document recognizing start-tags, end-tags, empty-element tags, and

PCDATA and to maintain a stack of the current element and its ancestors. Three modes of operation have been derived from this basic behavior:

1. Check the document for well-formedness.

   The maintenance of the ancestor stack provides the most basic well-formedness check—proper nesting. Several additional checks and recognition of other token types (declaration, processing instruction, comment, doctype, cdata) have been added to cover most of the other rules specified in the XML recommendation as well-formedness constraints (WFCs). However, entities are not checked as this exceeds the requirements of the documents for which this program is targeted.

2. Generate subroutine stubs for element-in-context transformation scripts.

   Mode number three will be to execute transformation subroutines for each event based on the state of the stack, that is, the element-in-context. The following element related events are recognized:

   - start-tag
   - PCDATA

     Mixed-content (elements intermixed with PCDATA) may cause multiple invocations of this event for a single element.

   - end-tag

   To facilitate the preparation of element-in-context subroutines an operation has been provided which writes out stub subroutines for each element-in-context encountered in a well-formed document

3. Execute event-specific element-in-context subroutines.

   The purpose of the subroutines will be to transform the document from XML into something else, in our examples, into HTML or RTF. The subroutines are simply included with the transwf core to make a document-specific transformation.

We would like to emphasize to the reader that *transwf* is not DTD controlled and does not, in fact, use a DTD at all. All processing is based on well-formed document instances.

The annotated code for *transwf* follows.

```
#!/usr/local/bin/perl
##############################################################
# transwf - Well-formed transformation program          #
#                                                        #
# transwf operates either as a CGI or a standalone       #
# program, determined by the $MODE variable.             #
# In standalone mode there are three possible operations: #
# gen, exec, and check.  In CGI mode only exec is the    #
# only operation.                                        #
#                                                        #
# check Checks an XML file for well-formedness as defined #
#       in the 07-Aug-97 XML Working draft with some     #
#       omissions with respect to entity validation.     #
# gen   Using a well-formed XML file as input will       #
#       generate stubs for the processing of each        #
#       element-in-context's start-tag, end-tag, and     #
#       pcdata.                                           #
# exec  Executes an element-in-context subroutine for    #
#       each start-tag, end-tag, empty-tag, and pcdata   #
#       found in a well-formed XML file.                 #
#                                                        #
# standalone command line                                #
# perl transwf -p [check|gen|exec] -f input.file         #
# -p    Type of process.  Default is check.              #
# -f    Input file.                                      #
# Output is written to stdout.                           #
#                                                        #
# CGI format                                             #
# cgi-bin/transwf/input.file                             #
#                                                        #
```

Figure 8–11

```
# Element-in-context subroutine names                   #
# Start tag subroutines are prefixed with an "st_", end #
# tags subroutines with an "et_" and pcdata subroutines #
# with "pc_".  The name of the subroutine is the name of #
# of the element followed by the name of its parent     #
# followed by name of its parent and so on up to the    #
# root.  Each element name is separated by an underscore. #
# Example (subroutine names for the HTML TITLE element): #
# st_title_head_html, pc_title_head_html,               #
# et_title_head_html.                                   #
#                                                       #
# exec processing                                       #
# As transwf will invoke the element-in-context         #
# subroutines they must be included with transwf.       #
#                                                       #
# Copyright Matthew Fuchs, Michael Leventhal, and David #
# Lewis, published in Designing XML Internet Applications #
# Prentice-Hall, 1998.  Permission for unrestricted use #
# as long as the authors are credited.                  #
#########################################################
# $MODE determines if the program is run standalone from
# the command line or as a CGI.
# $MODE = "CGI";
$MODE = "STANDALONE";
# Default processing is "exec".
$PROCESSING = "exec";
# If a CGI, where to find input files.
$CGIMODE_FILEPATH =  "/aimweb/homets";
# Disable record seperator so entire file can be read with
# the open statement.
undef($/);
if ($MODE eq "CGI") {
# For CGI processing: write content-type for sending back
# HTML, read input file from the PATH_INFO and open it,
# exiting if disaster strikes.
  print "content-type: text/html\n\n";
  $filename = $ENV{'PATH_INFO'};
  unless (open(DOC,"$CGIMODE_FILEPATH$filename")) {
   print "<html><head><title></title></head></head>
<body><p>Unsuccessful attempt to open $tsipath$filename</p>
</body></html>";
  exit; } }
```

Figure 8–11 (continued)

```
else {
# For standalone processing: read command line arguments to
# get input file and operation and open input file.
  $i = 0;
  while ($i < $#ARGV) {
    $param_type = $ARGV[$i++];
    $param_value = $ARGV[$i++];
    if ($param_type =~ /-p/i) {
      $PROCESSING = $param_value;
      $PROCESSING =~ tr/A-Z/a-z/; }
    elsif ($param_type =~ /-f/i) {
      unless (open(DOC,"$param_value")) {
        print "\nUnsuccessful attempt to open $file-
name.\n";
      exit; } }
  }
}
$file = <DOC>;
```

Figure 8–11 (continued)

The next line performs 90 percent of the lexical recognition performed by the program, a simple regular expression to recognize a start-tag or end-tag and any PCDATA that precedes it. Of course, angle brackets cannot appear within PCDATA for this to work; the standard character entities must be used. The file pointer is advanced after the match, ready for the next loop.

```
# I loop through the file, processing each start or end
# tag when it is seen.
while ($file =~ /([^<]*)<(\/)?([^>]+)>/) {
  $pcdata = $1;
  $st_or_et = $2;
  $gi = $3;
  $file = $';
```

Figure 8–12

An element-in-context subroutine will either be generated or executed for any PCDATA identified. The object which follows the PCDATA will either be an XML declaration, processing instruction, comment, doctype; cdata, or a start-, end-, or empty-element tag. In the next section shown in Figure 8-13 a processing routine is invoked

specific to each type and a flag is set for the type of object seen so that
well-formed checks related to order and duplication can be enforced.

```
# I recognize the following kinds of objects: XML declar-
# ation (a particular type of processing instruction),
# processing instructions, comments, doctype declaration,
# cdata marked sections, and elements.  Since the document
# production has order rules I set a flag when a particular
# type of object has been processed.  I invoke a subroutine
# to process each type of object.
  if ($pcdata =~ /[^\s]/) {
#  PCDATA processing.  Skip if just a well-formed check but
#  would do entity processing here if supported.  For "gen"
#  or "exec" invoke processing routines on pcdata with the
#  stack of parents and the subroutine prefix for pcdata.
    if ($PROCESSING eq "gen") {
      &write_sr(*ancestors,"","\&pc"); }
    elsif ($PROCESSING eq "exec") {
      &execute_sr(*ancestors,"\&pc"); } }
  if ($gi =~ /^\?XML/) {
    &process_decl;
    $decl_seen = 1;
  }
  elsif ($gi =~ /^\?/) {
    &process_pi;
    $misc_seen = 1;
  }
  elsif ($gi =~ /^!\-\-/) {
    &process_comment;
    $misc_seen;
  }
  elsif ($gi =~ /^!DOCTYPE/) {
    &process_doctype;
    $doctype_seen = 1;
  }
  elsif ($gi =~ /^\!\[CDATA\[/) {
    &process_cdata;
  }
  else {
    &process_element;
    $element_seen = 1;
  }
}
```

Figure 8–13

Some final checks are performed in the section shown in Figure 8–14 and the main routine of *transwf* is complete.

```
# There are some checks to catch various errors at the end.
# I make sure I have emptied the stack of all parents and I
# make sure there is no uncontained character data hanging
# around.
&check_empty_stack;
&check_uncontained_pcdata;
# Print a happy message if there are no errors.
&check_error_count;
#---------------------------------------------------------#
```

Figure 8–14

The following subroutines shown in Figure 8–15 perform various kinds of well-formedness checks.

```
#---------------------------------------------------------#
# Check to see if the ancestor stack containing all parents
# up to the root is empty.
sub check_empty_stack {
if ($#ancestors > -1) {
  &print_error_at_context;
}
}
#---------------------------------------------------------#
# Check to see if there is any uncontained PCDATA lying
# around (white space at the end of the document doesn't
# count).  I check also to see that a root to the document
# was found which catches a null file error.
sub check_uncontained_pcdata {
if ($file !~ /^\s*$/ || $ROOT eq "") {
  $error_count++;
  &printn("WFC Not well formed uncontained #PCDATA or null
file");
}
}
#---------------------------------------------------------#
# Check for a well-formed Name as defined in the Name
# production.
sub check_name {
local($name) = @_;
```

Figure 8–15

```perl
if ($name !~ /^[A-Za-z_:][\w\.\-:]*$/) {
  &printn("Invalid element or attribute name: $name");
  &print_error_at_context;
}
}
#----------------------------------------------------------#
#----------------------------------------------------------#
# Check that the XML declaration is coded properly and in
# the correct position (before any other object in the file
# and occuring only once.)
sub process_decl {
if ($decl_seen || $misc_seen ||
    $doctype_seen || $element_seen) {
  $error_count++;
  &printn("WFC XML declaration can only be at the head of
the document.");
}
# No checks are performed on processing instructions but
# the following will be used to store the PI in the $gi
# variable and advance the file pointer.
&process_pi;
# This is slightly lazy since we allow version='1.0".
# It is quite simple to fix just by making an OR of each
# parameter with either ' ' or " " quote marks.
if ($gi !~
/\?XML\s+version=[\'\"]1.0[\'\"](\s+encod-
ing=[\'\"][^\'\"]*[\'\"])?(\s+RMD=[\'\"](NONE|INTER-
NAL|ALL)[\'\"])?\s*\?/)
{
  $error_count++;
  &printn("WFC Format of XML declaration is wrong.");
}
}
#----------------------------------------------------------#
# Skip over processing instructions.
sub process_pi {
if ($gi !~ /\?$/) {
  $file =~ /\?>/;
  $gi = $gi.$`."?";
  $file = $';
}
}
#----------------------------------------------------------#
```

Figure 8–15 (continued)

```
#-------------------------------------------------------#
# Check that the Doctype statement is in the right position
# and, otherwise, make no attempt to parse its contents,
# including the root element.  The root element will
# determined from the element production itself and
# the "claim" of the Doctype won't be verified.
sub process_doctype {
if ($doctype_seen || $element_seen) {
  $error_count++;
  &printn("WFC Doctype can only appear once and must be
within prolog.");
}
if ($gi =~ /\[/ && $gi !~ /\]$/) {
  $file =~ /\]>/;
  $file = $';
  $gi = $gi.$`.$&;
}
}
#-------------------------------------------------------#
# Performs the well-formed check necessary to verify that
# CDATA is not nested.  We will pick up the wrong end of
# CDATA marker if this is the case so the error message is
# critical.
sub process_cdata {
if ($gi !~ /\]\]$/) {
  $file =~ /\]\]>/;
  $file = $';
  $gi = $gi.$`."]]";
}
$gi =~ /\!\[CDATA\[(.*)\]\]/;
$body = $1;
if ($body =~ /<\!\[CDATA\[/) {
  &printn("WFC Nested CDATA.");
  &print_error_at_context;
}
}
#-------------------------------------------------------#
```

Figure 8–15   (continued)

```
#-------------------------------------------------------#
# Performs the well-formed check of ensuring that '--' is
# not nested in the comment body which would cause problems
# for SGML processors.
sub process_comment {
if ($gi !~ /\-\-$/) {
  $file =~ /\-\->/;
  $file = $';
  $gi = $gi.$`."--";
}
$gi =~ /\!\-\-((.|\n)*)\-\-\-/;
$body = $1;
if ($body =~ /\-\-/) {
  $error_count++;
  &printn("WFC Comment contains --.");
}
}
#-------------------------------------------------------#
```

Figure 8–15   (continued)

The main subroutine of *transwf* follows *process_element*. Process element processes start-, end-, and empty-elements tags, manages the ancestor stack, and validates and stores attribute lists. An outline of process_element is shown in Figure 8–16.

1. Recognize empty-element tags. Empty-element tags will not be added to the stack.
2. Recognize attributes, scan them into name value pairs, save them in a associative array, and report well-formed errors related to attributes.
3. If we are processing an end-tag, check that we aren't at the root, execute or write element-in-context end-tag subroutine, and pop an ancestor off the ancestor stack.
4. If not end-tag it is either a start-tag or an empty-element tag(s). Push the element type name onto the ancestor stack and execute or write an element-in-context start-tag subroutine.
5. If an empty-element tag(s), pop the ancestor stack right away.

Figure 8–16   Outline of process_element

```
#-------------------------------------------------------
#
# This is the main subroutine which handles the ancestor
# stack (in an array) checking the proper nesting of the
# element part of the document production.
sub process_element {
# Distinguish between empty elements which do not add a
# parent to the ancestor stack and elements which can have
# content.
```

Figure 8–17

In the first line of the next section shown in Figure 8–18 we recognize the special syntax of empty-element tags.

```
if ($gi =~ /\/$/) {
    $xml_empty = 1;
    $gi =~ s/\/$//;
}
else {
    $xml_empty = 0;
}
```

Figure 8–18

In the next section shown in Figure 8–19 we parse attributes out of the $gi variable, check for attribute well-formedness and save the attribute name, value pairs in an associative array. That associative array will be available to the element-in-context routine.

```
# Check to see that attributes are well-formed.

if ($gi =~ /\s/) {
  $gi = $`;
  $attrline = $';
  $attrs = $attrline;
# This time we properly check to see that either ' '
# or " " is used to surround the attribute values.
  while ($attrs =~ /\s*([^\s=]*)\s*=\s*(("[^"]*")|('[^']*'))/)
{
# An end tag may not, of course, have attributes.
    if ($st_or_et eq "\/") {
      &printn("WFC Attributes may not be placed on end tags.");
      &print_error_at_context;
    }
    $attrname = $1;
    $attrvalue = $2;
     # cut the quote marks off the attribute value
    substr($attrvalue,0,1) = '';
    substr($attrvalue,-1,1) = '';
     # save in associative array
    $attrarray{"$attrname"} = $attrvalue;

# Check for a valid attribute name.
    &check_name($attrname);

    $attrs = $';
  }
  $attrs =~ s/\s//g;
# The above regex should have processed all the
# attributes.  If anything is left after getting rid
# of white space it is because the attribute
# expression was malformed.
  if ($attrs ne "") {
    &printn("WFC Malformed attributes.");
    &print_error_at_context;
  }
}
```

Figure 8–19

The code in Figure 8–20 recognizes if the current element is the document root and checks the well-formedness of the element type name.

```
if (!$element_seen) {
  $ROOT = $gi; }
# Check to see that the generic identifier is a
# well-formed name.
&check_name($gi);
```

Figure 8–20

In the listing in Figure 8–21 we recognize end-tags. We must check to make sure that the end-tag matches the last item on the stack; otherwise we have discovered the most basic well-formedness error. Next, we write or execute the end-tag element-in-context routine and pop the ancestor stack.

```
# If I have an end tag I just check the top of the stack,
# the end tag must match the last parent or it is an error.
# If I find an error I could either pop or not pop the stack.
# What I want is to perform some manner of error recovery so
# I can continue to report well-formed errors on the rest of
# the document.  If I pop the stack and my problem was caused
# caused by a missing end tag I will end up reporting errors
# on every tag thereafter. If I don't pop the stack and the
# problem was caused by a misspelled end tag name I will also
# report errors on every following tag.  I happened to chose
# the latter.
if ($st_or_et eq "\/") {
  $parent = $ancestors[$#ancestors];
  if ($parent ne $gi) {
    if (@ancestors eq $ROOT) { @ancestors = ""; }
    else {
      &print_error_at_context;
    }
  }
  else {
```

Figure 8–21

```
#   End-tag processing.  For "gen" or "exec" invoke
#   processing passing the stack of parents and the
#   end-tag prefix.
    if ($PROCESSING eq "exec") {
       &execute_sr(*ancestors,"\&et"); }
    elsif ($PROCESSING eq "gen") {
       &write_sr(*ancestors,"","\&et"); }
    pop @ancestors;
  }
}
```

Figure 8–21 (continued)

The code in Figure 8–22 shows start-tag processing. The element type name is pushed the onto the ancestor stack and we write or execute the element-in-context routine. If the tag was an empty-element tag, we immediately pop the element type name just added.

```
else {
# This is either an empty tag or a start tag.  Add the
# tag name to the ancestor stack.
  push (@ancestors, $gi);
# Start-tag processing.  For "gen" or "exec" invoke
# processing passing the stack of parents, the attribute
# associative array and the start-tag prefix.
  if ($PROCESSING eq "gen") {
    &write_sr(*ancestors,*attrarray,"\&st"); }
  elsif ($PROCESSING eq "exec") {
    &execute_sr(*ancestors,"\&st"); }
  undef(%attrarray);
# EMPTY tags should not stay on the stack as they won't be
# closed by an end tag.
  if ($xml_empty) {
    pop @ancestors; }
}
}
#--------------------------------------------------------#
```

Figure 8–22

Now we will look at the subroutine which is used in "gen" mode to write out element-in-context subroutine names. *write_sr* is passed the ancestor stack, the current element's attribute associative array, and a prefix for either start-tag, end-tag, or PCDATA. An outline of write_sr processing appears in Figure 8–23.

---

1. Create an element-in-context name by concatenating all ancestors, with each individual element type name separated by a '_'. For example, if the root element is RECORD and RECORD contains a HEAD and HEAD contains an ID, the element-in-context name will be

   _ID_HEAD_RECORD

   (The reader should note that the '_' is a valid character in an XML element names. Our processor may not work correctly if this character is, in fact, used in element names.)

   The event type prefix is "st" for a start-tag, "et" for an end-tag, and "pc" for PCDATA. The three subroutines for the above example will therefore be named

   - st_ID_HEAD_RECORD
   - pc_ID_HEAD_RECORD
   - et_ID_HEAD_RECORD

2. Loop through the attribute associative array and write a Perl comment containing the attribute name for each attribute for the convenience of the writer of the transformation rules.

3. Store subroutines in an associative array so that duplicate element-in-context rules can be checked for. If not a duplicate, write the element-in-context subroutine stub.

Figure 8–23   Outline of write_sr

```
#-----------------------------------------------------#
sub write_sr {
# This subroutine writes out an element-in-context
# subroutine stub.
  local(*elements,*attributes,$prefix) = @_;
  undef($sr_name);
  undef($at_name);
# Loop through all the parent elements and affix to the
# element name.
  foreach $element (@elements) {
    $sr_name = "_".$element.$sr_name; }
# Loop through all the attributes and write a comment
# which will identify the attribute name.
  foreach $attribute (keys %attributes) {
    $at_name = $at_name."# \$attrarray{\"$attribute\"}\n"; }
# To avoid writing duplicate subroutine stubs save the
# subroutine name in an associate array with a flag to
# indicate whether it has already been seen or not.
  if ($subroutines{"$prefix$sr_name"} ne "SEEN") {
    $subroutines{"$prefix$sr_name"} = "SEEN";
# Write the subroutines.
    if ($prefix eq "\&st") {
      &println("sub st$sr_name {\n$at_name;\n}"); }
    elsif ($prefix eq "\&pc") {
      &println("sub pc$sr_name {\n# \$pcdata\n;\n}"); }
    elsif ($prefix eq "\&et") {
      &println("sub et$sr_name {\n;\n}"); } }
}
#-----------------------------------------------------#
```

Figure 8–24

execute_sr, shown in Figure 8–25, calls an element-in-context subroutine. The subroutine name is constructed in exactly the same manner as was described for *write_sr.* Once the subroutine name is composed, the subroutine is executed with an eval statement.

```
#----------------------------------------------------------#
sub execute_sr {
# This subroutine executes an element-in-context
# subroutine.
  local(*elements,$prefix) = @_;
  undef($sr_name);
# Compose the name of the subroutine by looping through the
# parent stack.
  foreach $element (@elements) {
    $sr_name = "_".$element.$sr_name; }
  $sr_name = $prefix.$sr_name;
  eval $sr_name;
}
#----------------------------------------------------------#
```

Figure 8–25

print_error_at_context, listed in Figure 8–26, prints out the contents of the ancestor stack in order to identify the contextual position of a well-formedness error to the user.

```
#----------------------------------------------------------#
sub print_error_at_context {
# This routine prints out an error message with the contents
# of the ancestor stack so the context of the error can be
# identified.
# It would be most helpful to have line numbers.  In
# principle it is possible but more difficult since we
# choose to not process the document line by line.  We could
# still count line break characters as we scan the document.
# Nesting errors can cause every tag thereafter to generate
# an error so stop at 10.
if ($error_count == 10) {
  &printn("More than 10 errors ...");
  $error_count++;
}
else {
  $error_count++;
  &printn("Not well formed at context");
```

Figure 8–26

```
# Just cycle through the ancestor stack.
  foreach $element (@ancestors) {
    print "$first$element";
    $first = "->";
  }
  $first = "";
  &printn(" tag: <$st_or_et$gi $attrline>");
}
}
#----------------------------------------------------------#
```

Figure 8-26 (continued)

The last two routines, shown in Figure 8–27, of *transwf* check the error count and print out messages for either CGI or stand-alone modes.

```
#----------------------------------------------------------#
sub check_error_count {
if ($error_count == 0 && $PROCESSING eq "check") {
  &printn("INF This document appears to be well-formed.");
}
}
#----------------------------------------------------------#
sub printn {
local($string) = @_;
if ($MODE eq "CGI") {
    print "<pre>$string\n</pre>";
}
else {
  # $MODE eq "STANDALONE"
  print "$string\n";
}
}
#----------------------------------------------------------#
#----------------------------------------------------------#
```

Figure 8-27

8.3.2   *Element-in-Context Subroutines?*

At this point it may have occurred to the reader that transwf's element-in-context algorithm will lead to very long subroutine names when the document is deeply nested and a very large number of subroutines when there are many optional elements in content models. For even moderate examples of either or both of these conditions, in fact, *transwf's* simple approach to the evaluation of element-in-context subroutines is completely impractical.

This problem is easily remedied. We present in Figure 8–28 a simple algorithm which, when added to the *write_sr* and *exec_sr* subroutines, will cause the evaluation of the subroutine which is most specific with respect to the current context but does not require the full context. This algorithm also causes a default subroutine to be evaluated in the event that no subroutine exists for the current context, making *transwf* operational even when only a single default subroutine has been defined. The basic idea is to create a table (in Perl it would be conveniently implemented as an associative array) of subroutines which have been defined and to search that table for the most qualified element-in-context routine which exists each time a subroutine is to be evaluated.

```
AncestorStack set up to contain
   top     DEFAULT
   top-1   Current ELEMENT
   top-n   Parent of top-n+1
   0       sentinal (cannot match ELEMENT name)

depth = top AncestorStack

Subroutine = EventPrefix.AncestorStack[depth]
while ( Subroutine exists-in SubroutineTable )
      xSubroutine = Subroutine
      depth--
      Subroutine = Subroutine."_".AncestorStack[depth]

eval xSubroutine
```

Figure 8–28   Pseudocode for Most Qualified E-I-C Algorithm

Hallelujah! Now if we have a *P* element in 50 different contexts, we need write only one *P* subroutine to process them all. If we wish to apply a different transformation in just one particular context, for example, in list *LISTITEM*s, we may add one in-context subroutine, *P_LISTITEM,* which will override the less qualified *P* subroutine.

8.3.3 *Generation of Subroutine Stubs*

The operation of the gen mode has been described in the preceding discussion of the core routine *transwf.* The reader should be alert to the fact that gen mode works on a well-formed document instance. If there are optional elements or attributes not present in the well-formed document instance, they will not be part of the gen output. The gen mode is invoked as follows:

```
perl transwf -p gen -f well-formed-document-instance
```

An instance of a bulletin board message on which we will run gen is shown in Figure 8–29.

```
<RECORD><HEAD><ID>17</ID><PARENT>6</PARENT><CHILDREN></
CHILDREN>
<AUTHOR>bianca</AUTHOR><SUBJECT>Links</SUBJECT>
<TIME>858491557</TIME></HEAD>
<BODY>Hi Everybody!
Here is the link for SGML/XML on the Web page:
<RAW><a href="http://www.sil.org/sgml/sgml.html">http://
www.sil.org/sgml/sgml.html</a></RAW>
You can find the official W3C stuff about XML at:
<RAW><a href="http://www.w3.org/pub/WWW/xml">http://
www.w3.org/pub/WWW/xml</a></RAW>
Enjoy!
Bianca
</BODY></RECORD>
```

Figure 8–29   Bulletin Board Well-formed Document Instance discrec

The result of running gen on the above document instance follows in Figure 8–30:

```
sub st_RECORD { ; }
sub st_HEAD_RECORD { ; }
sub st_ID_HEAD_RECORD { ; }
sub pc_ID_HEAD_RECORD {
# $pcdata
; }
sub et_ID_HEAD_RECORD { ; }
sub st_PARENT_HEAD_RECORD { ; }
sub pc_PARENT_HEAD_RECORD {
# $pcdata
; }
sub et_PARENT_HEAD_RECORD { ; }
sub st_CHILDREN_HEAD_RECORD { ; }
sub et_CHILDREN_HEAD_RECORD { ; }
sub st_AUTHOR_HEAD_RECORD { ; }
sub pc_AUTHOR_HEAD_RECORD {
# $pcdata
; }
sub et_AUTHOR_HEAD_RECORD { ; }
sub st_SUBJECT_HEAD_RECORD { ; }
sub pc_SUBJECT_HEAD_RECORD {
# $pcdata
; }
sub et_SUBJECT_HEAD_RECORD { ; }
sub st_TIME_HEAD_RECORD { ; }
sub pc_TIME_HEAD_RECORD {
# $pcdata
; }
sub et_TIME_HEAD_RECORD { ; }
sub et_HEAD_RECORD { ; }
sub st_BODY_RECORD { ; }
sub pc_BODY_RECORD {
# $pcdata
; }
sub st_RAW_BODY_RECORD { ; }
sub st_a_RAW_BODY_RECORD {
# $attrarray{"href"}
; }
sub pc_a_RAW_BODY_RECORD {
# $pcdata
```

Figure 8–30

```
;  }
sub et_a_RAW_BODY_RECORD { ; }
sub et_RAW_BODY_RECORD { ; }
sub et_BODY_RECORD { ; }
sub et_RECORD { ; }
```

Figure 8–30 (continued)

The *$pcdata* variable is written as a comment in each PCDATA event subroutine because the element content will be stored in it. The *RAW* element has the special behavior of causing all markup within it to not be recognized (equivalent to a CDATA section) so we will want to remove the *a* element-in-context routines. In this next section we will see how we avoid having transwf attempt to execute an element-in-context routine for HTML nested with the *RAW* element.

A well-formed document instance for a contact database record follows in Figure 8–31.

```
<?XML version="1.0"?>
<!DOCTYPE ContactRec SYSTEM "ContactRec.dtd">
<ContactRec><Name>
<Honorific Title="Mr"></Honorific>
<First>William</First><Last>Shakespeare</Last></Name>
<Company><JobTitle>Principal Webmaster</JobTitle>
<CompanyName>Globe Theater</CompanyName></Company>
<Address>
<Street>1 James Street</Street>
<Street>Kingsthorpe</Street>
<City>London</City>
<Region>SW</Region>
<PostCode>NN2 6NY</PostCode>
<Country>United Kingdom</Country>
<Phone>
<DayTime>604-000000</DayTime>
<Fax>604-000000</Fax>
</Phone>
<Internet>
<Email>wshakespeare@immortality.com</Email>
<Web>http://www.sonnets.com</Web>
```

Figure 8–31 Contact Database Well-Formed Document Instance Contrec

```
</Internet>
</Address>
<Product SGMLEditor="Yes" ActiveViews="Yes"
SymposiaPro="Yes" SymposiaDocPlus="Yes"
SGMLEditorJapanese="No" SGMLEditorKorean="No"
XMLProducts="Yes" General="No"/>
<Contacts>
<Language Preference="English"/>
<History>
<Events>
<Date>
<Day>01</Day><Month>04</Month><Year>96</Year>
</Date>
<Venue>Conference for Computing in the Humanities</Venue>
<Notes>Very interested in XML software.  Please send me
information about an evaluation.</Notes>
</Events>
</History>
</Contacts>
</ContactRec>
```

Figure 8–31   (continued)

The results of running gen on this document are as would be expected from the prior example so we will reproduce only the generated subroutine for *PRODUCT* to illustrate the treatment of attributes.

```
sub st_Product_ContactRec {
# $attrarray{"SymposiaPro"}
# $attrarray{"General"}
# $attrarray{"SGMLEditorKorean"}
# $attrarray{"SGMLEditor"}
# $attrarray{"XMLProducts"}
# $attrarray{"SGMLEditorJapanese"}
# $attrarray{"ActiveViews"}
# $attrarray{"SymposiaDocPlus"}
;
}
```

Figure 8–32

8.3.4 *Bulletin Board Type Transformation*

A transformation script for bulletin board messages which may be run on the server as a CGI script is presented below in Figure 8–33 thru 8–36. The script, *transrec.pl*, is formed simply by appending the element-in-context subroutines to *transwf.* The element-in-context subroutines have been developed to cause the appropriate HTML to be output at each start-tag, end-tag, and PCDATA event.

```
#!/usr/local/bin/perl
############################################################
##
# transrec.pl - This is an application of transwf with    #
# element-in-context subroutines appended for             #
# transforming bulletin board messages to HTML.           #
############################################################
#
#----------------------------------------------------------
#
# Element-in-context subroutines                          #
#----------------------------------------------------------
#
sub st_RECORD {
        print "<html><head><title>Bulletin Board Message</
title></head>\n<body>"; }
sub et_RECORD {
        print "$msgid</body></html>"; }
sub st_HEAD_RECORD {
        print "<h1>Bulletin Board Message</h1>\n"; }
sub et_HEAD_RECORD { ; }
```

Figure 8–33

Looking at Figure 8–33, we see in subroutine st_RECORD that the start-tag *RECORD* causes an HTML document to begin the document *BODY* and to insert all the *HEAD* matter. The *RECORD* end-tag, in subroutine et_RECORD causes the HTML document to be completed. As element-in-context subroutines are executed between these first and last events, the body of the message will be output. The *BODY* close tag is preceded by the contents of the variable *$msgid*.

This variable contains information which was stored during execution of earlier event-triggered subroutines. This is shown in the code segment below. This illustrates how information can be reordered during the transformation.

```
sub st_ID_HEAD_RECORD {
        $msgid = "<table border=1
width=\"100%\">\n<tr><td>Message ID: "; }
sub pc_ID_HEAD_RECORD {
        $msgid .= "$pcdata"; }
sub et_ID_HEAD_RECORD { $msgid .= "</td>"; }
sub st_PARENT_HEAD_RECORD {
        $msgid .= "<td>Parent: "; }
sub pc_PARENT_HEAD_RECORD {
        $msgid .= "$pcdata"; }
sub et_PARENT_HEAD_RECORD { $msgid .= "</td>"; }
sub st_CHILDREN_HEAD_RECORD {
        $msgid .= "<td>Children: "; }
sub pc_CHILDREN_HEAD_RECORD {
        $msgid .= "$pcdata;"; }
sub et_CHILDREN_HEAD_RECORD {
        $msgid .= "</td></tr></table>\n"; }
```

Figure 8–34

In Figure 8–34 it can be seen that we decided to put the message, parent, and children numbers in a table at the bottom of the document even though they precede the message body in the XML document. We simply store our HTML output in a global variable which will output later in the processing.

```
sub st_AUTHOR_HEAD_RECORD {
print "<table><tr><td><p font=\"+2\"><b>AUTHOR:   </b></p></
td>"; }
sub pc_AUTHOR_HEAD_RECORD {
print "<td>$pcdata</td></tr>\n"; }
sub et_AUTHOR_HEAD_RECORD { ; }
sub st_SUBJECT_HEAD_RECORD {
print "<tr><td><p font=\"+2\"><b>SUBJECT:   </b></p></td>"; }
sub pc_SUBJECT_HEAD_RECORD {
print "<td>$pcdata</td></tr>\n"; }
sub et_SUBJECT_HEAD_RECORD { ; }
sub st_TIME_HEAD_RECORD {
```

Figure 8–35

```
print "<tr><td><p font=\"+2\"><b>DATE:   </b></p></td>"; }
sub pc_TIME_HEAD_RECORD {
            $date = &strftime(localtime($pcdata));
print "<td>$date</td></tr></td></table>\n"; }
sub et_TIME_HEAD_RECORD { ; }
sub st_BODY_RECORD {
print "<br><hr><br><pre>"; }
sub pc_BODY_RECORD {
print "$pcdata"; }
sub et_BODY_RECORD {
print "</pre>"; }
sub strftime
   {
   local ($sec, $min, $hour, $mday, $mon, $year,
         $wday, $yday, $isdst) = @_;
   local ($string);

   $string .= ($mon + 1) . "/" . ($mday) . "/" . ($year +
1900);
   return $string;
   }
```

Figure 8–35 (continued)

Of course, since our script is a Perl program like any other, we are able to use subroutines such as strftime shown above in Figure 8–35 within our element-in-context subroutines.

Within the body of the message we wish to preserve white space. Therefore we have started an HTML *PRE* section when we see the start-tag for *BODY.* In the next section shown in Figure 8-36 we will see how we handle *RAW* sections where we wish to pass HTML markup straight through and not interpret it as XML elements to be transformed. At the beginning of *RAW* sections we will turn the *PRE* off and set it back on at the end of the *RAW* section so that HTML markup will be recognized in the browser.

```
sub st_RAW_BODY_RECORD {
        $file =~ /<\/RAW>/i;
        print "</pre>$`<pre>";
        $file = $';
        pop @ancestors; }
sub pc_RAW_BODY_RECORD {
; }
sub et_RAW_BODY_RECORD {
; }
```

Figure 8–36

RAW processing has recourse to a dirty trick–no, we aren't too proud. It accesses the file pointer and advances to the end of the *RAW* section simply copying everything beforehand into the output. *RAW* also pops *RAW* off the ancestor stack as all *RAW* processing is completed in the start-tag routine .

The HTML output of the type transformation, shown in Figure 8–37, concludes this section.

```
<html><head><title>Bulletin Board Message</title></head>

<body><h1>Bulletin Board Message</h1>
<table><tr><td><p font="+2"><b>AUTHOR:   </b></p></
td><td>bianca</td></tr>
<tr><td><p font="+2"><b>SUBJECT:   </b></p></td><td>Links</
td></tr>
<tr><td><p font="+2"><b>DATE:   </b></p></td><td>3/16/
1997</td></tr></td></table>
<br><hr><br><pre>Hi Everybody!

Here is the link for SGML/XML on the Web page:

</pre><a href="http://www.sil.org/sgml/sgml.html">http://
www.sil.org/sgml/sgml.html</a><pre>
You can find the official W3C stuff about XML at:

</pre><a href="http://www.w3.org/pub/WWW/xml">http://
www.w3.org/pub/WWW/xml</a><pre>
```

Figure 8–37

```
Enjoy!

Bianca
</pre><table border=1 width="100%">
<tr><td>Message ID: 17</td><td>Parent: 6</td><td>Children:
</td></tr></table>
</body></html>
```

Figure 8–37   (continued)

8.3.5   *Contact Database Type Transformation*

We present the Contact Database XML to HTML type transformation script *transcon.pl* below in Figure 8–38 thru 8–43 with a few comments on the handling of attributes, the use of attributes, and conditional processing based on attribute values occasionally interspersed.

```perl
#!/usr/local/bin/perl
###############################################################
# transcon.pl - This is an application of transwf with   #
# element-in-context subroutines appended for            #
# transforming Contact Database records to HTML.         #
###############################################################
#-----------------------------------------------------------#
# Element-in-context subroutines                          #
#-----------------------------------------------------------#
sub st_ContactRec {
    print "<html><head><title>Contact Record</title></
head>\n<body>
<h1>Contact Record</h1><hr>\n";
}
sub st_Name_ContactRec {
;
}
sub st_Honorific_Name_ContactRec {
    $honorific = $attrarray{"Title"};
```

Figure 8–38

```
}
sub pc_Honorific_Name_ContactRec {
    $honorific = $pcdata;   }
sub et_Honorific_Name_ContactRec {
;
}
```

Figure 8–38   (continued)

Honorific may have the title in an attribute value or as the content
of an element. We handle this, as shown in Figure 8–38, by setting
the *$honorific* variable to the value of the *Title* attribute when we pro-
cess the start-tag event and override that value if there is PCDATA
which causes the *Honorific* PCDATA event subroutine to be invoked.
We will use the *$honorific* variable later.

```
sub st_First_Name_ContactRec {
;
}
sub pc_First_Name_ContactRec {
    $fname = $pcdata;
;
}
sub et_First_Name_ContactRec {
;
}
sub st_Last_Name_ContactRec {
;
}
sub pc_Last_Name_ContactRec {
    $lname = $pcdata;
    $lname =~ tr/a-z/A-Z/;
}
```

Figure 8–39

The PCDATA for *Last* is translated into all uppercase characters, as
shown in Figure 8–39. Of course, any programmatic transformation
of data content can be performed with Perl's powerful text-handling
facilities. This is among the strongest justifications for using Perl in
preference to other languages.

```perl
sub et_Last_Name_ContactRec {
;
}
sub et_Name_ContactRec {
    print "$lname, $fname ($honorific)<br>\n";
}
sub st_Company_ContactRec {
;
}
sub st_JobTitle_Company_ContactRec {
;
}
sub pc_JobTitle_Company_ContactRec {
    print "$pcdata<br>\n";
}
sub et_JobTitle_Company_ContactRec {
;
}
sub st_CompanyName_Company_ContactRec {
;
}
sub pc_CompanyName_Company_ContactRec {
    $pcdata =~ tr/a-z/A-Z/;
    print "$pcdata<br>\n";
}
sub et_CompanyName_Company_ContactRec {
;
}
sub et_Company_ContactRec {
;
}
sub st_Address_ContactRec {
;
}
sub st_Street_Address_ContactRec {
;
}
sub pc_Street_Address_ContactRec {
    $street_count++;
    print "#$street_count $pcdata<br>\n";
}
```

Figure 8–40

Let us consider the processing of *Street* shown in Figure 8–40. The *Street* element may repeat. From the point of view of element-in-context processing each *Street* will be the same. However we may use an internal counter, *$street_count*, to keep track of each invocation. Here we use the counter to output the street address line number. A similar technique may be used to deal with multiple instances of PCDATA in mixed content. For example, it may be useful to distinguish between the first and subsequent occurrences of PCDATA when, deciding if some kind of separator character should precede the text.

```
sub et_Street_Address_ContactRec { ; }
sub st_City_Address_ContactRec { ; }
sub pc_City_Address_ContactRec {
    print "$pcdata, ";
}
sub et_City_Address_ContactRec { ; }
sub st_Region_Address_ContactRec { ; }
sub pc_Region_Address_ContactRec {
    print "$pcdata ";
}
sub et_Region_Address_ContactRec { ; }
sub st_PostCode_Address_ContactRec { ; }
sub pc_PostCode_Address_ContactRec {
    print "$pcdata    ";
}
sub et_PostCode_Address_ContactRec { ; }
sub st_Country_Address_ContactRec { ; }
sub pc_Country_Address_ContactRec {
   print "$pcdata<br>\n";
;
}
sub et_Country_Address_ContactRec { ; }
sub st_Phone_Address_ContactRec { ; }
sub st_DayTime_Phone_Address_ContactRec { ; }
sub pc_DayTime_Phone_Address_ContactRec {
    print "DAY: $pcdata ";
}
sub et_DayTime_Phone_Address_ContactRec { ; }
```

Figure 8–41

```
sub st_Fax_Phone_Address_ContactRec { ; }
sub pc_Fax_Phone_Address_ContactRec {
   print "FAX:  $pcdata";
}
sub et_Fax_Phone_Address_ContactRec { ; }
sub et_Phone_Address_ContactRec {
   print "<br>\n";
}
sub st_Internet_Address_ContactRec { ; }
sub st_Email_Internet_Address_ContactRec { ; }
sub pc_Email_Internet_Address_ContactRec {
   print "$pcdata  ";
}
sub et_Email_Internet_Address_ContactRec { ; }
sub st_Web_Internet_Address_ContactRec { ; }
sub pc_Web_Internet_Address_ContactRec {
   print "$pcdata";
}
sub et_Web_Internet_Address_ContactRec { ; }
sub et_Internet_Address_ContactRec {
   print "<br>\n";
}
sub et_Address_ContactRec {
   print "<hr>";
}
sub st_Product_ContactRec {
   foreach $product (@attrarray) {
      if ($attrarray{"$product"} =~ /YES/i) {
         print "$product "; }
   }
   print "<br>\n";
}
```

Figure 8–41 (continued)

We see in the st_Product_ContactRec subroutine in Figure 8–41 that we cycle through the attribute array and test each attribute value for a value of "YES" in order to determine if the attribute name should be output. This is an example of output being conditional on an attribute value.

```
sub st_Contacts_ContactRec { ; }
sub st_Language_Contacts_ContactRec {
    $language = $attrarray{"Preference"};
    print "$language<br>\n";
}
sub st_History_Contacts_ContactRec { ; }
sub st_Events_History_Contacts_ContactRec { ; }
sub st_Date_Events_History_Contacts_ContactRec { ; }
sub st_Day_Date_Events_History_Contacts_ContactRec { ; }
sub pc_Day_Date_Events_History_Contacts_ContactRec {
    $day = $pcdata;
}
sub et_Day_Date_Events_History_Contacts_ContactRec { ; }
sub st_Month_Date_Events_History_Contacts_ContactRec { ; }
sub pc_Month_Date_Events_History_Contacts_ContactRec {
    $month = $pcdata;
}
sub et_Month_Date_Events_History_Contacts_ContactRec { ; }
sub st_Year_Date_Events_History_Contacts_ContactRec { ; }
sub pc_Year_Date_Events_History_Contacts_ContactRec {
   $year = $pcdata;
}
sub et_Year_Date_Events_History_Contacts_ContactRec { ; }
sub et_Date_Events_History_Contacts_ContactRec {
    if ($language =~ /english/i) {
        print "$month/$day/$year "; }
    else {
        print "$day/$month/$year "; }
}
```

Figure 8–42

We see in the et_Date_Events_History_Contacts_ContactRec subroutine shown in Figure 8–42 that output is again conditional on the value of an attribute seen earlier, in this case the *$language* attribute. We test to see if the preferred language is English or French and output the date in the customary American or European order, respectively.

```
sub st_Venue_Events_History_Contacts_ContactRec { ; }
sub pc_Venue_Events_History_Contacts_ContactRec {
    print "$pcdata<br>\n";
;
}
sub et_Venue_Events_History_Contacts_ContactRec { ; }
sub st_Notes_Events_History_Contacts_ContactRec { ; }
sub pc_Notes_Events_History_Contacts_ContactRec {
    print "<p>$pcdata</p>\n";
;
}
sub et_Notes_Events_History_Contacts_ContactRec { ; }
sub et_Events_History_Contacts_ContactRec { ; }
sub et_History_Contacts_ContactRec { ; }
sub et_Contacts_ContactRec { ; }
sub et_ContactRec {
  print "<hr></body></html>"; }
```

Figure 8–43

The HTML output of the *transcon.pl* script follows in Figure 8–44.

```
<html><head><title>Contact Record</title></head>
<body>
<h1>Contact Record</h1><hr>
SHAKESPEARE, William (Mr)<br>
Principal Webmaster<br>
GLOBE THEATER<br>
#1 1 James Street<br>
#2 Kingsthorpe<br>
London, SW  NN2 6NY    United Kingdom<br>
DAY:  604-000000  FAX:  604-000000<br>
wshakespeare@immortality.com  http://www.sonnets.com<br>
<hr><br>
English<br>
04/01/96 Conference for Computing in the Humanities<br>
<p>Very interested in XML software.  Please send me
information about an evaluation.</p>
<hr></body></html>
```

Figure 8–44

8.3.6 *Bulletin Board Export to RTF*

The export routine to RTF, *bb2rtf.pl*, the ASCII interchange format supported by Microsoft Word, does not differ in any significant way from the XML to HTML routine discussed earlier except that the markup language is RTF. We use this routine as our print composition engine since Word will paginate the document and apply other page formatting parameters to the document when we import it.

The code for bb2rtf.pl follows.

```perl
#!/usr/local/bin/perl
#############################################################
# bb2rtf.pl - This is an application of transwf with        #
# element-in-context subroutines appended for               #
# transforming bulletin board messages to RTF.              #
#############################################################
#-----------------------------------------------------------#
# Element-in-context subroutines                            #
#-----------------------------------------------------------#
sub st_RECORD {
print "{\\rtf1\\ansi
\\deff4\\deflang1033{\\fonttbl{\\f4\\fro-
man\\fcharset0\\fprq2 Times New
Roman;}{\\f5\\fswiss\\fcharset0\\fprq2 Arial;}}{\\col-
ortbl;\\red0\\green0\\blue0;\\red0\\green0\\blue255;\\red0\
\green255\\blue255;\\red0\\green255\\blue0;\\red255\\green0
\\blue255;\\red255\\green0\\blue0;\\red255\\green255\\blue0
;\\red255\\green255\\blue255;\\red0\\green0\\blue128;\\red0
\\green128\\blue128;\\red0\\green128\\blue0;\\red128\\green
0\\blue128;\\red128\\green0\\blue0;\\red128\\green128\\blue
0;\\red128\\green128\\blue128;\\red192\\green192\\blue192;}
{\\stylesheet{\\widctlpar \\f4\\fs20\\lang1036 \\snext0 Nor-
mal;}{\\s1\\sb240\\sa60\\keepn\\widctlpar
\\b\\f5\\fs28\\lang1036\\kerning28 \\sbasedon0\\snext0 head-
ing 1;}{\\*\\cs10 \\additive Default Paragraph
Font;}}{\\info{\\author Xxxx}{\\operator Xxxx}{\\crea-
tim\\yr1998\\mo10\\dy17\\hr4\\min32}{\\revtim\\yr1998\\mo10
\\dy19\\hr16\\min2}{\\version2}{\\edmins3}{\\nofpages1}{\\n
ofwords53}{\\nofchars307}{\\*\\company Xxxx
```

Figure 8–45

```
S.A.}{\\vern57431}}\\widowctrl\\ftnbj\\aend-
doc\\hyphcaps0\\formshade \\fet0\\sectd \\linex0\\endnhere
{\\*\\pnseclvl1\\pnu-
crm\\pnstart1\\pnindent720\\pnhang{\\pntxta
.}}{\\*\\pnseclvl2\\pnu-
cltr\\pnstart1\\pnindent720\\pnhang{\\pntxta
.}}{\\*\\pnseclvl3\\pndec\\pnstart1\\pnindent720\\pnhang{\\
pntxta
.}}{\\*\\pnseclvl4\\pnlcltr\\pnstart1\\pnindent720\\pnhang{
\\pntxta
)}}{\\*\\pnseclvl5\\pndec\\pnstart1\\pnindent720\\pnhang{\\
pntxtb (}{\\pntxta
)}}{\\*\\pnseclvl6\\pnlcltr\\pnstart1\\pnindent720\\pnhang{
\\pntxtb (}{\\pntxta
)}}{\\*\\pnseclvl7\\pnlcrm\\pnstart1\\pnindent720\\pnhang{\
\pntxtb (}{\\pntxta
)}}{\\*\\pnseclvl8\\pnlcltr\\pnstart1\\pnindent720\\pnhang{
\\pntxtb (}{\\pntxta
)}}{\\*\\pnseclvl9\\pnlcrm\\pnstart1\\pnindent720\\pnhang{\
\pntxtb (}{\\pntxta )}}\\pard\\plain
\\s1\\sb240\\sa60\\keepn\\widctlpar
\\b\\f5\\fs28\\lang1036\\kerning28 Bulletin Board Mes-
sage\\par \\pard\\plain \\widctlpar \\f4\\fs20\\lang1036 ";
}
sub et_RECORD {
        print "$msgid\\par }"; }
sub st_HEAD_RECORD { ; }
sub et_HEAD_RECORD { ; }
sub st_ID_HEAD_RECORD {
        $msgid = "\\par \\trowd \\trgaph108\\trleft-108
\\cellx2844\\cellx5796\\cellx8748 \\pard \\widctlpar\\intbl
Message ID: "; }
sub pc_ID_HEAD_RECORD {
        $msgid .= "$pcdata"; }
sub et_ID_HEAD_RECORD {
        $msgid .= " \\cell"; }
sub st_PARENT_HEAD_RECORD {
        $msgid .= " Parent: "; }
sub pc_PARENT_HEAD_RECORD {
        $msgid .= "$pcdata"; }
sub et_PARENT_HEAD_RECORD {
        $msgid .= " \\cell "; }
```

Figure 8–45 (continued)

```
sub st_CHILDREN_HEAD_RECORD {
        $msgid .= "Children: "; }
sub pc_CHILDREN_HEAD_RECORD {
        $msgid .= "$pcdata;"; }
sub et_CHILDREN_HEAD_RECORD {
        $msgid .= "\\cell \\pard \\widctlpar\\intbl \\row
\\pard \\widctlpar"; }
sub st_AUTHOR_HEAD_RECORD {
        print "\\par {\\b AUTHOR:\\tab }"; }
sub pc_AUTHOR_HEAD_RECORD {
        print "$pcdata\n"; }
sub et_AUTHOR_HEAD_RECORD { ; }
sub st_SUBJECT_HEAD_RECORD {
        print "\\par {\\b SUBJECT:\\tab }"; }
sub pc_SUBJECT_HEAD_RECORD {
        print "$pcdata\n"; }
sub et_SUBJECT_HEAD_RECORD { ; }
sub st_TIME_HEAD_RECORD {
        print "\\par {\\b DATE:        \\tab }"; }
sub pc_TIME_HEAD_RECORD {
        $date = &strftime(localtime($pcdata));
        print "$date\n"; }
sub et_TIME_HEAD_RECORD { ; }
sub st_BODY_RECORD {
        print "\\par
\\par _____
\\par
\\par "; }
sub pc_BODY_RECORD {
        $pcdata =~ s/\n/\n\\par /g;
        print "$pcdata"; }
sub et_BODY_RECORD { ; }
sub st_RAW_BODY_RECORD {
        if ($file =~ /<\/RAW>/) {
           $pos = index($file,"</RAW>",0);
           $len = length($file);
           $content = substr($file, 0, $pos);
           $file = substr($file, $pos + 6, $len);
           $content =~ s/<\/?[^>]*>//g;
           $content =~ s/\n/\n\\par /g;
           print "$content";
           pop @ancestors; } }
```

Figure 8–45   (continued)

```
sub pc_RAW_BODY_RECORD {
        print "$pcdata"; }
sub et_RAW_BODY_RECORD { ; }
sub strftime
   {
   local ($sec, $min, $hour, $mday, $mon, $year, $wday, $yday,
$isdst) = @_;
   local ($string);

   $string .= ($mon + 1) . "/" . ($mday) . "/" . ($year +
1900);
   return $string;
   }
```

Figure 8–45   (continued)

The output of *bb2rtf.pl* run on the XML bulletin board message
used in this chapter in shown below in Figure 8–45:

```
{\rtf1\ansi \deff4\deflang1033{\fonttbl{\f4\fro-
man\fcharset0\fprq2 Times New
Roman;}{\f5\fswiss\fcharset0\fprq2 Arial;}}{\col-
ortbl;\red0\green0\blue0;\red0\green0\blue255;\red0\green
255\blue255;\red0\green255\blue0;\red255\green0\blue255;\
red255\green0\blue0;\red255\green255\blue0;\red255\green2
55\blue255;\red0\green0\blue128;\red0\green128\blue128;\r
ed0\green128\blue0;\red128\green0\blue128;\red128\green0\
blue0;\red128\green128\blue0;\red128\green128\blue128;\re
d192\green192\blue192;}{\stylesheet{\widctlpar
\f4\fs20\lang1036 \snext0 Nor-
mal;}{\s1\sb240\sa60\keepn\widctlpar
\b\f5\fs28\lang1036\kerning28 \sbasedon0\snext0 heading
1;}{\*\cs10 \additive Default Paragraph
Font;}}{\info{\author Xxxx}{\operator Xxxx}{\crea-
tim\yr1998\mo10\dy17\hr4\min32}{\revtim\yr1998\mo10\dy19\
hr16\min2}{\version2}{\edmins3}{\nofpages1}{\nofwords53}{
\nofchars307}{\*\company Xxxx S.A.}{\vern57431}}\widowc-
trl\ftnbj\aenddoc\hyphcaps0\formshade \fet0\sectd
\linex0\endnhere
```

Figure 8–46

```
{\*\pnseclvl1\pnucrm\pnstart1\pnindent720\pnhang{\pntxta
.}}{\*\pnseclvl2\pnu-
cltr\pnstart1\pnindent720\pnhang{\pntxta
.}}{\*\pnseclvl3\pndec\pnstart1\pnindent720\pnhang{\pntxta
.}}{\*\pnseclvl4\pnlcltr\pnstart1\pnindent720\pnhang{\pntxt
a
)}}{\*\pnseclvl5\pndec\pnstart1\pnindent720\pnhang{\pntxtb
(}{\pntxta
)}}{\*\pnseclvl6\pnlcltr\pnstart1\pnindent720\pnhang{\pntxt
b (}{\pntxta
)}}{\*\pnseclvl7\pnlcrm\pnstart1\pnindent720\pnhang{\pntxtb
 (}{\pntxta
)}}{\*\pnseclvl8\pnlcltr\pnstart1\pnindent720\pnhang{\pntxt
b (}{\pntxta
)}}{\*\pnseclvl9\pnlcrm\pnstart1\pnindent720\pnhang{\pntxtb
 (}{\pntxta )}}\pard\plain \s1\sb240\sa60\keepn\widctlpar
\b\f5\fs28\lang1036\kerning28 Bulletin Board Message\par
\pard\plain \widctlpar \f4\fs20\lang1036 \par {\b
AUTHOR:\tab }bianca
\par {\b SUBJECT:\tab }Links
\par {\b DATE:        \tab }3/16/1997
\par
\par

\par
\par Hi Everybody!
\par
\par Here is the link for SGML/XML on the Web page:
\par
\par http://www.sil.org/sgml/sgml.html
\par
\par You can find the official W3C stuff about XML at:
\par
\par http://www.w3.org/pub/WWW/xml
\par
\par Enjoy!
\par
\par Bianca
\par \par \trowd \trgaph108\trleft-108
\cellx2844\cellx5796\cellx8748 \pard \widctlpar\intbl Mes-
sage ID: 17 \cell Parent: 6 \cell Children: \cell \pard
\widctlpar\intbl \row \pard \widctlpar\par }
```

Figure 8–46 (continued)

8.3.7 *Delayed Output and Forward References*

One very important transformation technique has not been covered in the preceding examples: forward references and delaying output. The reason we may need this technique is very simple. Very often in an XML transformation we would like to output a value which we will not know until we process the document further. For example, an author may wish to insert a reference to a figure using the figure title but the figure and its title are found later in the document. One way to address this problem is to write a marker in the place where the forward reference occurs which, in effect, says, replace this marker with its actual value once you know the actual value. We will write output to a delayed output stream and perform a second pass over this output stream replacing all markers with their values at the end of processing. Once this second pass is completed we can than write the output stream to our normal output channel. A short program is presented below which shows how to accomplish this in Perl.

In Figure 8–46 below the markers are strings adhering to the following format:

£ref#£

where # is unique marker identifier. A common way to make it unique is to simply increment a numeric value each time a new marker is created. The marker pattern may occur in strings and must be reserved. The delayed output stream is the variable *$output*. All output is accumulated here but is not printed until the markers are replaced with their final values.

```
# output stream is written to instead of stdout
# throughout element-in-context processing.
# When a forward reference is needed it is
# written to output stream as a ref# surrounded
# by the £ symbol.

$output = "Reply\n\n";

$output .= "Language Preference £ref1£\n";
$output .= "Comment\n£ref2£\n";

# At a later point in the processing we know
# the value of forward reference.  We write
# to an associative array which uses the forward
# reference name as the key.
$ref{"£ref1£"} = "Vietnamese";
$ref{"£ref2£"} = "Thiên can o tai long ta,
Chu tâm kia moi bang ba chu tai.";

# At the very end of processing we loop
# through the associative array of forward
# references replacing each referent name
# with the variable in the output stream.
# We can than write the output stream to
# stdout.

foreach $referent (keys %ref) {
  $refvalue = $ref{"$referent"};
  $output =~ s/$referent/$refvalue/g; }

print $output;
```

Figure 8–47

And the output, shown in Figure 8–47, is:

```
Reply

Language Preference Vietnamese
Comment
Thiên can o tai long ta,
Chu tâm kia moi bang ba chu tai.
```

Figure 8–48

Part Three

■ E-mail

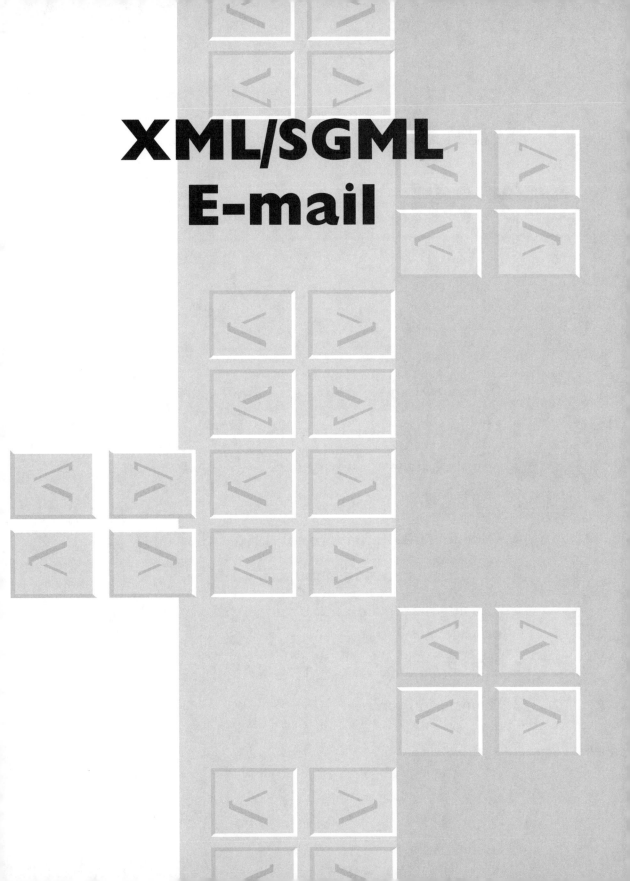

XML/SGML
E-mail

XML E-mail

Chapter

9

O ur discussion of XML in the Internet is not complete if it doesn't cover e-mail. Until recently there has been no standard means of e-mailing XML, but recent developments in both e-mail, such as the standardization of MIME, and XML/SGML, such as entity catalogs, finally make e-mail practical. This chapter discusses the implementation of a system to e-mail XML and SGML documents. It is mostly implemented in Perl and uses a modified version of SP to emit entity catalog information while parsing a document. It is designed to run on Unix systems but is easily ported to various other mail systems.

9.1 | Overview

Our first chapter introduced the notion of the various ways we manipulate our documents. Two that have received insufficient attention from the XML community are Send and Receive. In the Internet world, Send and Receive means e-mail, so this chapter will discuss e-mailing XML documents. E-mail, the first "killer app" of the Internet, remains one of its most important uses; in the corporate intranet, it is a major means of communication for geographically dispersed organizations. Web pages are fine for communicating information to a community of people, but you have to wait for them to come and get it. E-mail provides a means for point-to-point, almost instantaneous, communication. E-mail will remain an important means of communication for a long time to come. E-mailing XML gets XML into the day-to-day operation of your organization.

If you consider the variety of information representable in XML (all of it, to some degree), you will see the utility of exploiting it throughout your organization. Because of the centrality of e-mail in the modern enterprise, this cannot be done without the ability of e-mail XML—and display it as well-formatted text—from person to person. Memos, forms, notices—the usual set of business communications—can all be XML. XML also avoids many conformance issues by being platform independent; it doesn't require the recipient to have the same software as the sender to see a well-formatted document. Both the content, the XML message, and the format, a DSSSL stylesheet, are standard.

Push technology has received much attention lately. At this time, however, push technology has yet to become standardized. Most push technologies, however, are really "scheduled pull." New material is readied at a particular time. The client browsers arrange to retrieve that information at that time. This kind of push technology presents no new challenges—when the new material is retrieved it is displayed like previous material.

Up until now, e-mail has not been a popular means of disseminating XML/SGML, but recent developments in the SGML community are changing that situation. The problem in the past has been the dependence of an SGML document on other entities in the sender's environment. New developments, such as SGML Open Catalogs, MIME, Panorama, DSSSL, and even the Web, now make it possible to send a document from one location to another reliably.

Because commercial vendors have yet to take advantage of these new possibilities to provide e-mail for XML documents, we are providing the necessary software, called SGMaiL, on the accompanying CD-ROM. This is a "bare-bones" but serviceable implementation supporting DSSSL style sheets. The World Wide Web Consortium's Cascading Style Sheets could easily be supported as well. The rest of this chapter is devoted to explaining this agent and the two essential technologies behind it—SGML Open Catalogs and MIME. With this information in hand you will not only be able to use the existing agent but also extend it for your own needs.

9.2 | Why XML/SGML Is Hard to E-mail

The use of external entities makes a single document the hub of a collection of objects. These objects are combined to form the final document whose data are passed to the application. As we learned, entities are defined in the DTD and are located by either public or system identifiers.

Entities designated by public identifiers are normally entities whose contents are agreed to by some group or standards body and do not change. The HTML 3.2 DTD, for example, has "-//W3C//DTD HTML 3.2//EN" as its public identifier. A public entity can theoretically be retrieved from any location on the network (since it is the same everywhere), and once retrieved can be kept indefinitely.

System identifiers, on the other hand, simply refer to entities local to the system creating the document. There is little likelihood of finding the entity other than at the originating site, nor is there any promise of the entity's longevity. Its existence could be completely ad hoc.

As the parser cannot magically know where to find arbitrary entities, the declaration of an external entity in a DTD also needs to indicate, somehow, where the physical object (or objects) containing the entity is actually stored. In the "old days" this would be the name of a file. Of course, a file name only works on a particular machine or LAN. Suppose a document full of references to entities in the local file system is sent to another system. Unless all the entities just happen to be in the same location in the recipient's file system, the document becomes inaccessible.

The first fallback from this standpoint of total gibberish is to rely solely on public identifiers. But this only works if either

1. The sender and receiver agree on the set of allowable public identifiers, so the sender can be sure to use only ones known to the receiver. This is possible if the DTD is an industry standard, or the organizations have already agreed on the set, but this virtually eliminates ad hoc communication using smaller DTDs or customized DTDs

2. There is some acknowledged means of retrieving public entities. Up until now there has not been one, nor does any such agreement appear imminent.

The second approach might be to go through the document carefully to alter entity declarations so they point to locations on the recipient's system (skipping for the moment the question of finding out where these would be, or packaging the right material to send). This approach is not only complex and error-prone but also has the unfortunate side effect of creating a document different from the original.

A third approach, which is the one the SGML community has started taking, is to declare external entities in the DTD in a platform-independent way. The same entities can then be linked to different files on different systems without having to change the document. The means of doing this is the entity catalog.

9.3 | Entity Catalogs

The SGML Open Group (www.sgmlopen.com), an industry consortium addressing interoperability issues among SGML tools, has created an industry standard entity catalog format. The entity catalog represents another layer of indirection between the document and the file system. Entity declarations in documents no longer refer to the file system, but to entries in the catalog, and these entries refer to the file system. This additional layer frees the documents from the underlying environment;

they not only become more transportable but also easier to maintain. The physical location of entities can change arbitrarily. As long as the entity catalog is kept up-to-date, the documents will not be affected. Changing entries in a single file is much easier and more robust than updating every entity declaration in every DTD on the system.

The next sections will describe the structure of an entity catalog and will show, in general terms, how it can be used for constructing an e-mail message.

9.3.1 *Entity Catalog Structure*

An entity catalog is a file composed of a list of entries. With one exception, each entry has two or three parts. Tables 9–1 and 9–2 identify these two- and three-field entry types. These can be seen as instructions to the entity manager, the piece of software ultimately responsible for finding entities and handing them to the parser. The original specification for catalogs comes from SGML Open Technical Resolution 9401:1995, edited by Paul Grosso.

Entity type	*Declared Entity Identifier*	*System Identifier*
DOCTYPE LINKTYPE ENTITY PUBLIC	Either a public identifier or an entity name	Local name for resource, or, where supported, a URL

Table 9.1   Three-Field Catalog Entries

Entity type	*Field type*
SGMLDECL	System Identifier
DOCUMENT	System Identifier

Table 9.2   Two-Field Catalog Entries

9.3.2 *Catalog Entry Syntax*

As the general purpose of an entity catalog is to provide a mapping between identifiers used in documents and physical locations, we will start by describing those entries.

9.3.2.1   Catalog Syntax for Specifying Entities

These entities have three fields, with the following general meaning:

1. The type of entity being located. This can be one of the following:

   - DOCTYPE, indicating that the entry refers to a set of DTD declarations.
   - LINKTYPE, for a link type definition (linktypes are not yet part of XML, but are used in full SGML).
   - ENTITY (this holds for both general and parameter entities)
   - PUBLIC, indicating that this points to the location of a public entity.

2. The entity's name. Its format should correspond to the appropriate entity type. For example, if the entity is public, then the string should be a valid public identifier. If the entity is a parameter entity, then the name should start with a percent sign (%).
3. The system identifier, that is, the file name or other storage object identifier(s) for the entity. This is dependent on both the local system and the operating system. On systems supporting it, this field could be a URL; the system needn't be any smaller than the Internet.

Notice how entity declarations in the DTD should no longer include a system identifier. In other words, a declaration such as

```
<!ENTITY an-entity SYSTEM "an-entity.sgm">
```

should be shortened to

```
<!ENTITY an-entity SYSTEM>
```

and the catalog should have a declaration like

```
ENTITY an-entity "an-entity.sgm"
```

9.3.2.2   Other Catalog Entries

The entries with only two fields represent the SGML entities which aren't named:

- SGMLDECL, if the entry refers to an SGML Declaration. XML documents do not allow an SGML declaration, but full SGML documents do.
- DOCUMENT, meaning the entity will be a document. This becomes the default document if a parser is started with just the entity catalog and no explicit document.

Missing from all of these is a way of designating a style sheet for displaying the XML by the recipient. The SEMANTIC entry was proposed for this at one point. SEMANTIC indicates the location of the semantic information for the document, where this is possibly, but not necessarily, a style sheet. The fields for SEMANTIC are the following:

1. Semantic name identifies the particular semantics.
2. Semantic type would have a value such as DSSSL or CSS1.
3. Semantic title is an arbitrary string.
4. Storage object identifier gives a network location for the style sheet or program implementing the semantics.

```
SGMLDECL syssgml.decl
PUBLIC `ISO 8879-1986//ENTITIES Added Latin 1//EN//HTML'
ISOlat1.sgm
ENTITY product-name /usr/local/products/names.ent
ENTITY %rules /usr/local/sgml/parms.ent
ENTITY nonsense /dev/null
DOCTYPE myDTD myDTD.dtd
```

Figure 9–1   Example SGML Open Catalog

```
<!ENTITY % ISOlat1 ``ISO 8879-1986//ENTITIES Added Latin 1/
/EN//HTML''>
%ISOlat1;
<!ENTITY product-name system>
<!ENTITY % rules system>
<!ELEMENT root - - (#PCDATA, %rules;)>
```

Figure 9–2   DTD Declarations Declaring Entities in the Catalog

```
<!DOCTYPE myDTD system>
<root>
The product name is &product-name;.<rules>....</rules>
</root>
```

Figure 9–3   Document Using Entities from the Catalog

Figures 9–1 to 9–3 give a small example of an entity catalog at work. Figure 9–1 shows a small entity catalog with five entries defining entities of various types. The DTD in Figure 9–2 refers to three of these, making them accessible to the document in Figure 9–3. The document additionally references two entities—the default SGML declaration is used implicitly, and the DTD itself is referenced on the first line.

A parser faced with the document would require several files. A glance at the doctype declaration sends the parser back to the entity catalog to get the myDTD declarations in file myDTD.dtd. Parsing the DTD will reveal the rest of the entries in the catalog, except for the nonsense entry. However none of these are actually used in the document, except product-name, which will be substituted where referenced.

9.3.3 *Building an E-mail Message from a Catalog*

As mentioned before, the initial entity of a document is the hub of a collection of entities which together produce a final, parsed product. The problem is locating all the elements composing that final product without altering the original entities, both at the sender and at the receiver. Entity catalogs provide that possibility.

Given any initial entity, parsing that entity will reveal all of the entities actually used, directly or indirectly, by the document. If entity catalogs are used exclusively, then each of these entities will have an entry in a catalog. At the end of parsing, the e-mail agent will have a list of all the entities named and their actual system identifiers. From these it can compose a complete e-mail message.

This e-mail message will contain all the entities needed to construct the document at the recipient. They will be kept separate, rather than being all mixed into a larger single entity. The message will also contain a new entity catalog. This catalog contains all the identifiers encountered in parsing the original, but the system identifiers now refer to parts of the message, rather than locations in a file system. This total message—the initial document entity and all the entities needed to parse it—is e-mailed to the recipient.

The recipient's mail agent will decompose the message and find the catalog. The catalog tells the e-mail agent what each piece is. The agent stores them at the appropriate location in the local system and writes one final catalog—the same one it received, but with the system identifiers now pointing to actual locations in the receiver's file system.

This process sketches, in general terms, how an SGML e-mail agent works. Missing is a description of how the e-mail package itself is constructed. This requires some understanding of MIME, the Multipurpose Internet Mail Extensions.

9.4 | MIME

E-mail has been part of the Internet from its earliest days and has always been among its most significant technologies. For almost that entire time, e-mail has been limited to single chunks of 7-bit ASCII text—no colors, no graphics, no executables, and no attachments. Experiments were made with various kinds of multimedia mail, but the idea didn't really take off on the Internet until the standardization of MIME. MIME has three important elements for multimedia mail:

- A very simple means of composing/decomposing an e-mail of several pieces (called attachments).

- A straightforward protocol for describing the type of content each piece contains.

- A protocol for converting binary information to/from 7-bit ASCII.

Together these allow multipart, multimedia mail to "tunnel" through the preexisting Internet e-mail infrastructure. By tunneling we mean that several related objects, some of which are binary, are disguised as a single piece of 7-bit ASCII text for transmission through the Internet and then broken up again and converted back to their original form by the recipient.

We will explain the basic elements of the MIME protocol, the extensions proposed for XML, and how we still had to "cheat" a little to get around limitations of some current MIME e-mail agents. The goal here is not an exhaustive tutorial on MIME, but sufficient information to enable you to look at a MIME message and understand how it is composed. MIME is also of great interest as it is also part of the language of HTTP. If you look at an HTTP message from a server to a client, you will see a MIME header near the top.

9.4.1 *Parts of a MIME message*

The MIME standard is described in two IETF RFC's. The IETF, or Internet Engineering Task Force, is the main standards body for the Internet, to the extent that one exists. An RFC is a Request for Comments, and RFC 1521 describes the protocol for MIME messages. RFC 1521 extends RFC 822, the plain ASCII e-mail standard mentioned above. Like standard Internet e-mail, a MIME message is composed of a group of headers followed by a text body. Not surprisingly, MIME messages have more headers than plain vanilla e-mail.

9.4.1.1   MIME Headers

MIME messages can have several types of headers. Not all of them are obligatory, except the first two. These headers have the following syntax:

- The header name.
- A colon (:).
- Value for this header.
- Additional parameters. These are separated by semicolons (;), and of the form "parameter-name=value."

The important headers are as follows:

1. The MIME-Version indicates which version of MIME was used for the message. At the present time this is fixed to 1.0. Not coincidentally, this indicates to the e-mail agent that this is a MIME message.
2. The Content-Type indicates what kind of information is in the message. The content type consists of two parts, the type and subtype. The type indicates the general class, while the subtype indicates the specific encoding. Values for the type include:

- `text` can represent various kinds of textual information. Ordinary e-mail has the type `text/plain`, while Web documents are `text/html`.

- `multipart` indicates the message will have more than one part, known in the parlance as attachments. The most significant subtype here is `mixed`, indicating the attachments are of independent types. Each attachment will receive its own content type header.

- `application` indicates the contents will not fall into one of the standard types. The mail agent will not attempt to understand it but will send it to a special application for display. The subtype will indicate what the application is, such as a particular spreadsheet or word processor. If the subtype is not standard, then it should start "x."

3. `Content-Transfer-Encoding` indicates the format of the message data. Each attachment may have a different encoding. The default is the 7-bit ASCII of ordinary e-mail messages. Two other significant encodings are:

- `quoted-printable` is a mechanism for encoding 8-bit characters in ASCII. In particular, any character can be represented by "=" followed by two uppercase hexidecimal digits (i.e., the equal sign itself is "=3D"), and soft line breaks terminate with the same equal sign. This enables a mail message with long lines to be broken into the short lines required by the old mail protocol.

- `base64` is an encoding for binary data into ASCII, similar in intent to the `uuencode` algorithm from UNIX. This allows arbitrary binary data to be shipped using MIME. An attachment in base64 will display as a block of gibberish, with each line (except the last) exactly 76 characters.

There are two other encodings for pure binary information, but they are less frequently used.

MIME makes allowance for a proliferation of content types, especially through the `application` content type. However, developing new transfer encodings is particularly frowned upon. (Supporting a new type, as we will see, is very straightforward and requires no changes to the e-mail agent, while a new transfer encoding does require changes to the mail agent.)

Figure 9–4 presents a very simple MIME message. It has only one part, and that part is in ordinary ASCII text. The `charset` entry ensures this, although that is the default.

```
From: fuchs@localhost

To: fuchs@localhost

MIME-version: 1.0

Subject: not much

Content-type: text/plain; charset=us-ascii


This is my message to myself.
```

Figure 9–4   Short MIME Message

9.4.1.2   Attachments in Multipart Messages

The multipart header also has a `boundary` subheader. This subheader specifies an ASCII string used to separate the different attachments of the message. Each attachment is preceded by a line starting with two dashes followed by the boundary string and a new line. The last attachment is followed by a line containing only the boundary string with two dashes before it and two more after it. In Figure 9–5, for example, the `Content-Type` is `multipart/text`. The boundary string is `BOUNDARY=simple`. There are two parts, both just text, although the second one is actually an HTML page. The message ends with a final copy of the boundary string with two trailing dashes. Note that the boundary string must be chosen so that it not be confused with some part of the message. There is always a blank line between the last header and the start of the attachment body, even in a single- part message.

```
From: fuchs

To: fuchs

Subject: mimer

MIME-Version: 1.0

Content-Type: multipart/text; boundary="BOUNDARY=simple";


--BOUNDARY=simple

Content-type: text/plain; charset=us-ascii


This is the first part of a multipart MIME message.


--BOUNDARY=simple

Content-type: text/html; charset=us-ascii


<HTML>

<BODY>

<p>This is the second part of a multipart MIME message. This
attachment is part of an HTML page.

...

</HTML>


--BOUNDARY=simple--
```

Figure 9–5. Example Multipart MIME Message

Each attachment of a MIME message can also have a multipart content type, leading the pieces to form a tree (in which case each attachment would have its own boundary string). MIME is an example of a simple protocol which can be used to describe very complex objects.

9.4.2   *Handling MIME Messages*

Because they are short and in plain text, our example messages don't require special software to understand, but a system accepting MIME messages must be able to understand messages composed of a variety of esoteric content types, perhaps one per attachment. History has also shown that the menagerie of content types will continue to grow, so the MIME agent must be easily extensible.

To handle this, the MIME e-mail agent uses a divide and conquer strategy. It turns out that divide is very simple, and conquer infinitely extensible.

First it parses the message and separates the different attachments and places each one in a different temporary file. This can be done without any knowledge of the contents of the messages, just by reading the headers and searching for boundary strings. This is the divide phase. Base64-encoded attachments can also be decoded during this phase.

After chopping up the message into different files, each of a particular content type, the e-mail agent passes them to different programs, each for the appropriate content type. This is the conquer phase.

The choice of program to handle each content type is determined by the `mailcap` file. Just as the entity catalog connects entity names to files, the `mailcap` file connects content types to commands and programs to process them.

Each line in the `mailcap` file has two or three fields:

1. The `content-type` under consideration. This is any valid type, such as the `text/plain` used above.

2. A command to be executed for attachments of this content type. This command can have various parameters indicating the parameters of the command. These include:

- %s stands for the name of the file. The default entry for `text/plain` is `cat %s`, or display the file designated by `%s` (in UNIX). If there is no `%s` parameter, then the entire file will be sent to the program on the standard input.

- %t is replaced by the content type of the file.

- If the Content-Type header contained any extra parameters (as Figure 9–4 had `charset=us-ascii`), then these can be passed by name. The `us-ascii` can be sent by adding the parameter `%{charset}` to the command.

- %n is replaced by the number of attachments in the e-mail message.

- %F is replaced by a list of argument pairs, one pair for each attachment. The first element of each pair gives the content type of the attachment, and the second its location on disk.

3. The last field can take on various values which we will not be concerned with here.

The MIME agent searches through these records to find the appropriate content type for an attachment and then executes the associated command with the correct parameters. New content types can be added by installing the appropriate programs and updating the `mail-cap` file, making the agent easily extensible.

9.5 | Building the SGMaiL Agent

With these two standards, entity catalogs and MIME, we can start to develop a way to send XML via e-mail. A document flows from one desktop to another through the following stages:

1. The sender composes the document. The sender should have implemented catalogs, so that entity declarations are storage system independent (otherwise the receiver's file system will need to mimic the sender's).

2. The sender hands the document to their XML e-mail agent.

3. The e-mail agent parses the document, retrieving the identifiers and storage locations for all the entities referenced in the document. The agent needs to parse the document, and especially the DTD declarations, to determine the external entities actually accessed by the document, although a more simple agent could just parse the catalog and default to include all the entities it contains. However, the catalog may cover several DTDs and include many entities not included in the document.

4. The e-mail agent creates a multipart MIME message with all the storage entities used by the message (and any subdocuments). Each attachment is given a separate identifier.

5. The agent creates a new catalog specifically for the message and adds it as an attachment. This catalog provides the information necessary for the receiving agent to disassemble the arriving message.

6. The MIME message is sent.

7. The receiving agent disassembles the message and hands it to an XML agent.

8. The XML agent retrieves the catalog attachment and adjusts the entries to correspond to the temporary files housing the downloaded entities.

9. The message is parsed and displayed or otherwise processed.

The accompanying CD-ROM provides sample e-mail agents—one each for sender and receiver. The rest of this chapter will describe these agents and provide some examples of their use.

9.6 | The Sending Agent

The job of the sending agent is to look through the list of entities accessed directly or indirectly by the hub document and assemble them into a MIME message. This requires parsing the document and seeing where the entity references lead and then forming them into a new catalog.

The job of parsing the document and returning the names, types, and local system identifiers is given to an SP-based application, `createCatalog`. This application, when given an input file, will output an appropriate catalog, with correct system IDs, starting with the location of the document itself. From this we will locate all the appropriate local files, organize them in a MIME message, and send them to the receiver.

The task of organizing the files is conducted by a Perl script. The Perl script performs the following operations:

- Fork `createCatalog` and parse its output.
- Create the headers for a MIME message.
- Assemble the pieces from the catalog into a MIME message.
- Create a new catalog.
- Send the MIME message.

9.6.1 *Modifying SP for "createCatalog"*

A crucial element of implementing SGMaiL is parsing a document to locate all the constituent parts. To do this we have modified James Clark's SP parser to emit entity catalog information. This section will briefly describe how this was done.

SP is a complex system with two APIs:

1. A documented "external" API for basic applications. This external API reflects only information in the document instance, not information in the DTD. The external API is appropriate for applications only needing the information found in the parsed document structure (such as element type names, attributes, and content).

2. A currently undocumented "internal" API for more complex applications, such as an editor, which needs to know about the DTD and even the state of the parser.

Neither of these APIs is truly appropriate for our application. The first is insufficient because some external entities (such as parameter entities) are used exclusively in the DTD and are never reflected in the document instance. The second is overkill—we are interested in some very simple information, which is produced at a very specific point in the program. For our purposes, the simplest action is to derive a new SP application (described below) to suppress the usual output and then simply insert a few lines exactly where the parser encounters the declaration of an external entity to print the desired information.

9.6.1.1 Identifying the Entities in a Document

In building a catalog generator from a document we really require only a few pieces of information:

1. The entity's type, which can be only one of ENTITY, DOCTYPE, LINKTYPE, NOTATION, or PUBLIC. In Figure 9–9, they are declared in the array declArr. The

other catalog entry types aren't relevant here—they are specific to finding information given an existing catalog. In our case, SP has done all that work for us and will deliver the actual system identifier.

2. Either the entity's declared name in the DTD, or the Formal Public Identifier (FPI), if one exists. An FPI is a unique string designating a resource in the network.

3. Whether or not it is a parameter entity.

4. Its local system identifier.

The code fragment in Figure 9–6 shows how this is done. The code is inserted in the file Entity.cxx from the Jade distribution.

```
{
int nameLen, externLen;
const char *declArr[] = {"ENTITY", "DOCTYPE", "LINKTYPE",
                         "NOTATION", "PUBLIC"};
const char *decltp;
char *namePtr;
if (externalId().publicIdString()){
    decltp=declArr[4];
    delete [] namePtr;
    nameLen = externalId().publicIdString()->size();
    namePtr = new char[nameLen + 3];
    sprintf(namePtr, "\"%.*s\"",
        externalId().publicIdString()->size(),
        externalId().publicIdString()->data());
} else {
    nameLen = name().size();
    decltp=declArr[0];
    namePtr = new char[nameLen + 2];
    sprintf(namePtr, "\"%.*s\"", nameLen,
        name().data());
    switch(declType()){
    case generalEntity:
      break;
    case parameterEntity:
      sprintf(namePtr, "\"%%%.*s\"", nameLen,
        name().data());
```

Figure 9–6   Code Added into Jade Distribution in Entity.cxx

```
        break;
     case doctype:
        decltp=declArr[1];
        break;
     case linktype:
        decltp=declArr[2];
        break;
 }
}

 case notation:
        decltp=declArr[3];
        break;
        }
 }
externLen = externalId().effectiveSystemId().size();
printf("%s  %s  %.*s\n",
      decltp, namePtr,
     externLen-8, externalId().effectiveSystemId().data() +
8);
```

Figure 9–6 Code Added into Jade Distribution in Entity.cxx (continued)

The process is simplest if an FPI exists for the entity (in which case the entry will be simply *PUBLIC FPI SOI*). This is done by calling the method `externalId()`, which returns an `ExternalId` object, and then calling `publicIdString()`, which returns a `StringC` object, (essentially an array of `char*` and its length), if there is a public ID, and the `null` string otherwise. If there is, then `decltp` is set to point to the string `"PUBLIC"` and the public ID is stored in `namePtr`, surrounded (for safety's sake) by quotes.

If there is not an FPI for the entity, then we examine its declaration type [method `delType()`] and store the internal name. The only interesting item here is the need to insert the percent sign (%) for parameter entities.

Finally we get the system ID by calling the methods `externalID().effectiveSystemId().data()`. When looking at this string, the program indexes 8 bytes into the record, due to the presence of some other information in the string.

All the pieces are printed to STDOUT, essentially creating a catalog during the parse. The same program could be used on any legacy document to create a catalog from scratch.

9.7 | Parsing the Catalog and Creating the E-mail Message

Parsing the entity catalog and assembling the e-mail message is done by a Perl script. The script takes two parameters:

1. The initial, unparsed text of the e-mail message itself.
   The size of the message may grow precipitously once all the external entities are included.
2. A style file, such as a DSSSL style sheet, to be used by the recipient to format the incoming information.
   On the accompanying CD ROM, we've included Jade, a partial implementation of DSSSL from James Clark, the principal designer of DSSSL. Although not complete, Jade is sufficient to build many applications, including stylesheets.

To begin we must find the path to the source document, which is done by splitting the input file name, removing the last part, and concatenating the path back together (as shown in the following code fragment). The rest of the processing is done in the directory of the e-mail message.

Next a temporary file is opened to contain the resulting e-mail message. To get a unique file name, we take the local time (a string returned by the `localtime` function) and remove the spaces. The first items to be written to the file are the MIME headers:

```
my @fileParts = split /\//, $DOCFILE;
my $docFile = pop @fileParts;
my $docDir = join '/', @fileParts;
chdir $docDir;
```

```
print MSGFILE "MIME-Version: 1.0\n",
     "Content-Type: application/x-sgml; boundary=
      \"BOUNDARY=simple\";\n"
     " type = \"application/x-sgml\";\n\n";
```

Next a Perl script invokes the modified SP. The output catalog is collected in a single Perl array for manipulation, each entry line being a separate element of the array. Each of these entries is then matched against a regular expression to determine which kind of entry it is. The kinds of entry that could come out of the parse are either three-item entries (PUBLIC, ENTITY, DOCTYPE, and LINKTYPE), or two-item entries (SGMLDECL, DOCUMENT). The following regex breaks the entry into its constituents.

```
@pieces = m/(\w+)\s*(".*?"|'.*?'|\S+)\s*(\S+)/;
```

This isolates the first word, the second word or quoted string, and the final sysid.

For each incoming entry, a new outgoing entity is created for the catalog to go in the mail message. For the outgoing system ID, we use the last part of the current sysid (without the file path). This is just the original type, the original public identifier, and the file name. We also keep a table with the file names and their paths.

When each entry has been examined, we can start to write the output file. The first entry in the multipart MIME file is the catalog, which starts with the DOCUMENT entry and STYLESHEET entry if one is available. The print statements for this are as follows:

```
print MSGFILE "--BOUNDARY=simple\n";
print MSGFILE "Content-type: application/SGML-Open-Catalog\n";
print MSGFILE "Content-ID: catalog\n\n";
print MSGFILE "DOCUMENT ", $docFile, "\n";
if ($STYLESHEET) {
    print MSGFILE "STYLESHEET ", $styleFile, "\n";
    push @fileTable, [$styleFile, $STYLEFILE];
}
print MSGFILE $outCat;
```

where MSGFILE is the mail message temporary file, $docfile is the document name, $stylefile is the optional style sheet, and $outcat is the rest of the catalog created above.

Finally, we look through the list of files and generate a MIME partition for each one. This entails creating the appropriate header fields and appending the file to the end of the mail message. Then we close the file and exit.

The complete package is then handed to a local mail system with the names of the recipients. How this is done is very system dependent.

```
ENTITY %addrdef /usr/sgml/address.sgm
PUBLIC "ISO 8879-1986//ENTITIES Added Latin 1//EN//HTML"
                ISOlat1.sgm
DOCTYPE memo /usr/sgml/memo.dtd
```

Figure 9–7   An Example Catalog with Local System Identifers. The Full Catalog May Be Much Larger.

```
<!entity % addrdef system>
%addrdef;
<!element memo - - (from, to, salutation, p+, signature)>
<!element from - - (address)>
<!element to - - (address)>
<!element salutation - - (#pcdata)>
<!element p - - (#pcdata)>
<!element signature - - (#pcdata)>
```

Figure 9–8   File /usr/sgml/memo.dtd (Mentioned in the Catalog)

```
<!element address - - (#pcdata)>
```

Figure 9–9   File /usr/sgml/address.sgm (Mentioned in the Catalog)

```
<!doctype memo system>
<memo>
<from><address>Matthew Fuchs</address></from>
<to><address>Michael Leventhal</address></to>
<salutation>Fellow Author!</salutation>
<p>This is a tiny sample document</p>
<p>It will be used for demonstrating SGMaiL.</p>
<signature>See ya ma&ntilde;ana!</signature>
</memo>
```

Figure 9–10 A Memo Document

Figures 9–7 through 9–10 show a small XML document and its accompanying system-dependent catalog (the ñ entity is a small n with a tilde over it from the ISO Latin set). As this catalog may cover several DTDs, the entries relevant for this particular document comprise only a small part of the total file. Once it is passed through the parser, the MIME message in Figure 9–11 is output. Notice that the system identifiers in the catalog have been replaced with MIME ContentID fields. This is the message which is mailed.

Figure 9–11 shows the entire MIME message that will be sent through the Internet. Check carefully to make sure all the pieces are there!

In cases where XML or WebSGML are being used, it would not be necessary to send the full DTD. This example sends the DTD for two reasons:

1. It does not significantly change the code. In any case, many of the entity declarations would need to be sent anyway; they would be in the internal subset. For example, the ISO Added Latin 1 (ISOlat1) file is itself just a list of entity declarations for binary characters to be used in documents. For an XML application to use one of these char-

acters, the parser would have to have read the ISOlat1 file. But it could not do that unless it had been declared in the DTD subset included with the document.

2. Entity catalogs do not yet officially exist for XML at the time of this writing, although plans are underway and they will either be very similar or identical to the framework defined here. In any case, as there is no particular e-mail system generally available for e-mailing SGML or XML, it is worthwhile to make sure the code can be applied to both.

```
From: fuchs
To: fuchs
Subject: mimer
MIME-Version: 1.0
Content-Type: application/x-sgml; boundary="BOUNDARY=simple";
--BOUNDARY=simple
Content-type: Application/SGML-Open-Catalog
Content-ID: <199706021223.TPP122.0@localhost>
ENTITY %addrdef <199706021223.TPP122.3@localhost>
PUBLIC "ISO 8879-1986//ENTITIES Added Latin 1//EN//HTML"
        <199706021223.TPP122.4@localhost>
DOCTYPE memo <199706021223.TPP122.2@localhost>
--BOUNDARY=simple
Content-type: Application/X-sgml
Content-ID: <199706021223.TPP122.1@localhost>
<!doctype memo system>
<memo>
<from><address>Matthew Fuchs</address></from>
<to><address>Michael Leventhal</address></to>
<salutation>Fellow Author!</salutation>
<p>This is a tiny sample document</p>
<p>It will be used for demonstrating SGMaiL.</p>
<signature>See ya ma&ntilde;ana!</signature>
</memo>
```

Figure 9–11 A Full SGMaiL Message

```
--BOUNDARY=simple
Content-type: Application/X-sgml
Content-ID: <199706021223.TPP122.2@localhost>
<!entity % addrdef system>
%addrdef;
<!element memo - - (from, to, salutation, p+, signature)>
<!element from - - (address)>
<!element to - - (address)>
<!element salutation - - (#pcdata)>
<!element p - - (#pcdata)>
<!element signature - - (#pcdata)>
--BOUNDARY=simple
Content-type: Application/X-sgml
Content-ID: <199706021223.TPP122.3@localhost>
<!element address - - (#pcdata)>
--BOUNDARY=simple
Content-type: Application/X-sgml
Content-ID: <199706021223.TPP122.4@localhost>
... the larger ISOlat1 file ...
--BOUNDARY=simple--
```

Figure 9–11 A Full SGMaiL Message (continued)

9.8 | The Receiving Agent

The receiving agent must undertake the symmetrical task—parsing the MIME message, retrieving the different parts, storing them, re-creating the catalog, and running the parser on the resulting document.

Most of this process is straightforward. However, most e-mail agents will simply display the list of attachments, either in text or through a GUI, and let the user view each separately. XML differs from many other kinds of multipart e-mail because the pieces are related in a way that makes them useless on their own, so this approach is inappropriate. The `multipart/related` content type has been proposed for this and similar cases, but this is not understood by most e-mail agents. Therefore, we've resorted to parsing the MIME message and separating the attachments ourselves, but in a way that is easily upgraded when the necessary support comes into existence.

The SGML messages we are sending are defined as `application/x-sgml`, which will be opaque to the e-mail agent. All the attachments will be stored together in a single file, whose name will be passed to our SGMaiL agent.

Because all the attachments are in one file, the first line of the file will be the boundary string, and each attachment will include all its headers, which can be used to identify the parts.

The first step to processing the message is separating each attachment and placing it in its own file. These files are placed in the directory if it is not specified. When separating the attachments, the most important item is the `Content-ID` header, which uniquely identifies each attachment.

In the following code extract in Figure 9–13, `getSection` parses through the MIME file looking for the end of the partition. There is a first loop looking for a blank line, as long as there is no blank line, the input is a header, which is appended to the string `$type`. Once that's found, the rest of the file is appended to `$lines` until the separator is encountered. The important elements of the headers are returned along with the whole attachment.

```
sub getSection {
    my ($lines, $ding);
    my $type="";
    my ($separator, $infile) = @_;
    my $finished = 0;
    for ($ding = <$infile>; !(($ding eq "\n") || ($ding eq
"\r\n"));
 $ding = <$infile>){
$type .= $ding;
    }
    LOOP: while (<$infile>){
$ding = $_;
if (($_ eq $separator . "\n") || ($_ eq $separator .
"\r\n")){
    last LOOP;
} elsif (($_ eq $separator . "--\n") || ($_ eq $separator .
"--\r\n")){
    $finished = 1;
    last LOOP;
}
$lines .= $_;
    }
    # for type, we want content-type,
    # content-id, and description;
    my @contentType = $type =~ m|[Cc]ontent-[Tt]ype: ([\w-
]+/[\w-]+)?|;
    my @contentID = $type =~ m/[Cc]ontent-
[Ii][Dd]:\s*([^\s;\r\n]+)?[; \r\n]/;
    my @contentDescr =
$type =~ m/[Cc]ontent-[Dd]escription:\s*(.+)?[;\r\n]/;
    if (lc $contentID[0] eq catalog){
$catalog = $lines;
    }
    return ({type => $contentType[0],
     id => $contentID[0],
     descr => $contentDescr[0]},
    $lines, $finished);
}
```

Figure 9–12 Code to Divide Sections of MIME Message

The following loop (Figure 9-14) goes through the entire MIME message, calling getSection, above, until there are no partitions. Each partition body is stored in a separate file. The variable @fileMap contains an associative array relating the partition's Content-ID (which is used for the system identifier in the catalog shipped with the SGMaiL message) to the actual file.

```
do {
    ($typeArr, $lines, $fin) = getSection $separator, *MSGFILE;
    my $fileName = "/tmp/sgmldir/" . $typeArr->{'id'};
    $fileMap{${$typeArr}{'id'}} = [$fileName, $typeArr];
    open $fileName,">$fileName";
    print $fileName $lines;
    close $fileName;
} until ($fin);
```

Figure 9–13   Place MIME Attachments into Separate Files.

The only remaining step is to actually display the message. This is determined by the SEMANTICS entries in the catalog. The current agent accepts only DSSSL style sheets.

9.9 | Conclusion

The goal of this chapter was to describe the new technologies available for distributing SGML documents via e-mail. Until now this was not a viable option, but it has become possible due to these recent developments.

Because of the lack of implementations, we have developed and included a new e-mail agent, SGMaiL, for you to experiment with. SGMaiL provides limited functionality but can be customized as required to fit your needs. The appropriate files are included in the accompanying CD-ROM.

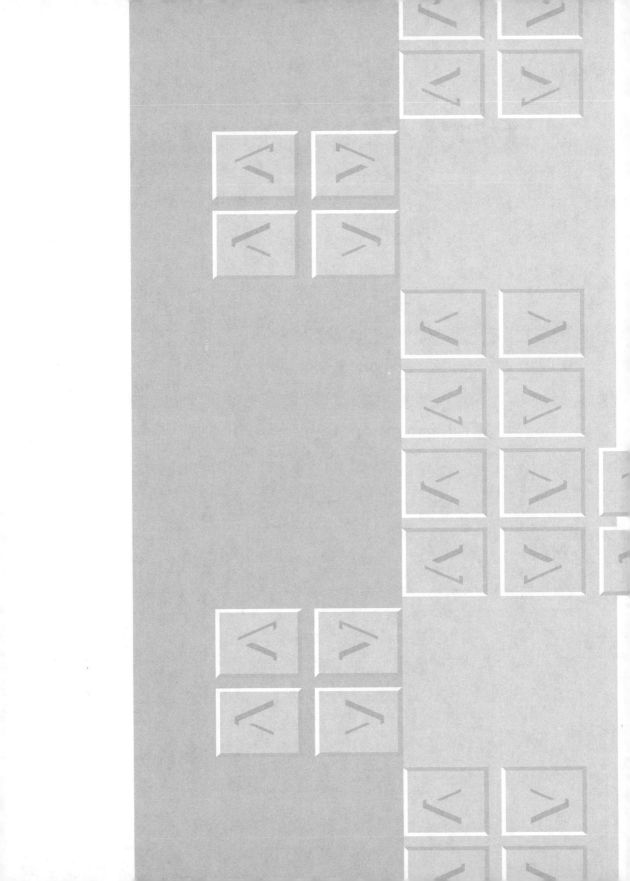

Part Four

XML and Java–
Parsers and APIs

XML Parsers and Application Programmer Interfaces

10

This chapter discusses how XML parsers and application programmer interfaces (APIs) serve developers of XML applications. We provide an overview of the capabilities and applications of XML parsers and then describe the major types of interfaces developers use to access these capabilities. We use existing parsers and proposed standard interfaces to illustrate these descriptions. The World-Wide Web Consortium's "Document Object Model" (DOM) is illustrated by a sample implementation of most of its features using the NXP parser as a basis. Finally, a sample application of the DOM that draws a graphic representation of an XML document is built on top of this implementation.

10.1 | Introduction

Many, if not most, applications which make use of XML require the services of an XML parser. In order to incorporate the capabilities of a parser within their applications, software developers generally employ either a command-line interface or some form of Application Programmer Interface (API). This chapter focuses on the latter of these interface types though it makes brief mention of the former. After some general background on XML parsers, we describe several generic types of parser interfaces, illustrating these with existing tools where possible. In the process, we introduce two XML parsers: NXP and AElfred. We then describe proposed standard interfaces: an event call-back interface named SAX, and an object model interface described in the World Wide Web Consortium's Working Draft Document Object Model (DOM)—Level 1. The DOM API is then illustrated by a sample implementation of it built on top of the NXP parser. Both NXP and this sample implementation of the W3C's DOM are written in Sun Microsystem's Java programming language. A simple application of the DOM interface is then presented. This application reads an XML document and then generates a graphic representation of its structure. The graphic representation emitted depicts the collection of DOM specified data structures which are made available to the developer through the DOM interface after the document is parsed . In this way we provide a sample application of the proposed DOM API as well as an illustration of the proposed standard itself.

10.2 | Parser Capabilities and Applications

This section summarizes the general capabilities which developers seek from an XML parser. Perhaps the two most common capabilities sought from an XML parser are verification that specific document instances are either conforming or valid, and document instance decomposition. More complicated and less frequently exploited capabilities are offered by some XML parsers which are based on their ability to access information relating to the DTDs and the current state of partial or "incremental" parses.

10.2.1 *Well-formedness and Validity Verification*

One of XML's greatest values is that it provides the basis for developing information representation languages. These languages are used both to facilitate information exchange between systems, or between humans and systems, and to provide for storage and recall of information on disk in a standard "serialized" form (disks only store information in serial form). Quality requirements for systems which use XML-based languages—e.g., as might be specified in contractual relationships between suppliers and purchasers—produce several applications for XML parsers. These exploit the capability of an XML parser to verify that specific document instances are well-formed or both well-formed and valid.

When a system is developed which expects to receive information that is represented using an XML-based language, it may or may not be a requirement that actual document instances received are well-formed or valid. The choice of whether to require documents to be well-formed (a minimum requirement if the documents are to be referred to as "XML" documents), or to require the more stringent condition of validity relative to a DTD, is one that must be made on an application-by-application basis according to the needs of the application. While this decision is generally outside the scope of this current discussion, just a couple of points will be made.

Primary factors affecting a decision to require and enforce well-formedness or validity should be the magnitude of harm which will result if a received document instance is not properly formed, and the reasonableness and cost of requiring and ensuring that proper form is used. In new applications, given the low cost of verifying well-formedness and validity, there is perhaps no reason not to require one or the other constraint. A reasonable exception to this is when the source of these instances is outside the developers control, and the need for them is sufficiently high as to warrant the cost of designing a system which can accommodate ill-formed instances.

In this chapter we assume there is some need for a parser. One consequence of the use of an XML parser is that the input provided to the parser will need to be either well-formed or valid; a parser will generally stop emitting output when these types of input errors are encountered and thus will not produce output that can be processed by the application. Thus even if the reasons for including a parser don't include verification of well-formedness or validity, this consequence will almost certainly necessitate introducing the requirement that XML input pass verification. This consequence may be avoided if means are provided to correct flaws in input form prior to offering it to the parser. Given that in the general case it takes the power of a parser to identify flaws in input form, only certain restricted classes of flaws are likely to be correctable in this situation. If the need to accept incorrectly formed input is high, and the requirement to include a parser is also unavoidable (e.g., to decompose input into components), one could look to advanced software language compiler techniques for approaches to automatic error detection and correction.

When XML documents are to be generated by humans, it is likely that *sans* availability of some form of quality control support, the document instances received from them will occasionally contain markup errors. Clearly when human-generated document instances are received by a system, the input will almost certainly need to be verified (the discussion in the prior paragraph excepted). In these situations, an XML parser may be used to verify markup is well-formed and (if required) valid before they are accepted as input.

Finally, an XML parser may be used to provision quality control support to authors so that the document instances they produce are well-formed and if required valid. This is the case, for instance, within an XML-aware editor. At the low end of these solutions, support may be offered by providing the author with a parser so that the quality of their product can be occasionally tested and any errors reported by the parser corrected. More sophisticated systems (e.g., general-purpose XML or

SGML editors) use parsing technology internally to provide interactive support to the author, providing guidance and even constraint in real time concerning which element types or attributes are acceptable or required at particular points in the document.

10.2.2 *Document Instance Decomposition*

Another major capability of a parser is that it can enable the decomposition of documents into subcomponents. In particular an XML parser can be used to provide a programmer with access to all the individual elements, attributes, text, DTD, entities, processing instructions, and so on, contained within a (valid or well-formed) document instance. This is perhaps the most common application for a parser. The parser serves as the front end within an input gathering system, decomposing ("parsing") a document into its subcomponents and then providing later stages of processing with access to these components. The latter portion of this chapter describes this in considerable detail.

10.2.3 *Parser Applications*

We now turn to the matter of identifying some general application areas for parsers within software systems. Given that XML is used to build information interchange languages, it should come as no surprise that the most common application of XML parsers is dealing with Input and/or Output (I/O) of information, whether this I/O involves interface to a file system, other components of a system, other systems, or to humans.

The short answer to the question of where XML parsers can find useful application is "anywhere XML-based languages find useful application." In general, an XML parser is most likely to serve a role in data input systems. Three high-level categories of applications are considered here:

- Configuration data receipt and interpretation.
- Intra- or intersystem communication
- Human interface

First, XML can easily replace many of the arcane formats used to store system configuration data in persistent storage (e.g., disk). While one might argue that adding an XML parser to an application just to read configuration files might be overkill, this may be an incorrect assessment when one considers first that a simple XML parser can be implemented very cheaply, and second, that XML parsers are likely to become standard equipment of application development frameworks and operating systems. Furthermore, if XML emerges to become the foundation of choice for the basis of document (or simply data) representation languages, the software machinery needed to complement the parser will also become commonly available. For example, standard machinery will provide, for example, programmer access to in-memory representation of received documents (e.g., as is the case with the W3C's DOM interface which is described below).

Support for intersystem communication is the classic XML application whereas its use in intrasystem communication is just emerging. For the same reasons that it was just suggested that XML parsers are likely to play an increasing role in configuration data management, so too is it likely to play roles in intrasystem data transfer applications. This represents a major new category of application area for SGML-related technology, an inroad into roles in mainstream data processing. Unlike document-oriented applications, these "nontraditional" SGML-technology applications will present new requirements on this technology base. For instance, we may find that many small fragments of XML-based content are manipulated in the course of a system's operation. As a result, the XML parser will likely be required to process multiple document instances during one continuous execution of the host program. These requirements on the parser need to be supported in parser APIs and also in the mechanics used to manage underlying system resources.

XML, and thus XML parsers, can play substantial roles in human interface systems. Applications in input gathering (from human users) were described earlier and will be formally associated with the concept of negotiation later in this book. There may be rare occasions when having a user directly type in XML text might make sense. A more likely role for XML in human interface systems is to facilitate communication between the various components of interface subsystems, and/or between interface subsystems and the rest of the application. For example, a GUI interface layer may be tasked with gathering data which is easily represented in XML for transport back to the primary application. This of course is just a particular form of the previous XML application category referred to as intrasystem communication, and thus similar parser roles and requirements as mentioned there will apply here as well.

10.3 | XML Parser Interfaces

We now discuss the means through which application software accesses XML parser capabilities. The software forming the application will invoke the services of the parser through some form of interface. The most common interfaces supported by XML parsers are

- Command-line interfaces
- ESIS event stream interfaces
- Event callback interfaces
- Object model interfaces

Each of these interfaces is described briefly in the following sections.

10.3.1 *Command-Line and ESIS Event Stream Interfaces*

Perhaps the simplest parser interface is the command-line interface. While not all XML parsers provide command-line interfaces, those that do can be put to immediate use in limited applications. When a command-line interface is provided by a parser, it almost certainly includes options to control the mode of parsing (e.g., whether XML validity or XML well-formedness constraints are tested), and what type of output is desired. One can generally specify, for instance, that output should indicate only whether the input satisfied the specified constraint. Many parsers (e.g., SP) also support a mode wherein output is generated which conforms to the definition of the standard stream interface known as element structure information set (ESIS).

The ESIS event stream output format is one of the oldest standard forms of interface to SGML parser output. It is sometimes provided as an interface to XML parsers, though over time this interface is likely to be eliminated as "higher-level" application programmer interfaces become standardized (for instance the SAX and DOM interfaces described below). This is because these higher level interfaces encapsulate (in the implementations which lay beneath them) functionality which the programmer would otherwise have to implement themselves. Still, the ESIS event stream is one of the simplest and easiest interfaces to use. It defines a set of events that can occur during parsing, such as the start of an element or the occurrence of an attribute, and then specifies for each a standard way to represent the information contained in this event on a stream (such as stdout). For example, when an element starts an indication of the event type ("element start") and the element type name will be included in the output. A parser which is invoked in a mode directing it to generate "ESIS" output will thus produce a stream in which the information about most events which occur during parsing is included (some events, such as occurrence of comments, may not be reported). The order of the events on the output is exactly the same as the order of their occurrence on the input. ESIS-formatted event information which is output by a parser may be used as input by a programmer. This is illustrated in Figure 10–1.

As an example of the command-line type of interface we offer the command-line interface offered by the NXP's parser. This interface is accessed via the following command-line form:

```
java NXP.Cl [-v] [-t] [-c] ( -u url | -f filename )
```

As with all Java programs, the NXP is invoked by running the Java run-time interpreter ("java" in this example) and providing it as a parameter with the name of a Java class which implements the "main()" method, "NXP.Cl" in the case of the NXP command-line interface. Parameters provided after the name of the Java class to run are provided to the main() method as an array of strings. The main() method in the NXP.Cl class accepts the following command-line options:

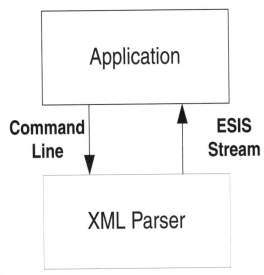

Figure 10–1

- -u: Go and fetch the XML file from the given URL
- -f: Go and fetch the XML file from the given file.
- -v: Switches on validation as defined in the XML draft (default: off)
- -t: Switch on talkative, or verbose mode, in other words (default: off)
- -c: Check for catalog before starting to parse (default: off)

The reader is referred to NXP documentation for details on these options.

10.3.2 *Event Callback Interfaces*

Another type of application programmer interface which may be provided is an event callback interface. This interface type is illustrated in Figure 10–2. In this type of parser interface, the application developer implements a set of "callback" methods or routines, each of which corresponds to an event which can occur during parsing of an XML document instance. This is in addition to any other code which might be required within the application (include a "main" routine for instance). The "callback" routines (normally) aren't called directly by any of the routines provided by the application developer but rather are called by the parser after it is started by the application. That is, at some point during execution of the application (e.g., just before a point where the result of parsing some XML input stream is needed) the application invokes the parser by calling the parser's main entry routine and then waits for the parser to complete and the routine to return. While the parser is running, it will discover events (such as a start or end of an element), and for each it will invoke the corresponding callback routine provided by the application programmer. When the parser calls the callback routines, it passes parameters which hold the details concerning the event which has occurred such

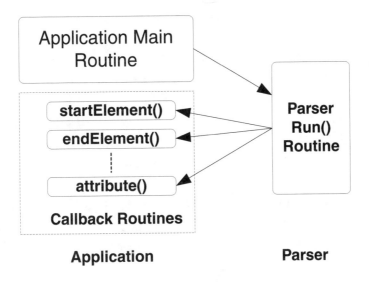

Figure 10–2

as the element type name for an element start event, or the attribute name and value for an attribute event.

The event callback interface is the type of interface provided by the NXP parser.[1] There is also a proposed standard for event callback type interfaces known as Simple API for XML or "SAX." Several implementations of this proposed standard callback type interface are now available. These interfaces are described in some detail in the following sections.

---

1. The NXP parser technology was acquired by Data Channel Software Ltd. and is now distributed under the name DXP. A version of NXP produced prior to this transfer is provided on the CDROM accompanying this book. This version is provided because it is the version used in the following examples.

10.3.2.1   NXP Event Callback Interface

In the case of NXP, the callback routines which must be implemented by the application developer correspond directly to the events which are defined in the ESIS stream interface. The full set of methods which must be implemented are specified within the NXP Java Interface called "ESIS" which is provided in the file named "esis.java." A sample implementation of this interface is provided by the Java class named "ESIS_stdout." The callback routines provided in the ESIS_stdout interface simply emit to the standard output stream all information provided to them by the parser. For a complete description of this interface, see the NXP distribution.

The following list of methods summarizes the ESIS interface.

- tag_open(String)—Indicates the start of an element.
- Attribute(String, int, String, String, Vector)—Attribute of an element.
- CDATA_Section(String)—CDATA section.
- data(String)—Data that were parsed.
- NDATA_Entity(String, Notation)—NDATA entity.
- PI_Entity(String, String)—PI entity.
- processing_instruction(String, String)—System data of a processing instruction.
- SDATA_Entity(String, String)—SDATA entity.
- tag_close(String)—Indicates the end of an element.

An example application of NXP and this interfaces is provided in the sample implementation of the W3C's DOM API described later in this chapter.

10.3.3 *Object Model Interfaces*

The final type of parser interface described here is the Object Model Interface. In this type of interface the programmer interacts with an object-oriented representation of the parser as well as the information which the parser generates as a result of parsing a document instance.

In the prototypical object model type interface, illustrated in Figure 10–3, the developer's initial interaction is with a "parser" object. Each instance of this object corresponds to a single instance of a parser. Most implementations of this type of interface will allow multiple instances of the parser to be created one at a time (serially), and some may allow multiple instances of the parser to exist simultaneously. In order to use a parser, the application creates an instance of the "parser" object with parameters to the creation method supplying the identity or contents of the document instance to be parsed (e.g., a file name, URL, or string). When the application needs to access the information contained in the document instance, it calls a method of the parser instance to begin the parsing process. The parser, while processing the input, builds an in-memory representation of the parsed document instance. This in-memory representation is itself constructed of objects, usually arranged in the form of a tree which mimics the structure described by the markup of the document instance. Once parsing is complete, this tree representation of the instance is returned to the application.

Thus the application creates and uses a parser instance to acquire an in-memory representation of the document instance. This "object model" representation usually takes the shape of a tree with a "document" object at the tree's root, and "element," "attribute," and "data" objects forming the interior and leaf positions. The application then accesses the information contained in this representation using methods provided by the classes to which the contained objects belong. An element type name, for example, may be retrieved from an ELEMENT object by using a "getElementTypeName" method.

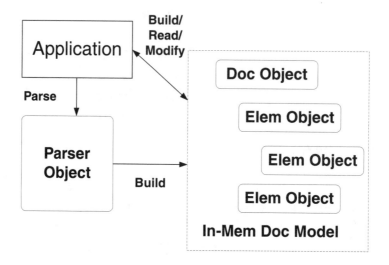

Figure 10–3

In some object model interfaces, the application may modify or even construct from scratch an in-memory representation of a document instance. Facilities may also be provided to generate a new document instance from the resulting in-memory representation. As we'll see, however, the current state of the interfaces (especially the proposed DOM standard interface) do not yet possess complete implementations of these particular features.

The World Wide Web Consortium's Document Object Model (DOM) is at once the prototypical object model interface to an XML parser and a proposed standard for this type of interface. It is described in some detail below.

10.4 | Sample XML Parsers

This section provides details concerning the XML parsers which are employed in demonstration projects later in this book. One of these,

Norbert Mikula's NXP, was introduced earlier in this chapter. Another, David Megginson's AElfred, is introduced here. As always, the reader is referred to Robin Cover's excellent SGML site, and to the XML Tools Page within that site, for references to currently available XML parsers.

10.4.1   *NXP XML Parser*

One of the first Java-based XML parsers, and in fact one of the first XML parsers of any kind, was Norbert Mikula's "NXP." It was developed very early in the life of the XML specification and because of this provided a test platform for many of the features included in this specification. This parser is also noteworthy because it makes use of Sun Microsystem's Java-based compiler compiler which is named JavaCC (see http://suntest.sun.com/JavaCC for more information). Unfortunately, NXP was, at the time of this writing, slightly out of date with the approved XML 1.0 specification. Now that the NXP technology has been acquired by Data Channel Software Ltd., the reader should contact this company (e.g., at http://www.datachannel.com) for the latest details on this tool.

10.4.1.1   Installing NXP

A version of the NXP parser can found on the CDROM accompanying this book. It is packaged into several compressed 'tar' format archives:

- Java source: Contains Java source files
- Precompiled class files: Compiled source
- JavaDoc NXP documentation

The source file archive includes the input files for JavaCC, as well as the output files produced by JavaCC when run on these files. Therefore, while you don't need to acquire JavaCC in order to compile NXP, you do have the option. Furthermore, if all you want to do is run NXP (including linking it into a larger Java application), all you need to acquire is the precompiled class files package. Norbert also has available on his site the documentation produced by JavaCC and ready-to-browse HTML files which are also provided in the Java-Doc NXP documentation package.

The NXP parser defines a Java package called "Nxp." Approximately 28 classes comprise the NXP package. The reader is referred to the NXP documentation for a full description of its capabilities and interface. The interface is partially described in a later section which focuses on the sample DOM API implementation which was built on top of NXP.

To install NXP, one may either start with the precompiled classes or acquire the source and compile classes. In either case, the resulting classes are placed in a directory named "Nxp" within a directory named in their CLASSPATH environment variable. The installation can be tested using NXP's command-line interface on a simple test file.

10.4.2 *AElfred XML Parser*

Another XML parser is AElfred which was created by David Megginson of Microstar Software Ltd. AElfred, like NXP, is written in Java and provides as its native interface an event callback type of application programmer interface. The design goals embodied in the AElfred implementation are stated in the readme file which comes with the AElfred distribution. Summarizing this list, the design goals include

- Minimal size—useful for applets where transfer time is important
- Few class files—again, useful for applet applications (though JAR files might reduce the need for this goal)

- Compatible with most or all Java implementations and platforms

- Use minimal amount of run-time memory possible

- Fast processing of documents

- Correct output for well-formed and valid documents, but need not reject every document that is not valid or not well-formed

- Full internationalization

In addition to supporting its own native application programmer's interface, both an event callback style interface (SAX—see below) and object model type interface (DOM—see below) have been constructed to work with AElfred. More information on AElfred can be obtained from the Microstar Software Ltd. Web site at http://www.microstar.com/xml. According to its readme file, AElfred is provided free for both commercial and noncommercial use.

10.5 | The SAX Event Callback API

A proposed event callback interface known as SAX, for "Simple API for XML," represents an attempt to standardize the details of a specific event callback interface. If such a standard can be established, then applications which require the services of an XML parser can be written to work with this interface and should then be able to make use of any parsers which support this standard. Such a standard could do for the event callback type interface what the ESIS standard has done for the event stream type interface. Given the experience and diversity of contributors who provided input into the definition of SAX and the generally high quality of the definition which resulted, it appears that SAX has a good chance of becoming a broadly supported XML parser interface.

Information about SAX is available on the Web site of one of its principal developers: David Megginson's SAX Home Page at http://www.microstar.com/xml/sax. Development of the SAX interface was a collaborative effort involving many people using the xml-dev e-mail list as a primary discussion venue. At the time of this writing SAX interfaces have been built on top of several parsers and numerous early applications of it have emerged. The reader is referred to the just mentioned SAX Home Page for more information on SAX. A brief summary of the proposal follows.

The proposed SAX definition specifies the interface which a programmer can use to access the capabilities of an XML parser. The application developer may acquire the an implementation of the SAX interface along with an XML parser (e.g., from some third party software provider), or may acquire a SAX implementation separate from an XML parser (an implementation which must be compatible with the parser they choose). The SAX interface can be provided directly by the parser, as illustrated in Figure 10–4a, or may be provided by an adapter layer which resides between a specific parser and the applica-

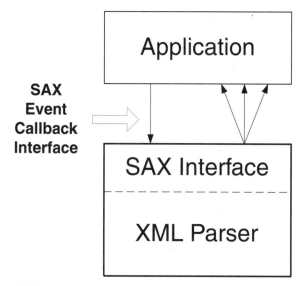

SAX Event Callback Interface

Figure 10–4a SAX in Parser

tion, as illustrated in Figure 10–4b. Regardless of whether the SAX interface is built into a XML parser or provided by an adapter, the SAX definition specifies what the "SAX Implementation" must provide to the application

The SAX definition specifies a primary "parser" method which must be provided by the SAX implementation and which is called by the application. It also specifies several event callback interfaces which must be provided by the application which will be called by the parser. In addition, the definition specifies methods which the SAX implementation must provide which the application calls to tell the parser which application routines will handle entity resolution, event callbacks, and error callbacks.

Like NXP's event callback interface, SAX requires the developer to implement several event callback methods which the SAX implementation will call when specific events occur during parsing. Whereas NXP's developer chose to use the list of ESIS-defined events as the basis for the list of events represented by the callback routine in NXP, the SAX developers took liberty to start fresh and define a new list of callback routines independent of the ESIS events. This may make

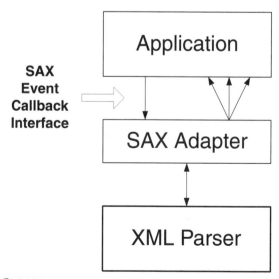

Figure 10–4b SAX via Adapter

sense given that the ESIS interface was developed primarily to serve as a canonical output format for SGML parsers. XML and XML parsers have to satisfy slightly different requirements, and an event callback type interface is quite different from a stream interface.

The event callback methods which an application must provide are collected within the DocumentHandler interface. These are summarized in the following list. The reader is referred to the SAX Home Page for the current detailed definition of these methods.

- startDocument()—beginning of the document
- endDocument()—end of the document.
- doctype(String name, String publicID, String systemID) —document type declaration.
- startElement(String name, AttributeMap attributes)— start of element
- endElement(String name)—end of element
- characters(char ch[], int start, int length)—characters in document instance
- ignorable(char ch[], int start, int length)—characters in document instance which are ignorable
- processingInstruction(String target, String remainder) — processing instruction

Additional SAX implementation-provided interfaces are also specified, as are additional application-provided interfaces.

David Megginson, in addition to providing substantial leadership to the development of the SAX definition, has built a SAX implementation. He built this implementation as an adapter layer and has provided drivers for several readily available XML parsers. As a result, the SAX interface is available regardless of which of these parsers a developer chooses to employ. Once again, the details (and in this case distribution) of this implementation can be found on the SAX Home Page.

10.6 | The W3C Document Object Model and API

The World Wide Web (WWW) has developed into one of the larger, if not the largest, applications for SGML. The World Wide Web Consortium (W3C), as the body responsible for steering the development of standards underlying the WWW, has been a major force behind this application. Considering this and their role in coordinating development of the XML standard itself, it is no surprise that the W3C has assumed a lead role in coordinating development of standard programmer interfaces to both HTML and XML. In particular, the W3C's Document Object Model (Core)—Level 1 (which will be referred to from here on as the DOM API, or simply DOM) is a working draft for a standard which describes, to quote the standard itself, "mechanisms for software developers and Web script authors to access and manipulate parsed HTML and XML content."

Quoting from the DOM area of the W3C's Web site: "The W3C DOM Working Group is developing a platform- and language-neutral program interface that will allow programs and scripts to access every element in a document and update the content and structure of documents in a standard way." A graphical presentation of structures defined by the DOM specification appears later in this chapter.

The resulting DOM (Core)—Level 1 is specified using English text and examples within the Working Draft. The Draft's appendices include two sample bindings of the proposed interface: one for the Object Management Group's Interface Definition Language (IDL) and another for the Java language. The DOM (XML) Level 1 specification was just released as this book went to press. It includes specification of means to represent XML specific information in a DOM compliant manner.

10.6.1 *Support and Implementation*

The W3C's draft standard DOM API appears to have the support of several major developers of software and WWW technology. In particular, the list of participants in the DOM standards work included (at the time of this writing): ArborText, Grif, IBM, Inso, Microsoft, Netscape, Novell, the Object Management Group, SoftQuad, and Sun Microsystems.

While it is currently still a working draft, there have already been several attempts to incorporate early versions of this API on top of XML parsers. Perhaps most prominent of these early implementations is Microsoft's attempt to include something close to the DOM interface within Internet Explorer (version 4 and up), and also as an interface to their "MSXML" XML parser.

Also of special note is the "SAXDOM" implementation which has been built by Don Park on top of the SAX event callback interface. This tool, by being built on top of SAX which itself is portable across a wide range of XML parsers, shows just how powerful a layered approach to interface construction can be. Don's SAXDOM implementation can be found at: http://users.quake.net/donpark/sax-dom.html or via Robin Cover's SGML website.

It should be noted that because of the newness of the DOM API specification and its current state as a working draft, the early implementations (e.g., Microsoft's and the simple example included below) can not be expected to conform without modification to any final DOM API specification that emerges. These implementations already take some liberties to extend and deviate from the specification; this is due both to the desire of the implementors to offer features which are simply not yet in the specification, and to the need to "localize" the interface to satisfy specific requirements and environments. Also, as new releases of the DOM specification are produced, there is a lagtime before they are implemented by various tools. This is the case at the time of this writing for those features described in the DOM (XML) Level 1 release of December 9, 1997.

10.6.2 *Acquiring Specifications.*

An area of the W3's Web site is devoted to the DOM. It can be found at http://www.w3c.org/DOM. In addition to the text of the specification itself, this area includes a Frequently Asked Question (FAQ) offering, requirements, and other documents related to the standard, and useful links to related technologies.

As always, additional information about this and most any other SGML-related technology can be found on Robin Cover's SGML Web site which is located at http://www.sil.com/sgml.

10.6.3 *Overview of the W3C's DOM Level-1 Interface*

The DOM API consists of a set of objects and interfaces with a pre-defined set of access methods for each. The primary classes specified in the DOM API are as follows:

- Document
- Node
- Element
- Text
- Attribute
- PI
- Comment

The Document class provides the top-level Node of the run-time, in-memory representation of an XML document. It provides access to a document instances root element as well as to the document type declaration associated with the document instance.

The Node class is a base class providing a fundamental run-time container for information which is to be arranged within a graph (tree) structure. It is subclassed to provide specific containers appropriate to particular document components such as Elements, text and Attributes. It also provides means for instances of Nodes (and its sub-classes) to be linked together into a tree. In particular, parent and children properties are maintained and accessible.

The Element class is, as the name suggests, the container information about elements contained in the document. In particular, each element occurring in the document will have an element object created for it within a run-time document object model. In addition to the properties of the Node, the element contains properties such as the tag name (which may soon be changed to element type name) and attributes.

The text class is provided to hold data content occurring in the read document instance. The actual data content contained in a Text class object is held in a list of nodes (a NodeList — see below), so that entities can be interspersed with actual character data.

The Attribute class is used to hold information contained in attribute occurrences appearing within the document. These objects are held within a helper class known as an AttributeList (see below). The PI and Comment classes provide for run-time representation of processing instructions and comments respectively. An appropriate set of methods is provided for setting and getting the properties associated with these XML data type.

In addition to the classes above which the DOM specification refers to as primary classes, a few of what are referred to as Auxiliary classes are specified. These classes include:

- NodeList
- EditableNodeList
- NodeEnumerator
- AttributeList
- DocumentContext
- DOM
- DOMFactory

The classes NodeList and EditableNodeList provide means for representing lists of Nodes. The NodeList represents a generic non-editable list of data objects of type Node or a subclass of type node. The

EditableNodeList, a subclass of type NodeList, expands upon the features of its parent class by providing methods for modifying the list of nodes it contains. The NodeEnumerator class provides representation for an iterator over a list of Nodes. It allows for traversing the list in forward and reverse directions, and allows for alternating directions. The AttributeList class provides representation for a list of Attribute objects each of which possess a unique name. Methods are provided by retrieving attributes by name and recording new attributes.

Class DocumentContext is included to represent information such as HTTP header fields that concern the context in which the document was found to occur. The DOMFactory class provides utilities used to create instances of the core DOM elements in their most frequently occurring form. Finally, the DOM class is included to provide, via a single (e.g., Java static) instance, means to create new instances of the DOMFactory class.

The specification release of December 9, 1997 includes a new set of classes intended to hold information about the XML DTD. It should be noted that at the time this was written the DOM API specification is a work in progress. Not surprisingly, it lacks some features the programmer might desire from such an interface. These include, for example, traversal and search methods and a full set of DOM instance construction methods. Some of these omissions are noted in the DOM specification and thus can be expected in future specification versions. The reader should obtain a current version periodically to see when and how new features are incorporated.

10.7 | Sample DOM Implementation

In this section we present a sample implementation of the W3C's document object model using NXP as the underlying parser. In the process we illustrate both the current definition of the proposed DOM standard and the integration of an XML parser into a DOM implementation.

The following subsections present all of the code comprising this sample DOM implementation. This includes the Java Interface definitions which comprise the W3C DOM specification itself as well as Java classes implementing each of the specified Interfaces. It is recommended that the reader first scan Section 10.7.1 to see a first level of detail of the Interface definitions. After doing this you should flip between a specific Interface definition and the class implementing this interface (which will appear in Sections 10.7.2.1 through 10.7.2.11), to gain a more detailed understanding of the interface and how it may be implemented.

Section 10.7.3 presents code which integrates this sample DOM implementation with the NXP parser. The result is a fully functional parser with DOM interface. After this, a sample application of this foundation is offered in Section 10.7.4.

10.7.1 *DOM Interface Definition*

The interfaces comprising a Java binding of the proposed W3C's DOM specification appears in Listing 10.1. It's worth emphasizing here that the following Interface definitions are defined by the W3C DOM specification; they are presented here in the form which was compiled and tested with the sample implementation which follows.

The Java Interface definitions which are presented in here appear on the accompanying CDROM each in an individual file (per Java language conventions). For the sake of presentation, the Java code comprising these definitions have been concatenated into one listing here:

```
=========================== Node.java
package org.w3c.dom;

public interface Node {
    // Node type enumeration
    public final int DOCUMENT   = 0;
    public final int ELEMENT = 1;
```

Listing 10.1

```
    public final int ATTRIBUTE = 2;
    public final int PI= 3;
    public final int COMMENT= 4;
    public final int TEXT= 5;

    int getNodeType();

    Node getParentNode();
    NodeListgetChildren();
    booleanhasChildren();
    NodegetFirstChild();
    NodegetPreviousSibling();
    NodegetNextSibling();

    void insertBefore(Node newChild, Node refChild)
throws NotMyChildException;

    Node replaceChild(Node oldChild, Node newChild)
throws NotMyChildException;

    Node removeChild(Node oldChild)
throws NotMyChildException;
}
========================== NodeList.java
package org.w3c.dom;

public interface NodeList {
    NodeEnumerator getEnumerator();

    Node item(long index)
throws NoSuchNodeException;

    long getLength();
}
========================== EditableNodeList.java
package org.w3c.dom;
```

Listing 10.1 *(continued)*

```
public interface EditableNodeList extends NodeList {
    void replace(long index, Node replaceNode)
throws NoSuchNodeException;

    void insert(long index, Node newNode)
throws NoSuchNodeException;

    Node remove(long index)
throws NoSuchNodeException;
};
========================= NamedNodeList.java
package org.w3c.dom;

public interface NamedNodeList {
    Node getNode(String name);
    Node setNode(String name, Node node);

    Node remove(String name)
throws NoSuchNodeException;

    Node item(long index)
throws NoSuchNodeException;

    long getLength();

    NodeEnumerator getEnumerator();
}
========================= NodeEnumerator.java
package org.w3c.dom;

public interface NodeEnumerator {
    Node getFirst();
    Node getNext();
    Node getPrevious();
    Node getLast();
```

Listing 10.1   *(continued)*

```
    Node getCurrent();

    // maybe

    boolean atStart();
    boolean atEnd();
}
========================= Element.java
package org.w3c.dom;

public interface Element extends Node {
    void setTagName(String name);
    String getTagName();

    AttributeList getAttributes();

    void setAttribute(Attribute newAttribute);

    NodeEnumerator getElementsByTagName(String name);
}========================= Attribute.java
package org.w3c.dom;

public interface Attribute extends Node {
    void setName(String name);
    String getName();

    void setValue(NodeList value);
    NodeList getValue();

    void setSpecified(boolean specified);
    boolean getSpecified();

    String toString();
}
```

Listing 10.1 *(continued)*

```
========================== AttributeList.java
package org.w3c.dom;

public interface AttributeList {
    Attribute getAttribute(String name);
    Attribute setAttribute(String name, Attribute attr);

    Attribute remove(String name)
throws NoSuchNodeException;

    Attribute item(int index)
throws NoSuchNodeException;

    long getLength();
}
========================== Text.java
package org.w3c.dom;

public interface Text extends Node {
    void setData(String data);
    String getData();

    void setIsIgnorableWhitespace(boolean newValue);
    boolean getIsIgnorableWhitespace();
}


========================== Comment.java
package org.w3c.dom;

public interface Comment extends Node {
    void setData(String data);
    String getData();
}========================== PI.java
package org.w3c.dom;

public interface PI extends Node {
```

Listing 10.1   *(continued)*

```
    void setName(String name);
    String getName();

    void setData(String data);
    String getData();
}========================= Document.java
package org.w3c.dom;

public interface Document extends Node {
    void setDocumentType(Node documentType);
    Node getDocumentType();

    void setDocumentElement(Element documentElement);
    Element getDocumentElement();

    NodeEnumerator getElementsByTagName(String name);
}========================= DocumentContext.java
package org.w3c.dom;

public interface DocumentContext {
    void setDocument(Document document);
    Document getDocument();
}
========================= NotMyChildException.java
package org.w3c.dom;

public class NotMyChildException extends Exception
{
}
========================= NoSuchNodeException.java
package org.w3c.dom;

public class NoSuchNodeException extends Exception {
    // adds nothing
}
```

Listing 10.1   *(continued)*

On a disk each of these interfaces would be carried in its own file and each file would begin with the following package declaration:

```
package w3c.dom;
```

This code is nearly identical to the sample Java binding of these DOM interfaces provided in the DOM specification; the differences concern minor points such as definition of events thrown in exception cases.

10.7.2 *DOM Interface Implementations*

We now present a set of classes which implements the major interfaces defined in the previous section. These classes are placed in a Java package called "negeng.dom." Thus, for instance, the implementation of the DOM w3c.dom.Node interface appears in class negeng.dom.Node. In-line Javadoc style documentation is provided in the code contained in these listings. Therefore the following comments are of a general nature rather than a line-by-line narration. The reader should thus look to the code and Javadoc comments for details.

Most of these classes include a "main()" method which contains code to test or at least exercise the methods defined in the class. These can be invoked from the command line. Using the class negeng.dom.Node as an example, a command to exercise this class would be

```
java negeng.dom.Node
```

All of the code presented below is contained on the accompanying CDROM; the reader is encouraged to compile and execute these test routines as a further illustration of the DOM and this sample implementation.

Most of these classes also provide a "print" method which emits a textual representation of the information they hold. These are used within the "main()" methods to present the results of sample uses of the associated classes.

10.7.2.1 Class negeng.dom.Node

Listing 10.2 presents the class which implements the w3c.dom.Node interface. The methods included in this class, as specified in the DOM, provide facilities to set and get "type," "parent," and "children" instance variables. The parent is represented as a reference to a Node while the children are represented using the "NodeList" class which is described below.

```
package negeng.dom;

import java.util.*;

/****************************************
 **
 * The basic node type.
 *
 */
public class Node implements org.w3c.dom.Node {
    /********************* Node ******************/
    /**
     * Basic constructor
     *
     */
    public Node(){
    }

    /********************* Node ******************/
    /**
     * Constructor with initial values.
     *
     * @param newNodeType Node type to assign
     *
     */
    public Node(int newNodeType){
```

Listing 10.2

```
type = newNodeType;
    }


    /********************* Node *******************/
    /**
     * Constructor with initial values.
     *
     * @param newNodeType Node type to assign
     * @param newNodeParent Parent of new node (add this as
child)
     *
     */
    public Node(int newNodeType, Node newNodeParent ){
type = newNodeType;
parentNode = newNodeParent;

// add to children of parent
if( parentNode != null ){
    if( parentNode.children == null){
parentNode.children = (NodeList) new NodeList();
    }
}

parentNode.children.items.addElement( this );
    }


    /********************* Node *******************/
    /*
     * Constructor with initial values
     *
     * @param newNodeType Node type to assign
     * @param newNodeParent Parent of new node (add this as
child)
     * @param newNodeChildren Children of new node
     *
     */
```

Listing 10.2   *(continued)*

```
    public Node(int newNodeType, Node newNodeParent, NodeList
newNodeChildren){
type = newNodeType;
children = newNodeChildren;
parentNode = newNodeParent;

// add to children of parent
if( parentNode != null ){
    if( parentNode.children == null){
parentNode.children = (NodeList) new NodeList();
    }
}

// add to children of parent
parentNode.children.items.addElement( this );
    }

    /****************** getNodeType ****************/
    /**
     * Get this node's type
     *
     * @return This node's type
     */
    public int getNodeType(){
return type;
    }

    /****************** setNodeType ***************/
    /**
     * Set the node's type
     *
     * @param newType The new type to assign
     *
     */
    protected void setNodeType(int newType){
 type = newType;
```

Listing 10.2 *(continued)*

```
    }

    /****************** getParentNode **************/
    /**
     * Get parent of Node
     *
     * @return The value of parent of this node
     */
    public org.w3c.dom.Node getParentNode(){
        return (org.w3c.dom.Node) parentNode;
    }

    /****************** setParentNode **************/
    /**
     * Set the parent node
     *
     * @param newParent The new parent node.
     *
     */
    protected void setParentNode(org.w3c.dom.Node newParent){
        this.parentNode = (Node) newParent;
    }

    /******************** setChildren ********/
    /**
     * Set children of node (extends org.w3c.dom.Node)
     * @param newChildren The new (NodeList) children to
assign.
     */
    protected void setChildren( org.w3c.dom.NodeList newChil-
dren ){
children = (NodeList) newChildren;
    }

    /******************** getChildren ************/
    /**
     * Get children of node
```

Listing 10.2   *(continued)*

```
     * @return The children (NodeList) of this node.
     */
    public org.w3c.dom.NodeList getChildren() {
if( children == null || children.getLength() < 1 ){
    // empty, return null
    return (org.w3c.dom.NodeList) null;
}
        return (org.w3c.dom.NodeList) children;
    }


    /******************** hasChildren ********/
    /**
     * Test for existence of children
     * @return true if children exist, false otherwise
     */
    public boolean hasChildren() {
if( children != null && (children.items.size() > 0) ){
    return true;
}
return false;
    }


    /******************** getFirstChild ***********/
    /**
     * Get the first child, null if none
     *
     * @return The first child, or null if no children exist
     */
    public org.w3c.dom.Node getFirstChild(){
if( children != null && children.items.size() > 0 ){
    return (org.w3c.dom.Node) children.items.firstElement();
}
return null;
    }


    /******************** getPreviousSibling ********/
```

Listing 10.2 *(continued)*

```
    /**
     * Get the previous sibling.
     * @return The previous sibling (Node), if parent exists
and parent has children and earlier(older) sibling exists.
     */
    public org.w3c.dom.Node getPreviousSibling(){
if( parentNode != null && parentNode.children != null ){
    int myIndex = parentNode.children.items.indexOf( this );

    if( myIndex > 0 ){
return (org.w3c.dom.Node)
  parentNode.children.items.elementAt( myIndex - 1 );
    } else {
// should continue backward breadfirst, not implemented
return null;
    }
}
return null;
    }


    /******************** getNextSibling ********/
    /**
     * Get the next sibling
     * @return The next sibling (Node), if parent exists, and
parent has children, and later(younger) sibling exists
     */
    public org.w3c.dom.Node getNextSibling(){
if( parentNode != null && parentNode.children != null ){
    int myIndex = parentNode.children.items.indexOf( this );

    if( parentNode.children.items.size() > myIndex + 2 ){
return (org.w3c.dom.Node)
  parentNode.children.items.elementAt( myIndex + 1 );
    } else {
// should continue forward breadth first trav, not impl.
return null;
    }
```

Listing 10.2 *(continued)*

```
        }
return null;
        }


    /******************** insertBefore ***********/
    /**
      * Insert child into before specified child of this node.
      * If refchild is null, append.
      *
      * @param newChild New child (Node) to insert
      * @param refChild Child before which new node is to be
inserted
      * @exception org.w3c.dom.NotMyChildException Thrown if
refchild is specified and not found.
      *
      */
      public void insertBefore(org.w3c.dom.Node newChild,
        org.w3c.dom.Node refChild)
throws org.w3c.dom.NotMyChildException {

if( refChild == null ){
    if( children == null) {
children = (NodeList) new NodeList();
    }

    children.items.addElement(newChild);
} else {
    int index = children.items.indexOf(refChild,0);

    if( index == -1 ){
throw new org.w3c.dom.NotMyChildException();
    }

    children.items.insertElementAt(newChild, index);
}
    }
```

Listing 10.2   *(continued)*

```java
/********************** appendChild ************/
/**
  * Append a child to list of children.
  *
  * @param newChild New child node to be appended
  *
  */
protected void appendChild(org.w3c.dom.Node newChild){
if(children == null){
    children = (NodeList) new NodeList();
}


children.items.addElement(newChild);
    }


/*********************** replaceChild **********/
/**
  * Replace a child with new child.
  *
  * @param newChild The new child (Node) to replace with
  * @param refChild The old child to be replaced
  * @exception org.w3c.dom.NotMyChildException Thrown if
refchild is specified and not found
  * @return The old child (Node)
  */
public org.w3c.dom.Node replaceChild(org.w3c.dom.Node
newChild,
      org.w3c.dom.Node refChild)
throws org.w3c.dom.NotMyChildException {

if( children == null){
    throw new org.w3c.dom.NotMyChildException();
}

int index = children.items.indexOf(refChild,0);

if( index == -1 ){
```

Listing 10.2   *(continued)*

```
            throw new org.w3c.dom.NotMyChildException();
}


Node oldChild = (Node) children.items.elementAt( index );

children.items.setElementAt(newChild, index);

return (org.w3c.dom.Node) oldChild;
        }

        /*********************** removeChild ***************/
        /**
          * Remove child
          *
          * @param refChild The child to remove
          * @exception org.w3c.dom.NotMyChildException Thrown if
refChild not found
          * @return The removed child (Node)
          *
          */
        public org.w3c.dom.Node removeChild(org.w3c.dom.Node ref-
Child)
throws org.w3c.dom.NotMyChildException {

if( children == null ){
        throw new org.w3c.dom.NotMyChildException();
}

int index = children.items.indexOf(refChild);

if( index == -1 ){
        throw new org.w3c.dom.NotMyChildException();
}

children.items.removeElementAt(index);

return refChild;
```

Listing 10.2   *(continued)*

```
        }


        /********************** print ****************/
        /**
         * Print the node with indentation
         * @param indent Number of spaces of indentation
         */
        public void print(int indent){
// derive a new indentString
String indentString = (new
String("
                            ")).substring(0, indent);

// emit this node
System.out.println(indentString + this);
System.out.println(indentString + "  type=" + type);


// emit child nodes
if( children != null ){
    System.out.println(indentString + "  children:");
    Enumeration childrenEnum = children.items.elements();

        while( childrenEnum.hasMoreElements() ){
        ((Node)childrenEnum.nextElement()).print( indent + 4
);
    }
} else {
    System.out.println(indentString + "  children: none");
}
        }


        /********************** print ****************/
        /**
         * Print the node (w/o indentation)
         *
         */
```

Listing 10.2   *(continued)*

```java
    public void print(){
print(0);
    }

    /********************** main *********************/
    /**
     * A class test routine.
     */
    public static void main(String argv[]){
// build root node
Node root = new Node();
System.out.println("root node built:");
root.print(4);

// test hasChildren w/o children
System.out.println("hasChildren (sb false) = " +
  root.hasChildren());

// build a few children
Node child1 = new Node(0,root);
Node child2 = new Node(0,root);
Node child3 = new Node(0,root);

System.out.println("three children built and added:");

root.print(4);

System.out.println("hasChildren (sb true) = " +
  root.hasChildren());

// test get first of root
Node childN = (Node) root.getFirstChild();
System.out.println("getFirstChild of root returned Node:");
childN.print(4);

  // test get siblings
```

Listing 10.2 *(continued)*

```
childN = (Node) child1.getNextSibling();
System.out.println("getNextSibling of child1 returned
Node:");
childN.print(4);


childN = (Node) child2.getPreviousSibling();
System.out.println("getPreviousSibling of child2 returned
Node:");
childN.print(4);


// test getChildren
NodeList rootChildren = (NodeList) root.getChildren();
System.out.println("getChildren of root returned NodeList:");
rootChildren.print(4);
    }

    /******************* member variables *************/
    /**
     * The type of this node (per org.w3c.dom def.)
     */
    protected int type;

    /**
     * The parent of this node
     */
    protected Node parentNode;

    /**
     * The children of this node
     */
    protected NodeList children;
}
```

Listing 10.2   *(continued)*

10.7.2.2 Class negeng.dom.NodeList

The next code listing, appearing in Listing 10.3, presents the negeng.dom.NodeList class which implements the w3c.dom.NodeList interface. In this implementation a java.util.vector type instance variable called "items" is used to hold a list of negeng.dom.Nodes. The DOM-specified methods for accessing the node list are implemented. The main() method builds a small node list to exercise these methods.

```
package negeng.dom;

import java.util.*;

/****************************************
 **
 * The nodelist class.
 */
public class NodeList implements org.w3c.dom.NodeList {

    /********************* Node ******************/
    /**
     * Basic construct.
     */
    public NodeList(){
items = new Vector( INITIAL_VECTOR_CAPACITY );
    }

    /********************** getEnumerator **************/
    /**
     * Get a NodeEnumerator for the nodelist
     *
     * @return A NodeEnumerator to iterate through nodes in
this nodelist
     */
```

Listing 10.3

```
    public org.w3c.dom.NodeEnumerator getEnumerator(){
return (org.w3c.dom.NodeEnumerator) new NodeEnumerator( this
);
    }


    /****************** item *************/
    /**
     * Get the item at a specific index
     *
     * @param index The index at which desired items exists.
     * @exception org.w3c.dom.NoSuchNodeException When no
node exists at index <i>index</i>
     * @return The Node existing at specified <i>index</i>
     */
    public org.w3c.dom.Node item(long index)
throws org.w3c.dom.NoSuchNodeException {

try {
    return (org.w3c.dom.Node) items.elementAt((int) index);
} catch ( ArrayIndexOutOfBoundsException e ) {
    throw new org.w3c.dom.NoSuchNodeException();
}
    }


    /******************** getLength ***************/
    /**
     * Get the length of this nodelist
     *
     * @return The length of this nodelist
     */
    public long getLength(){
return items.size();
    }


    /********************* print ***************/
    /**
     * Print list with indentation.
```

Listing 10.3   *(continued)*

```
     *
     * @param indent The number of spaces to prefix onto emit-
ted lines
     */
    public void print(int indent){
// derive a new indentString
String indentString = (new
String("
                        ")).substring(0, indent);


// emit this node
System.out.println(indentString + this);


// member vars
System.out.println(indentString + "  items:");


// emit member nodes
Enumeration itemEnumerator = items.elements();


while( itemEnumerator.hasMoreElements() ){
    ((Node) itemEnumerator.nextElement()).print( indent + 4
);
}
    }


    /******************** print ***************/
    /*
     * Print the node
     *
     */
    public void print(){
print(0);
    }


    /******************** main ********************/
    /*
     * A class test routine.
```

Listing 10.3   *(continued)*

```
      */
    public static void main(String argv[]){
// build a nodeList
NodeList aNodeList = new NodeList();
System.out.println("build nodelist");
aNodeList.print(4);

System.out.println("length=" + aNodeList.getLength() );

// should do more testing
    }

    /******************** member variablels *************/
    /**
     * The node list itself (as a vector)
     */
    protected Vector items;

    /**
     * Initial vector capacity
     */
    static int INITIAL_VECTOR_CAPACITY = 5;
}
```

Listing 10.3 *(continued)*

10.7.2.3   Class negeng.dom.EditableNodeList

The negeng.dom.EditableNodeList class is presented in Listing 10.4. It extends negeng.dom.NodeList with means for constructing and manipulating the classes it contains.

```
package negeng.dom;

import org.w3c.dom.*;
```

Listing 10.4

```
public class EditableNodeList
    extends NodeList
    implements org.w3c.dom.EditableNodeList {

    /******************** replace ***********/
    /**
     * Replace the node at index with replacementNode
     *
     * @param index Index at which existing node to be
replaced exists.
     * @param replacementNode The node to install as replace-
ment
     * @exception org.w3c.dom.NoSuchNodeException Thrown if
index is out of bounds.
     */
    public void replace(long index, org.w3c.dom.Node replace-
mentNode)
throws org.w3c.dom.NoSuchNodeException {

try {
    items.setElementAt( replacementNode, (int) index );
} catch ( ArrayIndexOutOfBoundsException e ){
    throw new org.w3c.dom.NoSuchNodeException();
}
    }

    /******************** append ***********/
    /**
     * Append <i>newNode</i> onto end of this nodelist
     *
     * @param newNode The node to append
     *
     */
    protected void append(org.w3c.dom.Node newNode){
items.addElement(newNode);
    }
```

Listing 10.4   *(continued)*

```
/******************** prepend ***********/
/**
 * Prepend <i>newNode</i> onto front of this nodelist
 *
 * @param newNode The node to prepend
 *
 */
protected void prepend(org.w3c.dom.Node newNode){
items.insertElementAt(newNode, 0);
}


/******************** insert ***********/
/**
 * Insert <i>newNode</i> into this nodelist before node
specified
 * by <i>index</i>.  If index is length of list, append
it.
 *
 * @param index index before which new node is to be
inserted
 * @param Node node
 * @exception org.w3c.dom.NoSuchNodeException Thrown if
new index is out of bounds
 *
 */
public void insert(long index, org.w3c.dom.Node newNode)
throws org.w3c.dom.NoSuchNodeException {

if( index == items.size() ){
    items.addElement(newNode);
}

try {
    items.insertElementAt(newNode, (int) index);
} catch ( ArrayIndexOutOfBoundsException e ){
    throw new org.w3c.dom.NoSuchNodeException();
```

Listing 10.4   *(continued)*

```
}

    }


    /******************** remove ************/
    /**
     * Remove node indexed by <i>index</i>
     * @param index Index of node to be removed.
     * @exception org.w3c.dom.NoSuchNodeException Thrown if
index is out of bounds
     */
    public org.w3c.dom.Node remove(long index)
throws org.w3c.dom.NoSuchNodeException{

org.w3c.dom.Node oldNode;
try {
    oldNode = (org.w3c.dom.Node) items.elementAt( (int) index
);
} catch( ArrayIndexOutOfBoundsException e ){
    throw new org.w3c.dom.NoSuchNodeException();
}

try { // this catch is redundant
    items.removeElementAt( (int) index );
} catch( ArrayIndexOutOfBoundsException e ){
    throw new org.w3c.dom.NoSuchNodeException();
}

return oldNode;
    }


    /*************** main *****************/
    /*
     * A class test routine.
     */
    public static void main(String argv[]){
// build an EditableNodeList
EditableNodeList aNodeList = new EditableNodeList();
```

Listing 10.4 *(continued)*

```
System.out.println("built editableNodeList");
aNodeList.print(4);

  // build and append two nodes
Node node1 = new Node();
aNodeList.append(node1);

Node node2 = new Node();
aNodeList.append(node2);

System.out.println("appended two nodes");
aNodeList.print(4);

// build and insert a node (no exception)
Node node3 = new Node();
try {
    aNodeList.insert(1,node3);
} catch (org.w3c.dom.NoSuchNodeException e) {
    System.out.println("no such node (bad)");
}
System.out.println("inserted node @ index=1(w/o exception)");
aNodeList.print(4);

// insert node (w/exception)
try {
    aNodeList.insert(999,node3);
} catch (org.w3c.dom.NoSuchNodeException e) {
    System.out.println("caught NoSuchNodeException (ok)");
}
System.out.println("inserted node beyond end, should have
just seen exception");

System.out.println("getLength()=" + aNodeList.getLength() );
    }
}
```

Listing 10.4   *(continued)*

10.7.2.4   Class negeng.dom.NamedNodeList

The next code listing, Listing 10.5, presents the negeng.dom.Named-NodeList class. As defined by the DOM, the nodes contained in this node list representation can be retrieved by name as well as through an enumeration. To facilitate this, both vector and hashtable instance variables are used. The vector is used to hold the actual negeng.dom.Node instances contained in the list while the hashtable is used to associate node names with the index in the vector where the node with this name appears. Again a main() method is provided to exercise this class

```
package negeng.dom;

import negeng.dom.*;

import java.util.*;

/*********************************************/
/**
 * A list of named nodes.
 *
 */

public class NamedNodeList implements org.w3c.dom.NamedN-
odeList {
    /****************** constructor **************/
    /**
     * Basic constructor.
     *
     */
    public NamedNodeList(){
items = new Vector();
nameHash = new Hashtable();
    }
```

Listing 10.5

```
/*********************** getNode *************/
/**
 * Get node associated with a particular name
 *
 * @param name The name of the node sought
 * @return The node associated with name.
 *
 */
    public org.w3c.dom.Node getNode(String name){
Node aNode;
Object indexObj;

if( (indexObj = nameHash.get(name)) == null ){
    // didn't find it
    return (org.w3c.dom.Node) null;
}

// found it, convert indexObj to index and fetch node from
items
return (org.w3c.dom.Node) items.elementAt( ((Integer) index-
Obj).intValue());
    }

/*********************** setNode ******************/
/**
 * Set a node: if node exists with name replace it, else
append a new.
 *
 * @param name Name of new or existing node
 * @param node The new or replacement node
 * @return If <i>name</i> references existing node,
return that node,
 * otherwise, return null.
 *
 */
```

Listing 10.5   *(continued)*

```
    public org.w3c.dom.Node setNode(String name,
org.w3c.dom.Node newNode){
Node oldNode;
Object indexObj;
int index;

if( (indexObj = nameHash.get(name)) != null ){
    // this is replacement!

    // convert indexObj to int
    index = ((Integer) indexObj ).intValue();

    // get the old value
    oldNode = (Node) items.elementAt( index );

    // replace it w/new
    items.setElementAt(newNode,index);

    // return oldNode (per org.w3c.dom spec)
    return (org.w3c.dom.Node) oldNode;
} else {
    // doesn't exist!
    // add to items
    items.addElement((org.w3c.dom.Node) newNode );
    index = items.size() - 1;

    // put index into hash table
    nameHash.put(name, new Integer(index) );

    // return null per org.w3c.dom.NamedNodeList spec
    return (org.w3c.dom.Node) null;
}
    }

    /********************** remove *******************/
    /**
```

Listing 10.5 *(continued)*

```
 * Remove node associated with name from named node list.
 *
 * @param name Name of node to be removed
 * @exception org.w3c.dom.NoSuchNodeException If name not
found.
 * @return If name references existing node, return that
node.
 *
 */
public org.w3c.dom.Node remove(String name)
throws org.w3c.dom.NoSuchNodeException {
Node oldNode;
Object indexObj;
int oldIndex;

// see if it is there
if( (indexObj = nameHash.get(name)) == null ){
    // whoops, not there
    throw new org.w3c.dom.NoSuchNodeException();
}

// convert indexObj to int
oldIndex = ((Integer) indexObj).intValue();

// remove from hash
nameHash.remove(name);

// retrieve then remove from items
oldNode = (Node) items.elementAt(oldIndex);
items.removeElementAt(oldIndex);

return (org.w3c.dom.Node) oldNode;
    }

/********************* item *********************/
/**
 * Get an item from NamedNodeList by index
```

Listing 10.5   *(continued)*

```
     *
     * @param index The index at which desired item exists
     * @exception org.w3c.dom.NoSuchNodeException If index
doesn't address existing node
     * @returns The indexed node, if it exists.
     *
     */
    public org.w3c.dom.Node item(long index)
throws org.w3c.dom.NoSuchNodeException {
Node theNode;

// get from items
try {
    theNode = (Node) items.elementAt( (int) index);
} catch ( ArrayIndexOutOfBoundsException e ){
    throw new org.w3c.dom.NoSuchNodeException();
}


return (org.w3c.dom.Node) theNode;
    }


    /********************** getLength *************/
    /**
     * Get the length of the named node list
     *
     * @return The number of nodes in named node list.
     */
    public long getLength(){
return items.size();
    }


    /********************** getEnumerator *************/
    /**
     * Get a NodeEnumerator for this named node list
     *
     * @return An NodeEnumerator which will iterate through
nodes in named node list.
```

Listing 10.5 *(continued)*

```
    */
    public org.w3c.dom.NodeEnumerator getEnumerator(){
return (org.w3c.dom.NodeEnumerator) new NodeEnumerator( this
);
    }


    /************** print ***********************/
    /**
     * Print the NamedNodeList structure with indent
     *
     * @param indent The indent to prefix onto emited lines
     *
     */
    public void print(int indent){
String indentString = (new
String("
                             ")).substring(0, indent);


System.out.println(indentString + this );
System.out.println(indentString + "  nameHash: " + nameHash);
System.out.println(indentString + "  items: ");
Enumeration en = items.elements();
Node aNode;
while(en.hasMoreElements()){
    aNode = (Node) en.nextElement();
    aNode.print(indent + 4);
}
    }


    /************** print ****************/
    /**
     * print the structure (no indent)
     */
    public void print(){
print(0);
    }
    /*************** main *********************/
```

Listing 10.5   *(continued)*

```
    /**
     * A class test routine
     *
     */
    public static void main(String argv[]){
// build a simple instance
NamedNodeList aNNL = new NamedNodeList();
System.out.println("built simple NamedNodeList");
aNNL.print();

// build and set a node with associated name
Node node1 = new Node();
Node aNode;
aNode = (Node) aNNL.setNode( "id", node1 );
if( aNode != null ){
    System.out.println("Error: found node and shouldn't
have");
} else {
    System.out.println("setNode(id) complete ok");
}

System.out.println("NNL now:");
aNNL.print();

// test getNode
if( (aNode = (Node) aNNL.getNode( "notThere" )) != null){
    System.out.println("ERROR: attempt to get non-existent
node succeeded");
} else {
        System.out.println("ok: attempt to get non-existent
node failed");
}

if( (aNode = (Node) aNNL.getNode( "id" ) ) == null){
    System.out.println("ERROR: attempt to get existent node
failed");
} else {
```

Listing 10.5   *(continued)*

```
    System.out.println("get node id back:");
    aNode.print(4);
}


// test setNode w/replacement
Node node2 = new Node();
if( ( aNode = (Node) aNNL.setNode( "id", node2 ) ) == null ){
    System.out.println("ERROR: replace didn't find exist-
ing");
} else {
    System.out.println("setNode to replace succeeded.  aNNL
now:");
    aNNL.print(4);
}


// test remove of nonexistent
boolean foundIt = true;
try {
    aNode = (Node) aNNL.remove( "notthere" );
} catch ( org.w3c.dom.NoSuchNodeException e ){
    foundIt = false;
}
if( foundIt ){
    System.out.println("ERROR: remove of nonexistent didn't
throw exception");
} else {
    System.out.println("remove of nonexistent threw excep-
tion: success");
}


// test remove of existent
foundIt = true;
try {
    aNode = (Node) aNNL.remove( "id" );
} catch ( org.w3c.dom.NoSuchNodeException e ){
    foundIt = false;
}
```

Listing 10.5   *(continued)*

```
if( foundIt ){
    System.out.println("remove of existent didn't throw
exception: success");
} else {
    System.out.println("ERROR: remove of existent threw
exception");
}

System.out.println("aNNL now:");
aNNL.print(4);

// test item
aNode = (Node) aNNL.setNode("id",node1);
aNode = (Node) aNNL.setNode("priv",node2);

System.out.println("inserted attributes 'id' and 'priv'");
foundIt = true;
try {
    aNode = (Node) aNNL.item(1);
} catch ( org.w3c.dom.NoSuchNodeException e ){
    foundIt = false;
}
if( foundIt ){
    System.out.println("aNNL.item(1) worked (?): found
node:");
    aNode.print(4);
} else {
    System.out.println("ERROR: aNNL.item(1) failed");
}

// test getLength
System.out.println("getLength()=" + aNNL.getLength() + "
(should be 2)");

// test getEnumerator
NodeEnumerator aNE = (NodeEnumerator) aNNL.getEnumerator();
System.out.println("getEnumerator returned: " + aNE);
```

Listing 10.5 *(continued)*

```
    }
    /*************** member variables ***************/


    /**
     * Vector containing items in the named node list.
     */
    protected Vector items;


    /**
     * hashtable associating name to index in items for each
node in named node list.
     */
    protected Hashtable nameHash;
    }
```

Listing 10.5 *(continued)*

10.7.2.5   Class negeng.dom.NodeEnumerator

Listing 10.6 presents the implementation of the w3c.dom.NodeEnumerator interface. Again a vector called "items" is used to hold the node list referenced by the enumerator. In this case the instance referred to by this instance variable is the vector contained in some source NodeList or NamedNodeList which is being enumerated. We don't make a second copy of the vector instance variable containing the node list to be enumerated but refer to it in-place. By doing this we achieve the DOM specified behavior of presenting, at any moment in time, the actual (perhaps mutated) contents of the NodeList or NamedNodeList which is being enumerated rather than a snapshot of that list taken at the time the enumerator was instantiated. Again a main() method is included to exercise this class.

```
package negeng.dom;

import org.w3c.dom.*;
import java.util.*;


/******************* NodeEnumerator *****************/
/**
 * Enumerator for node lists
 */
public class NodeEnumerator
    implements org.w3c.dom.NodeEnumerator {

    /********************* NodeEnumerator *************/
    /**
     * Constructor for enumerating NodeList's
     * @param nodes The NodeList which is to be enumerated.
     */
    NodeEnumerator(NodeList nodes){
items = nodes.items;
currentIndex = 0;
    }


    /********************** NodeEnumerator ************/
    /**
     * Constructor for enumerating NamedNodeList's
     * @param nodes The NamedNodeList which is to be enumer-
ated.
     */
    NodeEnumerator(NamedNodeList nodes){
items = nodes.items;
currentIndex = 0;
    }


    /********************** getFirst *************/
    /**
     * Get the first node in list and reset enumerator to this
node.
```

Listing 10.6

```
     *
     * @return The first node in list (if exists)
     *
     */
    public org.w3c.dom.Node getFirst() {

if( items.size() < 1 ){
    return (org.w3c.dom.Node) null;
}
currentIndex = 0;

return (org.w3c.dom.Node) items.elementAt(currentIndex);
    }


    /********************* getNext ******************/
    /**
     * Advance state of enumeration and return then current
Node.  If
     * enumeration already at last node, return null and leave
at this
     * last node.
     *
     * @return The next Node in list, null if at end
     */
    public org.w3c.dom.Node getNext(){
if( currentIndex == (items.size() - 1) ){
    // pointing at last already
    return (org.w3c.dom.Node) null;
}
return (org.w3c.dom.Node) items.elementAt(++currentIndex);
    }


    /********************* getPrevious ***************/
    /**
     * Reduce (move to earlier Node) state of enumeration and
return
```

Listing 10.6   *(continued)*

```
     * then current Node.  If already at first node, return
null and
     * leave enumeration at first node.
     *
     * @return The previous node if not already at first, else
null.
     * @exception org.w3c.dom.NoSuchNodeException Not thrown.
Return value of 'null' is used instead (inconsistency in dom
spec).
     */
    public org.w3c.dom.Node getPrevious(){
if( --currentIndex < 0 ){
    currentIndex = 0;
    return (org.w3c.dom.Node) null;
}
return (org.w3c.dom.Node) items.elementAt(currentIndex);
    }


    /******************** getLast *************/
    /**
     * Move state of enumeration to point to last node in
nodelist,
     * then return this last node.
     *
     * @return The last node in node list if not empty, else
null
     */
    public org.w3c.dom.Node getLast(){
if( items.size() > 0 ){
    currentIndex = items.size() - 1;
    return (org.w3c.dom.Node) items.lastElement();
} else {
    return (org.w3c.dom.Node) null;
}
    }


    /*********************** getCurrent *************/
```

Listing 10.6   *(continued)*

```
    /**
     * Get the current node pointed at by enumeration if node
list not
     * empty, else null
     *
     * @return Current node in enumeration if nodelist not
empty, else null
     */
    public org.w3c.dom.Node getCurrent(){
if( currentIndex < 0 || currentIndex > (items.size() - 1)){
    return (org.w3c.dom.Node) null;
}
return (org.w3c.dom.Node) items.elementAt(currentIndex);
    }


    /*********************** atStart **************/
    /**
     * Return indication of whether enumeration is at start
of nodelist.
     * Return true if nodelist is empty
     *
     * @return True if enumeration at start of nodelist, or
nodelist empty
     *
     */
    public boolean atStart(){
return (currentIndex == 0);
    }


    /********************** atEnd **************/
    /**
     * Return indication of whether enumeration is at end of
nodelist.
     * Return True if nodelist is empty
     *
     */
    public boolean atEnd(){
```

Listing 10.6 *(continued)*

```
if( items.size() == 0 ){
    return true;
}
return (currentIndex == (items.size() - 1)) ;
    }


    /*********************** print **************/
    /**
     * Print structure with indentation
     * @param indent Number of spaces indentation to prefix
to emitted lines.
     */
    public void print(int indent){
// derive a new indentString
String indentString = (new
String("
                          ")).substring(0, indent);

System.out.println(indentString + this);
System.out.println(indentString + "  Items:" + items);
System.out.println(indentString + "  currentIndex:" + cur-
rentIndex);
    }


    /*********************** print *************/
    /**
     * Print structure w/o indent
     */
    public void print(){
print(0);
    }


    /*********************** main **************/
    /**
     * A class test routine
```

Listing 10.6 *(continued)*

```
 * @exception org.w3c.dom.NoSuchNodeException This is
bogus due to getNext and getPrevious declarations in
org.w3c.dom.NodeEnumeration indicating it is thrown, but
really we use 'null' return.
 */
    public static void main(String argv[])
throws org.w3c.dom.NoSuchNodeException {
Node aNode; // temp for test purposes

// build a simple nodelist to enum
NodeList aNodeList = new NodeList();

NodeEnumerator aNE = (NodeEnumerator) new NodeEnumera-
tor(aNodeList);
System.out.println("NodeEnumerator for empty list:");
aNE.print(4);

System.out.println("build a non-empty nl");
Node node1 = new Node(1);
aNodeList.items.addElement(node1);
Node node2 = new Node(2);
aNodeList.items.addElement(node2);
Node node3 = new Node(3);
aNodeList.items.addElement(node3);
Node node4 = new Node(4);
aNodeList.items.addElement(node4);

// create a NodeEnum out of it
NodeEnumerator aNodeEnumerator = new NodeEnumera-
tor(aNodeList);

System.out.println("built an NodeEnumerator:");
aNodeEnumerator.print();

// test method getLast on this non-empty
if( (aNode = (Node) aNodeEnumerator.getLast()) == null){
```

Listing 10.6   *(continued)*

```
    System.out.println("ERROR: getLast() returned null even
though nodelist is non-empty");
} else {
    System.out.println("getLast() returned: " + aNode);
}


// test method getFirst on this non-empty
if( (aNode = (Node) aNodeEnumerator.getFirst()) == null ){
    System.out.println("ERROR: getFirst failed");
} else {
    System.out.println("getFirst() [on non-empty list]
returned: " + aNode );
}


// test method getNext
System.out.println("iterating w/getNext():");
while( ( aNode = (Node) aNodeEnumerator.getNext()) != null ){
    System.out.println("  getNext() = " + aNode);
}
System.out.println("getNext() returned null");


// test method getPrevious
System.out.println("iterating w/getPrevious():");
while( ( aNode = (Node) aNodeEnumerator.getPrevious()) !=
null ){
    System.out.println("  getPrevious() = " + aNode );
}
System.out.println("getPrevious() returned null");


// test method getCurrent (on non-empty)
if( (aNode = (Node) aNodeEnumerator.getCurrent()) == null){
    System.out.println("ERROR: getCurrent() returned null
even though nodelist is non-empty");
} else {
    System.out.println("getCurrent()=" + aNode);
}
```

Listing 10.6   *(continued)*

```
// test method atStart and atEnd
aNodeEnumerator.getLast();
System.out.println("moved to end w/getLast:");
System.out.println("  atStart()=" + aNodeEnumera-
tor.atStart());
System.out.println("  atEnd()=" + aNodeEnumerator.atEnd());
aNodeEnumerator.getFirst();
System.out.println("moved to start w/getFirst:");
System.out.println("  atStart()=" + aNodeEnumera-
tor.atStart());
System.out.println("  atEnd()=" + aNodeEnumerator.atEnd());
    }
    /***************** member variables ***********/
    protected Vector items;

    protected int currentIndex;

}
```

Listing 10.6   *(continued)*

10.7.2.6   Class negeng.dom.Element

Listing 10.7 below presents the code for class negeng.dom.Element. This implementation of interface w3c.dom.Element augments the Node class which it extends by providing both a String "name" instance variable, and a NamedNodeList "attributes" instance variable. The inherited NodeList "children" is used to hold the child nodes of the element. A main() class test method is provided. Please note that no method with signature "void setAttribute(Attribute newAttr)" is provided here. Implementation of this method is left as an exercise for the reader.

```
package negeng.dom;

import negeng.dom.*;

/*********************************/
/*
 * Class to hold Elements
 *
 */
public class Element
  extends Node
  implements org.w3c.dom.Element {
    /****************** Element ***************/
    /*
     * Constructor
     *
     */
    public Element(){
type = org.w3c.dom.Node.ELEMENT;
    }

    /****************** Element *************/
    /**
     * Constructor w/initializers
     *
     * @param newTagName Name for new elem
     */
    public Element(String newTagName){
type = org.w3c.dom.Node.ELEMENT;
tagName = newTagName;
    }

    /***************** Element ****************/
```

Listing 10.7

```
    /**
     * Constructor w/initializers
     *
     * @param newTagName Name for new elem
     * @param newAttributes AttributeList for new elem
     */
    public Element(String newTagName,
       org.w3c.dom.AttributeList newAttributes){
type = org.w3c.dom.Node.ELEMENT;
attributes = (AttributeList) newAttributes;
tagName = newTagName;
    }


    /****************** getTagName **************/
    /**
     * Get the element's name
     * @return The element's name
     */
    public String getTagName(){
return tagName;
    }


    /****************** setTagName **************/
    /**
     * Set the element's name
     * @param newName The name for the element
     *
     */
    public void setTagName(String newName){
tagName = newName;
    }


    /****************** getAttributes **********/
    /**
     * Get the attributes of this element.
     */
```

Listing 10.7   *(continued)*

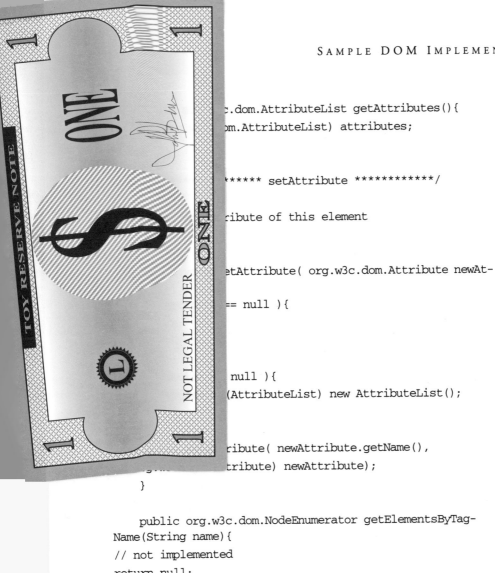

```
c.dom.AttributeList getAttributes(){
om.AttributeList) attributes;


****** setAttribute ************/

ribute of this element


etAttribute( org.w3c.dom.Attribute newAt-

== null ){



null ){
(AttributeList) new AttributeList();



ribute( newAttribute.getName(),
tribute) newAttribute);
    }


    public org.w3c.dom.NodeEnumerator getElementsByTag-
Name(String name){
// not implemented
return null;
    }


    /**************** print *************/
    /**
     * Print the element object
     *
     * @param indent Spaces to prefix to all emitted lines.
     *
     */
    public void print(int indent){
```

Listing 10.7 *(continued)*

```java
String indentString = (new
String("
                             ").substring(0,indent));

System.out.println(indentString + this);
System.out.println(indentString + "  tagName: " + tagName );


AttributeList attrList = (AttributeList) this.getAt-
tributes();

if( attrList != null && attributes.getLength() > 0 ){
    System.out.println(indentString + "  attributes: " );
    attrList.print(indent + 4);
} else {
    System.out.println(indentString + "  attributes: none");
}


if( children != null ){
    System.out.println(indentString + "  children: ");
    children.print(indent + 4);
 }
    }

    /******************** print ********************/
    /**
     * Print (w/o indent)
     */
    public void print(){
print(0);
    }


    /******************** main ********************/
    /**
     * A class test routine.
     */
    public static void main(String argv[]){
```

Listing 10.7 *(continued)*

```
// test simple constructor and setTagName
Element element1 = new Element();
element1.setTagName("para");
System.out.println("built elem, set tagName 'para':");
element1.print(4);

// test constructor w/tagName initializer
Element element2 = new Element("gobbledigook");
System.out.println("built 'gobbledigook' element:");
element2.print(4);

// test getAttributes (on empty list)
 AttributeList elem1attribs = (AttributeList) element1.getAt-
tributes();
System.out.println("getAttribs (when none) returned: "
  + elem1attribs );

// build  attrs for test
Attribute a1,a2,a3;
a1 = (Attribute) new Attribute("id","val1");
a2 = (Attribute) new Attribute("id2","val2");

// now add them to the node's attributes
a3 = (Attribute) elem1attribs.setAttribute("id",a1);
a3 = (Attribute) elem1attribs.setAttribute("id2",a2);

System.out.println("added 2 attr: now:");
element1.print(4);

/*
// add first child, w/grandchild
Node child1 = new Node("child 1");
child1.addAttribute("fname", "betty");
child1.addAttribute("lname", "lewis");
node1.addChild(child1);
```

Listing 10.7   *(continued)*

```java
    Node grandchild11 = new Node("grandchild 1.1");
    grandchild11.addAttribute("fname", "darleen");
    grandchild11.addAttribute("lname", "lewis-doe");
    child1.addChild(grandchild11);

    // add 2nd child, w/grandchild
    Node child2 = new Node("child 2");
    child2.addAttribute("fname", "fred");
    child2.addAttribute("lname", "flintstone");
    node1.addChild(child2);

    Node grandchild21 = new Node("grandchild 2.1");
    grandchild21.addAttribute("fname", "pebbles");
    grandchild21.addAttribute("lname", "flintstone");
    child2.addChild(grandchild21);

    node1.print();
    */
        }


    /*************************** member vars
***************/
        /**
         * The name of tag (element type)
         */
        private String tagName;

        /**
         * The attributes of this class
         */
        protected AttributeList attributes;
}
```

Listing 10.7   *(continued)*

10.7.2.7   Class negeng.dom.Attribute

This next listing, Listing 10.8, presents class negeng.dom.Attribute which implements w3c.dom.Attribute. It appears that the only place this class is used in the other portions of the DOM interface is as the type of the argument provided in the setAttribute() method of the class w3c.dom.Element, which coincidentally was not built in this sample implementation. Nonetheless, a main() method is provided in order to test it and illustrate its behavior.

```
package negeng.dom;

import negeng.dom.*;
import java.util.*;

/********************************
/**
  * Class for holding attributes
  */
public class Attribute
   extends Node
   implements org.w3c.dom.Attribute {

    /*************** constructor ***********/
    /**
      * Basic constructor.
      */
    public Attribute(){
type = org.w3c.dom.Node.ATTRIBUTE;
name = new String("");
value = new NodeList();
specified = true;
    }

    /*************** Attribute *************/
```

Listing 10.8

```
    /**
     * Constructor w/initialing values
     *
     * @param newName Name of new attribute
     * @param newValue Value (nodelist) of new attribute.
     */
    public Attribute(String newName, org.w3c.dom.NodeList
newValue){
type = org.w3c.dom.Node.ATTRIBUTE;
name = newName;
value = (NodeList) newValue;
specified = true;
    }


    /*************** Attribute **************/
    /**
     * Constructor w/initializing values.  Build a new
Attribute
     * and initialize with value of NL with single Text node
which
     * itself is initialized from <i>newValue</i> parameter.
     *
     * @param newName The name of the new attribute
     * @param newValue String value of new attribute
     *
     */
    public Attribute(String newName, String newValue){
type = org.w3c.dom.Node.ATTRIBUTE;
name = newName;
Text valText = new Text(newValue);
value = new NodeList();
value.items.addElement( valText );
specified = true;
    }


    /*************** getName **************/
    /**
```

Listing 10.8   *(continued)*

```
     * Get the name of this attribute
     * @return Name of this attribute.
     */
    public String getName(){
return name;
    }


    /*************** setName ****************/
    /**
     * Set the name of this attribute
     *
     * @param name The new name for this attribute
     *
     */
    public void setName(String newName){
name = newName;
    }


    /*************** getValue ***************/
    /**
     * Get the value of this attribute
     *
     * @return The value of this attribute (NodeList)
     */
    public org.w3c.dom.NodeList getValue(){
return (org.w3c.dom.NodeList) value;
    }


    /*************** setValue ***************/
    /**
     * Set the value of this attribute
     *
     * @param newValue The new value (NodeList) to assign as
this attribute's value
     */
    public void setValue(org.w3c.dom.NodeList newValue){
```

Listing 10.8 *(continued)*

```
value = (NodeList) newValue;
    }

    /*************** getSpecified ***********/
    /**
     * Get the value of specified flag
     *
     * @return The current <i>specified</i> flag
     */
    public boolean getSpecified(){
return specified;
    }

    /*************** setSpecified ***********/
    /*
     * Set the value of specified flag
     *
     * @param newSpecified The new value for specified
     *
     */
    public void setSpecified(boolean newSpecified){
specified = newSpecified;
    }

    /*************** toString ***************/
    /**
     * Convert value to string and return
     *
     */
    public String toString(){
// not implemented
return "";
    }

    /************* print ****************/
    /*
```

Listing 10.8   *(continued)*

```
      * print the attribute structure
      *
      */
    public void print(int indent){
String indentString = (new
String("
                          ")).substring(0,indent);

System.out.println(indentString + super.toString());
System.out.println(indentString + "  name: " + name );
System.out.println(indentString + "  specified: " + specified
);
System.out.println(indentString + "  value: " + value );
value.print(indent + 4);
    }


    /*************** print ***********/
    /**
      * Print (w/o indent)
      *
      */
    public void print(){
print(0);
    }


    /************* main **************/
    /**
      * A class test routine.
      *
      */
    public static void main(String argv[]){
// build a simple test attribute
Attribute attr1 = new Attribute();
System.out.println("simple, empty, attribute");
attr1.print();

// build a more complext test attribute value (first value)
```

Listing 10.8 *(continued)*

```
Node node1 = new Node();
NodeList nodeList1 = new NodeList();
nodeList1.items.addElement(node1);
Attribute attr2 = new Attribute("id", nodeList1 );

System.out.println("initialized attribute:" + attr2);
attr2.print();

// test construct with initial name string value
Attribute attr3 = new Attribute("name", "negeng");
System.out.println("initialized attribute:" + attr3);
attr3.print();
    }

    /************* member variables ************/
    /**
      * The name of this attribute.
      */
    String name;
    /**
      * The value of this attribute.
      *
      */
    NodeList value;

    /**
      * The <i>specified</i> flag for this attribute.   (see
org.w3c.dom specification)
      */
    boolean specified;
}
```

Listing 10.8   *(continued)*

10.7.2.8 Class negeng.dom.AttributeList

The class negeng.dom.AttributeList, presented in Listing 10.9, provides a container to hold the list of attributes associated with an element. The usual means for getting, setting and removing list items are provided. It is very nearly identical to the NamedNodeList helper class which was introduced in an earlier version of the DOM specification and which in this earlier version provided the function of holding attributes which this class now provides.

```
package negeng.dom;

import negeng.dom.*;
import negeng.*;

import java.util.*;

/**********************************************/
/**
 * A list of attributes
 *
 */

public class AttributeList implements
org.w3c.dom.AttributeList {
    /****************** constructor **************/
    /**
     * Basic constructor.
     *
     */
    public AttributeList(){
items = new Vector();
nameHash = new Hashtable();
    }
```

Listing 10.9

```
/*********************** getAttribute **************/
/**
 * Get attribute associated with a particular name
 *
 * @param name The name of the attribute sought
 * @return The Attribute associated with name.
 *
 */
public org.w3c.dom.Attribute getAttribute(String name){
Attribute aNode;
Object indexObj;

if( (indexObj = nameHash.get(name)) == null ){
    // didn't find it
    return (org.w3c.dom.Attribute) null;
}


// found it, convert indexObj to index and fetch node from
items
return (org.w3c.dom.Attribute) items.elementAt( ((Integer)
indexObj).intValue());
    }


/*********************** setAttribute
******************/
/**
 * Set an Attribute: if name exists replace assoc. item,
else append a new.
 *
 * @param name Name of new or existing attribute
 * @param node The new or replacement attribute
 * @return If <i>name</i> references existing attr,
return it,
 * otherwise, return null.
 *
 */
```

Listing 10.9   *(continued)*

```
    public org.w3c.dom.Attribute setAttribute(String name,
org.w3c.dom.Attribute newAttr){
Node oldAttr;
Object indexObj;
int index;

if( (indexObj = nameHash.get(name)) != null ){
    // this is replacement!

    // convert indexObj to int
    index = ((Integer) indexObj ).intValue();

    // get the old value
    oldAttr = (Node) items.elementAt( index );

    // replace it w/new
    items.setElementAt(newAttr,index);

    // return oldAttr (per org.w3c.dom spec)
    return (org.w3c.dom.Attribute) oldAttr;
} else {
    // doesn't exist!
    // add to items
    items.addElement((org.w3c.dom.Attribute) newAttr );
    index = items.size() - 1;

    // put index into hash table
    nameHash.put(name, new Integer(index) );

    // return null per org.w3c.dom.AttributeList spec
    return (org.w3c.dom.Attribute) null;
}
    }

    /********************** remove ********************/
    /**
```

Listing 10.9   *(continued)*

```
      * Remove attr associated with name
      *
      * @param name Name of attr to be removed
      * @exception org.w3c.dom.NoSuchNodeException If name not
found.
      * @return If name references existing node, return that
node.
      *
      */
     public org.w3c.dom.Attribute remove(String name)
throws org.w3c.dom.NoSuchNodeException {
Node oldAttr;
Object indexObj;
int oldIndex;

// see if it is there
if( (indexObj = nameHash.get(name)) == null ){
    // whoops, not there
    throw new org.w3c.dom.NoSuchNodeException();
}

// convert indexObj to int
oldIndex = ((Integer) indexObj).intValue();

// remove from hash
nameHash.remove(name);

// retrieve then remove from items
oldAttr = (Node) items.elementAt(oldIndex);
items.removeElementAt(oldIndex);

return (org.w3c.dom.Attribute) oldAttr;
    }


/********************** item **********************/
/**
    * Get attribute from AttributeList by index
```

Listing 10.9   *(continued)*

```
     *
     * @param index The index at which desired item exists
     * @exception org.w3c.dom.NoSuchNodeException If index
doesn't address existing node
     * @returns The indexed node, if it exists.
     *
     */
    public org.w3c.dom.Attribute item(int index)
throws org.w3c.dom.NoSuchNodeException {
Attribute theAttr;

// get from items
try {
    theAttr = (Attribute) items.elementAt(index);
} catch ( ArrayIndexOutOfBoundsException e ){
    throw new org.w3c.dom.NoSuchNodeException();
}

return (org.w3c.dom.Attribute) theAttr;
    }

    /********************** getLength *************/
    /**
     * Get the length of the named node list
     *
     * @return The number of nodes in named node list.
     */
    public long getLength(){
return items.size();
    }

    /*************** print ********************/
    /**
     * Print the AttributeList structure with indent
     *
     * @param indent The indent to prefix onto emited lines
```

Listing 10.9   *(continued)*

```
        *
        */
    public void print(int indent){
String indentString = (new
String("
                            ")).substring(0, indent);

System.out.println(indentString + this );
System.out.println(indentString + "   nameHash: " + nameHash);
System.out.println(indentString + "   items: ");
Enumeration en = items.elements();
Attribute anAttr;
while(en.hasMoreElements()){
    anAttr = (Attribute) en.nextElement();
    anAttr.print(indent + 4);
}
    }


    /*************** print ****************/
    /**
     * print the structure (no indent)
     */
    public void print(){
print(0);
    }
    /*************** main ********************/
    /**
     * A class test routine
     *
     */
    public static void main(String argv[]){
// build a simple instance
AttributeList aAL = new AttributeList();
System.out.println("built simple AttributeList");
aAL.print();

// some attribs to work with
```

Listing 10.9   *(continued)*

```
Attribute anAttr, attr1, attr2;

// build a sample attribute and add to aAL
attr1 = new Attribute("id","val1");
anAttr = (Attribute) aAL.setAttribute( "id", attr1 );

System.out.println("added attr1: AL now:");
aAL.print();

// test getAttr
if( (anAttr = (Attribute) aAL.getAttribute( "notThere" )) !=
null){
    System.out.println("ERROR: attempt to get non-existent
node succeeded");
} else {
        System.out.println("ok: attempt to get non-existent
node failed");
}

if( (anAttr = (Attribute) aAL.getAttribute( "id" ) ) ==
null){
    System.out.println("ERROR: attempt to get existent node
failed");
} else {
    System.out.println("get node id back:");
    anAttr.print(4);
}

// test setNode w/replacement
attr2 = new Attribute("id2","val2");
if( ( anAttr = (Attribute) aAL.setAttribute( "id", attr2 ) )
== null ){
    System.out.println("ERROR: replace didn't find exist-
ing");
} else {
    System.out.println("setNode to replace succeeded.  aAL
now:");
    aAL.print(4);
```

Listing 10.9 *(continued)*

```
}

// test remove of nonexistent
boolean foundIt = true;
try {
    anAttr = (Attribute) aAL.remove( "notthere" );
} catch ( org.w3c.dom.NoSuchNodeException e ){
    foundIt = false;
}
if( foundIt ){
    System.out.println("ERROR: remove of nonexistent didn't
throw exception");
} else {
    System.out.println("remove of nonexistent threw excep-
tion: success");
}

// test remove of existent
foundIt = true;
try {
    anAttr = (Attribute) aAL.remove( "id" );
} catch ( org.w3c.dom.NoSuchNodeException e ){
    foundIt = false;
}
if( foundIt ){
    System.out.println("remove of existent didn't throw
exception: success");
} else {
    System.out.println("ERROR: remove of existent threw
exception");
}

System.out.println("aAL now:");
aAL.print(4);

// test item
anAttr = (Attribute) aAL.setAttribute("id",attr1);
```

Listing 10.9 *(continued)*

```
anAttr = (Attribute) aAL.setAttribute("id2",attr2);

System.out.println("inserted attributes 'id' and 'id2'");
foundIt = true;
try {
    anAttr = (Attribute) aAL.item(1);
} catch ( org.w3c.dom.NoSuchNodeException e ){
    foundIt = false;
}
if( foundIt ){
    System.out.println("aAL.item(1) worked (?): found
node:");
    anAttr.print(4);
} else {
    System.out.println("ERROR: aAL.item(1) failed");
}

// test getLength
System.out.println("getLength()=" + aAL.getLength() + "
(should be 2)");
    }
    /*************** member variables ***************/

    /**
     * Vector containing items in the named node list.
     */
    protected Vector items;

    /**
     * hashtable associating name to index in items for each
node in named node list.
     */
    protected Hashtable nameHash;
}
```

Listing 10.9   *(continued)*

10.7.2.9   Class negeng.dom.Text

Listing 10.10 presents the class negeng.dom.Text which implements interface w3c.dom.Text. The two instance variables, String "data" and boolean "isIgnorableWhiteSpace" are used to provide the required class behavior as specified in the DOM interface definition. A very simple main() routine is provided.

```
package negeng.dom;

import negeng.dom.*;

/***************************************/
/**
 * The subclass of node which contains text
 */
public class Text extends Node implements org.w3c.dom.Text {
    /******************** constructor ***********/
    /**
     * Basic constructor
     */
    public Text(){
data = new String("");
type = org.w3c.dom.Element.TEXT;
isIgnorableWhitespace = false;
    }

    /***************** constructor *************/
    /**
     * Constructor with initial data as param
     *
     * @param newData The value of data to initialize with.
     *
     */
    public Text(String newData){
data = newData;
```

Listing 10.10

```java
type = org.w3c.dom.Element.TEXT;
isIgnorableWhitespace = false;
    }


    /******************** getData **************/
    /**
     * Get data in this text node
     *
     * @return The text in this text node
     *
     */
    public String getData(){
return data;
    }


    /****************** setData ***************/
    /**
     * Set the data in this text node
     */
    public void setData(String newData){
data = newData;
    }


    /*********** getIsIgnorableWhitespace *******/
    /**
     * Get the value of the <i>isIgnorableWhiteSpace</i>
flag.
     *
     * return The value of the <i>isIgnorableWhiteSpace</i>
flag.
     */
    public boolean getIsIgnorableWhitespace(){
return isIgnorableWhitespace;
    }


    /*********** getIsIgnorableWhitespace *******/
    /**
```

Listing 10.10   *(continued)*

```
    * Set the value of the <i>isIgnorableWhiteSpace</i>
flag.
    *
    * @param newValue The new value to for the <i>isIgnor-
ableWhiteSpace</i> flag.
    */
    public void setIsIgnorableWhitespace(boolean newValue){
isIgnorableWhitespace = newValue;
    }


    /***************** print ****************/
    /**
    * Print with indent
    *
    * @param indent The number of spaces to prepend in emit-
ted lines
    */
    public void print(int indent){
String indentString = (new
String("
                         ")).substring(0,indent);

System.out.println(indentString + "Text:" + this );
System.out.println(indentString + "  data: <------------\n"
+
  data + "\n" + indentString + "  ------------->");
System.out.println(indentString + "  isIgnorableWhitespace: "
+ isIgnorableWhitespace);
    }


    /***************** print ****************/
    /**
     * Print w/o indent
     */
    public void print(){
print(0);
    }
```

Listing 10.10   *(continued)*

```
/***************** main *****************/
/**
 * A class test routine
 */
public static void main(String argv[]){
// build Text node then test setData
Text text1 = new Text();
text1.setData("Today is the first day of the rest of our
lives");

System.out.println("Built and then setData a new Text
node:");
text1.print();

// test setIsIgnorableWhitespace
text1.setIsIgnorableWhitespace(true);
System.out.println("setIsIgnorableWhitespace(true):");
text1.print();
    }
    /*************** member variables *************/
    /**
     * The data (text) in this text node.
     */
    private String data;

    /**
     * The isIgnorableWhitespace flag associated with this
text node
     */
    private boolean isIgnorableWhitespace;
}
```

Listing 10.10   *(continued)*

10.7.2.10   Class negeng.dom.Document

Listing 10.11 below presents an implementation of the DOM specified interface w3c.dom.Document. The primitiveness of this class
reflects the early stage of development of the DOM definition itself at
the time of this writing. No details are provided as to the contents of
the document type declaration, for instance. Still, this provides a basic
top-level interface to the in-memory representation of the results of a
parsing of an XML document. Rather than provide a class test main()
method here, a sample client to the services of this class is presented
in the next section.

```java
package negeng.dom;

import negeng.dom.*;

/*********************************/
/**
 * Class to hold Document
 *
 */
public class Document
  extends Node
  implements org.w3c.dom.Document {
    /****************** Document ***************/
    /**
     * Constructor
     *
     */
    public Document(){
type = org.w3c.dom.Node.DOCUMENT;
documentType = null;
documentElement = null;
    }
```

Listing 10.11

```
/****************** Document *************/
/**
 * Constructor w/initializer
 *
 * @param documentElement The root Element of the docu-
ment.
 */
public Document(Element newDocumentElement){
type = org.w3c.dom.Node.DOCUMENT;
documentType = null;
documentElement = newDocumentElement;
}


/****************** getDocumentType *************/
/**
 * Get the documentType node
 *
 * @return The current document type of this document.
 */
public org.w3c.dom.Node getDocumentType(){
return documentType;
}


/****************** setDocumentType *************/
/**
 * Set the document type of this document.
 *
 * @param newDocumentType The new document type for this
document.
 **/


public void setDocumentType(org.w3c.dom.Node newDocument-
Type){
documentType = (Node) newDocumentType;
}


/****************** getDocumentElement **********/
```

Listing 10.11   *(continued)*

```
    /**
     * Get the document element of document.
     **/
    public org.w3c.dom.Element getDocumentElement(){
return (org.w3c.dom.Element) documentElement;
    }


    /***************** setDocumentElement ***********/
    /**
     * Set the document element of document.
     *
     * @param newDocumentElement The new doc elem of docu-
ment.
     **/
    public void setDocumentElement( org.w3c.dom.Element new-
DocumentElement ){
documentElement = (Element) newDocumentElement;
    }


    /***************** getElementsByTagName ***********/
    /**
     * Get decendent elements by tag name
     *
     * @param name The name of elements to get
     *
     **/


    public org.w3c.dom.NodeEnumerator getElementsByTag-
Name(String name){
return documentElement.getElementsByTagName(name);
    }


    /***************** print *************/
    /**
     * Print the document
     *
     * @param indent Spaces to prefix to all emitted lines.
```

Listing 10.11   *(continued)*

```
     *
     */
    public void print(int indent){
String indentString = (new
String("
                         ").substring(0,indent));

System.out.println(indentString + this);
System.out.println(indentString + "   documentType: " + docu-
mentType );
System.out.println(indentString + "   documentElement: " +
documentElement );
this.documentElement.print(indent + 4);
    }

    /******************** print ********************/
    /**
     * Print (w/o indent)
     */
    public void print(){
print(0);
    }

    /******************** main ********************/
    /**
     * A class test routine.
     */
    public static void main(String argv[]){
    }

    /*********************** member vars
**************/
    /**
     * The document type of this document.
     */
    protected Node documentType;
```

Listing 10.11   *(continued)*

```
    /**
     * The document element of this document
     */
    protected Element documentElement;
}
```

Listing 10.11   *(continued)*

10.7.2.11   Class negeng.dom.DOMFactory

The last of the DOM classes illustrated here is the DOMFactory presented in Listing 10.12. This class simply provides the user with means to create the core elements required during construction of a DOM tree. This class was introduced in the December 9, 1997 release of the DOM specification.

```
package negeng.dom;

public class DOMFactory implements org.w3c.dom.DOMFactory {

    public DOMFactory(){
    }

    public org.w3c.dom.Document createDocument(){
return (org.w3c.dom.Document) new Document();
    }

    public org.w3c.dom.DocumentContext createDocumentCon-
text(){
return (org.w3c.dom.DocumentContext) new DocumentContext();
    }

    public org.w3c.dom.Element createElement(String tagName,
        org.w3c.dom.AttributeList attributes){
return (org.w3c.dom.Element) new Element(tag-
Name,attributes);
```

Listing 10.12

```
        }

    public org.w3c.dom.Text createTextNode(String data){
return (org.w3c.dom.Text) new Text(data);
        }

    public org.w3c.dom.Comment createComment(String data){
return (org.w3c.dom.Comment) null; // not implemented
        }

    public org.w3c.dom.PI createPI(String name, String data){
return (org.w3c.dom.PI) null; // not implemented
        }

    public org.w3c.dom.Attribute createAttribute(String name,
        org.w3c.dom.NodeList value){
return (org.w3c.dom.Attribute) new Attribute(name, value);
        }
}
```

Listing 10.12 *(continued)*

10.7.3 *Integrating the DOM Implementation*

We now demonstrate integration of the DOM interface implementation just presented with an XML parser. This is provided within the "XSpec" utility class which provides a client application means to load and parse XML documents. While these facilities should be provided within the DOM implementation itself, no definition for them was included in the DOM as of the time of this writing. For that reason, these facilities are provided on top of, rather than within, the DOM implementation.

This application also provides a simple main() routine which uses the print() methods built into the DOM implementation to generate as output a textual representation of the in-memory model of the document which was built. A sample of this output, and the input it was produced from, is offered below. Three new classes are presented in the following sections: negeng.Tree, negeng.XEsis, and negeng.XSpec. The first two of these classes serve as utilities which the negeng.XSpec class makes use of to actually parse XML documents.

10.7.3.1   Class negeng.Tree

The class negeng.Tree, which is presented in Listing 10.13, extends the class negeng.dom.Document with facilities to construct a tree while parsing a document. In particular, it adds a stack on which partially processed nodes can be kept, along with a means to push and pop nodes on and off of this stack. It also provides means to add attributes and children to the node which is on the top of the stack which, by the definition used here, is the current focus of a tree construction process. The element associated with the node on top of the stack is "open"; attributes and child elements which are encountered before it is "closed" (and associated node popped off the stack) are related to with this element and thus the DOM data structures built as a result of these events appearing on the input are attached to this "current" node. No main() test method is provided; rather the classes which are presented below form a sample application of this class.

```
package negeng;

import java.util.*;

import negeng.*;
import negeng.dom.*;

/************************************************/
/*
```

Listing 10.13

```
 * A tree root upon which to build a document
 *
 * <ul>
 *     <li>member 'stack' holds focus of construction
 *         Top is current focus, lower stack elements
holdbaldy79
 *         path into tree of current node.
 *     <li>methods to alter focus (push, pop)
 *     <li> methods to add attributes and children to Element
which is
 *         current focus.
 * </ul>
 */
public class Tree extends Document {
    /****************** Tree ******************/
    /*
     * Basic constructor.  Build tree w/root element w/name
'TreeRoot'.
     *
     */
    public Tree() {
// no document element till set
documentElement = null;

// nothing on the stack
    }

    /****************** appendChild ****************/
    /**
     * Append a node to children of node
     * currently on top of stack.
     *
     * @param newChild The child node to be appended
     *
     */
    public void appendChild(Node newChild){
Node current = (Node) stack.peek();
```

Listing 10.13   *(continued)*

```
    try {
        current.insertBefore((org.w3c.dom.Node) newChild,
            (org.w3c.dom.Node) null);
    } catch( org.w3c.dom.NotMyChildException e ) {
    }
        }


        /******************** addAttribute ****************/
        /**
         * Create an attribute node with value <i>value</i> and
add
         * it to attributes of Element on top of stack
         *
         * @param name The name of attribute
         * @param value The value of attribute
         *
         */
        public void addAttribute(String name, String value){
Attribute newAttribute = new Attribute( name, value );

((Element)stack.peek()).setAttribute(newAttribute);
        }


        /********************* push *******************/
        /**
         * Push a new Element onto top of stack (existing top
         * becomes top-1).  This node becomes current focus
         * of attribute and child manipulation methods.
         *
         * @param elem The node to push and have become current
top
         *
         */
        public void push(Element elem){
            stack.push( elem );
        }
```

Listing 10.13   *(continued)*

```
/******************** pop ********************/
/**
 * Pop a node off of top of stack.  Top-1 becomes
 * new top thus focus of attribute and child
 * manipulation methods.
 *
 * @returns The Node previously at top.
 */
public Element pop(){
return (Element) stack.pop();
}


/******************** print ******************/
/**
 * Print tree w/indent
 *
 * @param indent Number of spaces of indent
 */
public void print(int indent){
String indentString = (new
String("
                        ")).substring(0,indent);

System.out.println(indentString + this );
System.out.println(indentString + "  documentElement: " );
documentElement.print(indent + 4);
}

/******************* member variables **********/
/**
 * A stack used during traversal.
 */
protected Stack stack = new Stack();
}
```

Listing 10.13 *(continued)*

10.7.3.2   Class negeng.XEsis

The class negEng.XEsis, presented in Listing 10.14, provides the call-back routines which the NXP parser calls during the parsing of an XML document, that is, this class implements the NXP.ESIS interface. The callback routines in turn call on the facilities of the negeng.Tree class, and on the DOM implementation upon which it is in turn built, in order to construct appropriate elements of the DOM tree for ESIS events. The features of the DOMFactory class were not utilized in this example. A single instance variable of type negeng.Tree provides the construction site where a new document tree can be built. For example, the "tag_open" event causes a new negeng.dom.Element node to be constructed and then appended onto the list of children for the node currently on top of the stack. It then "pushes" this new element onto the stack to record that it has become the current focus of construction. The element previously on top of the stack is left under this new element and will reappear as the current focus of construction once this new node's end-tag appears. The method tag_close() sees to this.

```
package negeng;

import NXP.*;
import negeng.*;
import negeng.dom.*;

/*****************************************/
/**
 * An ESIS interface for parser call-backs.
 *
 */
public class XEsis implements NXP.Esis {
    /********************* XEsis ************/
    /**
     * Basic constructor
```

Listing 10.14

```
     *
     * @param tree A (empty) tree object which ESIS will build
upon
     *
     */
    public XEsis(Tree tree){
        this.tree = tree;

        //super.Esis_Stdout();
    }

    /***************** SetTree **********/
    /**
     * Set the Tree upon which ESIS is to build
     *
     * @param tree The new tree to build upon
     *
     */
    public void SetTree(Tree tree){
        this.tree = tree;
    }

    /**************** setDebugLevel ************/
    /**
     * Set the debug level
     *
     * @param newLevel The new debug level
     *
     */
    public void setDebugLevel(int newLevel){
debugLevel = newLevel;
    }

    /******************** tag_open **************/
    public void tag_open(String name){
if(debugLevel > 0){
```

Listing 10.14   *(continued)*

```
                System.out.print("XEsis.tag_open: " + name +
"\n");
}


        // create node for element
        negeng.dom.Element elem = new negeng.dom.Element(
name );

// is this first open, i.e., documentElement
if( tree.getDocumentElement() == null ){
    // no doc elem yet, make this it
    tree.setDocumentElement( elem );
} else {
    // is doc elem, this is child
    tree.appendChild( elem );
}

        // make this elem. current
        tree.push( elem );
    }

    public void tag_close(String name){
if(debugLevel > 0){
        System.out.println("XEsis.tagclose: " + name);
}

        // pop elem stack
        tree.pop();
    }

    public void data(String data){
if(debugLevel > 0){
        System.out.println("XEsis.data: \"" + data +
"\"");
}

        Text newText = new Text( data );
```

Listing 10.14 *(continued)*

```
tree.appendChild( newText );
    }

    public void processing_instruction(String target, String
pi){
if(debugLevel > 0){
            System.out.println("XEsis.p_i:");
}
    }

    public void Attribute(String name, int declValType,
       String declVal, String defaultVal, java.util.Vector
specifiedVal){
if(debugLevel > 0){
            System.out.println("XEsis.Attribute: " + name);
    System.out.println("  declValType=" + declValType );
    System.out.println("  declVal=" + declVal );
    System.out.println("  defaultVal=" + defaultVal );
    System.out.println("  specifiedVal=" + specifiedVal );
}

        tree.addAttribute(name, (String) specifiedVal.elemen-
tAt(0));
    }

    public void SDATA_Entity(String name, String text){
if(debugLevel > 0){
            System.out.println("XEsis.SDATA_Entity");
}
    }

    public void CDATA_Section(String data){
if(debugLevel > 0){
            System.out.println("XEsis.CDATA_ Section:");
}
    }
```

Listing 10.14   *(continued)*

```
    public void NDATA_Entity(String name, Notation not){
if(debugLevel > 0){
            System.out.println("XEsis.NDATA_Entitity: " +
name);
}
    }


    public void PI_Entity(String name, String text){
if(debugLevel > 0){
    System.out.println("XEsis.PI_Entitiy: " + name);
}
    }


    /************** member variables *************/
    /**
     * The tree to build upon
     */
    private Tree tree;

    /**
     * The debug level ( >0 will produce output )
     */
    private int debugLevel;
}
```

Listing 10.14   *(continued)*

10.7.3.3   Class negeng.XSpec

The final class of the sample DOM integration is negeng.XSpec which is presented in Listing 10.15. This class offers a high-level interface to the facilities provided by the negeng.dom.*, negeng.Tree, NXP*, and negeng.XEsis classes. In particular, the XSpec class is intended to represent an arbitrary specification which in serial form is represented in XML but which after being parsed is represented (accessible) via the DOM interface. Means are provided to instantiate new XSpecs and to initialize them from an XML instance which is

stored either in a String or file. The method parse() calls on the underlying facilities to parse the provided XML document instance and
build and return a DOM representation of it.

```
package negeng;

import negeng.*;
import negeng.dom.*;

import java.io.*;

/*******************************************************/
/**
 * Container object holding specification object.
 *
 */

public class XSpec extends java.lang.Object
{
    /******************** XSpec *********************/
    /**
     * Basic constructor.
     */
    public XSpec(){
        tree = new Tree();
xEsis = new XEsis( tree );
    }

    /******************** XSpec *********************/
    /**
     * XSpec constructor : sets inputFile and loads from this
file
     *
     * @param inputFile The name of a file containing spec
     *
     */
```

Listing 10.15

```java
    public XSpec( File inputFile ) {
        tree = new Tree();
xEsis = new XEsis( tree );

        this.inputFile = inputFile;
        xmlParser = new NXP.XMLParser(this.inputFile.get-
Path(),
  NXP.XML.FILE_INPS, true, false, false);

        xmlParser.setEsis( xEsis );

//xEsis.setDebugLevel(1);
    }

    /******************** XSpec **********************/
    /**
     * XSpec constructor : sets inputString and loads
     *
     * @param specString A string containing spec
     *
     **/
    public XSpec( String inputString ){
this.inputString = inputString;

inputByteInputStream =
  new ByteArrayInputStream( this.inputString.getBytes());

        tree = new Tree();
xEsis = new XEsis( tree );

        xmlParser = new NXP.XMLParser(this.inputByteInput-
Stream);

        xmlParser.setEsis( xEsis );
    }
```

Listing 10.15   *(continued)*

```
/******************** setInputFile
**********************/
    /**
      * Set the inputFile member of XSpec and prepare to parse.
      *
      * @param inputFile File object from which to get spec.
      *
      */
    public void setInputFile(File inputFile){
this.inputFile = inputFile;

        xmlParser = new NXP.XMLParser(this.inputFile.get-
Path(),
  NXP.XML.FILE_INPS, true, false, false);

        xmlParser.setEsis( xEsis );
    }

    /******************** setInputString
**********************/
    /**
      * Set the inputString member of XSpec and prepare to
parse
      *
      * @param inputString String containing spec in XML
      *
      */
    public void setInputString(String inputString){
this.inputString = inputString;

inputByteInputStream =
  new ByteArrayInputStream( this.inputString.getBytes());

        tree = new Tree();
xEsis = new XEsis( tree );
```

Listing 10.15 *(continued)*

```
        xmlParser = new NXP.XMLParser(this.inputByteInput-
Stream);

        xmlParser.setEsis( xEsis );
    }

    /******************** parse ********************/
    /**
     * parse Initiate a parse of the spec.
     *
     */
    public int parse(){
        xmlParser.startParsing();

        return 1;
    }

    /******************** print ********************/
    /**
     * Print XSpec with indent
     *
     * @param indent Number of spaces of indent.
     */
    public void print(int indent){
String indentString = (new
String("
                        ")).substring(0,indent);

System.out.println(indentString + "XSpec: " + this );
System.out.println(indentString + "  Tree: " );
tree.print(indent + 4);
    }

    /******************** loadAndParseFile **********/
    /**
     * Load and parse spec from file
     *
```

Listing 10.15   *(continued)*

```
    * @param fileName Name of file from which to load spec
    *
    */
   public void loadAndParseFile( String filePath ){
//* read xspec from file containing xml
System.out.println("#Test getting XSpec from file: " + file-
Path );

File inputFile = new File( filePath );
setInputFile(inputFile);

System.out.println("#created XSpec from file, begin
parse...");

parse();

System.out.println("#Parse complete:");
   }

   /******************** loadAndParseString ***********/
   /**
    * Load and parse spec from string
    *
    * @param inputString String containing spec.
    *
    */
   public void loadAndParseString( String inputString ){
//* read xspec from string containing xml
System.out.println("Test fetching of XSpec from string");

setInputString( inputString );
System.out.println("set input String, begin parse... ");

parse();

System.out.println("Parse complete");
   }
```

Listing 10.15   *(continued)*

```
/******************** main **********************/
/**
 * main  A class test method
 *
 *   options: [-v] [filename]
 **/
public static void main(String argv[]) {
int argi = 0;
boolean visualize = false;
if( argv.length > 0 ){
    // first arg may be option
    if( argv[0].equals("-v")){
argi++;
visualize = true;
    }
}


XSpec anXSpec = new XSpec();
if( argv.length - argi > 0){
    // arg contains file name
    anXSpec.loadAndParseFile( argv[argi] );

} else {
    // arg empty - synthesize example
    String specString;
    specString = new String("<hi><here id=\"loc1\"/
><there>yup</there></hi>\n");

    anXSpec.loadAndParseString( specString );
}

if( visualize ){
    XSpecVizer aVizer = new XSpecVizer();
```

Listing 10.15   *(continued)*

```
        aVizer.emitDocElemAsDot("a",(Element)anXSpec.tree.getDoc-
   umentElement());
   } else {
        anXSpec.print(4);
   }
       }

       //****** instance (member) variables
       private File inputFile;
       private String inputString;

       private ByteArrayInputStream inputByteInputStream;
       private NXP.XMLParser xmlParser;
       private NXP.Esis_Stdout esis;

       XEsis xEsis;
       Tree tree;
   }
```

Listing 10.15   *(continued)*

A simple main() method is provided so that the facilities provided
by negeng.XSpec may be exercised in a demonstration mode from the
command line. To exercise it, type at the command line:

```
java negeng.XSpec [-v] [filename]
```

If the name of a file containing an XML document instance is supplied as the filename argument, then this file is parsed and the resulting DOM tree is printed. If no file name is supplied then the
following sample document instance is supplied:

```
<hi><here id="loc1"/><there>yup</there></hi>
```

The output generated when this string is parsed appears in Listing 10.16 below. The meaning of the "-v" option is described in the next section..

```
Test fetching of XSpec from string
set input String, begin parse...
Parse complete
    XSpec: negeng.XSpec@1ee793
      Tree:
        negeng.Tree@1ee7bf
          documentElement:
            negeng.dom.Element@1eeadf
              tagName: HI
              attributes: none
              children:
                negeng.dom.NodeList@1eeb27
                  items:
                    negeng.dom.Element@1eeb2a
                      tagName: HERE
                      attributes:
                        negeng.dom.AttributeList@1eeb7d
                          nameHash: {ID=0}
                          items:
                            negeng.dom.Attribute@1eeb86
                              name: ID
                              specified: true
                              value:
negeng.dom.NodeList@1eeb82
                                  negeng.dom.NodeList@1eeb82
                                    items:

Text:negeng.dom.Text@1eeb83
                                      data: <-------------
loc1
                                      ------------->
```

Listing 10.16

```
                           isIgnorableWhitespace:
false

               negeng.dom.Element@1eeb6e
                 tagName (element type name): THERE
                 attributes: none
                 children:
                   negeng.dom.NodeList@1eeb67
                     items:
                       Text:negeng.dom.Text@1eeb68
                       data: <-------------

yup

                       ------------->
                       isIgnorableWhitespace: false
```

Listing 10.16   *(continued)*

The levels of indentation in this output indicate depth in the resulting in-memory representation of the structure built as a result of parsing. In this example, an negeng.XSpec object has an instance variable called "Tree" which holds a negeng.Tree object. This node in turn has an instance variable documentElement which holds an element with a tagName of "HI." This element node is the root of the tree representing an element of type "HI," and all its children. Its instance variable "children" holds a NodeList which contains two nodes representing elements of types "HERE" and "THERE." The element node with tagName "HERE" has an instance variable "attributes" which contains an AttributeList in which an attribute node occurs that holds the information known about the attribute "ID." The element node with tagName "THERE" contains as children a node list in which a text node appears in order to hold the string "yup." The next section presents a tool for generating graphical representations of these structures as further application of the framework presented above.

10.7.4   *The XSpecViser Application*

As a final exercise of the DOM interface, an application which generates graphic representations of DOM structures is presented. A class negeng.XSpecVizor implements this application. Invoking the negeng.XSpec main() main routine with the "-v" option causes routines in this class to be called upon to generate this graphic representation.

10.7.4.1   Lefty, Dotty, and Dot

The graphs produced by XSpecVizor are presented with the help of the graphic tools known as Graphviz which are available thanks to John Ellison, Eleftherios Koutsofios and Stephen North of ATT Labs. These tools are available under both commercial and non-commercial license terms and can be retrieved easily from the web site located at: http://www.research.att.com/sw/tools/reuse. The following tools are contained in this package:

- Lefty—A customizable graphic editor
- Dotty—A customizable graph viewer written in Lefty
- Dot—A batch program for drawing directed graphs with hierarchies

These programs were developed on Unix for X-Windows and have since been ported to the Microsoft Windows environment.

The current application generates visual representations of DOM data structures by emitting appropriate graph representations in the format which the tool Dot uses as input. Dot converts this textual graph representation into graphic representations of these graphs. It should be noted that this application uses only a small subset of the capabilities presented in these tools. For example, none of the interactive capabilities of Lefty or Dotty are employed in this application.

10.7.4.2   negeng.XSpecVizor Class

The Java implementing the class negeng.XSpecVizor is presented in
Listing 10.17. Methods are provided to emit "Dot" representations
for each of the major DOM classes. Each of these routines accepts, in
addition to a reference to the DOM structure itself, a name which
will be used to identify the corresponding node in the resulting Dot
produced graph.

```java
package negeng;

import negeng.*;
import negeng.dom.*;

public class XSpecVizer {
    /***************** constructor ************/
    public XSpecVizer(){
    }

    /***************** emitTextAsDot ****************/
    /**
      * Emit Text as dot graph
      * @param myName (New) name for dot node to gen
      * @param attr The attribute to emit
      **/
    private void emitTextAsDot(String myName, Text textNode){
String data = textNode.getData();
int endIndex = ( data.length() > 7 ) ? 6 : data.length();

String outRep = new String( data.substring(0,endIndex) );

// hide specials
outRep = outRep.replace('\n',' ');
outRep = outRep.replace('\r',' ');
```

Listing 10.17

```
System.out.println(
   "     " + myName + "[label = \"{ Text | " +
 outRep + " }\"];\n");
   }


 /****************** emitNodeAsDot *****************/
 /**
  * Emit Node as dot graph
  * @param myName (New) name for dot node to gen
  * @param attr The attribute to emit
  **/
 private void emitNodeAsDot(String myName, Node theNode){
switch( theNode.getNodeType() ){
 case org.w3c.dom.Element.DOCUMENT:
   break;
 case org.w3c.dom.Element.ELEMENT:
   emitElementAsDot(myName, (Element) theNode);
   break;
 case org.w3c.dom.Element.ATTRIBUTE:
   emitAttributeAsDot(myName, (Attribute) theNode);
   break;
 case org.w3c.dom.Element.PI:
   break;
 case org.w3c.dom.Element.COMMENT:
   break;
 case org.w3c.dom.Element.TEXT:
   emitTextAsDot(myName, (Text) theNode);
   break;
}
   }
 /****************** emitNodeListAsDot *************/
 /**
  * Emit NodeList as dot graph
  * @param myName (New) name for dot node to gen
  * @param attr The attribute to emit
  */
```

Listing 10.17 *(continued)*

```
    private void emitNodeListAsDot(String myName, NodeList
theNL){
System.out.print(
"     " + myName + "[label = \"{<i> NL | {\\\n          ");


int i;
String sep = new String(); // separator of rec cells
for(i=0;i<theNL.getLength();i++){
    System.out.print(sep + "<n" + i + "> " );
    if( i == 0 ) { sep += "| "; }
}


// close my def
System.out.println(" }}\"];\n");


// emit children
Node node;
for(i=0;i<theNL.getLength();i++){
    node = null;
    try {
node = (Node) theNL.item((long) i);
    } catch( org.w3c.dom.NoSuchNodeException e ){
System.out.print("ERROR: item on NL failed");
System.exit(1);
    }


    // emit child i
    emitNodeAsDot(myName + "_n" + i, node);


    // emit arc btwn me and child i
    System.out.println("    " + myName + ":n" + i + " -> " +
      myName + "_n" + i + ":i;\n");
}
    }
    /****************** emitAttributeAsDot ***************/
    /**
```

Listing 10.17   *(continued)*

```
    * Emit Attr as dot graph
    * @param myName (New) name for dot node to gen
    * @param attr The attribute to emit
    **/
   private void emitAttributeAsDot(String myName, Attribute
attr){
// emit my dot node def, initial
System.out.println(
"    " + myName + "[label = \"{<i> Attr | \\\n" +
"      Name: " + attr.getName() + "| <nl> NL }\"];\n");

// emit child nodeList
emitNodeListAsDot( myName + "_nl", (NodeList)
attr.getValue());

// emit arcs from me to children
System.out.println(
"    " + myName + ":nl -> " + myName + "_nl:i;\n");
   }


   /******************** emitAttributeListAsDot
*****************/
   /**
     * Emit Attr List as dot graph
     * @param myName (New) name for dot node to gen
     * @param attribs The attribute list to emit
     **/
   private void emitAttributeListAsDot(String myName,
     AttributeList attribs ){
// emit my dot node def, initial material
System.out.print(
"    " + myName + "[label = \"{<i> AttrList | { \\\n       ");

int i;

// my def, record content def
String sep = new String(); // separator of rec cells
```

Listing 10.17   *(continued)*

```
for(i=0;i<attribs.getLength();i++){
    Attribute attr = null;
    try {
attr = (Attribute) attribs.item(i);
    } catch ( org.w3c.dom.NoSuchNodeException e ){
System.out.println("ERROR: emitting dot code for attr");
System.exit(1);
    }

    System.out.print(sep + "<a" + i + "> " + attr.getName());

    if( i == 0 ) { sep += "| "; }
}
System.out.println("}}\"];\n"); // done w/my node def

// emit def of sub nodes
for(i=0;i<attribs.getLength();i++){
    Attribute attr = null;
    try {
attr = (Attribute) attribs.item(i);
    } catch ( org.w3c.dom.NoSuchNodeException e){}

    emitAttributeAsDot(myName + "_a" + i, attr);

    // emit arc from me to this child node
     System.out.println("     " + myName + ":a" + i +
      " -> " + myName + "_a" + i + ":i;\n");
}
    }

    /****************** emitElementAsDot ****************/
    /**
     * Emit Element as dot graph definition
     * @param myName Name for the new node to gen
     * @param elem The elem to visualize
     **/
```

Listing 10.17 *(continued)*

```
        private void emitElementAsDot(String myName, Element elem
) {
/** emit dot language to visualize this node **/
System.out.println(
"       " + myName + "[label = \"{<i> Element |\\\n" +
"         Tag: " + elem.getTagName() + "| \\\n" +
"         { <attribs> Attribs |<children> Children }}\"];\n");

    // emit attributes
    AttributeList attribs = (AttributeList) elem.getAttributes();
    if( attribs != null && attribs.getLength() > 0 ){
        // emit this child
        emitAttributeListAsDot(myName + "_al", attribs);

        // emit arc from me to this child
        System.out.println("    " + myName + ":attribs -> " +
          myName + "_al:i;\n");
    }

    // emit children
    NodeList children = (NodeList) elem.getChildren();
    if( children != null && children.getLength() > 0 ){
        emitNodeListAsDot( myName + "_cl", children );

        // and arc to this child
        System.out.println("    " + myName + ":children -> " +
          myName + "_cl:i;\n");
    }
    }

    /******************** emitDocElemAsDot
********************/
    /** emitDocElemAsDot()
      * Emit DocElem as a dot specification
      * @param myName The name for the dot node emitted
      * @param theDocElem The doc elem to emit.
      **/
```

Listing 10.17   *(continued)*

```
    public void emitDocElemAsDot(String myName, Element the-
DocElem ) {
StringBuffer lineBuf = new StringBuffer(256);

lineBuf.append(
"digraph domgraph { \n" +
"    node[shape = record];\n\n" +
"    doc0 [label = \"{<i> Document | { \\\n" +
"        <dtd> DocType |<docElem> DocElem}}\"];\n\n");

System.out.print( lineBuf );
        emitElementAsDot("doc0_docElem", theDocElem);

System.out.println("    doc0:docElem -> doc0_docElem:i;");

System.out.println("}");
    }


}
```

Listing 10.17 *(continued)*

Listing 10.18 presents a very simple XML document which is used to illustrate both the output of XSpecVizor and the resulting graphical representation produced by Lefty, Dot and Dotty. Listing 19 presents the DOT textual representation of the DOM tree which is built for this simple XML input. Figure 10–5 shows the same DOM structures in the graphical form produced by XSpecVizor. The sequence of commands to generate an on-screen rendition of the this graphical representation is:

- java negeng.XSpec -v s1.xml > ofile
- sed -e '1,/complete/d' ofile > s1.dot
- dotty s1.dot

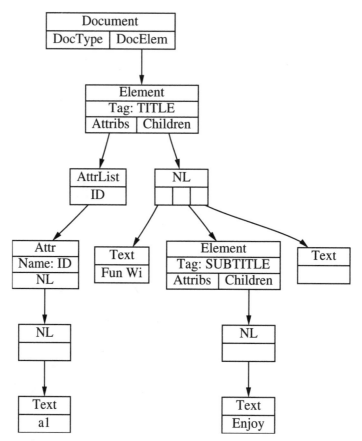

Figure 10–5

This assumes the sample XML is in a file named s1.xml. For those unfamiliar with the wonders of the "sed" command, it performs stream-editing functions. The sed command above removes lines from line 1 up to and including a line which contains the string "complete." These lines contain extraneous output produced by the program.   An menu command in the dotty tool may be used to send this graphic representation to a printer.

```
<title id="a1">Fun With XML
<subtitle>Enjoy Weekends Too</subtitle>
</title>
```

Listing 10.18

```
digraph domgraph {
    node[shape = record];

    doc0 [label = "{<i> Document | { \
      <dtd> DocType |<docElem> DocElem}}"];

    doc0_docElem[label = "{<i> Element |\
      Tag: TITLE| \
      { <attribs> Attribs |<children> Children }}"];

    doc0_docElem_al[label = "{<i> AttrList | { \
      <a0> ID}}"];

    doc0_docElem_al_a0[label = "{<i> Attr | \
      Name: ID| <nl> NL }"];

    doc0_docElem_al_a0_nl[label = "{<i> NL | {\
      <n0>  }}"];

    doc0_docElem_al_a0_nl_n0[label = "{ Text | a1 }"];

    doc0_docElem_al_a0_nl:n0 -> doc0_docElem_al_a0_nl_n0:i;

    doc0_docElem_al_a0:nl -> doc0_docElem_al_a0_nl:i;

    doc0_docElem_al:a0 -> doc0_docElem_al_a0:i;

    doc0_docElem:attribs -> doc0_docElem_al:i;

    doc0_docElem_cl[label = "{<i> NL | {\
      <n0> | <n1> | <n2>  }}"];
```

Listing 10.19

```
doc0_docElem_cl_n0[label = "{ Text | Fun Wi }"];

doc0_docElem_cl:n0 -> doc0_docElem_cl_n0:i;

doc0_docElem_cl_n1[label = "{<i> Element |\
  Tag: SUBTITLE| \
  { <attribs> Attribs |<children> Children }}"];

doc0_docElem_cl_n1_cl[label = "{<i> NL | {\
  <n0>  }}"];

doc0_docElem_cl_n1_cl_n0[label = "{ Text | Enjoy }"];

doc0_docElem_cl_n1_cl:n0 -> doc0_docElem_cl_n1_cl_n0:i;

doc0_docElem_cl_n1:children -> doc0_docElem_cl_n1_cl:i;

doc0_docElem_cl:n1 -> doc0_docElem_cl_n1:i;

doc0_docElem_cl_n2[label = "{ Text |     }"];

doc0_docElem_cl:n2 -> doc0_docElem_cl_n2:i;

doc0_docElem:children -> doc0_docElem_cl:i;

doc0:docElem -> doc0_docElem:i;
}
```

Listing 10.19   *(continued)*

As a final illustration of both the DOM data structures and the XSpecVizor visualizer, a longer example of XML input is presented in Listing 10.20, and the graphical representation of the DOM tree which results is presented in Figure 10–6.

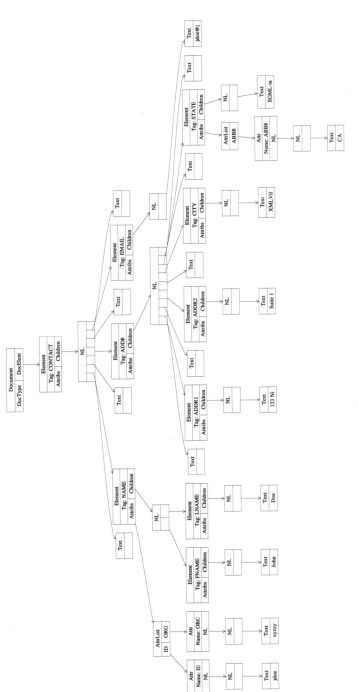

Figure 10-6

```
<contact>
  <name id="jdoe" org="xyzzy"><fname>John</
fname><lname>Doe</lname></name>
  <addr>
    <addr1>123 Nice Place</addr1>
    <addr2>Suite 1</addr2>
    <city>XMLVil</city>
    <state abbr="CA">SGML-ia</state>
  </addr>
  <email>jdoe@jstud.com</email>
</contact>
```

Listing 10.20

10.8 | Chapter Summary

This chapter has presented a general background on XML parsers and the application programmer interfaces through which developers access them. It described in some detail several generic types of APIs which are common or emerging for XML parsers: command-line interfaces, ESIS event stream interface, event callback interfaces, and object model interfaces. Two XML parsers, Norbert Mikula's "NXP" and David Megginson's AElfred, were introduced as examples and in preparation for their use in later demonstrations.

We introduced the emerging standard APIs known as "Simple API for XML" (SAX), an event callback type interface and the Document Object Model (Core)—Level 1 (DOM), an object model type interface. An overview of the major structure of each of these was presented. With these two standards gaining support and implementation, the need to build custom interfaces to XML parsers may eventually be eliminated and replaced with a well-known practice of utilizing XML parsers to solve day-to-day problems.

As XML grows in popularity, XML parsers are likely to become standard equipment within development and production platforms.

Over time provisioning of XML parsing will likely become a feature of core environments such as the Java core classes and libraries provided by common operating systems. At the same time advanced features such as incremental compilation will likely become common and cost/performance equations even better.

While the parser may represent core XML technology long into the future, the interfaces through which developers access structured content will almost certainly become a more immediate concern. That standards such as SAX and DOM are being proposed is a promising trend as well-accepted standards in this area have the power to serve as a new level of stable platforms upon which to build information systems. Widely accepted standard means for accessing and manipulating structured documents within software will complement our emerging ability to interchange this information which SGML and XML offer. Used together these technologies have the potential to make communication and manipulation of structured information widely accessible to automation.

Part Five

Input Gathering and Negotiation using XML

Future – Agents and all that

Input Gathering and Negotiation using XML

This chapter describes features found in many input gathering problems and how XML can be used within solutions to some of these problems. The notion of negotiation forms the basis of formalisms used to think about input gathering problems and systems. We describe how formal specification of negotiation problems may include using an XML-based language for defining what constitutes acceptable output or agreements for negotiation problems. It is shown that specification of negotiation problems can themselves be carried in an XML-based language. We discuss combining such a "negotiation specification language" with a software negotiation agent to implement a form of computational negotiation. Data types become "negotiable" when their specification includes information which can drive negotiation. Generalizing, we present the use of XML in "language-agent" solution architectures which use near-optimal specification languages to carry characteristics of problem instances to agents which configure themselves before producing some desired behavior.

11.1 | Introduction

11.1.1 *The Ubiquitous Problem of Input Gathering*

Gathering data—or "input"—from users is one of the most funda-mental and frequent problems encountered during information sys-tems operation. Virtually every software application encountered, whether found on an intranet or on the Internet at large, will include some form of data gathering capabilities. This ubiquity is directly reflected in the training and practice of the information systems pro-fessional. From a very first "hello world" program, the student pro-grammer is tasked with writing programs which solicit, receive, and then use input provided by the user. In the simplest cases, few limits are placed on what the program will "accept" as input; for instance, it may accept a restricted length sequence of characters terminated by a line end character. As the complexity of input gathering problems increases, system developers are tasked with facilitating complex user-system communication.

This chapter describes features found in a wide variety of input gathering problems and then describes how XML can play a signifi-cant role within solutions to real-world input gathering problems you may encounter during Internet or intranet application development. It does this using formalisms which enable a clear statement of the roles available for XML in negotiation. As a logical progression in the development of these formalisms we frame the issue of "specification" as a problem in itself. Deliberate development of "specification envi-ronments" is promoted as a natural complement to software-based agents which accept specification language as input and produce desirable behavior as output. The need for a common basis for creat-ing "near-optimal" specification languages further motivates use of XML in "input gathering systems." Finally, in the last part of this chapter, we attempt to balance the use of abstraction and formalism which is developed in the first part with a simple illustration of how some of the concept which are offered may be put to use.

11.1.2   *Input Gathering and Negotiation*

Whether simple or complex, many systems exhibit a common pattern of communication: bidirectional communication with a user expressly undertaken to facilitate gathering of data. Managing the complexity of input gathering problems, and their solutions, can be a formidable problem. The concept of negotiation is used here first as an aid to describing the nature of input gathering problems, and then as a source of ideas for systems design and implementation for new systems.

The concept of negotiation used here is that of a communication process in which information is exchanged among involved parties or agents until an "agreement" or termination of communication results. In the case of input gathering systems, the core of the agreement is a data set or possibly compound data object, which satisfies the constraints and interests of both user and system. To apply this concept of negotiation, an input gathering problem is viewed as a problem of negotiation and a software solution is constructed so that the resulting system behaves much like an agent participating in a negotiation.

XML can play at least two important roles in input gathering problems. First, the output of an input gathering system (i.e., the "agreement" produced out of a successful negotiation) is generally represented in some machine-readable language. Not surprisingly, XML may be used as the basis of such a language and when it does it serves as the basis of a "specification language" in the sense that it carries information ("specifications") from specification producers to consumers. Secondly, a system development methodology may be used while developing an input gathering (or negotiation) system which requires that input gathering problems encountered be specified in a formal manner so that this specification may act as input to a configurable "negotiation engine." In this approach a generalized negotiation engine accepts as input a specification of a negotiation problem and then interacts with a user so as to negotiate, or gather, input satisfying the negotiation problem specified.

There is clearly a history of using notions of negotiation in information systems practice. In some large data processing applications involving order entry, for instance, the notion of negotiation is used to label the task of gathering input from users. On a much lower level (in the sense of ISO data communication layers), negotiation is commonly used to describe and model the process of parameter exchange and establishment in data communications protocols. This current discussion differs from these prior efforts in that it concerns application of XML to specify negotiation problems, and upon the gathering, or negotiation, of data which are represented (in the output of the negotiation system) using an XML-based language. Finally, it focuses primarily on human-computer interaction; a perhaps equally rich range of applications for combining the notion of negotiation with XML exists in computer-computer interactions (e.g., negotiation of data transfer lexicon and grammar).

11.1.3   Negotiation Processes from 20,000 Feet

Negotiation and input gathering commonly involve a series of exchanges of information between user and system. The following list highlights the types of exchanges found in common practice.

- Presentation of general information about the nature of the negotiation to be undertaken and data to be collected.
- Exchanges aimed at acquiring user preferences related to the negotiation.
- Exchanges aimed at acquiring specific items of data.
- Exchanges allowing the user to confirm that previously negotiated values are in fact agreeable to them.

The general information presented at the start of an input gathering process typically informs (or reminds) the user of the nature of the process to be followed and data to be collected. Information concerning the mechanics of negotiation may be offered at this point. User preference information may concern either the process or the product (data) to be developed. For example, during a typical software installation process the user may be asked to select the language in which negotiation is to occur or the style of interaction (e.g., "expert" versus "typical") to be presented.

Exchanges concerning acquisition of specific items of data form the core of the negotiation. These exchanges may focus on just one "variable" at a time, or a related series of exchanges may focus on fixing values to a set of variables. Frequently, a system offers or proposes default values for variables. Some of the system-proposed values may not be negotiable. For those variables which are negotiable, the user is provided with some means of manipulating (altering or replacing) any default values proposed, or providing new values if no defaults are proposed. Once a user is satisfied with a value or set of values, he or she submits them to the system which then considers (i.e., calculates) whether the returned values are acceptable and then replies with an appropriate response. This response may in effect express dissatisfaction with the value(s) proposed by the users (i.e., present an error message), in which case a new opportunity to manipulate the value(s) in question may be offered. Alternatively, the system may indicate (implicitly or explicitly) that a particular set of variable-value bindings was acceptable and move on with the negotiation process.

Eventually, a "complete" set of data may be acquired. The user may be asked to review this and explicitly indicate either that it is acceptable as is, that it needs further revision, or the negotiation should be "canceled." A revision process, or continuation of the larger process of which the input gathering process is a component, then occurs as appropriate.

Similar patterns of communication occur when "negotiation" is undertaken by humans. Involved parties generally discuss the nature of negotiations to be undertaken upfront. Following this they proceed to make a series of "moves," such as requesting or proposing additions, deletions, or modifications to draft agreements, offering criticisms to proposals previously offered, or offering information on their individual or shared interests. Eventually one or the other party may suggest that a particular draft is sufficiently developed to be raised to the status of "final agreement." If both parties agree, this action is taken, "final details" are worked out, an agreement is made (or parties return to the negotiation table or cancel), and the negotiation terminates. Either party may terminate negotiation at any time. While conduct of negotiation by humans isn't explicitly discussed in the following material, it may be useful to occasionally reflect on it while reading the following, or during later consideration of negotiation systems, as there is likely considerable insight to be gained by such consideration.

11.2 | Negotiation and Language-Agent Architectures

11.2.1 *Negotiation Problem Specification*

Input gathering operations, and negotiation processes in general, are carried out by agents acting in deliberate ways to accomplish specific goals. The input gathering component of a simple software application will, for instance, conduct a series of information exchanges with the user until some set of required data has been collected. In order to behave as it does, the software application must have within it, in some form or another, specification of the input gathering problem it is to solve during the course of successful execution. For example, the specification of what is to be collected may consist of a list of data items with, for each, type declaration, prompt language, default generating expressions, and so on.

In many software applications, the required input gathering capabilities are hardcoded; the "specification" of the input gathering problem is not expressed in machine-readable form "on its own" but rather is tightly intertwined with the code comprising the application. This may be a fine approach when solving a one-of-a kind problem and thus building a one-of-a-kind implementation as a solution to this problem. It may lead to inefficiencies however when a series of similar input gathering problems appear in each of a series of applications. In these situations, the construction of the solution for each application is likely to include a reimplementation of certain mechanics (software structures) found in earlier solutions. In a moment, we'll discuss how the output of input gathering systems can be represented in XML, and how the resulting series of similar input gathering problems may be solved using a configurable negotiation engine. First, however, we consider this situation on an abstract, language-basis-neutral, level.

11.2.2 *Specification Problems and Language-Agent Architecture*

The need to specify and solve negotiation problems is a classic case of the generic problem of specification and solution development in software systems. When a pattern appears in a series of software problems, it is frequently useful to consider which, if any, aspects of the individual problems reappear over the problem series.[1] Looking at the individuals in the series as a collection, one may find that portions of the problem specifications are common across the series. The portion

---

1. Note that we are referring to "patterns in problems" as opposed to "patterns in solutions," (or patterns in software design). While these notions are clearly related it is important here that we begin our discussion with the earlier of these notions.

of the problem specifications which differs from one problem to the next can be thought of as characterizing the individual problems in the series. The remaining portion of the problem specifications will, by definition, remain constant over the series of problems.

Separating that which differs from that which remains constant over a series of problems is a first step toward building an efficient solution architecture for the series of problems as a whole. A generic solution architecture for "specification" problems such as this is to combine a custom language for specifying that which characterizes individual problems in a series with a software-based agent which embodies a solution to the portion of the problem's specification which remains constant over the series. This is referred to here as the "language-agent" solution architecture. This is illustrated in Figure 11–1. The language component of this solution architecture is expressly designed to carry the information which characterizes individuals in the problem series. The agent portion of this solution architecture possesses the capability to exhibit the behavior described in a solution to the common portion of the problem specification which is "configurable." That is, it accepts as input the specification of the characteristics of a particular problem and then exhibits behavior which represents a solution to that particular problem. This solution combines the behavior appropriate given the characteristics of the particular problem instance with behavior appropriate given the common features of the series of problems.

As stated above, some input gathering problems can be modeled as negotiation problems. If we consider "negotiation problems" as our series of problems, we find that the specification of what is to be collected, along with certain ancillary information such as prompt wording, default, and validation expressions, and so on, characterize individual negotiation problems. The specification of the behavior of a configurable agent capable of conducting a negotiation constitutes the portion of the input gathering problems which remains constant over the series of negotiation problems. This is illustrated in Figure 11–2.

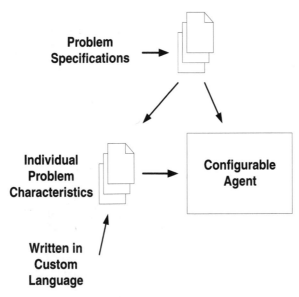

Figure 11–1   Language-Agent Solution Architecture

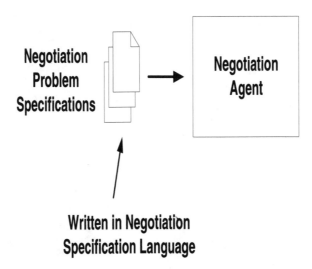

Figure 11–2   Language-Agent Negotiation System

The discussion of the language-agent solution architecture is carried just a bit further in the next section which describes the notion of "optimal specification environment." Subsequent sections first enumerate interesting features of negotiation (e.g., those facilitating negotiation problem specification) and then proceed to consider implementation of generic solutions to the problem of negotiating XML-based input data.

11.2.3 *Optimal Specification Environments*

There are at least two major categories of benefits to be sought by employing the language-agent solution architecture just described. First, reuse of certain portions of implementation in multiple applications may produce more consistent behavior at the user interface of resulting applications. Secondly, the reuse of portions of implementation will likely produce many of the classic cost benefits of software reuse. These involve primarily reduced cost of development and maintenance.

While these benefits are generally available through software reuse, a specific benefit results when a language-agent architecture is employed which may not appear in other reuse schemes. Synthesis of a language for specifying that which varies from problem instance to problem instance provides an opportunity to optimize the authoring or "specification" environment used by the people (e.g., developers) tasked with generating and maintaining these specifications. Because they are freed from the burden of handling details which recur over the series of problems, the author or editor of these specifications will be able to concentrate a larger fraction of his or her energy on that which actually characterizes the individual problems and solutions.

The notion of optimal specification environment should be recognized by folks familiar with SGML as it is a frequent (but often unstated) natural benefit to the separation of logical markup ("abstractions") from presentation markup ("renditions") which SGML enthusiasts advocate. In both cases, the result is a focusing of author energy and attention on the substance of created work rather than on details of some particular rendering of it. Carrying this parallel in the other direction on a slight tangent, one should consider whether multiple renditions of information contained in a negotiation specification are possible. As stated later in this chapter, this suggests that information able to facilitate negotiation be contributed to the pool of meta-information maintained for data objects (classes) so that it may be used (rendered) in as many ways as reasonable.

It is worth noting that XML, as it is a tool for constructing languages and thus specification environments, represents an exciting addition to the information system developer's tool chest. It offers a standard meta-language from which to develop specific near-optimal specification environments which in turn are employed within solutions based upon language-agent solution architectures. Use of XML as the basis for constructing near-optimal specification environments happens to produce a series of similar negotiation problems (negotiation of XML document instances) which can also benefit from the language-agent solution architecture. Thus XML may be paired with the language-agent solution architecture to produce an integrated high-level methodology for information systems development. This methodology becomes accessible primarily because XML has emerged as a tool which enables us to employ "language" in information system solutions. As such, XML offers to release human kind's latent capacity to invent language to solve problems so that this capacity can be applied more freely than ever to our information management problems.

11.3 | Description of Negotiation Problems

This section discusses various ways in which negotiation problems, or input gathering problems, may be described. In doing so it develops a set of features of negotiation which together may serve within a descriptive language for characterizing individual negotiation problems. This descriptive language is used later in Section 11.4.5 as the basis for an example XML application aimed at facilitating specification of negotiation problems.

11.3.1 *Negotiation Problem Output and Structure*

The primary characterizing feature of input gathering or negotiation problems is the specification of the input which is to be gathered or negotiated, that is, specification of the output of negotiation. While a later section will discuss negotiation output (e.g., output specification "language") in some depth, this current section focuses on the high-level structure of negotiation problems. Considering our focus on XML and then on how it can be used to describe output specification languages, we focus here on the structure of the problem's output specification language.

Clearly many negotiation problems possess discernible structure (e.g., as just described, the output of negotiation will possess certain structural features). In this section, we illustrate this by considering just a couple of the forms of structure found in typical negotiation problems. In particular, a negotiation problem may possess the following structural features:

- Division into subcomponents
- Repeating and alternative components
- Inclusion of common components
- Division of responsibility for various aspects of negotiation into "layers"

While this is certainly only a partial list of the structures which can be found in negotiation problems, we'll elaborate on just these for illustration purposes.

11.3.1.1 Division into Subcomponents

The division of a negotiation problem into subcomponents is perhaps the most common form of structure found or enforced in negotiation problems. When a negotiation problem is divided into components, the target "complete data set" (or data object) will likely be divided into components in a manner dictated by the problem's definition. For example, input gathering in support of order entry might be divided into "filling the shopping cart," as one component, and "checking out" as another component. The output of this negotiation might similarly be divided into data related to the filled shopping cart and data related to being checked out.

Components of negotiation problems may be nested within one another. Using the preceding example again, the problem of negotiating data comprising shopping cart contents may be further divided into the problem of negotiating the data comprising each of perhaps several items in the shopping cart. Each of these problems may be further divided into the problem of negotiating quantity, part identification, part features, and so on.

11.3.1.2 Repeating and Alternative Components

Components may be found to repeat in a negotiation problem (i.e., components of output structure may repeat themselves.). Clearly this is the case in the shopping cart example where, for instance, negotiation of details of an item to add to the shopping cart will reappear for each item added. Also, within the negotiation of checkout data, depending on the payment option chosen, one of several alternative negotiation problem (sub-)components will appear.

11.3.1.3   Inclusion of Common Components— Component Architecture

A specific component of a negotiation problem may appear within numerous negotiation problems. Consider for example the negotiation which occurs during download of software containing encryption from a Web site located in the United States. The negotiation of information sufficient to satisfy the U.S. government's encryption export laws is generally carried out independent of the negotiation of the parameters of the particular software to be downloaded. The same subproblem occurs every time a download must be negotiated for a non-U.S. export product.

There is clearly a case for a "component architecture" in negotiation. Such an architecture will allow for (relatively) small negotiation problems to be specified independently of one another and then for larger negotiation problems to be constructed and solved using these "common" negotiation problems and their solutions as "components." That is, we can isolate a component which reappears in multiple negotiation problems and specify it as a problem in isolation.

As in the general case stated above, the key feature of a component negotiation problem is the data set (or object) which is concerned with negotiation. Thus a component architecture for negotiation is best thought of as being derived from a component architecture for the data which a series of negotiation problems aim to gather. In general, whenever a data object is found to appear in multiple applications, it is a good candidate to become a member of a component library built to contain data common to the multiple applications.

Given that most component libraries are now built using an object-oriented paradigm, we may consider negotiation as simply another behavior (or method) which an object may be expected to exhibit. When a new data item is added to a component library, one should consider where specification of instances of the object come from and then extend its definition with properties which facilitate negotiation of instances with these specification sources. Thus a component architecture for negotiation may be built as an extension to a general-purpose component architecture for data objects.

11.3.1.4   Layering

Negotiation problems may also be structured as a series of "layers" with each layer containing a different aspect of the overall problem. A bank clerk, for instance, may be responsible for checking that all the fields of a submitted loan application are filled in, while a higher-level bank agent is responsible for verifying the submitted information is correct, and yet an even higher-level agent is responsible for either approving or rejecting the requested loan. As an example computer application, consider an input gathering system employing a three-tier architecture: a lightweight client, Web server-based middleware, and a data processing center database server. In such a system an HTML page-resident script may be responsible for ensuring that certain field prerequisite and syntactical requirements are met prior to submitting a response to a Web server. In the Web server, additional application logic may be responsible for validating interform field relations prior to submitting a proposed change to a data store. The data store itself might then enforce further validation constraints.

11.3.2   *Negotiation Problem Output— Agreements*

The solution for a negotiation problem is some form of "agreement" and a commitment by involved parties to its terms. The first of these components of an agreement is generally specified by enumerating a set of "terms of the agreement." In the case of an input gathering problem, the most prominent result or product of a successful input gathering event is the data set, or variable bindings which result. Since the definition of "agreement" is quite relevant to Internet commerce applications (which themselves are appearing with increasing frequency on the Internet), some further comment on this subject is in order.

A simplistic attempt to apply a model of negotiation to input gathering problems might have us define that the data set resulting from an input gathering event constitutes the "terms of agreement" of the negotiation which was in effect carried out. Clearly, however, this is only a part of what the law would consider as the "agreement" produced. In particular, much of the information presented by the system during the input gathering process might also be considered part of the agreement. The material constituting the prompts presented by the system, and some of the information presented peripherally to the prompts (pricing or performance data, for instance) might also reasonably be considered part of the resulting agreement. Now, if a "specification" of a negotiation problem were to exist separate from, and as input to, a "negotiation engine" (or agent), it might be the case that it contains a large fraction of what the law might consider, apart from the produced data object, as constituting the agreement. It might be reasonable, then, to employ the language-agent architecture along with "version control" devices as means to enable reconstruction of "terms of agreement" produced by input gathering systems. The need to be able to construct legally meaningful "terms of agreement" is especially high when the value of goods discussed in negotiated agreements is substantial, such as when commerce is conducted on the Internet. Even so the "terms of agreement" are just one component of the solution to a negotiation.

The specification of terms of agreement are generally only the most tangible (immediate) product of a successful negotiation. Less tangible but perhaps equally important (especially in Internet applications) are the commitments of the involved parties to abide by, that is, "live by," the terms carried in its specification. Depending on the value of the agreement (i.e., of goods discussed within it, and/or of conformance or departure from its terms by one party to another party), and the nature of the trust relationship shared by the parties, the existence of such a commitment may or may not need to be explicitly recorded. Generally we record a commitment to abide by terms of an agreement by rendering signatures on a nonmutable form of the specification of these terms. While this is commonly the case in agreements produced by negotiation conducted by humans, it is presently rarely the case in input gathering systems. Clearly this must change as the value of agreements negotiated with the aid of computers increases, and also as the trust relationship between users and computer operators changes. Again, this is especially the case in electronic commerce applications conducted at a distance (e.g., over the Internet) where the product of input gathering is specification of terms of an agreement, and where preexisting trust relationships are rare. Thus, in addition to sharing attributes of negotiation vis-à-vis the exchange of information conducted to fix values to variables, some input gathering problems share this additional attribute with negotiation problems: Recording of commitment to terms of agreement by involved parties may be necessary. The use of XML as the means to carry output specification may provide a convenient implementation of a rendering of signature to agreement. That is, digital signature technology may be applied to the resulting XML data objects. If the resulting XML data object were to contain (perhaps by reference) the negotiation problem specification, then a fairly complete agreement would result.[2] Alternatively, signatures could be rendered to human-readable renditions of the resulting agreement and then appropriate means used to store and associate this rendition of the agreement with its internal (e.g., XML) form (e.g., by including this rendition as an entity reference).

---

2. A user might not wish to "sign" a representation of an agreement which wasn't in a language they didn't understand, and thus standards for specification of the product of negotiation may be required. Clearly this is a direction being pursued by the CommerceNet project and related endeavors. For more information on this topic, see, for instance, www.commercenet.net.

11.3.3 *Recurring Negotiation Problems*

A common feature of both input gathering and negotiation is that in some situations (particularly in a single-application area) a series of very similar negotiation problems will arise. This is the situation, for example, solved by virtually all information systems; they are typically executed repeatedly and for each execution cycle the input gathering or negotiation component of the problem it solves will in effect reappear and be solved anew. Likewise, some negotiation problems involving only humans can be seen to recur frequently. For example, numerous instances of the common tenant lease are negotiated over time. We standardize the structure of terms of agreement in these situations to simplify and make more efficient the task of negotiating new agreements; that is, develop reusable agreement "templates" which can be reapplied within each of a series of similar negotiation problems. This leads us to our next topic, "output specification languages."

11.3.4 *Output Specification Languages*

A standard structure or template may in effect serve as an "output specification language." The term "language" is used here in the formal computer science sense.[3] An output specification language may be associated with a negotiation problem to describe that only agreements allowed by this language may be considered valid agreements (or solutions) for that specific negotiation problem. Alternatively, a negotiation may be said to be "constrained" to emit only agreements allowed by an associated output specification language.

Similarly, an output specification language may be associated with a recurring negotiation problem (or class of negotiation problems) as a way of describing that only agreements allowed by this language may be considered valid output for any specific problem instance belonging to the recurring negotiation problem. Said another way, a negotiation process conducted to solve a specific instance of a recurring negotiation problem which has an output specification language associated with it must, if it produces an agreement, produce an agreement which conforms to this language. In more practical terms, when software is constructed to solve an input gathering problem, it is usually the case that the output of the software will be constrained by some output specification language. In fact, as stated above, the output specification language constitutes a substantial part (but certainly not all) of the definition of the negotiation problem.

The preceding discussion coupled with an appreciation of the nature of XML should lead the reader to start thinking that XML would be a fine tool for constructing output specification languages. Given that the early professional discipline of the principal author of the SGML standard was law, one may even wonder whether agreement specification was the initial target application for XML's parent, SGML. Still, we should continue with our "descriptive" treatment of negotiation and the parallels between it and input gathering before proceeding to the "prescriptive" considerations, such as how well XML may be equipped to serve as the basis for output languages in negotiation systems.

---

3. A "language" is a set of sentences. In the present application, we say that an input gathering or negotiation process can produce any of a restricted set of data sets as output. From the perspective of the formal definition of language, each possible output of some negotiation process is a sentence and the set of all outputs which the negotiation process can produce is the language which defines its output. One may define a language by enumerating all sentences which are within the language. Alternatively, one may define a language by specifying rules for constructing sentences which, if followed without exception, will only produce sentences in the language. For example, an XML document type definition specifies a set of rules (grammar productions) for constructing documents which are valid with respect to that DTD. One can view such construction rules as restricting membership in the language to only those sentences which can be built without violating them.

11.3.5 *Constraints on Valid Agreement*

The ability of an output specification language to describe constraints to the range of agreements valid in a particular problem was deliberately limited in the preceding discussion. In particular, the definition of an output specification language was crafted to allow that not all agreements which are allowed by a given output specification language are necessarily valid agreements for a particular recurring negotiation problem. We should and do allow that the task of discerning whether a particular agreement is valid within a particular domain may require capabilities beyond those exhibited by an negotiation system employing no more information than that contained in a (limited) description of an output specification language. The definition above specified that when an output specification language is associated with a negotiation problem, only those proposed agreements which are allowed by (lie within) this language "may" be considered valid agreements. If a proposed agreement isn't allowed by an output specification language, it can not be an agreement to the negotiation problem. That an agreement is found in an output specification language is a requirement to that agreement's being a valid agreement but is not sufficient by itself to guarantee that the agreement is valid. To illustrate this, consider that one can clearly produce a nonsensical tenant agreement using a standardized tenant agreement template, or that one can produce a nonsensical repair manual using an Air Transport Association airframe maintenance manual DTD.

All agreements which can be written using a template or DTD "may" be considered valid with respect to these output specification languages; however not all agreements (i.e., documents) which are valid in this respect are valid given the context of their larger application domain. In practice, additional "domain-specific" information, knowledge, or skills may be required both in order to generate a valid agreement, and during attempts to discern whether an agreement is valid.

In light of the deliberate weakness of an output specification language to describe constraints on agreements, as just mentioned, an additional descriptive device is introduced—what we label "constraints on valid agreement." Using this device, the full range of agreements which are valid for a given negotiation problem are specified using an associated set of "constraints on valid agreement." An output specification language which is associated with a negotiation problem is one form of constraint on valid agreement for that problem. As stated above, only agreements allowed by the output specification language may be valid agreements. Additional forms of constraints on valid agreement may exist. Or said another way, when there are some agreements which are allowed by a given output specification language but which are still not valid for some associated negotiation problem, there must be "constraints on valid agreement" other than the output specification language which preclude the inclusion of these agreements in the set of valid agreements for the problem.

Constraints on valid agreement are associated with negotiation problems in the same way as output specification languages. The means by which constraints on valid agreement are specified can take many forms. One of the most frequent ways to specify such constraints, is to enumerate a set of rules (e.g., expressions) which must be satisfied by a candidate agreement before it can be considered valid in the domain. An expression might specify, for instance, that a particular variable in some negotiation problem may take on only values contained in an enumeration (e.g., a "color" property for a product specification may take on only values corresponding to colors in which the product is available). The rules or expressions constraining valid agreements may include reference to other items in the agreement (e.g., variables negotiated earlier) or to data outside of the agreement (e.g., a database). This is illustrated in Figure 11–3. In the hypothetical case illustrated, a constraint is specified which restricts the total cost of items negotiated to be less than an available data value stored in a database.

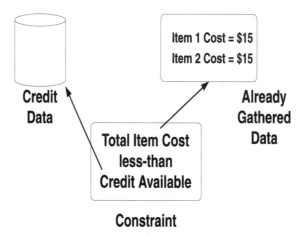

Figure 11–3 Constraints on Valid Agreement

The constraints on valid agreement associated with a given negotiation problem may not be fully specified (in machine-readable form). Some of the constraints on valid agreement for a particular negotiation problem may not be computable. This may be due to there not existing sufficient machine-readable representation of a constraint, or may be due to some required computation's being intractable. In any particular implementation of a negotiation problem, some subset of the constraints on valid agreement will be enforced.

11.3.6 *Practical Enforcement of Output Constraints*

While complete specification of constraints on valid agreement expresses the theoretical limits imposed on agreements satisfying the associated negotiation problem, in practice one must likely choose to enforce only a fraction of these constraints. For example, the notion of output specification language is intended to carry practical (e.g., computationally tractable) constraints on valid agreement. Which constraints on valid agreement are enforced within a given solution to a negotiation problem is a practical matter.

Multiple output specification languages may be associated with a single negotiation problem. Each such language may embody a different subset of the constraints on valid agreement associated with this overarching problem. Each leaves a different subset of constraints on valid agreement unspecified, and thus untestable. Each suggests a different partial solution to the over-overarching negotiation problem. The practical application of this notion is that given a negotiation problem, different degrees of guidance and constraint may be provided to the user depending on their needs for this aid. A trusted expert in a field of specification may require no guidance from an input gathering subsystem. He or she can craft valid agreements all day long with pen and paper. On the other hand, the wisdom of relying on a user to craft valid agreements with few tool-enforced constraints depends both on their expertise with the structure and substance of the agreement desired, and the trust relationship shared between the user and their counterpart in negotiations. Successful negotiation requires both guidance and constraint.

As another example of this distinction between constraints on valid agreement and output specification languages, consider an hypothetical order negotiation problem. The theoretical constraints on valid agreements could dictate, for instance, that only agreements which describe orders which the business can reasonably fulfill and which come from living and financially capable customers may be negotiated. In practice, a particular solution built to aid negotiation of new orders will probably enforce a much less rigorous standard on the agreements it produces. It may not, for instance, possess the capacity to determine if a user's claimed identity is associated with a live, financially capable person. The resulting order entry tool may still be useful even if means outside of its operation will need be brought to bear on the overarching negotiation problem to ensure that only valid agreements are produced in the end.

In practice, all constraints specified in the output specification language will be enforced while perhaps only some constraints on valid agreement will be enforced. Somewhat different mechanisms may be used in each case. For example, if an XML document type declaration is used to define the output specification language, an XML parser may be used to validate that output conforms to the output specification language. Some additional constraints beyond those specified in the XML document type declaration, which would be considered constraints on valid agreement, may be expressed in a full-featured programming language.

11.3.7 *Examples from Current Systems Practice*

Surveying existing software systems, we find many examples of negotiation already at play. For example, many interfaces to transaction-oriented systems exhibit characteristics of negotiation systems. Bank teller machines and on-line banking systems negotiate specification of financial transactions, product and service order entry tools negotiate specification of a set of line items to be delivered or elements of a service agreements to be fulfilled, and on-line travel reservation systems negotiate specification of itineraries. "Form processing" systems are aimed squarely at the task of negotiating mutually agreeable specifications. While some of these applications have historically placed a human agent between input gathering system and end user, this is increasingly not the case in current and newly developed systems. With this phenomenon, comes an increasing burden on systems developers to formalize input gathering more explicitly. The argument and ideas presented here are intended to motivate and provide direction to the use of XML in these formalisms.

As another example consider an on-line order entry system. The product of an interaction with such a tool (i.e., an input gathering or negotiation operation) is the specification of a particular "order."

While frequently the product of such an interaction is stored in one or more database tables, one may generally represent the same information in a serial form (e.g., within a data structure represented as a string conforming to some grammar). When we do this, one can consider that the set of all possible order specifications which can be produced by the system (set of strings) constitutes a language. As a corollary, a language may be imagined which serves to constrain the range of agreements that a given order entry system can negotiate to those expressible using this language. Such a language might require, for instance, a "customer information" section, a "shipping section," "billing section," as well as one or more "line item" sections. Within each section, a set of attributes or variables may be used to carry specific agreed-to data values. Restrictions may limit the range of values acceptable for particular attributes. The output of a specific interaction, that is, negotiation, between a user and such a system is thus "specification" of an order constrained by a particular output specification language.

As another example, let us consider the general-purpose word processor. A word processor gathers natural language information along with presentation and logical "markup" information. It does this by having certain user actions (e.g., selecting a collection of content and choosing to emphasize it) cause "markup" to be inserted within the in-system representation of the document. An interaction with a word processor produces as output a document containing the information which the user provided carried within the internal "mark-up" representation language used by the particular system. The word processor program's input gathering capabilities in effect negotiate with the user to collect specification of an agreement—the document. The document produced is necessarily constrained such that it will be recognized by the word processor's various modules (e.g., those managing storage, export, and rendering functions). If it fails to constrain its product to its internal representation language, the product of its application will be unusable to the other modules of the program. The product of this negotiation is thus restricted to that which is expressible using the system's internal document representation language. On the other hand, without a grammar checker or other device for bringing domain restrictions to play, "negotiation" of an agreement with a word processor can produce any document which can be represented in this output specification language.

Finally, consider as an example the contemporary validating XML or SGML editor. Clearly the product of an interaction with such a tool is a specific data set (document instance) which is valid according to a particular language; in this case the language is the one specified by the particular document type declaration active during the interaction. The validating XML or SGML editor can produce only document instances which conform to the language specified in the DTD. To the extent that the constraints restricting the range of valid agreement negotiation problems are expressible using the DTD specification language, the validating SGML or XML editor is a general-purpose negotiation system. If the application dictates enforcement of constraints on valid agreement which aren't expressible within a DTD, however, the contemporary validating XML or SGML editor will fall short of serving as a negotiation tool on its own. In these cases we must rely on means outside of the editor, for instance in a companion postprocessor or in the knowledge of the user, to ensure conformance to the constraints not represented in the DTD.

In all three of these cases, a successful interaction with a system generates a product in the form of a specification expressible in, and conforming to, a particular language. They vary in the extent and manner in which each constrains the range of output they may produce. The word processor and general validating SGML or XML editor enforce relatively few limits, when compared to those enforced by an order entry system. This is a consequence of differences in their respective application areas, and in the system's role in enforcement of constraints on agreement. A word processor and, in traditional applications, the validating XML or SGML editor, are aimed at facilitating specification of documents containing natural language, whereas the order entry application concerns specification of sentences from a far more restricting artificial language. Of particular note here is that in the domain of order entry, as in many domains arising in information systems practice, the constraints which must be applied during input gathering exceed the capacity of a word processor or "even" validating an XML or SGML editor's ability to represent and enforce constraints on output language. If we were prescribing features of a negotiation system for these applications, and we sought to employ XML or SGML in such a system, we'd have to look beyond contemporary validating XML or SGML editors for a solution. We might seek a more powerful "configurable negotiation agent" which embodied both the capabilities for validating XML document instances plus facilities for representing and enforcing more general constraints on valid agreement.

11.4 | Manufacturing Negotiator Behavior

Up to this point we've focused on describing features of negotiation problems. We now turn to the problem of building negotiation systems, that is, of constructing software which exhibits the behavior of a negotiator. The solution architecture employed, as introduced earlier, combines a language for carrying specification of what is to be negotiated with software implementing a configurable negotiation agent. In this section we develop a sample inventory of what must be carried in a language used to specify characteristics of negotiation problems.

11.4.1 *Overview of Information Used by a Negotiator*

As stated early on in this chapter, an input gathering or negotiation system invariably must (at least) appear to employ a specification of the negotiation problem it solves while it operates. Here is one possible enumeration of the information which a negotiator may be expected to require in order to negotiate the gathering of input in a particular negotiation problem. Clearly there is more information which may be employed by a negotiator, and other ways of partitioning this information into categories.

An enumeration of categories of information employed during negotiation of input is as follows:

- Specification of introductory information or other ancillary information not related to specific negotiable variables which is presented to the user during negotiation
- Specification of the negotiable variables including, for each, prompt information, default generating expressions, and so forth.
- The structure of negotiation, for example, division into a series of components with each concerned with negotiation of subsets of the negotiable variables.
- Description of the output specification language and instance generation

11.4.2 *Introductory and Ancillary Information*

This first category includes any information offered during startup of the negotiation and may also include header or footer information offered during negotiation of specific topics (see below) or variable bindings throughout the negotiation. In a Web page-oriented negotiation, this information may simply be an introductory "splash" page plus header and footer information which wraps around each page of the negotiation proper. If the negotiation is divided into a series of components, call them "topics," then splash pages and headers and footers may be provided for each topic.

11.4.3 *Information about Negotiable Variables*

The second category is among the most critical and substantial of those listed. This consists principally of a list of negotiable variables. For each variable, its specification must include all information required to negotiate and validate values for the variable. This could include, for example,

- Prompting material.
- Variable type information
- Value manipulation device specification
- Default specification
- Validation specification
- Conditional inclusion specification

11.4.3.1 Prompting Material

The prompting material includes all the information offered to the user during negotiation of binding a value to the variable. It may be divided into subcomponents:

- Labeling information. Used to identify the variable or its value in, for instance, a confirmation page. For example, "First Name" or "Part Number."

- Preamble information. Offered in advance of presenting an actual enquiry for a user-supplied value. For example, "We now need to ask you for the 'ship-to address' which is the address where we'll send the products you've ordered."

- Prompt wording proper. Wording specifically aimed at prompting the user to provide (or manipulate) a value for this variable. For example, "What is your daytime telephone number?"

- Prologue and footnote material. Offered as additional material to expand on the material offered in the preamble or prompt proper. Footnote material may be provided which could be presented separately from the rest of the prompt material, that is, as a page footnote. For example, "Please note that we cannot ship your products to a post office box."

The prompting material may be specified in exactly the form in which it is to be presented, for example, in HTML if the GUI uses a Web browser, or it may be specified in logical markup and then rendered into the specific GUI's markup language when needed. While the former might be simpler, the latter enables this same information to be used in a variety of presentation contexts, for example, whether a CGI-bin or client-side scripting solution is used. If the target negotiation agent has natural language generation capabilities, specific renditioning of this language may be left to this agent.

Prompting material may be static, but it may also need to be dynamically generated. It may be desirable to include previously negotiated values within prompt material. This can enable, for instance, a user-provided name to be included in headers. Prompt material which must be dynamically generated may be specified as an expression which is evaluated at the time it is to be used. These expressions may make use of material negotiated earlier in the negotiation and may also make use of other data stores (e.g., results of data store queries).

11.4.3.2   Negotiable Variable Type Information

Specification of type information for negotiable variables is required so that the negotiation agent can ensure that the appropriate sort of value is requested and assigned for each variable. The type of a particular variable may be one of a simple enumeration of available types. It could be, for example, that each negotiable variable is identified as an integer, string, one-of-enumeration, or many-of-enumeration. More complex types such as "date," "date-range," and so on may be added to the possible types if needed. Compound types may also be supported. A negotiable variable may consist of a list of contained variables; for this a type identifier of "variable-list" may be allowed. A grammar-defined type may be allowed. That is, the value of a variable of a grammar-defined type must consist of a set of component variables arranged according to a grammar (e.g., an XML DTD model group). Finally, domain-specific types could also be employed; for instance "part-number" may refer to a specific syntactical form used within a specific company to specify part numbers.

In addition to specification of basic type, some type parameters may be required. For example, if the type is "string," then a "string length" parameter may also be required. Likewise, if the type is an enumeration, then the list of values (or source of list of values), along with labels to identify each value, may need to be specified. If a variable is of a compound type, such as "variable list," then specification of the structure required will be required.

11.4.3.3   Value Manipulation Devices

It may be required or desirable to specify or state a preference for a "value manipulation device" for some or all negotiable variables. This specification identifies the user interface device (e.g., the graphical user interface device) which should be employed to enable a user to manipulate the value of a variable. For example, if a variable is of type string, then either a (single-line) text field, or a (multiple-line) text box may be presented to enable the user to input (or manipulate) a string value for a variable. While in some cases it may be possible for the negotiation agent to automatically select an input device depending on the negotiable variable's type or other information, in other cases it may be necessary or desirable to select this device explicitly. For example, when a variable is of type "one-of-enumeration," one may employ either a radio box set, or a picklist to enable the user to specify a value for the variable.

An argument can be made for separating the specification of actual value manipulation devices (negotiation presentation structure detail), from specification of what is to be negotiated (negotiation logical structure detail). Just as style specification may be used to direct generation of specific renditions of logically marked-up documents, a style specification can also be used to direct generation of negotiation behavior possessing different presentation forms.

11.4.3.4   Default Specification

For each negotiable variable it may be necessary or desirable to provide (propose) a value to be included as a default when an input manipulation device is offered to the user. The value to use as such a default may be a simple constant, but it may need to be specified using the capability of an arbitrary expression. Again, such an expression may act on previously negotiated values and on data stores outside the negotiation such as a database.

11.4.3.5   Validation Specification and Expressions

Once a user has provided their preferred value for a negotiable variable, it will usually be necessary to validate that the user-provided value is acceptable to the system. Perhaps the lowest level of validation is simply to allow a variable to be marked "required" and then to ensure that a value is provided for it. Another level of validation is to ensure that when a value is provided, it satisfies constraints defined according to the type of the variable. For instance, the value of a variable of type "date" can be checked to ensure it is in fact in a valid format for a date. Finally, arbitrary domain-specific validation may be specified using a boolean expression operating over previously negotiated variable values and external data stores.

11.4.3.6   Inclusion Conditions

It may be that certain negotiable variables aren't relevant within a specific negotiation process given what has been previously negotiated (and perhaps given external state information). For instance, after a variable concerning "method of payment" is negotiated, it may or may not be necessary to negotiate the value of a variable concerned with details of a specific method of payment. Thus it may be necessary to indicate for a negotiable variable the conditions under which negotiation of a value for this variable should be included in the negotiation process. Again, a boolean expression operating over previously negotiated values, and possibly external data, may be used to specify those conditions under which to include negotiation of such optional variables.

11.4.4 *Negotiation Structure*

A previous section discussed the structure of negotiation problems and the possible relation of this structure to the structure of the data set or object which is to be produced as output for the problem. We now turn to the related topic of the structure of the behavior of the negotiation agent. The negotiation agent (software application) will likely play some role in managing the structure of interaction with the user. For instance, the negotiation agent may walk the user through a series of topics, where within each topic a set of variables are negotiated. Alternatively, the agent may take a more passive role and provide the user with the means of directing attention to specific topics themselves (for instance using a row of "tabs" which the user can use to direct focus to a particular topic). In any case, the structure of the negotiation may be viewed as a set of topics with each in turn consisting of a list of variables to be negotiated.[4]

If, for illustration purposes, we assume that a negotiation will be structured into topics, one component of the specification of the negotiation will be specification of a set of topics. For each topic certain information must be specified:

- The list of negotiable variables to include in the topic
- Introductory material or header and footer material that should be presented when focusing on the topic.
- Specification of conditions under which to include the topic, if it happens to be a topic which is not always to be included.

Details of specification of this information aren't presented here but should easily be inferred given the related discussion above.

It should be assumed that the negotiation agent will play some role in directing attention to specific topics—otherwise there could be no assurance that all topics needed to produce a valid agreement would receive needed focus. The question then is by what means to specify how a negotiation agent is to direct attention to specific topics. Perhaps the simplest solution to this problem is simply to list the topics to be focused on in the order in which they should be attended to. Given that specification of a topic may include specification of conditions under which to include them, this solution actually offers considerable flexibility and has been known to satisfy the needs of real-world negotiation problems quite well.

Another possible source for directing the order of presentation of topics is the output specification language. This possibility requires

---

4. Topics may in effect serve as containers for a set of variables. Thus they may serve a role akin to a compound variable. In this regard, the distinction between topics and variables may be somewhat arbitrary.

however, that we first consider specification of the output specification language and is thus delayed momentarily.

11.4.5 *Output Specification Language and Instance Generation*

The final component required to specify a negotiation problem is the specification of the language in which the output of the negotiation will reside and the means of generating an instance in this language as output to a specific negotiation process. Presuming this language is an application of XML, the first part of the output language specification is defined using a document type definition. The second part of this final component is specification of the manner in which specific output for a given negotiation will be generated; that is, how an instance of a document conforming to the XML DTD will be generated. While the first of these problems can be solved simply (e.g., using a DTD), the second of these problems is not solved as easily.

11.4.5.1 Simple XML-based Output Language

A simple outpute language DTD might, for example, contain no repeatable element occurrence indicators, contain only "seq" (strictly ordered) model group connectors, and contain no mixed content. The order of element types in negotiation output that conform to such a DTD will be fixed, though some elements may be optional.

One can partially specify how to generate instances of this document type by treating the element types as though they were elements, listing them, with appropriate nesting, in the order they should be generated. Figure 11–4 presents a DTD for such a simple output language. Clearly given the simplicity of the model group presented here, a simple list of elements to emit, in the order they should be emitted, would suffice to specify how to emit instances conforming to this

DTD. In fact, this information could be derived from the DTD itself in this and similar cases.

```
<!-- *********************************************

     Sample Output Specification Language DTD

     ********************************************* -->

<!DOCTYPE BDayEntry [

<!ELEMENT BDayEntry ( Name, Date, GiftRequest )

<!ELEMENT Name ( #PCDATA )>

<!ELEMENT Date ( #PCDATA )>

<!ELEMENT GiftRequest ( #PCDATA )>
]>
```

Figure 11–4

In addition to an ordered, nested listing of element types in the order in which their instances should be generated, we must specify how to generate the data content of those elements which occupy leaf positions in the resulting tree (interior elements can't contain data since mixed content was prohibited). A simple way of doing this is to associate with each leaf element one negotiable variable.

While we are presently concerned only with what information is needed to enable negotiation and generation of output and with creation of a language for carrying this information, it is worth testing the viability of actually conducting negotiation and generating output given a proposed negotiation specification. We'll do this for our simple output language now. To negotiate and then generate a document instance in a simple XML-based output language, one could first negotiate all topics (e.g., in some fixed order) and then traverse this list of elements to emit output. For each nonleaf element we emit the element start-tag, recurse to emit each element nested beneath it, then emit the element end-tag. For leaf elements, we emit the element start tag, then the value of the associated negotiable variable, and finally the element end-tag. A leaf element may be omitted if it is marked optional and the associated negotiable variable has either a conditional include expression which evaluates to false, or a value which is empty.

Specification of the inclusion of attributes as an extension to such a simple output language specification can be accomplished in a simple manner. One need only augment the list of element types with an ordered list of attributes for each of them, along with, for each, where a value is to come from. This suffices to specify the attributes and their order for each element. To specify how to generate attribute content, one can again associate a negotiable variable with each appearance of an attribute in an element.

It may be that a simple one-to-one association of negotiable variables to leaf elements and element attribute occurrence may not provide enough power to generate the desired output. It may be, for instance, that given data contained in a given element must be composed from the value of numerous separately negotiated variables. In these cases, we may associate with selected leaf elements and element attribute occurrences some specific expression operating over the negotiated variables and external data. That is, the contents of an emitted element or attribute may be derived by evaluating an expression whose constituent terms include references to various negotiated variables, or to external data.

11.4.5.2 Sample Negotiation Specification DTD

Before moving on to consider more complex output specification languages we'll illustrate the material presented thus far with a simple example. Figure 11–5 presents a sample DTD for specifying negotiation. One can see that the design of this DTD is such that the features of negotiation described above can be represented in conforming document instances. It is assumed that some expression language will be used to specify the default value to recommend, any value check conditions which should be tested on returned values, and any "conditional include" conditions which should be tested before including negotiation of a variable in a particular negotiation process.

```
<!-- *******************************************

     Sample Negotiation Specification Language DTD

     ******************************************* -->


<!DOCTYPE NegSpec [

<!-- ********* Top level is 'NegSpec'    ********* -->
<!ELEMENT NegSpec ( Context,
    ( NegVar+ | Topic+),
    NegApp,
    EmitSpec ) >

<!-- ******* Context - optional header/footer **** -->
<!ELEMENT Context ( Header?, Footer? )>

<!ELEMENT Header ( #PCDATA )>
<!ELEMENT Footer ( #PCDATA )>

<!-- *********** NegVar ******** -->
<!ENTITY % NegVarAttrDefs
      "Length CDATA #IMPLIED" >

<!ELEMENT NegVar ( Type, PrePrompt?, Prompt,
   PostPrompt?, Default,
   Check, IncludeCond)>
```

Figure 11–5

```
<!ATTLIST NegVar
NameID#REQUIRED
Type( String |
   Integer |
   YesNoBool ) "String"
%NegVarAttrDefs; >




<!-- ******** Prompting Material ******** -->
<!ELEMENT PrePrompt ( #PCDATA ) >
<!ELEMENT Prompt ( #PCDATA ) >
<!ELEMENT PostPrompt ( #PCDATA ) >
<!ELEMENT Default ( #PCDATA ) >
<!ELEMENT Check ( #PCDATA ) >
<!ELEMENT IncludeCond ( #PCDATA ) >

<!-- ************* Topic ********** -->
<!ELEMENT Topic ( Header?, NegVarList, Footer? ) >

<!ELEMENT NegVarList ( #PCDATA ) >

<!-- ************ App and its Props ******** -->
<!ELEMENT NegApp EMPTY >
<!ATTLIST NegApp
TopicList IDREFS #REQUIRED>

<!-- ******** Output Emit Spec ****** -->
<!ELEMENT EmitSPec ( #PCDATA ) >
]>
```

Figure 11–5   (continued)

A sample document conforming to our Negotiation Specification DTD is presented in Figure 11–6. This document instance specifies the negotiation of data objects described using the DTD in Figure 11–4. One can see that the "EmitSpec" in this example is quite simple indeed, which is as expected given the simplicity of the DTD defining the target output specification language.

```xml
<!-- *********************

     Sample Negotiation Specification Document

     ********* ************** -->

<!-- <?xml version="1.0"?> -->

<!-- <!DOCTYPE NegSpec> -->

<NegSpec>
<Context>
    <Header>Birthday Information Inquiry</Header>
    <Footer>XML Negotiation Example</Footer>
</Context>

<NegVar Name="name" Type="string" Length="25">
    <Label>Name</Label>
    <Prompt>What your name?</Prompt>
</NegVar>

<NegVar Name="date" Type="string">
    <Label>Birthday</Label>
    <Prompt>What your birthday?</Prompt>
</NegVar>

<NegVar Name="gift" Type="string">
    <Label>Gift Request</Label>
    <Prompt>What do you want for your birthday?</Prompt>
</NegVar>

<Topic name="bdayEntry">
    <Header>Birthday Book Entry</Header>
    <NegVarList>name date bdayEntry</NegVarList>
</Topic>

<NegApp TopicList="bdayEntry"/>
```

Figure 11–6

```
<!-- associate variables with XML elements -->
<EmitSpec>
     BDayEntry {
Name name
Date date
GiftRequest gift
    }
</EmitSpec>

</NegSpec>
```

Figure 11–6   (continued)

11.4.5.3   Complex XML-based Output Language

There are situations when the output of a negotiation or input gathering process is more complex than allowed by the restrictions in the previous section. We'll consider just one of these situations in limited detail here and then briefly comment on approaches for treating more general cases.

Frequently an element must be allowed to appear repeatedly within the output of a negotiation. This is the case, for instance, when an element's contents (i.e., nested elements and/or text) are used to carry specification of a product selection in an order entry system, and multiple products may be selected in a single order. This situation occurs in general whenever a particular component of specification must be allowed to appear repeatedly in an output specification.

When an element is allowed to repeat, it will be the case that some number of the variables, or perhaps whole topics, present in the negotiation problem will have to be negotiated multiple times. That this is the case can be specified by augmenting the specification of properties of a variable or topic with a means for indicating whether multiple instances of it may be negotiated. The implementation of a configurable negotiation agent which accepts specifications containing such repeating negotiation components must then be equipped to carry out the specified behavior.

When still more complex output language is required, employing, for example, mixed content, repeatable occurrence indicators, and so on, more traditional SGML/XML editing solution techniques may be required. In particular, the direction of focus of negotiation to specific topics is perhaps best driven by a negotiation planner which has access to an XML parser with "incremental parsing" capabilities. With this technology available, the negotiation agent, given a partial input, can determine the set of valid data that can occur next (and at particular points within the already collected information). This is the same technology that allows a DTD-aware editor to limit the set of elements and content which can be inserted at specific points during the authoring of a traditional XML or SGML document. Used within a negotiation planner, such a parser can enable the negotiation agent to efficiently negotiate output constrained by complex DTDs.

11.5 | Chapter Summary

This chapter developed the analogy between input gathering and negotiation, first at an abstract level and then in increasing detail. It did so with the aim of developing formalism to the description of input gathering problems which would help us characterize and classify them and which would help us to understand and develop the roles which XML may play in solutions to input gathering problems. It discussed characteristics of negotiation problems as background for subsequent discussion of requirements for language designed to carry specification of negotiation problems. It introduced a solution architecture for building input gathering or negotiation systems which utilize such a language coupled with a configurable negotiation agent. We described how such an agent may accept instances of negotiation specification written in negotiation specification language as input which enables it to produce the behavior required to collect the sought-after input. It was argued that this language-agent solution architecture was itself a valuable tool for aiding systems development. We pointed out that this architecture enables creation of "near-optimal specification environments" and that XML can serve as a key tool for creation of these environments, and thus for creating information systems in general.

The final section focused on the negotiation specification side of the problem of generating the behavior of a negotiator. A detailed enumeration of the information which could be carried within a real-world negotiation specification language was offered. Finally, comments were offered regarding how a few more complex negotiation problems can be handled.

Hopefully this material has heightened your appreciation for the role of negotiation in information systems and how XML can be employed in these systems. Information systems depend at the most fundamental level on language as the means for carrying specification between agents. This exchange of information requires common language and mutually appropriate communication behavior. XML provides the basis for constructing common languages and negotiation is by definition communication behavior appropriate for facilitating information exchange. Every system developer should have both ready for service in their personal toolbox.

INDEX

E

▌ M

▌ N

∎ T

Java™ Development Kit
Version 1.1.x
Binary Code License

This binary code license ("License") contains rights and restrictions associated with use of the accompanying software and documentation ("Software"). Read the License carefully before installing the Software. By installing the Software you agree to the terms and conditions of this License.

1. Limited License Grant. Sun grants to you ("Licensee") a non-exclusive, non-transferable limited license to use the Software without fee for evaluation of the Software and for development of Java™ compatible applets and applications. Licensee may make one archival copy of the Software. Licensee may not re-distribute the Software in whole or in part, either separately or included with a product. Refer to the Java Runtime Environment Version 1.1 binary code license (http://www.javasun.com/products/JDK/1.1/index.html) for the availability of runtime code which may be distributed with Java compatible applets and applications.

2. Java Platform Interface. Licensee may not modify the Java Platform Interface ("JPI", identified as classes contained within the "java" package or any subpackages of the "java" package), by creating additional classes within the JPI or otherwise causing the addition to or modification of the classes in the JPI. In the event that Licensee creates any Java-related API and distributes such API to others for applet or application development, Licensee must promptly publish an accurate specification for such API for free use by all developers of Java-based software.

3. Restrictions. Software is confidential copyrighted information of Sun and title to all copies is retained by Sun and/or its licensors. Licensee shall not modify, decompile, disassemble, decrypt, extract, or otherwise reverse engineer Software. Software may not be leased, assigned, or sublicensed, in whole or in part. **Software is not designed or intended for use in on-line control of aircraft, air traffic, aircraft navigation or aircraft communications; or in the design, construction, operation or maintenance of any nuclear facility. Licensee warrants that it will not use or redistribute the Software for such purposes.**

4. Trademarks and Logos. This License does not authorize Licensee to use any Sun name, trademark or logo. Licensee acknowledges that Sun owns the Java trademark and all Java-related trademarks, logos and icons including the Coffee Cup and Duke ("Java Marks") and agrees to: (i) comply with the Java Trademark Guidelines at http://java.sun.com/trademarks.html; (ii) not do anything harmful to or inconsistent with Sun's rights in the Java Marks; and (iii) assist Sun in protecting those rights, including assigning to Sun any rights acquired by Licensee in any Java Mark.

5. Disclaimer of Warranty. Software is provided "AS IS," without a warranty of any kind. ALL EXPRESS OR IMPLIED REPRESENTATIONS AND WARRANTIES,

INCLUDING ANY IMPLIED WARRANTY OF MERCHANTABILITY, FITNESS FOR A PARTICULAR PURPOSE OR NON-INFRINGEMENT, ARE HEREBY EXCLUDED.

6. Limitation of Liability. SUN AND ITS LICENSORS SHALL NOT BE LIABLE FOR ANY DAMAGES SUFFERED BY LICENSEE OR ANY THIRD PARTY AS A RESULT OF USING OR DISTRIBUTING SOFTWARE. IN NO EVENT WILL SUN OR ITS LICENSORS BE LIABLE FOR ANY LOST REVENUE, PROFIT OR DATA, OR FOR DIRECT, INDIRECT, SPECIAL, CONSEQUENTIAL, INCIDENTAL OR PUNITIVE DAMAGES, HOWEVER CAUSED AND REGARDLESS OF THE THEORY OF LIABILITY, ARISING OUT OF THE USE OF OR INABILITY TO USE SOFTWARE, EVEN IF SUN HAS BEEN ADVISED OF THE POSSIBILITY OF SUCH DAMAGES.

7. Termination. Licensee may terminate this License at any time by destroying all copies of Software. This License will terminate immediately without notice from Sun if Licensee fails to comply with any provision of this License. Upon such termination, Licensee must destroy all copies of Software.

8. Export Regulations. Software, including technical data, is subject to U.S. export control laws, including the U.S. Export Administration Act and its associated regulations, and may be subject to export or import regulations in other countries. Licensee agrees to comply strictly with all such regulations and acknowledges that it has the responsibility to obtain licenses to export, re-export, or import Software. Software may not be downloaded, or otherwise exported or re-exported (i) into, or to a national or resident of, Cuba, Iraq, Iran, North Korea, Libya, Sudan, Syria or any country to which the U.S. has embargoed goods; or (ii) to anyone on the U.S. Treasury Department's list of Specially Designated Nations or the U.S. Commerce Department's Table of Denial Orders.

9. Restricted Rights. Use, duplication or disclosure by the United States government is subject to the restrictions as set forth in the Rights in Technical Data and Computer Software Clauses in DFARS 252.227-7013(c) (1) (ii) and FAR 52.227-19(c) (2) as applicable.

10. Governing Law. Any action related to this License will be governed by California law and controlling U.S. federal law. No choice of law rules of any jurisdiction will apply.

11. Severability. If any of the above provisions are held to be in violation of applicable law, void, or unenforceable in any jurisdiction, then such provisions are herewith waived to the extent necessary for the License to be otherwise enforceable in such jurisdiction. However, if in Sun's opinion deletion of any provisions of the License by operation of this paragraph unreasonably compromises the rights or increases the liabilities of Sun or its licensors, Sun reserves the right to terminate the License and refund the fee paid by Licensee, if any, as Licensee's sole and exclusive remedy.

LICENSE AGREEMENT AND LIMITED WARRANTY

READ THE FOLLOWING TERMS AND CONDITIONS CAREFULLY BEFORE OPENING THIS CD PACKAGE, *DESIGNING XML INTERNET APPLICATIONS.* THIS LEGAL DOCUMENT IS AN AGREEMENT BETWEEN YOU AND PRENTICE-HALL, INC. (THE "COMPANY"). BY OPENING THIS SEALED CD PACKAGE, YOU ARE AGREEING TO BE BOUND BY THESE TERMS AND CONDITIONS. IF YOU DO NOT AGREE WITH THESE TERMS AND CONDITIONS, DO NOT OPEN THE CD PACKAGE. PROMPTLY RETURN THE UNOPENED CD PACKAGE AND ALL ACCOMPANYING ITEMS TO THE PLACE YOU OBTAINED THEM FOR A FULL REFUND OF ANY SUMS YOU HAVE PAID.

1.   **GRANT OF LICENSE:** In consideration of your purchase of this book, and your agreement to abide by the terms and conditions of this Agreement, the Company grants to you a nonexclusive right to use and display the copy of the enclosed software program (hereinafter the "SOFTWARE") on a single computer (i.e., with a single CPU) at a single location so long as you comply with the terms of this Agreement. The Company reserves all rights not expressly granted to you under this Agreement.

2.   **OWNERSHIP OF SOFTWARE:** You own only the magnetic or physical media (the enclosed CD) on which the SOFTWARE is recorded or fixed, but the Company and the software developers retain all the rights, title, and ownership to the SOFTWARE recorded on the original CD copy(ies) and all subsequent copies of the SOFTWARE, regardless of the form or media on which the original or other copies may exist. This license is not a sale of the original SOFTWARE or any copy to you.

3.   **COPY RESTRICTIONS:** This SOFTWARE and the accompanying printed materials and user manual (the "Documentation") are the subject of copyright. The individual programs on the CD are copyrighted by the authors of each program. Some of the programs on the CD include separate licensing agreements. If you intend to use one of these programs, you must read and follow its accompanying license agreement. You may not copy the Documentation or the SOFTWARE, except that you may make a single copy of the SOFTWARE for backup or archival purposes only. You may be held legally responsible for any copying or copyright infringement which is caused or encouraged by your failure to abide by the terms of this restriction.

4.   **USE RESTRICTIONS:** You may not network the SOFTWARE or otherwise use it on more than one computer or computer terminal at the same time. You may physically transfer the SOFTWARE from one computer to another provided that the SOFTWARE is used on only one computer at a time. You may not distribute copies of the SOFTWARE or Documentation to others. You may not reverse engineer, disassemble, decompile, modify, adapt, translate, or create derivative works based on the SOFTWARE or the Documentation without the prior written consent of the Company.

5.   **TRANSFER RESTRICTIONS:** The enclosed SOFTWARE is licensed only to you and may not be transferred to any one else without the prior written consent of the Company. Any unauthorized transfer of the SOFTWARE shall result in the immediate termination of this Agreement.

6.   **TERMINATION:** This license is effective until terminated. This license will terminate automatically without notice from the Company and become null and void if you fail to comply with any provisions or limitations of this license. Upon termination, you shall destroy the Documentation and all copies of the SOFTWARE. All provisions of this Agreement as to warranties, limitation of liability, remedies or damages, and our ownership rights shall survive termination.

7.   **MISCELLANEOUS:** This Agreement shall be construed in accordance with the laws of the United States of America and the State of New York and shall benefit the Company, its affiliates, and assignees.

8.   **LIMITED WARRANTY AND DISCLAIMER OF WARRANTY:** The Company warrants that the SOFTWARE, when properly used in accordance with the Documentation, will operate in substantial conformity with the description of the SOFTWARE set forth in the Documentation. The

Company does not warrant that the SOFTWARE will meet your requirements or that the operation of the SOFTWARE will be uninterrupted or error-free. The Company warrants that the media on which the SOFTWARE is delivered shall be free from defects in materials and workmanship under normal use for a period of thirty (30) days from the date of your purchase. Your only remedy and the Company's only obligation under these limited warranties is, at the Company's option, return of the warranted item for a refund of any amounts paid by you or replacement of the item. Any replacement of SOFTWARE or media under the warranties shall not extend the original warranty period. The limited warranty set forth above shall not apply to any SOFTWARE which the Company determines in good faith has been subject to misuse, neglect, improper installation, repair, alteration, or damage by you. EXCEPT FOR THE EXPRESSED WARRANTIES SET FORTH ABOVE, THE COMPANY DISCLAIMS ALL WARRANTIES, EXPRESS OR IMPLIED, INCLUDING WITHOUT LIMITATION, THE IMPLIED WARRANTIES OF MERCHANTABILITY AND FITNESS FOR A PARTICULAR PURPOSE. EXCEPT FOR THE EXPRESS WARRANTY SET FORTH ABOVE, THE COMPANY DOES NOT WARRANT, GUARANTEE, OR MAKE ANY REPRESENTATION REGARDING THE USE OR THE RESULTS OF THE USE OF THE SOFTWARE IN TERMS OF ITS CORRECTNESS, ACCURACY, RELIABILITY, CURRENTNESS, OR OTHERWISE.

IN NO EVENT, SHALL THE COMPANY OR ITS EMPLOYEES, AGENTS, SUPPLIERS, OR CONTRACTORS BE LIABLE FOR ANY INCIDENTAL, INDIRECT, SPECIAL, OR CONSEQUENTIAL DAMAGES ARISING OUT OF OR IN CONNECTION WITH THE LICENSE GRANTED UNDER THIS AGREEMENT, OR FOR LOSS OF USE, LOSS OF DATA, LOSS OF INCOME OR PROFIT, OR OTHER LOSSES, SUSTAINED AS A RESULT OF INJURY TO ANY PERSON, OR LOSS OF OR DAMAGE TO PROPERTY, OR CLAIMS OF THIRD PARTIES, EVEN IF THE COMPANY OR AN AUTHORIZED REPRESENTATIVE OF THE COMPANY HAS BEEN ADVISED OF THE POSSIBILITY OF SUCH DAMAGES. IN NO EVENT SHALL LIABILITY OF THE COMPANY FOR DAMAGES WITH RESPECT TO THE SOFTWARE EXCEED THE AMOUNTS ACTUALLY PAID BY YOU, IF ANY, FOR THE SOFTWARE.

SOME JURISDICTIONS DO NOT ALLOW THE LIMITATION OF IMPLIED WARRANTIES OR LIABILITY FOR INCIDENTAL, INDIRECT, SPECIAL, OR CONSEQUENTIAL DAMAGES, SO THE ABOVE LIMITATIONS MAY NOT ALWAYS APPLY. THE WARRANTIES IN THIS AGREEMENT GIVE YOU SPECIFIC LEGAL RIGHTS AND YOU MAY ALSO HAVE OTHER RIGHTS WHICH VARY IN ACCORDANCE WITH LOCAL LAW.

ACKNOWLEDGMENT

YOU ACKNOWLEDGE THAT YOU HAVE READ THIS AGREEMENT, UNDERSTAND IT, AND AGREE TO BE BOUND BY ITS TERMS AND CONDITIONS. YOU ALSO AGREE THAT THIS AGREEMENT IS THE COMPLETE AND EXCLUSIVE STATEMENT OF THE AGREEMENT BETWEEN YOU AND THE COMPANY AND SUPERSEDES ALL PROPOSALS OR PRIOR AGREEMENTS, ORAL, OR WRITTEN, AND ANY OTHER COMMUNICATIONS BETWEEN YOU AND THE COMPANY OR ANY REPRESENTATIVE OF THE COMPANY RELATING TO THE SUBJECT MATTER OF THIS AGREEMENT.

Should you have any questions concerning this Agreement or if you wish to contact the Company for any reason, please contact in writing at the address below.

Robin Short

Prentice Hall PTR

One Lake Street

Upper Saddle River, New Jersey 07458

Use of this software is subject to the Binary Code License terms and conditions on page 583. Read the license carefully. By opening this package, you are agreeing to be bound by the terms and conditions of this license from Sun Microsystems, Inc.